HEGEL
SELECTIONS

EDITED BY

J. LOEWENBERG

CHARLES SCRIBNER'S SONS

NEW YORK

For permission to use selections from Hegel's works we are indebted to the
following: Houghton Mifflin Company for "Contrite Consciousness" from
The Phenomenology of Mind, translated by Josiah Royce, included in Dr.
B. Rand's *Modern Classical Philosophers;* The Macmillan Company for
the "Preface to the Phenomenology of Mind," translated by J. B. Baillie;
Oxford University Press for "The Doctrine of Essence," "Objective Mind,"
and "Absolute Mind" from the *Encyclopaedia of the Philosophical Sciences,*
translated by W. Wallace.

B-11.72[M]

Printed in the United States of America
SBN 684-12526-9

CONTENTS

CONTENTS

INTRODUCTION

Hegel is a philosopher whom one neglects at one's peril. His learning was vast, his discernment keen, his penetration deep. He had an encyclopedic mind, and his vision was synoptic. Nothing human—aye, nothing divine, say the facetious—was foreign to him. So great was his passion for catholicity that he sought to harness to his prodigious system the most divergent and discordant of themes. Second only to his passion for synthesis was his passion for sardonic analysis of the very themes he was eager to harmonize. Clearly, a philosophy so universal in scope is imposing. Has the omnivorous mind of Hegel, we naturally ask, anticipated the thoughts we cherish as our own? Has his metaphysical genius pondered and transcended our deepest ideas and concepts? Hegel thought he had provided a system sufficiently spacious to include in it in sublimated form all the typical ways of responding to the world and all the typical categories by which to describe it. The truth is the whole, he said, and his philosophy, he claimed, was the whole truth. It is poetic justice perhaps that in our own day the rebuke to such an extravagant claim should have taken the form of ignoring it. But to ignore a claim is not to dispute it. The very extravagance with which Hegel proclaimed the truth of his philosophy is a challenge to the prevailing neglect of it. The tenets associated with his name, though their pretentiousness be offensive, may well be worth our knowing.

It is his doctrine rather than his life that particu-

larly arrests our attention. His biography offers nothing
to stir the imagination. He was born at Stuttgart, Au-
gust 27, 1770. His family belonged to the upper middle
class. His early education he received at the public
schools of his native town. Hegel was not a brilliant
pupil learning with ease and rapidity. He was sure and
steady. His understanding, not surprisingly quick, was
uncommonly sound. Neither at the gymnasium in Stuttgart nor at the university in Tübingen (which he entered in 1788 as student of theology) did Hegel display
exceptional qualities of mind. The certificate which he
received upon leaving the university in 1793 mentions
his good character, commendable acquaintance with
theology and philology, and—curiously enough—inadequate knowledge of philosophy. Of genius Hegel appears to have given no promise during the formative
period of his life. After leaving the university he
spent seven years as a private tutor, partly in Switzerland (1793-96), and partly in Frankfort (1797-1800).
The letters and essays written during these years show
how slow was the process of Hegel's philosophical
growth. His was a long apprenticeship. In 1801,
when he was past thirty, Hegel entered upon his
academic career at Jena. His first appointment was
that of a mere lecturer (*Privat-Docent*), yet he immediately took his place as a leader in philosophy.
In 1802-03, in collaboration with Schelling, he edited
the *Journal für Philosophie*. The independence of his
philosophical position dates from 1803, when Schelling
left Jena. His ability was soon recognized. His
promotion to a professorship came in 1805; the battle of Jena, however, terminated for the time being a
university career so auspiciously begun. Ten years
elapsed between the battle of Jena and his appointment
as professor of philosophy at Heidelberg: two of these

he spent as the editor of a newspaper in Bamberg (1806-08), the remaining eight as the director of the gymnasium at Nuremberg (1808-16). The professorship at Heidelberg he held for but two years. In 1818 he was called to Berlin. And in Berlin he remained till his death in 1831, the acknowledged dictator of one of the most powerful philosophic schools in the history of thought.

Hegel's chief works fall into two groups. One group consists of books which he published during his life. They alone offer, of course, a wholly authoritative account of his philosophy. Of these, in the order of publication, are the following: *Die Phaenomenologie des Geistes,* 1807; *Wissenschaft der Logik,* 1812-16; *Encyclopaedie der philosophischen Wissenschaften im Grundrisse,* 1817 (second enlarged edition, 1827; third edition, 1830); *Grundlinien der Philosophie des Rechts,* 1820. The other group comprises Hegel's posthumous works. They are reports of his lectures, edited and published by his pupils, not from manuscripts of his own, but rather from the collated notes of different students. Obviously they cannot be regarded as possessing indisputable authenticity. These reports of his lectures bear the following titles: *Vorlesungen über die Philosophie der Religion,* edited by P. Marheineke, 1832 (second altered edition, 1840); *Vorlesungen über die Geschichte der Philosophie,* edited by K. L. Michelet, 1833-36 (second edition, 1842); *Vorlesungen über die Aesthetik,* edited by H. G. Hotho, 1835-38 (second edition, 1840-43); *Vorlesungen über die Philosophie der Geschichte,* edited by E. Gans, 1837 (second edition, 1840). The complete edition of Hegel's works, as prepared and revised by his pupils, numbers eighteen volumes; his son later added a nineteenth volume containing Hegel's letters.

What is Hegel's philosophy as embodied in all these
volumes? The question is vexatious. Hegel's philosophy defies summary restatements. Interpreters of
Hegel, according to one of his interpreters, "have con-
tradicted each other, almost as variously, as the several
commentators on the Bible." The comparison is not
altogether inept. The Bible, of course, is not a single
system of thought, the product of a single thinker, the
unwinding of a single dialectical thread. Yet what extraordinary likeness Biblical and Hegelian writings do
manifest in vastness, massiveness, opulence, redundance,
obscurity, and depth! By deft selection and emphasis
isolated themes culled from any source may be made to
assume contradictory shapes. Scriptural and Hegelian
teachings are peculiarly liable to distortion when abstracted from their proper context: their meaning lies
in their own recondite terms, their own dark imagery,
their own prolix style, their own leisurely digressions.
The paraphrase of the Bible in the abbreviated language
of formal logic would indeed be a parody of it. No
less anomalous is the quintessential account of Hegel's
philosophy in nomenclature not his own.

The indissoluble union between the content of his
philosophy and its form is the chief obstacle to an
understanding of Hegel. His system of thought and
the esoteric language in which it is expressed are related in circular fashion: to grasp the meaning of the
strange words Hegel has coined an understanding of his
system must already be in one's possession, yet the system seems unutterable without the use of the bizarre
language in which he himself clothed it. To reproduce
the spirit of Hegel's philosophy without its letter is to
sacrifice subtlety, to reproduce it with its letter is to renounce intelligibility. Hegel's style is unquestionably
scandalous. Yet the scandal does not lie in its inar-

ticulateness. On the contrary, Hegel's expressions are laden with too much meaning. The opulence of his language is the source of its greatest obscurity. One example will illustrate the point. The verb *aufheben*, one of his characteristic key-words, is employed by Hegel to convey at once three distinct meanings. Among other things, the word signifies to annul, to preserve, to elevate. These meanings are manifestly not synonymous. In ordinary parlance it is quite clear from the context in what sense the word is to be understood. Hegel's parlance, however, is not ordinary. When the verb is used by him we are required to think simultaneously of significations that are at loggerheads. When something in Hegel's text is characterized as *aufgehoben* we must understand it to be cancelled and conserved and exalted all at once. How? Why? Hegel's entire system is the answer. It is an essential part of that system to show that everything has a rhythmic destiny: it comes to fruition, it comes to grief, it enters a higher truth. This, according to Hegel's philosophy, is the rhythmic pattern manifested by the career of anything, be it a scientific concept, a literary movement, a national policy, a religious creed, a political institution, an economic system, a philosophic principle. Everything vanishes into its opposite, and nothing ever passes away. The equal truth of these two assertions, seemingly incompatible, Hegel thought he could establish by a rigorous method involving the use of an esoteric nomenclature. Under the word *aufgehoben*, for instance, we have epitomized the universal law of rhythmic change which everything is fated to exemplify. But this is a relatively simple illustration of a mode of argument couched in peculiar speech. To disengage the deep spirit of Hegel's philosophy from its occult letter is indeed like trying to separate Siamese twins.

The circular relation between his philosophy and the terms needed to express it is not the only paradox fathered by Hegel. Still greater is the paradox involved in the relation between the result of his philosophy and the method necessary to achieve it. The result is conceived by Hegel as a final expression of ultimate truth; the method, however, is a sort of Wandering Jew, condemning itself to perpetual peregrination. Of two things one (as the French say)—either the method is valid, in which case any result achieved by its means must generate its own antithesis, thus rendering the result abortive; or if some particular mode of synthesis (Hegel's own, for example) is singled out as the *dénouement* of the dramatic conflict of concepts and attitudes, then the validity of the method would seem to suffer shipwreck at the very point where its coerciveness is most urgently needed. The logic in terms of which Hegel exhibits the relativity of all particular views of the world, on the ground that "the truth is the whole," is a strange logic to invoke for the demonstration that his own unique vision is the final truth. Just because the truth is the whole, no single philosophy, however complete it may appear, can claim exemption from the universal principle requiring that every synthesis produce on its own level the antithesis proper to it. For the principle on which Hegel's philosophy rests, rebuking as it does any particular concept or partisan attitude, must condemn likewise any single system or individual synthesis. Hegel's logic, if valid, can never terminate in a supreme synthesis. His logic, playing the double rôle of uniting opposites and of providing a negative mate for the synthesis issuing from such union, suffers no philosophy to escape from the fate it decrees. Hegel's own method decrees that his own system be ultimately jettisoned. It too must become *aufgehoben.* In logic, alas, the exception never proves the rule. And the rule is relentless: universal and perpetual transition of everything to something else. Hegel's logic is well symbolized by Shelley in the impetuous and uncontrollable West Wind—the wild spirit which is moving everywhere, tameless and swift and proud, at once the destroyer and preserver of every kind of truth, Hegel's included.

The task of Hegel's interpreter is thus not an easy one. He is between the devil and the deep sea. What shall he single out as characteristic? Shall he emphasize the truth of Hegel's positive views? Or shall he lay stress on the negative method? Hegel himself considered the results of his thinking and the manner of vindicating them as inseparable; the severance by the interpreter of Hegel's philosophical product and the mode of its production is like the familiar divorce of Hamlet from the Prince of Denmark. But what in this case corresponds to the prince? Over this question interpreters of Hegel may well differ. There are those who think that in Hegel's chief tenets lies the truth unveiled. Convinced of the irrefragable nature of his constructive ideas, they venture to abandon his tortuous course in favor of arguments free from tergiversation. What the master taught, not how he taught it, they hold to be of permanent value. The princely portion of Hegel's philosophy is the final doctrine; Hegel's way of propounding it they ascribe to idiosyncrasy or perversity. Others, however, assert that Hegel's genius is to be found in his peculiar method. Hegel's distinct contribution, they emphatically declare, lies in the manner of his thinking rather than in the product of it. His views on many things—on religion, art, morality, history, logic, or the state—derive their value from the singular way by which he un-

folded them. Those for whom the secret of Hegel
lies in the method would not share his sanguine belief
in the validity of the special consequences he derived
from it. The Hegelian method may sanction deductions
quite at variance with those cherished by the master and
his followers. The notorious quarrels between the "Left-
Hegelians" and the "Right-Hegelians" show how attenuated is the bond between the dialectical method and
its consequences. But whatever the consequences, the
method itself must be regarded as the royal leaven of
Hegel's thought.

We agree with those for whom the distinguishing
mark of Hegel's genius is his method. What is it?
It is called "dialectical." The history of its use is old.
It is certainly as old as Socrates and Plato. Hegel
did not regard himself as the inventor of the dialectical method. "Dialectic," he says in his *Encyclopaedie,*
"is no novelty in philosophy. Among the ancients Plato
is termed the inventor of Dialectic: and his right to the
name rests on the fact, that the Platonic philosophy first
gave the free scientific, and thus at the same time the
objective, form to Dialectic. Socrates, as we should
expect from the general character of his philosophizing,
has the dialectical element in a predominantly subjective shape, that of Irony. He used to turn his Dialectic,
first against ordinary consciousness, and then especially
against the Sophists. In his conversations he used to
simulate the wish for some clearer knowledge about the
subject under discussion, and after putting all sorts
of questions with that intent, he drew on those with
whom he conversed to the opposite of what their first
impressions had pronounced correct. . . . In modern
times it was, more than any other, Kant who resusci-
tated the name of Dialectic, and restored it to its post of
honor. He did it . . . by working out the antinomies of

reason. The problem of these antinomies is no mere
subjective piece of work oscillating between one set
of grounds and another; it really serves to show that
every abstract position of understanding, taken precisely as it is given, naturally veers round into its opposite." The dialectical method is thus no invention
of Hegel's. New is merely Hegel's universal and systematic application of it. But it is no simple matter
to state to what precisely Hegel considered his method
relevant. For here once more interpreters differ. Shall
the method be regarded as applicable to terms of discourse or to characteristic views of the world? Is it
to be taken as expressing a logic of concepts or a logic
of life? As elaborated by Hegel in his *Wissenschaft der
Logik* (1812-16), it is clearly a logic of categories; as
it is displayed in *Die Phaenomenologie des Geistes*
(1807) it is rather, to use a suggestive phrase of Josiah
Royce's, a "logic of passion."

Those who take their clue from Hegel's later works,
beginning with the *Logic,* are inclined to place in the
foreground the application of the method to objects of
thought. The governing idea of the dialectic, as applied to *categories,* involves at once analysis and synthesis. From the point of view of analysis, dialectic
is a method whereby each concept may be seen to imply
its own opposite as a necessary and inseparable part
of itself. Taken merely as a mode of analysis the dialectical method is productive of a situation which is
logically absurd, showing as it does that any concept is
burdened with a meaning antithetical to it. This situation can be relieved only by synthesis, by the admission
of a wider idea in which the original concept and its
generated antithesis are reconciled. Synthesis or fed-
eration of antithetical categories is what the dialectical
logic is designed to accomplish. This repetitive pat-

tern—mutual antagonism and consequent reconciliation —is the fate to which *all* concepts must submit. Such a pattern provides a scheme for their combination into a single hierarchical system, demanding and justifying an ultimate distinction between "lower" and "higher" categories. This in brief is what Hegel is supposed to mean by his doctrine that all concepts are "dialectically" related: concepts advance in meaning from lower to higher by an inherent rhythm of logical opposition and unison. But dialectic as here used, it must be remembered, is a dialectic of abstract concepts; indirectly, indeed, it applies to all concrete things, since all concrete things to be conceived or expressed require general terms by which to think or to describe them. Directly and in the first instance, however, the dialectical logic is a logic of conceptual entities.

Those, on the other hand, who find in the earlier and neglected *Phenomenology* the key to the meaning of Hegel's method tell a different story. It is a story of momentous vision and beliefs. The dialectical logic, as displayed in this book, is the logic, not of abstract terms or categories, but of the perennial types of human experience. Here Hegel sets in opposition passionate conceptions rather than bloodless concepts. Different and recurrent views of life—sensuous and intellectual, emotional and reflective, practical and theoretical, mystic and philistine, sceptical and dogmatic, empirical and speculative, conservative and radical, selfish and social, religious and secular—are here induced to voice the will to believe in their own exclusive reasonableness. And reasonable each does appear from the point of view of its own perspective. But, alas, each human attitude in the process of contending for mastery always finds its claim to power rebuked and impugned. For there is no human view or belief without its rival. And the rival is no less emphatic in asseveration of its rights. Life, as Hegel conceives it, is an incessant strife of partisan views. They are partisan because they are particular. Indeed, partisanship and particularity are synonymous. Whatever is particular—a particular art, a particular religion, a particular philosophy —is self-absorbed and self-centered and hence never free from bias. The truth is that every particular point of view ineluctably suffers from a warped perspective. The unavoidable tendency of everything particular to emphasize its own particularity Hegel discerns to be the source of all the fatal collisions that render human life so everlastingly unstable. The dialectical method, taken merely as a mode of analysis, simply consists in laying siege to every typical attitude or belief by rendering its partisan claims logically ridiculous.

The *Phenomenology,* intent as it is upon uncovering the logical ridiculousness in our typical and warped ways of reacting to the world, reveals Hegel's philosophical vision more felicitously than does the *Logic.* In the earlier use of it rather than in the later does the dialectical method appear as a genuine instrument of philosophic discourse. In the *Logic,* the method bears too much the stamp of artificiality; in the *Phenomenology,* it shows rather signs of unusual artistry. There is cleverness in the *Logic;* in the *Phenomenology* there is genius. Despite its occult style, the *Phenomenology* must be ranked as a work of art, the distinguishing qualities of which are histrionic and comic.

Histrionic and comic Hegel's cast of mind certainly was. The dialectical method, as exhibited in the *Phenomenology,* means two things: it means a subjective pose and it means an objective situation. The attitude demanded for the application of the dialectical method is a certain kind of impersonation. The only

way to understand a point of view is by intellectual
sympathy to impersonate it.   For no point of view,
so Hegel teaches, can be grasped from without.   To
appreciate it truly one must insert oneself inside it and
reproduce by an act of sympathetic imagination its intrinsic nature.   The dialectical critic's art is like that
of the dramatist or of the actor: he must identify himself with the character he is portraying.   To be sure,
only a great artist—a Shakespeare—can with skill hide
his own true face behind an alien mask.   Dramatic or
histrionic sincerity is not ordinary sincerity: the artist
must always pretend to be what he himself is not.   He
must play a part.   On its subjective side, then, the dialectical method is simply a method of portrayal, requiring an initial distinction, so Hegel tells us in his
characteristic language, between what a thing is *für
uns* and what it is *für sich*.   To discover what it is
"for itself" is to understand it from within, is to adopt
its unique standpoint.   Suppose it is the mystic point of
view we are interested in understanding.   What mysticism is "for us," the external observers and critics, is
obviously not the mysticism of the mystic.   The mystic's
is the only true version of mysticism.   To the outsider
it must inevitably appear as a meaningless fiction unless he is able to recover the vital experience of which
it is the fervent expression.   We must see mysticism
through mystic eyes if we are to understand its indig-
enous character.   For non-mystics an experiment of
this sort involves strenuous effort and superb art.   It
is no less difficult than the impersonation of Hamlet by
an actor of sanguine temper and resolute will.   Yet precisely such histrionic art is requisite for the portrayal
from its own centre of any point of view foreign to our
nature.   The mastery of this art it is which Hegel exacts

for the application of the dialectical method. And of this art his own philosophy is a singular illustration.

But the histrionic art demanded for the application of the dialectical method is only one side of it. When the method is actually *applied* to any given point of view the ensuing result appears to be essentially comic, if we heed George Meredith's observation that "the life of comedy is in the idea." "Folly," says this panegyrist of the Comic Spirit in his well known *Essay on Comedy*, "is the natural prey of the Comic, known to it in all her transformations, in every disguise; and it is with the springing delight of hawk over heron, hound after fox, that it gives her chase, never fretting, never tiring, sure of having her, allowing her no rest." This is a wonderful epitome of one aspect of the dialectical method, especially if we assent to Meredith's statement that "there are questions, as well as persons, that only the Comic can fitly touch." There is indeed a comedy of ideas as there is a comedy of persons. The comic spirit is nourished and sustained by various kinds of incongruity: ideas and beliefs no less than persons and situations may be instances of the ludicrous. Ideas and beliefs, too, may be pretentious, pedantic, fantastic, bizarre, grotesque, inept, perverse, reckless, blind, and blatant. The logic called dialectical is the logic of comedy *par excellence*. It is the logic by which ideas and beliefs are made to whip themselves, as it were, in the process of exhibiting their internal contradictions. But instead of showing us the absurdities of men and women inflicting evil upon themselves and each other in their blindness and self-delusion, as does the comic poet, the comic philosopher, whose weapon is dialectic, uncovers the antitheses of ideas and aberrations of beliefs, the aim of the two being the same, namely, to kindle "thoughtful laughter" at the sight of folly so everlastingly rampant.

Two illustrations, winnowed from Hegel's text, will show better than abstract analysis the comic spirit in its dialectical form. They are particularly instructive, for the logical absurdity of empiricism and scepticism is supposed indirectly to aid and abet Hegel's own rationalism and gnosticism.

Consider empiricism, and consider the unsophisticated expressions of it. Lovers of tangible facts, are they not disdainful of theory and speculation? They invariably appeal to the certainty of perception and to the palpable nature of the objects confronting us here and now. One may distinguish empiricists by the lavish use they make of the expressions "here" and "now." That which can be characterized by these two words, is this not, they will ask, a solid fact? What, indeed, may vie with it in solidity? The man of "common sense" will always applaud Dr. Johnson's refutation of Bishop Berkeley's denial of matter in behalf of an esoteric empiricism. Dr. Johnson accepted with alacrity Boswell's challenge to refute Berkeley's proof of the non-existence of matter. Striking his foot with mighty force against a large stone, Johnson simply said, "I refute it *thus.*" What a crushing rebuke to philosophical sophistry! The appeal to what is present here and now is assumed to enjoy indefeasible finality. Such a typical attitude Hegel selects for comic castigation. And his procedure is quite simple: it consists in undermining the self-assurance of the empiricist by reducing to absurdity the uncritical use of the terms "here" and "now." For these two labels are amazingly democratic. There is not a thing in the world to which they cannot be attached. But when something is said to be "here" or "now," *where* precisely is it, and *when* does it occur?

"Here" and "now" have elastic boundaries. If it is not to contract into a point without extension, "here" manifestly suggests any part of space. "Now," too, connotes any portion of time, if it is not to collapse into an instant without duration. Hence what we intend to convey by these two terms is quite flexible in meaning. Is a thing "here" because found in this room, in this country, on this continent, on this planet? So vast in extent is the term that "here" may be stretched to include everything located within our solar system as contrasted with what presumably falls outside it. And what we call "present" is equally catholic. For the word may qualify a moment, a day, a generation, a century. There is a definite sense in the contrast between the present geological age and a past period similarly immense in duration. So immeasurable is the span of time which with perfect propriety we may designate as the "present."

It is obvious that not a little analysis is needed to render intelligible what precisely we are to understand by the expressions "here" and "now." Their meaning is far from self-luminous. The man of empirical temper is thus called upon to define their application. But as soon as he begins to dabble in analysis and definition he is lost. Hegel, "impersonating" the point of view of such a man, shows how egregiously childish are his essays in generalizations about space and time. How absurd is "common sense" whenever it is induced to elucidate its understanding of abstract concepts! *Sobald er philosophiert ist er ein Kind.* This remark of Goethe about Byron is of much wider application. Its appositeness is borne out by many men of genius—whether artists or scientists—who in speculative innocence invade the field of philosophy. If Dr. Johnson, instead of crushing by his famous gesture

Berkeley's argument, had only confided to Boswell his thoughts about matter and mind, space and time, substance and cause, appearance and reality! What a "comic tragedian" is he who invokes his random perceptions to settle in cavalier fashion the formidable questions that daunted the brain of a Plato or a Kant! He is indeed the dupe of his own simplicity and ignorance. There is a *personne ingénue* in the realm of reason as there is in ordinary life. And Hegel's dialectical analysis of the philosophical simpleton is no less comical than Molière's portrayal of Agnès in *l'Ecole des Femmes*.

But, of course, all empiricism is not uncouth. It is not merely the inveterate belief that "seeing is believing." Empiricism may be entertained as a sophisticated theory. It is a refined doctrine, resting on the argument that perceptual immediacy is a type of cognition first in the order of genesis and second to none in absolute certitude. Is this, too, ridiculous? Yes, says Hegel, if the *objects* of perceptual immediacy are regarded as demonstrably particular. If we define the empirical way of knowing as a way concerned exclusively with particular objects—and thus Hegel "impersonates" sophisticated empiricism—what can rival it in absurdity? For particulars—things that are "here" and "now," endowed with "individual" qualities and relations—are essentially unutterable. We are obliged to introduce universals, "general" qualities and relations applicable to heterogeneous existences, in any attempt to describe the particular objects we experience. We perceive, for instance, a particular rose, but the description of it in terms of fragrance, shape, and color is general, relevant to every kind of flower. We never succeed in specifying the particular save in terms that define the *type* or the *class* of things to which it belongs. Perceptual immediacy and discursive language are incompatible. The immediate is ineffable; descriptions are compendious and catholic, never disclosing what is individual and incommensurable in the objects directly apprehended. Speech inevitably signifies the dominance of the common denominator. Hence empiricism, though intending to safeguard the reality of the particular, is doomed to silence, since it cannot without abandoning the particularity of its objects name or specify them. Empiricism, in a word, cannot say what it *means* (i.e. particulars) and it cannot mean what it *says* (i.e. universals). Either speechlessness or self-contradiction—this is the dilemma to which philosophical empiricism is reduced. As long as it chooses to be articulate, empiricism ceases to be true to itself; in equating the immediately perceived object with the conceptually described object, it becomes in fact indistinguishable from its rival. Not content with silence empiricism turns into rationalism. It becomes, as Hegel says, "its own other." Can anything be more comic?

The other attitude shown by Hegel in comic perspective is scepticism. The comedy of scepticism lies in its audacity. Temperate scepticism is not necessarily hilarious. Disciplined doubt, indeed, is the essence of sanity and good sense. We are not called upon to believe everything whenever we are exhorted not to be sceptics. Doubt and belief are inseparable. We are all a curious blend of faith and incredulity. It is the *objects* of belief and doubt that divide us: one man's god is another man's devil. What Hegel finds ridiculous is not negation of something definite, which is a corollary from the belief in its opposite, but the attitude of doubt when directed equally at everything. He portrays a doubting Thomas, not uncommon in philosophy and life, who is dominated by the idea that complete incredulity is a speculative privilege not to be curbed in the interest of freedom of thought. Doubt without restraint, however, is self-stultifying. Hegel has no difficulty in reducing it to absurdity. For the incongruity of complete scepticism lies in its fated incompleteness. The audacious sceptic is bound to find an insurmountable barrier to his temerity.

The freedom to doubt *everything,* if taken seriously, demands of course universal extension. And if all things without exception may be the prey of doubt, the doubter himself must obviously be included. But this is arrant nonsense. It is not possible to doubt one's own existence and yet continue existing to doubt it. The consciousness that doubts, as Descartes has shown, would seem to be in a privileged position; it remains invulnerable above the wreck wrought by universal negation. Yet, this very immunity from doubt is the sceptic's heel of Achilles; for if he cannot doubt himself he cannot doubt everything, and if he cannot doubt everything, he is not a complete sceptic, and if he is not a complete sceptic, his much vaunted freedom of thought is in jeopardy. *Absolute* doubt stayed by an unavoidable surd becomes absurd. The method of absolute doubt employed in behalf of absolute certainty, the famous Cartesian method, turns out to be ludicrous. The assumption of the *universal* applicability of doubt is either valid or invalid. If valid, everything is disproved, including the doubter, which is nonsense; if invalid, nothing is proved, save the impossibility of complete scepticism even as a pose.

Once universal scepticism is logically shaken, seeing that the sceptic at least is not in the grip of doubt, Hegel calls attention to a lesser and more common absurdity in which the inordinate doubter is involved. The intellectual freedom to deny is inconsistent with the practical necessity to affirm the recalcitrant facts of life. The sceptic, too, must live; he also must submit to the hard conditions nature imposes upon all creatures, thus negating in practice negations entertained in theory. The clash between theory and practice is laughable wherever discerned. Consider those who in the name of religion solemnly declare that all existence is vanity while hoarding wealth and pursuing pleasure! In the confirmed sceptic this clash is too patently comic, coerced as he is at every turn by the exigencies of life to repudiate his speculative pose. Unlimited negation, then, is self-contradictory in theory and impossible in practice. Doubt is a critical weapon of a positive sort. It can be used to attack insecure beliefs only from the vantage-ground of truth. Doubt implies a standard for testing the adequacy of human beliefs. Such a standard, Hegel's philosophy, based on the notion that "the truth is the whole," endeavors to furnish and to render operative. But it is a standard for the justification of which the dialectical method is indispensable, the method of impersonating all human points of view (including the point of view of the inveterate sceptic) as if they were adequate in order to uncover the incongruity inherent in them.

These two instances must suffice to indicate Hegel's discernment of the logically incongruous. Empiricism and scepticism are, however, obvious examples of the comic. Hegel does not confine himself to the obvious. In the *Phenomenology* he submits to comic analysis beliefs more profound and ideas more subtle. Nothing, indeed, escapes his dialectical scourge. Science and religion, morality and art, logic and history, heaven and earth—they are all shown to be replete with every form of fantastic folly. Hegel gives short shrift to whatever is finite and particular. His philosophy is a condemnation of the partial masquerading as the complete. Whatever is one-sided is absurd, suffering from the illusion of perspective and from the blindness of partisanship. This is the constant refrain. It culminates in the *Logic* in the drastic dictum that *"alle Dinge sind an sich selbst widersprechend."*

The incongruous character of "all things," disclosed by Hegel's method, is subject to two modes of interpretation, depending upon which aspect of the dialectic is singled out as primary. As a mode of insinuating oneself into the heart of every concept and attitude, the dialectical logic is one thing; as a way of discerning and revealing ubiquitous contradictions and absurdities, it is quite another. The histrionic use of the dialectic turns it into an instrument of transition and growth; the comic use of it transforms it into an objective weapon of observation and analysis. In the one case, the subject's protean impersonations occupy the stage; in the other, the substantial character of the world becomes the relevant focus. One implies idealism, the other realism.

The idealism to which the histrionic use of the dialectic is conducive is not unlike the idealism suggested by the cardinal principle of romanticism. The comparison will shock those who regard Hegel as the apostle of "panlogism" of which romanticists are indeed the passionate adversaries. None the less, the dialectical logic as a method of impersonation may be seen to lie cheek by jowl with the spirit of romanticism. For romanticism glorifies the self, and the self it exalts is a dynamic being of versatile genius, able to embrace and transcend all possible moods and experiences. The romantic individual is nothing if not experimental. All things must be tried, but all things must be left behind. His aim is self-enlargement or self-expansion by means of successive experiments with all phases of life. As artist, as critic, as lover, as philosopher, the romanticist is always inspired by a longing for an absolute ideal; and this longing at once justifies and condemns the attempt to see in every particular a hint or token of his unattainable ideal. The ideal, being literally nowhere, is symbolically everywhere. The romanticist can thus afford to be at once eclectic and fickle. Nothing is ever too jejune to be neglected or perfect enough to be espoused. Hence the expansiveness and waywardness of romantic art and life. Multifarious artistic forms, things of beauty, objects of love, noble passions—they are all but intimations of a transcendent ideal too deep for adequate utterance or embodiment. Of the tendency to test and to shun all particular expressions of the ideal, romantic irony is a singularly instructive illustration. It consists in the power to impersonate in rapid succession heterogeneous moods, passions, and attitudes, with apparent seriousness and sincerity, in order to show through subsequent parody and ridicule the artist's complete mastery over them. Romantic irony is an art essentially histrionic. It is the actor's art of concealing himself behind a character not his own, and then, the play being over, appearing without his mask to receive the plaudits for his masterly simulation, thus destroying the illusion of identity between himself and his rôle. Admiration for his creative art is enhanced by the recognition of disparity between his true and his assumed character. The actor, indeed, is genuinely most himself when he is least himself. He is never identical with the apparent character with which his art for the moment identifies him. And so with the romanticist. Never to be completely identical with what he chooses now and then to identify himself—this is his constant endeavor. His irony is a deliberate attempt to destroy the illusion his art has fashioned, thus riveting attention from the play to the player, from the art to the artist, from the character to the impersonator. It is a mode of making focal the creative personality of the artist rather than the moods and the passions he set out to personify. His power and freedom over the objects of his passion and imagination become manifest when from behind his mask the laughing countenance of the histrionic genius is suddenly visible.

> All forms of all faces,
>   All works of all hands
> In unsearchable places
>   Of time-stricken lands,
> All death and all life, and all reigns and all
>   ruins, drop through me as sands.

Romantic irony is employed to *display* this creative might of the self. The self is glorified through his power to transcend everything imaginable and everything thinkable. All ideas and all forms drop through him "as sands."

In Hegel's dialectical method, one may see, then, not inaptly, an application on a grand scale of the histrionic principle involved in romantic irony. This of course does not mean that we can "derive" Friedrich Hegel from Friedrich Schlegel. How far Schlegel, who elaborated the principle of romantic irony, directly influenced our philosopher, is a tantalizing problem not easy to solve. Hegel's method has various affinities. To Kant, to Fichte, to Schelling, Hegel's historical relations were intimate; and these thinkers had already made use of the dialectical method long before Hegel applied it on so vast a canvas in the *Phenomenology*. But it is precisely as it finds expression in that extraordinary book that the dialectical method invites comparison with the mobile and voracious spirit of romantic irony. "In my

view," says Hegel in the preface to the *Phenomenology,*
"everything depends on grasping and expressing the
ultimate truth not as Substance but as Subject as well."
A dark saying this, characteristically Hegelian. Who
and what is the "subject?" The little word, indeed,
epitomizes Hegel's romantic idealism. For by the subject, as the *Phenomenology* gradually discloses, Hegel
means a dynamic and histrionic being dramatically impersonating and ironically dissolving all possible views
of reality. That reality requires for its comprehension
just these histrionic and dissolving views is the insight
in which the subject's multiform experiments culminate.
But it is a final not an initial insight. It is a sort of
promised land, lending impetus and direction to the dialectical voyage of discovery. Though "assumed" before the "phenomenological" pilgrimage can be set in
motion, the contention that reality itself has a dialectical form and rhythm is supposed to be "proved" with
increasing coerciveness by the pilgrim's dialectical progress. The dialectical nature of reality, in brief, is deduced by Hegel from the dialectical way of knowing it.
Dialectic, being *primarily* a mode of experience, thus
imposes upon the "subject" the necessity of experiment-
ing in romantic fashion with all possible concepts and
all possible attitudes. They must all be successively
entertained and successively superseded. The subject of
knowledge, identifying itself with each, is identical with
none. It can attain its goal, defined by Hegel as *absolute knowledge,* only by alternately enacting and abandoning a series of cognitive rôles. To reach perfection
in the art of knowing, the "subject," like a versatile
actor, must constantly rehearse new parts. In the interest of truth it must mimic in progression a host of incompatible ideas and beliefs. Hence the significance
of Hegel's phrase, often quoted, that "truth is the

whole." Truth is what the "subject" experiences; and
since ways of experiencing are many and various and
conflicting, they are *all* true, but true progressively and
synoptically. To be *absolutely* true, then, the whole
requires a series of gradual and continuous approxima-
tions; but each member of the series, not being the whole
truth, is inevitably tainted with falsehood. The result
is that truth is a whole, each integral part of which is
mutilated or truncated. Hegel uses a rather violent
simile to convey this paradoxical form of truth, likening
it to a "bacchanalian revel, where not a soul is sober,"
yet "the revel is just as much a state of transparent unbroken calm." This conception of truth is the boldest
expression in philosophic dress of the cardinal principle
of romanticism. Truth is restless, experimental, elastic,
catholic. And the "subject" of all the distorted or "in-
ebriated" truths, constituting the "bacchanalian revel,"
is essentially insatiable, omnivorous, fastidious, protean.

Is the "subject," required to grasp and to express
"ultimate truth," a human self? Hegel's answer is not
unambiguous. From one point of view, it is a human
self (Hegel, the author of the *Phenomenology,* or we,
the readers of it) that must reproduce by successive
impersonations the continuous series of gradual approxi-
mations to absolute knowledge. Absolute knowledge is
the insight that "the truth is the whole." And such truth
is actually embodied in a human system of philosophy,
namely, the Hegelian, in so far as it can show that it has
traced the essential nature of reality in its self-development, and has encompassed the entire objective world
in its rational necessity. But from another point of view,
absolute knowledge means the knowledge of an absolute. The subject necessary for the comprehension and
expression of "ultimate truth" must be commensurate
with it. Only an "absolute" subject can grasp and per-

sonify the "whole" truth. Conversely, the "whole" truth, manifested in time's infinite stretches and requiring countless forms to body it forth, must be the object of a mind universal in extent and preternatural in quality. The actual "grasp" of such a truth (*Begriff* is Hegel's word, on which he rings numerous changes), obviously calls for a spirit with prodigious tentacles, so to speak, to clutch it. When the dialectic, viewed as a vehicle of human discourse, has actually reached its goal, the goal by a sort of *tour de force* turns out to be a super-human mind whose dialectical experience constitutes the stupendous wealth and labor of the objective world. The *absolutely known,* which the dialectical logic finally succeeds in revealing, coalesces in the end with the reality of an *absolute knower.* The known *is* the knower; thought and being are one. This is Hegel's avowed idealism—the identification of the essence and evolution of the universe with the activity of an all-pervading mind—resulting from making central the dialectical process as a mode of insatiable experience.

When, however, the dialectical method is envisaged not as an organ of spiritual growth but as an instrument of comic discernment, the philosophy consonant with it is that of realism, if realism is a name for the belief that things are "substantial" rather than "subjective," that reality possesses an independent nature not conforming to mind but rather exacting submission from it. This indeed is a fundamental tenet of Hegel's philosophy, in behalf of which the dailectical logic is so generously employed, so long as mind is understood to be *merely* human. The comedy or tragi-comedy of the human mind, as Hegel portrays it, consists in its blindness, ignorance, conceit, delusion, and impotence in the face of a stubborn world that is too much with us. The mind that seeks to dominate or to reform this vener-

able world of ours, to use or to malign it, to be happy
in it or to flee from it, soon discovers the solidity and
the perversity of things. Mind proposes but the world
disposes. The world triumphs in the end. The countless efforts to assimilate a recalcitrant reality to the
mind's particular needs and purposes must in the long
run come to grief. Hegel shows in comic perspective
our inevitable propensity to feel and think and act as
if the world were nothing else than the servant of our
interests and the minister of our wants. Humanity is
but human; the universe must be drawn to a vaster
scale. The human mind is continually enmeshed in folly
precisely because it *is* human: it is finite, limited, self-
centered, partisan, fatuous. To be sure, a super-human
mind, a spirit that "grasps" truth in its wholeness, is
supposed to express itself in all the forms of human
folly, to require them for its dynamic life, and to reconcile them by its eternal reason; this, indeed, is the
paradoxical view entertained by Hegel to render human
unreason itself *ultimately* rational. But the eventual
sublimation of folly does not cancel its actual absurdity.
The dialectical analysis of the human mind to which
Hegel treats us demands as a matter of fact at every
turn a "substantial" world with which consciousness
vehemently collides. That *in the end* the world loses its
ordinary substantiality and comes to be identified with
an absolute "subject" in the fullness of whose histrionic
life all incongruities form a divine harmony is irrelevant
for the comic situations we are bidden to witness. These
situations are comic not because a super-human spirit
requires to absorb and transmute a host of absurdities
but simply because these absurdities *are* absurd, inherently and indefeasibly.

The logic of this is simple. If short of the "whole",
as Hegel teaches, everything is the prey of self-contra-

diction, then the "parts", being but parts, are necessarily
infected with the poison of irrationality. It is this pois-
onous infection—Hegel calls it *absolute Negativitaet*—
which causes the universal urge towards wholeness; but
the whole is a "bacchanalian revel", a whole of parts
all vainly struggling to be more than mere parts. In the
self-aggrandizement of each part, which the whole at
once incites and defeats, lies its intrinsic and eternal
comedy. Hegel expresses this by saying, in the cryptic
and esoteric style of his *Phenomenology*, that *"jedes
Moment, weil es Moment des Wesens ist, muss selbst
dazu gelangen, als Wesen sich darzustellen"*. This
means (rendered freely) that the parts of which the
world consists all suffer from an exaggerated sense of
their importance, each seeking to draw all the others
within its particular orbit, each regarding itself as the
essential and favored representative of the whole. The
conflicts between science and religion, art and morality,
one national culture and another—are they not instances
of the peculiar and perpetual error of the human mind
to magnify out of proportion in the name of *all* truth or
all civilization a *particular* set of interests or values?
The four classes of "idols" which beset men's minds,
made famous by Francis Bacon, they too spring perpetually from the illusions of perspective to which intellectual pretension, moral arrogance, and emotional
aberration are always subject. The human mind is
incurably "idolatrous" because it moves in concentric
circles. It worships at this shrine or that shrine the
particular gods that attract and excite it.

Now the inexhaustible source of genuine comedy lies
in the perception and exhibition of human extravagance.
All comedy achieves its effect by rendering ridiculous
those ailing from the illusion of perspective. Aristophanes, Rabelais, Voltaire, Cervantes, Fielding, Molière,

George Meredith, Anatole France, Bernard Shaw—to
mention some of the most renowned masters of comic
discernment—show by different means of form and expression how folly or delusion is perennially gnawing
at the flesh of the human spirit. Folly or delusion—
it matters little by which name we designate the generic
condition that produces specific absurdities and incongruities—is of course a many-headed monster, sliding
into various shapes, appearing in different guises, recurring under different forms. Can the myriad aspects
of folly or delusion be brought under a common formula?
The formula provided by Hegel's philosophy is certainly not lacking in comprehensiveness. Delusion is
narrowness of perspective. Folly is straining of the
particular. The constant object of comic observation
and laughter, is it not the disproportionate excess of
something particular—a particular passion, a particular
interest, a particular belief, a particular attitude, a particular ideal? In uncovering without scruple the logical
ridiculousness of everything steeped in its own inordinate particularity, Hegel has supplied comedy with a
metaphysical underpinning of great depth and solidity.

But this metaphysical underpinning, it can now be
shown, has greater affinity with realism than with idealism. For in Hegel's philosophy mind itself is the comic
dramatis persona. Mind itself in all its *human* manifestations, is an overweening and unregenerate particular. Every mode of human experience is deluded by its
own partial vision, mistaking for absolute what is but
relative, and drawing everything from its illusory perspective. The disproportionate excesses of the human
mind are thus sadly in need of correction. How?
Hegel's own answer in terms of his idealism is itself a
comic instance; the dialectical method renders it absurd. The perspective of human experience, so he

maintains, can only be corrected by rising above it to an absolute or super-human experience with which it is continuous. The *Phenomenology* (the English translator of this work remarks in his preface) "enables us to determine the position of Absolute Truth, and the parallax of the Absolute can only be found if we take as our base-line the diameter of the orbit of human experience." This statement, though its astronomical idiom is foreign to Hegel's thought, is not an infelicitous rendering of his deepest conviction: in the spiritual life of humanity are to be found the lineaments however distorted of what is ultimately most real and most true. Man is the image of the divine. The human state is the god on earth. Human art, human religion, human philosophy are the steps of Jacob's ladder leading to the heaven of the Absolute Mind. But all this is a refined version of anthropomorphism. It demands that we interpret the whole in terms of the part, and that part especially to which as human beings we are not altogether impartial. The folly of drawing the whole to the scale of the part is just what the dialectical method singles out as proper food for the Comic Spirit. Can Hegel's idealism escape the scourge of his own method? We wonder. His method, designed as it is to chastise everything particular, must impugn necessarily the idolatrous attempt to exalt the human mind by regarding its characteristic forms of experience and discourse as the measure of the Absolute. The apotheosis of mind has its logical source in the propensity peculiar to every particular part of the whole to magnify its own importance and to endow with preëminence its congenital and provincial interest. From this point of view, idealism is indeed inevitable; the identification of absolute reality with mind or spirit is in conformity with the principle of self-aggrandizement governing all partial and partisan perspectives. But though inevitable, as nationalism is inevitable, idealism is not less comic, since it too represents the universal intent to enshrine the whole in some favored part. In so far, then, as the dialectical method is used by Hegel to render ridiculous the usurpation of reality by any of its particular manifestations, the apotheosis of mind is obviously a delectable theme for comic treatment. Of idealism Hegel's logic is thus not unambiguously the pet purveyor. It drives us rather into the arms of realism, provided realism be understood as a theory that assigns to spirit no privileged place in the economy of substantial things.

Hegel's method leads to results that are not free from ambiguity. It is a double-edged sword. The idealism it establishes is certainly equivocal. Of this idealism Mr. Santayana has said, perhaps harshly but not unjustly, that it "is simply contempt for all ideals, and a hearty adoration of things as they are." This is an adequate judgment of but half of Hegel's story; for in Hegel all depends upon whether the point of view taken is human or non-human. The comic portrayal of everything human is hardly conducive to an unflinching apology for the established order of things. Hegel's dialectical analysis of life involves a merciless criticism of whatever is prized as permanent and invincible. Nations, creeds, sentiments—they are all unstable and doomed to be fugitive. The recognition that change is the lord of the world is usually not regarded as the dominant trait of conservatism. Radicalism towards all things *temporal* is what Hegel's logic most inexorably proclaims. But this is only one edge of the dialectical sword. There is the other edge. The oscillations of fortune in history are not merely temporal; they are the necessary beats of a universal rhythm. Viewed *logically,* things mutable are unchangeable parts of a rational order. From the point of view of a superhuman mind, a mind omnipresent and omniscient, all things and events are indispensable manifestations of a spiritual cosmos. Whatever happens can thus be justified in advance. The institutions that prevail, seen in their timeless necessity and truth, are as spiritual as it is possible for them to be. Not entirely misguided are those who accuse Hegel's philosophy of collusion with the dominant interests and powers of the nation or of the world. The cross-purposes which different races or ages strive to bring to fruition are all grist to the mill of the absolute: whatever happens must be regarded as inevitable and rational and good. It belongs to the pathos of Hegel's idealism to permit "a hearty adoration of things as they are." The established order is *always* the right order. *Realpolitik* is the legitimate child of Hegel's logic. Whatever is, is. And whatever is, is right.

Is Hegel's philosophy a vindication of optimism or of pessimism? Here again his position is equivocal. In one sense, Hegel's philosophy is a *Theodicy,* a justification of the ways of God. It stoutly maintains, as does Browning's poetry, that

> God's in His heaven—
> All's right with the world!

Appearances notwithstanding, the universe is a paragon of goodness and rationality. As an *organic whole,* the universe absorbs and transmutes all its unspiritual parts; as a *perpetual process,* it overcomes and transcends them. An absolute subject, with which the universe is identified, enacts and supersedes all the seemingly irrational gyrations in nature and history, and in so doing renders them ultimately spiritual. Nothing evil, however diabolical, is sufficiently impregnable to resist the ubiquitous process of dialectical sublimation. With

apparent sincerity Hegel could pronounce the famous
judgments that "what is real is rational" and that "what
is rational is real." Optimism could hardly go farther.
In the face of the trials and the tragedies of life, which
none better than he knew how to descry, Hegel actually
believed in the possibility of exhibiting that a symmetrical relation obtains between reality and rationality. Yet,
in another sense, Hegel's philosophy may be characterized as a *Demonodicy*, a justification of the ways of the
devil. From the human vantage-point the world appears as essentially unsublimated. The world inhabited
by the human mind is the scene of pain and sorrow, sin
and anguish, struggle and defeat. Grave is the life of
mind as human history displays and unfolds it. What
could be graver than the vision of life as comic? What
more tragic than the view that human folly is universal
and ineradicable? Hegel has himself, with characteristic love of paradox, called attention to the tragic
implications of comedy. The issues that hang in the balance in Greek comedy—this at all events is the view expressed in the *Phenomenology*—are far more tragic than
are those dealt with in Greek tragedy. Indeed, Greek
comedy may well be regarded as the most tragic turning point in ancient civilization; for in Greek comedy the
ideals and values acknowledged and reverenced in Greek
tragedy are mercilessly abandoned to scorn and ridicule.
The tragic significance of Greek comedy lies in its
sweeping iconoclasm. That behind the most sacred
things lurks ignorance or delusion is a terrifying revelation. That holiness is born of folly is an agonizing insight. Such an insight if suffered to become dominant
must necessarily lead to universal despair; and that
Greek comedy succeeded in engendering the despair that
prepared the soil of the human mind for the reception
of Christianity is Hegel's main theme. The Christian

religion is here interpreted as affording an escape from the pessimism rendered imperative by comedy. Be that as it may, the comic spirit, if seen to hover over all things earthly, is surely one of the parents of pessimism. And the pessimism which Hegel adroitly discerns as the outcome of Greek comedy is equally implied by his dialectical analysis of the human scene. Everything human is subject to folly. Life is a perpetual comedy. Nothing is free from incongruity. Contradiction pervades all human ideas and beliefs.

Hegel's philosophy regarded eulogistically is a sort of *divine* comedy. For Hegel and his disciples the saving grace is in the adjective. The world, indeed, is a comedy, since all its parts are awry and absurd, but these very parts are "the great world's altar-stairs, that slope through darkness up to God." The *whole* is spiritual. The infernal work of Satan is necessary for supernal triumph. The march of the world, which is the march of the Absolute itself, is through Hell and Purgatory. This divine comedy, holding in solution all the mundane torments and defeats, is too sublime for laughter. Hegel's cosmic comedy is as awe-inspiring as Dante's: folly, being divinely appointed, is no longer ludicrous. Comedy thus deeply conceived ceases to be comic. Only the "happy ending," so to speak, in a preternatural sense and on a cosmic scale, saves Hegel's picture of the world (as well as Dante's) from assuming the character of an unmitigated tragedy.

Not lacking in impressiveness is Hegel when robbed of his grand manner. His philosophy may be envisaged in a less eulogistic fashion. Without the beatific vision of the all-encompassing Absolute it is ultimately intent upon, his philosophy retains the value of a *human* comedy more comprehensive and more diversified than any of its kind. It is a tragi-comic biography of human experience, encyclopedic in scope and of unrivalled detachment in observation and criticism. In an altogether unique way, it sums up the myriad attempts of mankind, recurring rhythmically as do the seasons, to adapt an obdurate universe to certain preferential ideas and interests. Hegel's strength lies in his clear perception of the actual. "Merely as a reporter of certain empirical aspects of the actual," as William James says of him, "Hegel is great and true." Hegel's philosophical comedy is "great and true" in revealing, as does literary comedy, what transpires in our actual world. The violent opposition of ideas and the wanton antagonism of wills are venerable themes; the variations of them discerned by all comic writers have but the appearance of novelty. For this reason genuine comedy neither preaches nor does it scold: it emanates from a realistic conception that human follies are patterns of behavior not of to-day or of yesterday. What inspires and directs all great comedy is the shrewd observation of a repetitive rhythm in human delusions and contradictions. Of this Hegel's dialectic is a singular expression. With all its abstruseness and obfuscation it is an ingenious instrument of comic art. When all the technical trappings are laid aside Hegel emerges as a comic genius of the first water. He is the laughing philosopher, but his laughter is sober, his laughter is sad.

It is hardly feasible to settle the question whether this or that interpretation of Hegel is the right key to the secret of his system. In Hegel's system there are many mansions, and many are the doors leading to the treasures that are laid up in them. The diversity of opinion on a system so commodious, so catholic, so recondite is not unnatural. Conflicting explanations are bound to be offered of a philosophy which in conception and utterance gives every appearance of a labyrinth. And so of "keys" to Hegel there is a bewildering plenitude, all succeeding in opening some obscure chambers of thought or inspiration. But the "Secret of Hegel" (borrowing the phrase from the title of a book which purports to unriddle his philosophy) is still a secret.

J. LOEWENBERG.

SHORT BIBLIOGRAPHY

Croce, B. What is living and what is dead in the Philosophy of Hegel. Translated by D. Ainslie. London, 1915. [An excellent bibliography of Hegel is appended to the German and French translations of this book]

McTaggart, J. M. E. Studies in the Hegelian Dialectic. 2nd ed. Cambridge, 1922.

Reyburn, H. A. The ethical theory of Hegel. Oxford, 1921.

Royce, J. Lectures on Modern Idealism. chs. 6-10. New Haven, 1919.

Stace, W. T. The Philosophy of Hegel. London, 1924.

Wallace, W. Prolegomena to the Study of Hegel's Philosophy. 2nd ed. Oxford, 1894.

HEGEL
Selections

PHENOMENOLOGY OF MIND

PREFACE

Translated by J. B. Baillie

In the case of a philosophical work it seems not only superfluous, but, in view of the nature of the subject, even inappropriate and inexpedient to begin, as writers usually do, with a preface explaining the end the author had in mind, the circumstances which gave rise to the work, and the relation in which the writer takes it to stand to other treatises on the same subject, written by his predecessors or his contemporaries. For whatever it might be suitable to state about philosophy in a preface—say, an historical sketch of the main drift and point of view, the general content and results, a string of desultory assertions and assurances about truth—this cannot be accepted as the form and manner in which to expound philosophical truth.

Moreover, because philosophy has its being essentially in the element of universality, which encloses the particular within it, the end or final result seems, in the case of philosophy more than in that of other sciences, to have absolutely expressed the complete fact itself in its very nature, for which the mere process of bringing it to light would seem, properly speaking, to have no essential significance. On the other hand, in the general idea of e.g. anatomy—the knowledge of the parts of the body regarded as lifeless—we are quite sure we do not possess the objective concrete fact, the actual

1

content of the science, but must, over and above, be concerned with particulars. Further, in the case of such a collection of items of knowledge, which has no real right to the name of science, any talk about purpose and such-like generalities is not commonly very different in manner from the descriptive and superficial way in which the contents of the science—these nerves and muscles, etc.—are themselves spoken of. In philosophy, on the other hand, it would at once be felt incongruous were such a method made use of and yet shown by philosophy itself to be incapable of grasping the truth.

In the same way too by determining the relation which a philosophical work professes to have to other treatises on the same subject, an extraneous interest is introduced, and obscurity is thrown over the point at issue in the knowledge of the truth. The more the ordinary mind takes the opposition between true and false to be fixed, the more is it accustomed to expect either agreement or contradiction with a given philosophical system, and only to see the one or the other in any explanation about such a system. It does not conceive the diversity of philosophical systems as the progressive evolution of truth; rather, it sees only contradiction in that variety. The bud disappears when the blossom breaks through, and we might say that the former is refuted by the latter; in the same way when the fruit comes, the blossom may be explained to be a false form of the plant's existence, for the fruit appears as its true nature in place of the blossom. These stages are not merely differentiated; they supplant one another as being incompatible with one another. But the ceaseless activity of their own inherent nature makes them at the same time moments of an organic unity, where they not merely do not contradict one another, but where one is as necessary as the other; and this equal necessity of all moments constitutes from the outset the life of the whole. But contradiction in the case of a philosophical system is not usually conceived in this way; and again, the mind perceiving the contradiction does not commonly know how to relieve it or keep it free of onesidedness, or to recognise in what seems conflicting and inherently antagonistic the presence of mutually necessary moments.

The demand for such explanations, as also the attempts to satisfy this demand, very easily pass for the essential business philosophy has to undertake. Where could the inmost truth of a philosophical work be found better expressed than in its purposes and results? and in what way could these be more definitely known than through their distinction from what is produced during the same period by others working in the same field? If, however, such procedure is to pass for more than the beginning of knowledge, if it is to pass for actually knowing what a philosophical system is, then we must, in point of fact, look on it as a device for avoiding the real business at issue, an attempt to combine the appearance of being in earnest and taking trouble about the subject with an actual neglect of the subject altogether. For the real subject-matter is not exhausted in its purpose, but in working the matter out; nor is the mere result attained the concrete whole itself, but the result along with the process of arriving at it. The purpose by itself is a lifeless universal, just as the general drift is a bare activity in a certain direction, which is still without its concrete realisation; and the naked result is the corpse of the system which has left its guiding tendency behind it. Similarly, the distinctive difference of anything is rather the boundary, the limit, of the subject; it is found at that point where the matter stops, or it is what the matter is *not*. To trouble oneself in this fashion with the purpose and results, or again with the differences, the positions taken up and judgments passed by one thinker and another, is therefore an easier task than perhaps it seems. For instead of laying hold of the matter itself, a procedure of that kind is all the while away from the subject altogether. Instead of dwelling within it and becoming absorbed by it, knowledge of that sort is always grasping at something else; such knowledge, instead of keeping to the subject-matter and giving itself up to it, never gets away from itself. The easiest thing of all is to pass judgments on what has a solid substantial content; it is more difficult to grasp it, and most of all difficult to do both together and produce the systematic exposition of it.

The beginning of culture and of the struggle to get out of the unbroken immediacy of naïve psychical life has always to be made by acquiring knowledge of universal principles and points of view, by striving, in the first instance, to work up simply to the *thought* of the subject-matter in general, not forgetting at the same time to give reasons for supporting it or refuting it, to apprehend the concrete riches and fullness contained in its various determinate qualities, and to know how to furnish a coherent, orderly account of it and a responsible judgment upon it. This beginning of mental cultivation will, however, very soon make way for the earnestness of actual life in all its fullness, which leads to a living experience of the subject-matter itself; and when, in addition, conceptual thought strenuously penetrates to the very depths of its meaning, such knowledge and style of judgment will be relegated to their due place in everyday thought and conversation.

The systematic development of truth in scientific form can alone be the true shape in which truth exists. To help to bring philosophy nearer to the form of science—

that goal where it can lay aside the name of *love* of knowledge and be actual *knowledge*—that is what I have set before me. The inner necessity that knowledge should be science lies in its very nature; and the adequate and sufficient reason for this is simply and solely the systematic exposition of philosophy itself. The external necessity, however, so far as this is apprehended in a universal way, and apart from the accident of the personal element and the particular occasioning influences affecting the individual, is the same as the internal: it lies in the form and shape in which the process of time presents the existence of its moments. To show that the time has come to raise philosophy to the level of scientific system would, therefore, be the only true justification of the attempts which aim at proving that philosophy must assume this character; because the temporal process would thus bring out and lay bare the necessity of it, nay, more, would at the same time be carrying out that very aim itself.

When we state the true form of truth to be its scientific character—or, what is the same thing, when it is maintained that truth finds the medium of its existence in notions or conceptions alone—I know that this seems to contradict an idea with all its consequences which makes great pretensions and has gained widespread acceptance and conviction at the present time. A word of explanation concerning this contradiction seems, therefore, not out of place, even though at this stage it can amount to no more than a dogmatic assurance exactly like the view we are opposing. If, that is to say, truth exists merely in what, or rather exists merely *as* what, is called at one time intuition, at another immediate knowledge of the Absolute, religion, Being—not being in the centre of divine love, but the very Being of this centre, of the Absolute itself—from that point of view it is rather the opposite of the notional or conceptual form which would be required for systematic philosophical exposition. The Absolute would not be grasped in conceptual form, but felt, intuited; it is not its conception, but the feeling of it and intuition of it that are to have the say and find expression.

If we consider the appearance of a claim like this in its more general setting, and look at it from the level which the self-conscious mind at present occupies, we shall find that self-consciousness has got beyond the substantial fullness of life, which it used to carry on in the element of thought—beyond this naïve immediacy of belief, beyond the satisfaction and security arising from the sense of certainty which conscious life possessed regarding its reconciliation with ultimate reality wherever present, whether inner or outer. Self-conscious mind has not merely passed beyond that to the opposite extreme of insubstantial reflection of self into self, but beyond this too. It has not merely lost its essential and concrete life, it is also conscious of this loss and of the transitory finitude characteristic of its content. Turning away from the husks it has to feed on, and confessing that it lies in wickedness and sin, it reviles itself for so doing, and now desires from philosophy not so much to bring it to a knowledge of what it is, as to obtain once again through philosophy the restoration of that comfortably solid and substantial mode of existence it has lost. Philosophy is thus expected not so much to meet this want by opening up the compact solidity of substantial existence, and bringing this to the light and level of self-consciousness—is not so much to get chaotic conscious life brought back to the orderly ways of thought, and the simple unity of the concept, as to run together what thought has divided asunder, suppress the notion with its distinctions, and restore the *feeling* of existence. What it wants from philosophy is not so much insight as edification. The beautiful, the holy, the eternal, religion, love—these are the bait required to awaken the desire to bite: not the notion, but ecstasy, not the march of cold necessity in the subject-matter, but ferment and enthusiasm—these are to be the ways by which the wealth of the concrete substance is to be stored and spread out to view.

With this demand there goes the strenuous effort, almost perfervidly zealous in its activity, to rescue mankind from being sunken in what is sensuous, vulgar, and of fleeting importance, and to raise men's eyes to the stars; as if men had quite forgotten the divine, and were on the verge of finding satisfaction, like worms, in mud and water. Time was when man had a heaven, decked and fitted out with endless wealth of thoughts and pictures. The significance of all that is, lay in the thread of light by which it was attached to heaven; instead of dwelling in the present as it is here and now, the eye glided away over the present to the Divine, away, so to say, to a present that lies beyond. The mind's gaze had to be directed under compulsion to what is earthly, and kept fixed there; and it has needed a long time to introduce that clearness, which only celestial realities had, into the crassness and confusion shrouding the sense of things earthly, and to make attention to the immediate present as such, which was called Experience, of interest and of value. Now we have apparently the need for the opposite of all this; man's mind and interest are so deeply rooted in the earthly that we require a like power to get them raised above that level. His spirit shows such poverty of nature that it seems to long for the mere pitiful feeling of the divine in the abstract, and to get refreshment from that, like a wanderer in the desert craving for the

merest mouthful of water.   By the little which can thus
satisfy the needs of the human spirit we can measure
the extent of its loss.

This easy contentment in receiving, or stinginess in
giving, does not suit the character of science.   The man
who only seeks edification, who wants to envelop in mist
the manifold diversity of his earthly existence and
thought, and craves after the vague enjoyment of this
vague and indeterminate Divinity—he may look where
he likes to find this: he will easily find for himself the
means to get something he can rave over and puff
himself up with.   But philosophy must beware of the
wish to be edifying.

Still less must this kind of contentment, which holds
science in contempt, take upon itself to claim that raving obscurantism of this sort is something higher than
science.   These apocalyptic utterances pretend to occupy the very centre and the deepest depths; they look
askance at all definiteness and preciseness (ὅρος) of
meaning; and they deliberately hold back from conceptual thinking and the constraining necessities of
thought, as being the sort of reflection which, they say,
can only feel at home in the sphere of finitude.   But
just as there is a breadth which is emptiness, there is a
depth which is empty too: as we may have an extension
of substance which overflows into finite multiplicity
without the power of keeping the manifold together, in
the same way we may have an insubstantial intensity
which, keeping itself in as mere force without actual
expression, is no better than superficiality.   The force
of mind is only as great as its expression; its depth only
as deep as its power to expand and lose itself when
spending and giving out its substance.   Moreover, when
this unreflective emotional knowledge makes a pretext
of having immersed its own very self in the depths of

the absolute Being, and of philosophising in all holiness and truth, it hides from itself the fact that instead of devotion to God, it rather, by this contempt for all measurable precision and definiteness, simply confirms in its own case the fortuitous character of its content, and on the other endows God with its own caprice. When such minds commit themselves to the unrestrained ferment of sheer emotion, they think that, by putting a veil over self-consciousness, and surrendering all understanding, they are thus God's beloved ones to whom He gives His wisdom in sleep. This is the reason, too, that in point of fact what they do conceive and bring forth in sleep is dreams.

For the rest it is not difficult to see that our epoch is a birth-time, and a period of transition. The spirit of the age has broken with the world as it has hitherto existed, and with the old ways of thinking, and is in the mind to let them all sink into the depths of the past and to set about its own transformation. It is indeed never at rest, but carried along the stream of progress ever onward. But it is here as in the case of the birth of a child; after a long period of nutrition in silence, the continuity of the gradual growth in size, of quantitative change, is suddenly cut short by the first breath drawn—there is a break in the process, a qualitative change—and the child is born. In like manner the spirit of the time, growing slowly and quietly ripe for the new form it is to assume, loosens one fragment after another of the structure of its previous world. That it is tottering to its fall is indicated only by symptoms here and there. Frivolity and again ennui, which are spreading in the established order of things, the undefined foreboding of something unknown —all these are hints foretelling that there is something else approaching. This gradual crumbling to pieces, which did not alter the general look and aspect of the whole, is interrupted by the sunrise, which, in a flash and at a single stroke, brings to view the form and structure of the new world.

But this new world is perfectly realised just as little as the new-born child; and it is essential to bear this in mind. It comes on the stage to begin with in its immediacy, in its bare generality. A building is not finished when its foundation is laid; and just as little is the attainment of a general notion of a whole the whole itself. When we want to see an oak with all its vigour of trunk, its spreading branches, and mass of foliage, we are not satisfied to be shown an acorn instead. In the same way science, the crowning glory of a spiritual world, is not found complete in its initial stages. The beginning of the new spirit is the outcome of an extensive transformation of manifold forms of spiritual culture; it is the reward which comes after a chequered and devious course of development, and after much struggle and effort. It is a whole which, after running its course and laying bare all its content, returns again to itself; it is the resultant abstract notion of the whole. But the actual realisation of this abstract whole is only found when those previous shapes and forms, which are now reduced to ideal moments of the whole, are developed anew again, but developed and shaped within this new medium, and with the meaning they have thereby acquired.

While the new world makes its first appearance merely in general outline, merely as a whole lying concealed and hidden within a bare abstraction, the wealth of the bygone life, on the other hand, is still consciously present in recollection. Consciousness misses in the new form the detailed expanse of content; but still more the developed expression of form by which distinctions are definitely determined and arranged in their precise relations. Without this last feature science has no general intelligibility, and has the appearance of being an esoteric possession of a few individuals—an esoteric possession, because in the first instance it is only the essential principle or notion of science, only its inner nature that is to be found; and a possession of few individuals, because, at its first appearance, its content is not elaborated and expanded in detail, and thus its existence is turned into something particular. Only what is perfectly determinate in form is at the same time exoteric, comprehensible, and capable of being learned and possessed by everybody. Intelligibility is the form in which science is offered to everyone, and is the open road to it made plain for all. To reach rational knowledge by our intelligence is the just demand of the mind which comes to science. For intelligence, understanding (*Verstand*), is thinking, pure activity of the self in general; and what is intelligible (*Verständige*) is something from the first familiar and common to the scientific and unscientific mind alike, enabling the unscientific mind to enter the domain of science.

Science, at its commencement, when as yet it has neither got as far as detailed completeness nor perfection of form, is exposed to blame on that account. But to suppose this blame to attach to its essential nature would be as unjust, as it is inadmissible not to be ready to recognise the demand for that further development in fuller detail. In the contrast and opposition between these two aspects (the initial and the developed stages of science) seems to lie the critical knot which scientific culture at present struggles to loosen, and about which it is so far not very clear. One side parades the wealth of its material and the intelligibility of its ideas; the other pours contempt at any rate on the latter, and makes a parade of the immediate intuitive rationality and divine quality of its content. Although the first is reduced to silence, perhaps by the inner force of truth alone, perhaps, too, by the noisy bluster of the other side, and though having regard to the reason and nature of the case it did feel overborne, yet it does not therefore feel satisfied as regards those demands for greater development; for those demands are just, but still unfulfilled. Its silence is due only in part to the victory of the other side; it is half due to that weariness and indifference which are usually the consequence when expectations are being constantly awakened by promises which are not followed up by performance.

The other side * no doubt at times makes an easy enough matter of getting a vast expanse of content. They haul in a lot of material—already familiar and arranged in order; and since they are concerned more especially about what is exceptional, strange, and curious, they seem all the more to be in possession of the rest, which knowledge in its own way was finished and done with, as well as to have control over what was unregulated and disorderly. Hence everything appears brought within the compass of the Absolute Idea, which seems thus to be recognised in everything, and to have succeeded in becoming a system *in extenso* of scientific knowledge. But if we look more closely at this expanded system we find that it has not been reached by one and the same principle taking shape in diverse ways; it is the shapeless repetition of one and the same idea, which is applied in an external fashion to different material, the wearisome reiteration of it keeping up the semblance of diversity. The Idea, which by itself is no doubt the truth, really never gets any farther than just

* Schelling and his school.

where it began, as long as the development of it consists in nothing else than such a repetition of the same formula. If the knowing subject carries round everywhere the one inert abstract form, taking up in external fashion whatever material comes his way, and dipping it into this element, then this comes about as near to fulfilling what is wanted—viz., a self-origination of the wealth of detail, and a self-determining distinction of shapes and forms—as any chance fancies about the content in question. It is rather a monotonous formalism, which only comes by distinction in the matter it has to deal with, because this is already prepared and well known.

This monotonousness and abstract universality are maintained to be the Absolute. This formalism insists that to be dissatisfied therewith argues an incapacity to grasp the standpoint of the Absolute, and keep a firm hold on it. If it was once the case that the bare possibility of thinking of something in some other fashion was sufficient to refute a given idea, and the naked possibility, the bare general thought, possessed and passed for the entire substantive value of actual knowledge; we find here similarly all the value ascribed to the general idea in this bare form without concrete realisation; and we see here, too, the style and method of speculative contemplation identified with dissipating and resolving what is determinate and distinct, or rather with hurling it down, without more ado and without any justification, into the abyss of vacuity. To consider any specific fact as it is in the Absolute, consists here in nothing else than saying about it that, while it is now doubtless spoken of as something specific, yet in the Absolute, in the abstract identity $A = A$, there is no such thing at all, for everything is there all one. To pit this single assertion, that "in the Absolute all is one," against the organised whole of determinate and complete knowledge, or of knowledge which at least aims at and demands complete development—to give out its Absolute as the night in which, as we say, all cows are black—that is the very *naïveté* of vacuous knowledge.

The formalism which has been deprecated and despised by recent philosophy, and which has arisen once more in philosophy itself, will not disappear from science, even though its inadequacy is known and felt, till the knowledge of absolute reality has become quite clear as to what its own true nature consists in. Having in mind that the general idea of what is to be done, if it precedes the attempt to carry it out, facilitates the comprehension of this process, it is worth while to indicate here some rough idea of it, with the hope at the same time that this will give us the opportunity to set aside certain forms whose habitual presence is a hindrance in the way of speculative knowledge.

In my view—a view which the developed exposition of the system itself can alone justify—everything depends on grasping and expressing the ultimate truth not as Substance but as Subject as well. At the same time we must note that concrete substantiality implicates and involves the universal or the immediacy of knowledge itself, as well as the immediacy which is being, or immediacy *qua* object *for* knowledge. If the generation which heard God spoken of as the One Substance * was shocked and revolted by such a characterisation of his nature, the reason lay partly in the instinctive feeling that in such a conception self-consciousness was simply submerged, and not preserved. But partly, again, the opposite position, which maintains thinking to be merely subjective thinking, abstract universality as such, is ex-

* Spinoza.

actly the same bare uniformity, is undifferentiated, un-moved substantiality.* And even if, in the third place, thought combines with itself the being of substance, and conceives immediacy or intuition (*Anschauung*) as think-ing, it is still a question whether this intellectual intui-tion does not fall back into that inert, abstract simplic-ity, and exhibit and expound reality itself in an unreal manner.†

The living substance, further, is that being which is truly subject, or, what is the same thing, is truly real-ised and actual (*wirklich*) solely in the process of positing itself, or in mediating with its own self in tran-sitions from one state or position to the opposite. As subject it is pure and simple negativity, and just on that account a process of splitting up what is simple and undifferentiated, a process of duplicating and set-ting factors in opposition, which [process] in turn is the negation of this indifferent diversity and of the opposition of factors it entails. True reality is merely this process of reinstating self-identity, of reflecting into its own self in and from its other, and is not an original and primal unity as such, not an immediate unity as such. It is the process of its own becoming, the circle which presupposes its end or its purpose, and has its end for its beginning; it becomes concrete and actual only by being carried out, and by the end it involves.

The life of God and divine intelligence, then, can, if we like, be spoken of as love disporting with itself; but this idea falls into edification, and even sinks into in-sipidity, if it lacks the seriousness, the suffering, the patience, and the labour of the negative. *Per se* the divine life is no doubt undisturbed identity and oneness with itself, which feels no anxiety over otherness and

* Kant and Fichte.
† Schelling.

estrangement, and none over the surmounting of this estrangement. But this "per se" is abstract generality, where we abstract from its real nature, which consists in its being objective to itself, conscious of itself on its own account (*für sich zu sein*); and where consequently we neglect altogether the self-movement which is the formal character of its activity. If the form is declared to correspond to the essence, it is just for that reason a misunderstanding to suppose that knowledge can be content with the "per se," the essence, but can do without the form, that the absolute principle, or absolute intuition, makes the carrying out of the former, or the development of the latter, needless. Precisely because the form is as necessary to the essence as the essence to it, absolute reality must not be conceived of and expressed as essence alone, i.e. as immediate substance, or as pure self-intuition of the Divine, but as form also, and with the entire wealth of the developed form. Only then is it grasped and expressed as really actual.

The truth is the whole. The whole, however is merely the essential nature reaching its completeness through the process of its own development. Of the Absolute it must be said that it is essentially a result, that only at the end is it what it is in very truth; and just in that consists its nature, which is to be actual, subject, or self-becoming, self-development. Should it appear contradictory to say that the Absolute has to be conceived essentially as a result, a little consideration will set this appearance of contradiction in its true light. The beginning, the principle, or the absolute, as at first or immediately expressed, is merely the universal. If we say "all animals," that does not pass for zoology; for the same reason we see at once that the words absolute, divine, eternal, and so on do not express what is implied

in them; and only mere words like these, in point of
fact, express intuition as the immediate. Whatever is
more than a word like that, even the mere transition to
a proposition, is a form of mediation, contains a process
towards another state from which we must return once
more. It is this process of mediation, however, that is
rejected with horror, as if absolute knowledge were
being surrendered when more is made of mediation than
merely the assertion that it is nothing absolute, and
does not exist in the Absolute.

This horrified rejection of mediation, however, arises
as a fact from want of acquaintance with its nature,
and with the nature of absolute knowledge itself. For
mediating is nothing but self-identity working itself out
through an active self-directed process; or, in other
words, it is reflection into self, the aspect in which the
ego is for itself, objective to itself. It is pure negativity, or, reduced to its utmost abstraction, the process
of bare and simple becoming. The ego, or becoming in
general, this process of mediating, is, because of its
being simple, just immediacy coming to be, and is immediacy itself. We misconceive therefore the nature of
reason if we exclude reflection or mediation from ultimate truth, and do not take it to be a positive moment
of the Absolute. It is reflection which constitutes truth
the final result, and yet at the same time does away
with the contrast between result and the process of arriving at it. For this process is likewise simple, and
therefore not distinct from the form of truth, which
consists in appearing as simple in the result; it is indeed just this restoration and return to simplicity.
While the embryo is certainly, in itself, implicitly a
human being, it is not so explicitly, it does not take
itself to be a human being (*für sich*); it is only the
latter in the form of developed and cultivated reason,

which has made itself to be what it is implicitly. Its
actual reality is first found here. But this result arrived at is itself simple immediacy; for it is self-
conscious freedom, which is at one with itself, and has
not set aside the opposition it involves and left it there,
but has made its account with it and become reconciled
to it.

What has been said may also be expressed by saying
that reason is purposive activity. Extolling so-called
nature at the expense of thought misunderstood, and
more especially the rejection of external purposiveness,
have brought the idea of purpose in general into dis-
repute. All the same, in the sense in which Aristotle,
too, characterises nature as purposive activity, purpose
is the immediate, the undisturbed, the unmoved which is
self-moving; as such it is subject. Its power of moving,
taken abstractly, is its existence for itself, or pure negativity. The result is the same as the beginning solely
because the beginning is purpose. Stated otherwise, what
is actual and concrete is the same as its inner principle
or notion simply because the immediate *qua* purpose
contains within it the self or pure actuality. The realised purpose, or concrete actuality, is movement and
process of development. But this very unrest is the
self; and it is one and the same with that immediacy
and simplicity characteristic of the beginning just for
the reason that it is the result, and has returned upon
itself—while this latter again is just the self, and the
self is self-referring and self-relating identity and
simplicity.

When thinking of the Absolute as subject, men have
made use of statements like 'God is the eternal,' the
'moral order of the world,' or 'love,' etc. In such propositions ultimate truth is just barely stated to be Subject,
but not set forth as the process of reflectively mediating

itself within itself. In a proposition of that kind we
begin with the word God. By itself this is a meaningless
sound, a mere name; the predicate says afterwards *what*
it is, gives it content and meaning: the empty beginning
becomes real knowledge only when we thus get to the
end of the statement. So far as that goes, why not
speak alone of the eternal, of the moral order of the
world, etc., or, like the ancients, of pure conception
such as being, the one, etc., i.e. of what gives the
meaning without adding the meaningless sound at all?
But this word just indicates that it is not a being or
essence or universal in general that is put forward,
but something reflected into self, a subject. Yet at the
same time this acceptance of the Absolute as Subject
is merely anticipated, not really affirmed. The subject is
taken to be a fixed point, and to it as their support the
predicates are attached, by a process falling within the
individual knowing about it, but not looked upon as
belonging to the point of attachment itself; only by
such a process, however, could the content be presented
as subject. Constituted as it is, this process cannot belong to the subject; but when that point of support is
fixed to start with, this process cannot be otherwise
constituted, it can only be external. The anticipation
that the Absolute is subject is therefore not merely not
the realisation of this conception; it even makes realisation impossible. For it makes out the notion to be a
static point, while its actual reality is self-movement,
self-activity.

Among the many consequences that follow from what
has been said, it is of importance to emphasise this, that
knowledge is only real and can only be set forth fully in
the form of science, in the form of system; and further,
that a so-called fundamental proposition or first principle of philosophy, even if it is true, is yet none the less

false just because and in so far as it is merely a fundamental proposition, merely a first principle. It is for
that reason easily refuted. The refutation consists in
bringing out its defective character; and it *is* defective
because it is merely the universal, merely a principle,
the beginning. If the refutation is complete and thorough, it is derived and developed from the nature of
the principle itself, and not accomplished by bringing
in from elsewhere other counter assurances and chance
fancies. It would be strictly the development of the
principle, and thus the completion of its deficiency, were
it not that it misunderstands its own purport by taking
account solely of the negative aspect of what it seeks
to do, and is not conscious of the positive character of
its process and result. The really positive working out
of the beginning is at the same time just as much the
very reverse, it is a negative attitude towards the principle we start from, negative, that is to say, of its one-
sided form, which consists in being primarily immediate,
a mere purpose. It may therefore be regarded as a
refutation of what constitutes the basis of the system;
but more correctly it should be looked at as a demonstration that the *basis* or principle of the system is in
point of fact merely its *beginning*.

That the truth is only realised in the form of system,
that substance is essentially subject, is expressed in the
idea which represents the Absolute as Spirit (*Geist*)—
the grandest conception of all, and one which is due to
modern times and its religion. Spirit is the only Reality. It is the inner being of the world, that which essentially is, and is *per se;* it assumes objective, determinate form, and enters into relations with itself—it is
externality (otherness), and exists for self; yet, in this
determination, and in its otherness, it is still one with
itself—it is self-contained and self-complete, in itself

and for itself at once. This self-containedness, however, is first something known by us, it is implicit in its
nature (*an sich*); it is Substance spiritual. It has to
become self-contained *for itself,* on its own account; it
must get knowledge of spirit, and must be consciousness
of itself as spirit. This means, it must be presented to
itself as an object, but at the same time straightway
annul and transcend this objective form; it must be its
own object in which it finds itself reflected. So far as
its spiritual content is produced by its own activity, it
is only *we* [the thinkers] who know spirit to be for
itself, to be objective to itself; but in so far as spirit
knows itself to be for itself, then this self-production,
the pure notion, is the sphere and element in which its
objectification takes effect, and where it gets its exis-
tential form. In this way it is in its existence aware of
itself as an object in which its own self is reflected.
Mind, which, when thus developed, knows itself to be
mind, is science. Science is its realisation, and the
kingdom it sets up for itself in its own native element.

A self having knowledge purely of itself in the absolute antithesis of itself, this pure ether as such, is the
very soil where science flourishes, is knowledge in universal form. The beginning of philosophy presupposes
or demands from consciousness that it should feel at
home in this element. But this element only attains
its perfect meaning and acquires transparency through
the process of gradually developing it. It is pure
spirituality as the universal which assumes the shape of
simple immediacy; and this simple element, existing as
such, is the soil of science, is thinking, and can be only
in mind. Because this medium, this immediacy of mind,
is the mind's substantial nature in general, it is the
transfigured essence, reflection which itself is simple,
which is aware of itself as immediacy; it is being, which

is reflection into itself. Science on its side requires the individual self-consciousness to have risen into this high ether, in order to be able to live with science, and in science, and really to feel alive there. Conversely the individual has the right to demand that science shall hold the ladder to help him to get at least as far as this position, shall show him that he has in himself this ground to stand on. His right rests on his absolute independence, which he knows he possesses in every type and phase of knowledge; for in every phase, whether recognised by science or not, and whatever be the content, his right as an individual is the absolute and final form, i.e. he is the immediate certainty of self, and thereby is unconditioned being, were this expression preferred. If the position taken up by consciousness, that of knowing about objective things as opposed to itself, and about itself as opposed to them, is held by science to be the very opposite of this position: if, when in knowing it keeps within itself and never gets beyond itself, science holds this state to be rather the loss of mind altogether—on the other hand the element in which *science* consists is looked at by consciousness as a remote and distant region, in which consciousness is no longer in possession of itself. Each of these two sides takes the other to be the perversion of the truth. For the naïve consciousness to give itself up completely and straight away to science is to make an attempt, induced by some unknown influence, all at once to walk on its head. The compulsion to take up this attitude and move about in this position, is a constraining force it is urged to fall in with, without ever being prepared for it and with no apparent necessity for doing so. Let science be *per se* what it likes, in its relation to naïve immediate self-conscious life it presents the appearance of being a reversal of the latter;

or, again, because naïve self-consciousness finds the
principle of its reality in the certainty of itself, science
bears the character of unreality, since consciousness 'for
itself' is a state quite outside of science. Science has
for that reason to combine that other element of self-
certainty with its own, or rather to show that the other
element belongs to itself, and how it does so. When
devoid of that sort of reality, science is merely the content of mind *qua* something implicit or potential (*an
sich*); purpose which at the start is no more than something internal; not spirit, but at first merely spiritual
substance. This implicit moment (*Ansich*) has to find
external expression, and become objective on its own
account. This means nothing else than that this moment
has to establish self-consciousness as one with itself.

It is this process by which science in general comes
about, this gradual development of knowing, that is set
forth here in the *Phenomenology of Mind.** Knowing,
as it is found at the start, mind in its immediate and
primitive state, is without the essential nature of mind,
is sense-consciousness. To get the length of genuine
knowledge, or produce the element where science is
found—the pure conception of science itself—a long
and laborious journey must be undertaken. This process towards science, as regards the content it will bring
to light and the forms it will assume in the course of its
progress, will not be what is primarily imagined by leading the unscientific consciousness up to the level of
science: it will be something different, too, from establishing and laying the foundations of science; and
anyway something else than the sort of ecstatic enthusiasm which starts straight off with absolute knowledge, as if shot out of a pistol, and makes short work

* "Being the first part of the *System of Science*" (first
edition; omitted in later edition).

of other points of view simply by explaining that it is
to take no notice of them.

The task of conducting the individual mind from its
unscientific standpoint to that of science had to be
taken in its general sense; we had to contemplate the
formative development (*Bildung*) of the universal [or
general] individual, of self-conscious spirit. As to the
relation between these two [the particular and general
individual], every moment, as it gains concrete form
and its own proper shape and appearance, finds a place
in the life of the universal individual. The particular
individual is incomplete mind, a concrete shape in whose
existence, taken as a whole, one determinate characteristic predominates, while the others are found only in
blurred outline. In that mind which stands higher than
another the lower concrete form of existence has sunk
into an obscure moment; what was once substantial objective fact (*die Sache selbst*) is now only a single
trace: its definite shape has been veiled, and become
simply a piece of shading. The individual, whose substance is mind at the higher level, passes through these
past forms, much in the way that one who takes up a
higher science goes through those preparatory forms of
knowledge, which he has long made his own, in order
to call up their content before him; he brings back the
recollection of them without stopping to fix his interest
upon them. The particular individual, so far as content is concerned, has also to go through the stages
through which the general mind has passed, but as
shapes once assumed by mind and now laid aside, as
stages of a road which has been worked over and lev-
elled out. Hence it is that, in the case of various kinds
of knowledge, we find that what in former days occupied
the energies of men of mature mental ability sinks to
the level of information, exercises, and even pastimes for

children; and in this educational progress we can see the
history of the world's culture delineated in faint outline.   This by-gone mode of existence has already become an acquired possession of the general mind, which
constitutes the substance of the individual, and, by thus
appearing externally to him, furnishes his inorganic
nature.   In this respect culture or development of mind
(*Bildung*), regarded from the side of the individual,
consists in his acquiring what lies at his hand ready for
him, in making its inorganic nature organic to himself,
and taking possession of it for himself.   Looked at,
however, from the side of universal mind *qua* general
spiritual substance, culture means nothing else than
that this substance gives itself its own self-consciousness, brings about its own inherent process and its own
reflection into self.

Science lays before us the morphogenetic process of
this cultural development in all its detailed fullness and
necessity, and at the same time shows it to be something that has already sunk into the mind as a moment
of its being and become a possession of mind.   The
goal to be reached is the mind's insight into what knowing is.   Impatience asks for the impossible, wants to
reach the goal without the means of getting there.   The
length of the journey has to be borne with, for every
moment is necessary; and again we must halt at every
stage, for each is itself a complete individual form, and
is fully and finally considered only so far as its determinate character is taken and dealt with as a rounded
and concrete whole, or only so far as the whole is looked
at in the light of the special and peculiar character
which this determination gives it.   Because the substance of individual mind, nay, more, because the universal mind at work in the world (*Weltgeist*), has had
the patience to go through these forms in the long

stretch of time's extent, and to take upon itself the prodigious labour of the world's history, where it bodied forth in each form the entire content of itself, which each is capable of grasping; and because by nothing less could that all-pervading mind ever manage to become conscious of what itself is—for that reason, the individual mind, in the nature of the case, cannot expect by less toil to grasp what its own substance contains. All the same, its task has meanwhile been made much lighter, because this has historically been implicitly (*an sich*) accomplished, the content is one where reality has already given place to spiritual possibilities, where immediacy has been overcome and brought under the control of reflection, the various forms and shapes have been already reduced to their intellectual abbreviations, to determinations of thought (*Gedankenbestimmung*) pure and simple. Being now a thought, the content is the possession of the substance of mind; existence has no more to be changed into the form of what is inherent and implicit (*Ansichseins*), but only the implicit—no longer merely something primitive, nor lying hidden within existence, but already present as a recollection—into the form of what is explicit, of what is objective to self (*Fürsichseins*).

We have to state more exactly the way this is done. At the point at which we here take up this movement, we are spared, in connection with the whole, the process of cancelling and transcending the stage of mere existence. This process has already taken place. What is still to be done and needs a higher kind of transformation, is to transcend the forms as ideally presented and made familiar to our minds. By that previous negative process, existence, having been withdrawn into the mind's substance, is, in the first instance, transferred to the life of self only in an immediate way. The possession the self has thereby acquired, has still the same character of uncomprehended immediacy, of passive indifference, which existence itself had; existence has in this way merely passed into the form of an ideal presentation. At the same time, by so doing, it is something familiar to us, something "well-known," something which the existent mind has finished and done with, and hence takes no more to do with and no further interest in. While the activity that is done with the existent is itself merely the process of the particular mind, of mind which is not comprehending itself, on the other hand, *knowledge* is directed against this ideal presentation which has hereby arisen, against this "being-familiar" and "well-known"; it is an action of *universal* mind, the concern of *thought*.

What we are "familiar with" is not intelligently known, just for the reason that it is "familiar." When engaged in the process of knowing, it is the commonest form of self-deception, and a deception of other people as well, to assume something to be familiar, and give assent to it on that very account. Knowledge of that sort, with all its talk, never gets from the spot, but has no idea that this is the case. Subject and object, and so on, God, nature, understanding, sensibility, etc., are uncritically presupposed as familiar and something significant, and become fixed points from which to start and to which to return. The process of knowing flits between these secure points, and in consequence goes on merely along the surface. Apprehending and demonstrating consist similarly in seeing whether every one finds what is said corresponding to his idea too, whether it is familiar and seems to him so and so or not.

Analysis of an idea, as it used to be carried out, did anyhow consist in nothing else than doing away with its character of familiarity. To break up an idea into its ultimate elements means returning upon its moments, which at least do not have the form of the idea as picked up, but are the immediate property of the self. Doubtless this analysis only arrives at thoughts which are themselves known elements, fixed inert determinations. But what is thus broken up into parts, this unreal entity, is itself an essential moment; for just because the concrete fact is self-divided, and turns into unreality, it is something self-moving, self-active. The action of separating the elements is the exercise of the force of Understanding, the most astonishing and greatest of all powers, or rather the absolute power. The circle, which is self-enclosed and at rest, and, being a substance, holds its own moments, is an immediate condition, the immediate, continuous relation of elements with their unity, and hence arouses no sense of wonderment. But that an accident as such, when cut loose from its containing circumference,—that what is bound and held by something else and actual only by being connected with it,—should get an existence all its own, gain freedom and independence on its own account—this is the portentous power of the negative; it is the energy of thought, of pure ego. Death, as we may call that unreality, is the most terrible thing, and to keep and hold fast what is dead demands the greatest force of all. Beauty, powerless and helpless, hates understanding, because the latter exacts from it what it cannot perform.* But the life of mind is not one that shuns death, and keeps clear of destruction; it endures its death and in death maintains its being. It only wins to its truth when it finds itself in utter desolation. It is this mighty power, not by being a positive which turns away from the negative, as when we say of anything it is nothing or it is false, and, being then done with it, pass off to

* This is directed against Novalis and the cult of beauty.

something else; on the contrary, mind is this power only by looking the negative in the face, and dwelling with it. This dwelling beside it is the magic power that converts the negative into being. That power is just what we spoke of above as subject, which by giving determinateness a place in its substance, cancels abstract immediacy, i.e. immediacy which merely *is,* and, by so doing, becomes the true substance, becomes being or immediacy that does not have mediation outside it, but is this mediation itself.

This process of making what is objectively presented a possession of pure self-consciousness, of raising it to the level of universality in general, is merely one aspect of mental development; spiritual evolution is not yet completed. The manner of study in ancient times is distinct from that of the modern world, in that the former consisted in the cultivation and perfecting of the natural mind. Testing life carefully at all points, philosophising about everything it came across, the former created an experience permeated through and through by universals. In modern times, however, an individual finds the abstract form ready made. In straining to grasp it and make it his own, he rather strives to bring forward the inner meaning alone, without any process of mediation; the production of the universal is abridged, instead of the universal arising out of the manifold detail of concrete existence. Hence nowadays the task before us consists not so much in getting the individual clear of the level of sensuous immediacy, and making him a substance that thinks and is grasped in terms of thought, but rather the very opposite: it consists in actualising the universal, and giving it spiritual vitality, by the process of breaking down and superseding fixed and determinate thoughts. But it is much more difficult to make fixed and definite thoughts

fuse with one another and form a continuous whole than
to bring sensuous existence into this state. The reason
lies in what was said before. Thought determinations
get their substance and the element of their existence
from the ego, the power of the negative, or pure reality; while determinations of sense find this in impotent
abstract immediacy, in mere being as such. Thoughts
become fluent and interfuse, when thinking pure and
simple, this inner immediacy, knows itself as a moment,
when pure certainty of self abstracts from itself. It
does not "abstract" in the sense of getting away from
itself and setting itself on one side, but of surrendering
the fixed quality of its self-affirmation, and giving up
both the fixity of the purely concrete—which is the ego
as contrasted with the variety of its content—and the
fixity of all those distinctions [the various thought-
functions, principles, etc.] which are present in the
element of pure thought and share that absoluteness of
the ego. In virtue of this process pure thoughts become
notions and conceptions, and are then what they are in
truth, self-moving functions, circles, are what their
substance consists in, are spiritual entities.

   This movement of the spiritual entities constitutes the
nature of scientific procedure in general. Looked at as
the concatenation of their content, this movement is the
necessitated development and expansion of that content
into an organic systematic whole. By this movement,
too, the road, which leads to the notion of knowledge,
becomes itself likewise a necessary and complete evolv-
ing process (*Werden*). This preparatory stage thus
ceases to consist of casual philosophical reflections,
referring to objects here and there, to processes and
thoughts of the undeveloped mind as chance may direct;
and it does not try to establish the truth by miscellane-
ous ratiocinations, inferences, and consequences drawn

from circumscribed thoughts. The road to science, by
the very movement of the notion itself, will compass
the entire objective world of conscious life in its rational necessity.

Further, a systematic exposition like this constitutes
the first part of science,* because the positive existence
of mind, *qua* primary and ultimate, is nothing but the
immediate aspect of mind, the beginning; the beginning,
but not yet its return to itself. The characteristic feature distinguishing this part of science [Phenomenology]
from the others is the element of positive immediate existence. The mention of this distinction leads us to
discuss certain established ideas that usually come to
notice in this connection.

The mind's immediate existence, conscious life, has
two aspects—cognition and objectivity which is opposed to or negative of the subjective function of knowing. Since it is in the medium of consciousness that
mind is developed and brings out its various moments,
this opposition between the factors of conscious life is
found at each stage in the evolution of mind, and all the
various moments appear as modes or forms (*Gestalten*)
of consciousness. The scientific statement of the course
of this development is a science of the experience
through which consciousness passes; the substance and
its process are considered as the object of consciousness. Consciousness knows and comprehends nothing
but what falls within its experience, for what is found
in experience is merely spiritual substance, and, moreover, object of its self. Mind, however, becomes object,
for it consists in the process of becoming an other to
itself, i.e. an object for its own self, and in transcending this otherness. And experience is called this very
process by which the element that is immediate, unex-

* v. note p. 23.

perienced, i.e. abstract—whether it be in the form of
sense or of a bare thought—externalises itself, and then
comes back to itself from this stage of estrangement,
and by so doing is at length set forth in its concrete
nature and real truth, and becomes too a possession of
consciousness.

The dissimilarity which obtains in consciousness between the ego and the substance constituting its object,
is their inner distinction, the factor of negativity in general. We may regard it as the defect of both opposites,
but it is their very soul, their moving spirit. It was on
this account that certain thinkers long ago took the
void to be the principle of movement, when they conceived the moving principle to be the negative element,
though they had not as yet thought of it as self. While
this negative factor appears in the first instance as a
dissimilarity, as an inequality, between ego and object,
it is just as much the inequality of the substance with
itself. What seems to take place outside it, to be an
activity directed against it, is its own doing, its own
activity; and substance shows that it is in reality subject. When it has brought out this completely, mind
has made its existence adequate to and one with its
essential nature. Mind is object to itself just as it
is, and the abstract element of immediacy, of the separation between knowing and the truth, is overcome. Being
is entirely mediated; it is a substantial content, that is
likewise directly in the possession of the ego, has the
character of self, is notion. With the attainment of
this the *Phenomenology of Mind* concludes. What mind
prepares for itself by the argument of the *Phenomenology*
is the element of true knowledge. In this element the
moments of mind are now set out in the form of thought
pure and simple, which knows its object to be itself.
They no longer involve the opposition between being

and knowing; they remain within the undivided simplicity of the knowing function; they are the truth in the form of truth, and their diversity is merely diversity of the content of truth. The process by which they are developed into an organically connected whole is Logic and Speculative Philosophy.

Now, because the systematic statement of the mind's experience embraces merely its ways of appearing, it may well seem that the advance from that to the science of ultimate truth in the form of truth is merely negative; and we might readily be content to dispense with the negative process as something altogether false, and might ask to be taken straight to the truth at once: why meddle with what is false at all? The point formerly raised, that we should have begun with science at once, may be answered here by considering the character of negativity in general regarded as something false. The usual ideas on this subject particularly obstruct the approach to the truth. The consideration of this point will give us an opportunity to speak about mathematical knowledge, which the unphilosophical mind looks upon as the ideal which philosophy ought to try to attain, but has so far striven in vain to reach.

Truth and falsehood as commonly understood belong to those sharply defined ideas which claim a completely fixed nature of their own, one standing in solid isolation on this side, the other on that, without any community between them. Against that view it must be pointed out, that truth is not like stamped coin * that is issued ready from the mint and so can be taken up and used. Nor, again, *is* there something false, any more than there *is* something evil. Evil and falsehood are indeed not so bad as the devil, for in the form of the devil they get the length of being particular subjects;

* *Cp.* Lessing, *Nathan der Weise*, IV.6.

qua false and evil they are merely universals, though they have a nature of their own with reference to one another. Falsity (that is what we are dealing with here) would be *otherness,* the negative aspect of the substance, which [substance], *qua* content of knowledge, is truth. But the substance is itself essentially the negative element, partly as involving distinction and determination of content, partly as being a process of distinguishing pure and simple, i.e. as being self and knowledge in general. Doubtless we can know in a way that is false. To know something falsely means that knowledge is not adequate to, is not on equal terms with, its substance. Yet this very dissimilarity is the process of distinction in general, the essential moment in knowing. It is, in fact, out of this active distinction that its harmonious unity arises, and this identity, when arrived at, is truth. But it is not truth in a sense which would involve the rejection of the discordance, the diversity, like dross from pure metal; nor, again, does truth remain detached from diversity, like a finished article from the instrument that shapes it. Difference itself continues to be an immediate element within truth as such, in the form of the principle of negation, in the form of the activity of Self. All the same, we cannot for that reason say that falsehood is a moment or forms even a constituent part of truth. That "in every case of falsity there is something true" is an expression in which they are taken to be like oil and water, which do not mix and are merely united externally. Just in the interest of their real meaning, precisely because we want to designate the aspect or moment of complete otherness, the terms true and false must no longer be used where their otherness has been cancelled and superseded. Just as the expressions "unity of subject and object," of "finite and infinite," of "being and thought," etc., are absurd if subject and object, etc., are taken to mean what they are *outside* their unity, and are thus in that unity not meant to be what its very expression conveys. In the same way falsehood is not, *qua* false, any longer a moment of truth.

Dogmatism as a way of thinking, whether in ordinary knowledge or in the study of philosophy, is nothing else but the view that truth consists in a proposition, which is a fixed and final result, or again which is directly known. To questions like "When was Ceasar born?", "How many feet made a furlong?", etc., a straight answer ought to be given; just as it is absolutely true that the square of the hypotenuse is equal to the sum of the squares of the other two sides of a right-angled triangle. But the nature of a so-called truth of that sort is different from the nature of philosophical truth.

As regards truth in matters of historical fact—to deal briefly with this subject—so far as we consider the purely historical element, it will be readily granted that they have to do with the sphere of particular existence, with a content in its contingent and arbitrary aspects, features that have no necessity. But even bare truths of the kind, say, like those mentioned, are impossible without the activity of self-consciousness. To get to know any one of them, there has to be a good deal of comparison, books must be consulted, or in some way or other inquiry has to be made. Even in a case of direct perception, only when we know it along with the reasons behind it, is it held to be something of real value; although it is merely the naked fact itself that we are, properly speaking, supposed to be concerned about.

As to mathematical truths, we should be still less inclined to consider anyone a geometer who had got Euclid's theorems by heart (*auswendig*) without knowing the proofs, without, if we may say so by way of contrast, getting them into his head (*inwendig*). Similarly, if anyone came to know by measuring many right-angled triangles that their sides are related in the way everybody knows, we should regard knowledge so obtained as unsatisfactory. All the same, while proof is essential in the case of mathematical knowledge, it still does not have the significance and nature of being a moment in the result itself; the proof is over when we get the result, and has disappeared. *Qua* result the theorem is, no doubt, one that is seen to be true. But this eventuality has nothing to do with its content, but only with its relation to the knowing subject. The process of mathematical proof does not belong to the object; it is a function that takes place outside the matter in hand. Thus, the nature of a right-angled triangle does not break itself up into factors in the manner set forth in the mathematical construction which is required to prove the proposition expressing the relation of its parts. The entire process of producing the result is an affair of knowledge which takes its own way of going about it. In philosophical knowledge, too, the way existence, *qua* existence, comes about (*Werden*) is different from that whereby the essence or inner nature of the fact comes into being. But philosophical knowledge, for one thing, contains both, while mathematical knowledge sets forth merely the way an existence comes about, i.e. the way the nature of the fact gets to ʿbe in the sphere of knowledge as such. For another thing, too, philosophical knowledge unites both these particular movements. The inward rising into being, the process of substance, is an unbroken transition into outwardness, into existence or being for another; and conversely the coming of existence into being is withdrawal into the inner essence. The movement is the twofold process in

which the whole comes to be, and is such that each at
the same time posits the other, and each on that account
has in it both as its two aspects. Together they make
the whole, through their resolving each other, and making themselves into moments of the whole.

In mathematical knowledge the insight required is an
external function so far as the subject-matter dealt
with is concerned. It follows that the actual fact is
thereby altered. The means taken, construction and
proof, contain, no doubt, true propositions; but all the
same we are bound to say that the content is false.
The triangle in the above example is taken to pieces,
and its parts made into other figures to which the construction gives rise in the triangle. It is only at the
end that we find again reinstated the triangle we are
really concerned with; it was lost sight of in the course
of the construction, and was present merely in fragments, that belonged to other wholes. Thus we find
negativity of content coming in here too, a negativity
which would have to be called falsity, just as much
as in the case of the movement of the notion where
thoughts that are taken to be fixed pass away and disappear.

The real defect of this kind of knowledge, however,
affects its process of knowing as much as its material.
As to that process, in the first place we do not see any
necessity in the construction. The necessity does not
arise from the nature of the theorem: it is imposed; and
the injunction to draw just these lines, an infinite number of others being equally possible, is blindly acquiesced
in, without our knowing anything further, except that,
as we fondly believe, this will serve our purpose in
getting at the proof. Later on this purposive device
then comes out, and is therefore merely external in
character, just because it is only after the proof is

found that it comes to be known. In the same way,
again, the proof takes a direction that begins anywhere we like, without our knowing as yet what relation this beginning has to the result to be brought out.
In its course, it takes up certain specific elements and
relations and lets others alone, without its being directly
obvious what necessity there is in the matter. An external purpose controls this process.

The evidence peculiar to this defective way of knowing—an evidence on the strength of which mathematics
plumes itself and proudly struts before philosophy—
rests solely on the poverty of its purpose and the defectiveness of its material, and is on that account of a
kind that philosophy must scorn to have anything to
do with. Its purpose or principle is quantity. This is
precisely the relationship that is non-essential, alien to
the character of the notion. The process of knowledge
goes on, therefore, on the surface, does not affect the
concrete fact itself, does not touch its inner nature or
notion, and is hence not a conceptual way of comprehending. The material which is to enable mathematics
to proffer these welcome treasures of truth consists of
space and numerical units (*das Eins*). Space is that
kind of existence on which the concrete notion inscribes
the diversity it contains—an empty, lifeless element in
which its differences likewise subsist in passive, lifeless
form. What is concretely actual is not something
spatial, such as is treated of in mathematics. With un-
realities like the things mathematics takes account of,
neither concrete sensuous perception nor philosophy has
anything to do. In an unreal element of that sort we
find, then, only unreal truth, fixed lifeless propositions.
We can call a halt at any of them; the next begins of
itself *de novo*, without the first having led up to the
one that follows, and without any necessary connexion

having in this way arisen from the nature of the subject-matter itself. So, too—and herein consists the
formal character of mathematical evidence—because of
that principle and the element where it applies, knowledge advances along the lines of bare equality, of
abstract identity. For what is lifeless, not being self-
moved, does not bring about distinction within its essential nature; does not come at essential opposition
or unlikeness; and hence involves no transition of one
opposite element into its other, no qualitative, immanent
movement, no *self*-movement. It is quantity, a form of
difference that does not touch the essential nature,
which alone mathematics deals with. It abstracts from
the fact that it is the notion which separates space into
its dimensions, and determines the connections between
them and in them. It does not consider, for example,
the relation of line to surface, and when it compares the
diameter of a circle with its circumference, it runs up
against their incommensurability, i.e. a relation in terms
of the notion, an infinite element, that escapes mathematical determination.

Immanent or so-called pure mathematics, again, does
not oppose time *qua* time to space, as a second subject-
matter for consideration. Applied mathematics, no
doubt, treats of time, as also of motion, and other concrete things as well; but it picks up from the experience synthetic propositions—i.e. propositions expressing
relations, relations determined by their essential nature
—and merely applies its formulae to those propositions
assumed to start with. That the so-called proofs of
propositions like that stating the equilibrium of the
lever, the relation of space and time in gravitation, etc.,
which applied mathematics frequently gives, should be
taken and given as proofs, is itself merely a proof
of how great the need is for knowledge to have a

process of proof, seeing that, even where proof is not
to be had, knowledge yet puts a value on the mere
semblance of it, and gets thereby a certain sense of
satisfaction. A criticism of these proofs would be as
instructive as it would be significant, if the criticism
could strip mathematics of this artificial finery, and
bring out its limitations, and thence show the necessity
for another type of knowledge.

As to time, which we are asked to think of as the
counterpart to space, and as constituting the object-
matter of the other division of pure mathematics, it is
the notion itself in the form of existence. The principle of quantity, of difference which is not determined
by the notion, and the principle of equality, of abstract, lifeless unity, are incapable of dealing with that
sheer restlessness of life and its absolute and inherent
process of differentiation. It is therefore only in an
arrested, paralysed form, only in the form of the quantitative unit, that this essentially negative activity becomes the second object-matter of this way of knowing,
which, itself an external operation, degrades what is
self-moving to the level of mere matter, in order thus to
get an indifferent, external, lifeless content.

Philosophy, on the contrary, does not deal with a
determination that is non-essential, but with a determination so far as it is an essential factor. The abstract
or unreal is not its element and content, but the real,
what is self-establishing, has life, within itself, existence in its very notion. It is the process that creates
its own moments in its course, and goes through them
all; and the whole of this movement constitutes its
positive content and its truth. This movement includes,
therefore, within it the negative factor as well, the element which would be named falsity if it could be considered one from which we had to abstract. The element

that disappears has rather to be looked at as itself essential, not in the sense of being something fixed, that has to be cut off from truth and allowed to lie outside it, heaven knows where; just as similarly the truth is not to be held to stand on the other side as an immovable lifeless positive element. Appearance is the process of arising into being and passing away again, a process that itself does not arise and does not pass away, but is *per se,* and constitutes reality and the life-movement of truth. In this way truth is the bacchanalian revel, where not a soul is sober; and because every member no sooner gets detached than it *eo ipso* collapses straightway, the revel is just as much a state of transparent unbroken calm. Judged by that movement, the particular shapes which mind assumes do not indeed subsist any more than do determinate thoughts or ideas, but they are, all the same, as much positive and necessary moments, as negative and transitory. In the entirety of the movement, taken as an unbroken quiescent whole, that which gets distinctness in the course of its process and secures specific existence, is preserved in the form of a self-recollection, in which existence is self-knowledge, and self-knowledge, again, is immediate existence.

It might well seem necessary to state at the outset the chief points in connexion with the *method* of this process, the way in which science operates. Its nature, however, is to be found in what has already been said, while the proper systematic exposition of it is the special business of Logic, or rather is Logic itself. For the method is nothing else than the structure of the whole in its pure and essential form. In regard, however, to what has been hitherto currently held on this point, we must be sensible that the system of ideas bearing on the question of philosophical method, belongs also to a stage of mental culture that has now passed away. This may

perhaps seem somewhat rough-handed or revolutionary;
and I am far from adopting an attitude of that sort; but
it is significant that the scientific régime bequeathed by
mathematics—a régime of explanations, divisions, axioms, an array of theorems, with proofs, principles, and
the consequences and conclusions drawn from them—
all this has already come to be generally considered as
at any rate out of date. Even though there is no clear
idea why it is unsuitable, yet little or no use is made
of it any longer; and even though it is not condemned
outright, it is all the same not in favour. And we must
have the prejudice and conviction that what is excellent
can turn itself to practical account, and make itself
acceptable. But it is not difficult to see that the method
of propounding a proposition, producing reasons for it
and then refuting its opposite by reasons too, is not
the form in which truth can appear. Truth moves itself by its very nature; but the method just mentioned
is a form of knowledge external to its material. Hence
it is peculiar to mathematics and must be left to mathematics, which, as already indicated, takes for its principle the relation of quantity, a relation alien to the notion,
and gets its material from lifeless space, and the equally
lifeless numerical unit. Or, again, such a method, adopting a freer style, one involving more of arbitrariness
and chance, may have a place in ordinary life, in a
conversation or in supplying matter-of-fact instruction
for the satisfaction of curiosity rather than knowledge,
very much like what a preface does. In every-day life
the mind finds its content in different kinds of knowledge, experiences of various sorts, concrete facts of
sense, thoughts, too, and principles, and, in general, in
whatever lies ready to hand, or passes for a solid stable
entity, or real being. The mind follows wherever this
leads, sometimes interrupting the connection by an un-

restrained caprice in dealing with the content, and takes up the attitude of determining and handling it in quite an external fashion. It runs the content back to some touchstone of certainty or other, even though it be but the feeling of the moment; and conviction is satisfied if it reaches some familiar resting-place.

But when the necessity of the notion banishes from its realm the loose procedure of the "raisonnements" of conversation, as well as the pedantic style of scientific pomposity, its place, as we have already mentioned, must not be taken by the disconnected utterance of presageful surmise and inspiration, and the arbitrary caprice of prophetic utterance; for this does not merely despise that particular form of scientific procedure, but contemns scientific procedure altogether.

Now that the triplicity, adopted in the system of Kant—a method rediscovered, to begin with, by instinctive insight, but left lifeless and uncomprehended—has been raised to its significance as an absolute method, true form is thereby set up in its true content, and the conception of science has come to light. But the use this form has been put to in the Kantian system has no right to the name of science. For we see it there reduced to a lifeless schema, to nothing better than a mere shadow, and scientific organisation to a synoptic table. This formalism—about which we spoke before in general terms, and whose procedure we wish here to state more fully—thinks it has comprehended and expressed the nature and life of a given form when it proclaims a determination of the schema to be its predicate. The predicate may be subjectivity or objectivity, or again magnetism, electricity, and so on, contraction or expansion, East or West, and such like—a form of predication that can be multiplied indefinitely, because according to this way of working each determination, each mode, can be applied as a form or schematic element in the case of every other, and each will thankfully perform the same service for any other. With a circle of reciprocities of this sort it is impossible to make out what the real fact in question is, or what the one or the other is. We find there sometimes constituents of sense picked up from ordinary intuition, determinate elements that certainly should mean something else than they express; at other times what is inherently significant, viz. pure determinations of thought —like subject, object, substance, cause universality, etc. —these are applied just as uncritically and unreflectingly as in every-day life, are used much as people employ the terms strong and weak, expansion and contraction. As a result that type of metaphysics is as unscientific as those ideas of sense.

Instead of the inner activity and self-movement of its own actual life, such a simple determination of direct intuition (*Anschauung*)—which means here sense-knowledge—is expressed in terms of a superficial analogy, and this external and empty application of the formula is called "construction." The same thing happens here, however, as in the case of every kind of formalism. A man's head must be indeed dull if he could not in a quarter of an hour get up the theory that there are enervating, innervating, and indirectly enervating diseases and so many cures, and who could not— since not so long ago instruction of that sort sufficed for the purpose—in as short a time be turned from being a man who works by rule of thumb into a theoretical physician. Formalism in the case of speculative Philosophy of Nature (*Naturphilosophie*) takes the shape of teaching that understanding is electricity, animals are nitrogen, or equivalent to south or north and so on. When it does this whether as baldly as it is here expressed or concocted with even more terminology, such forceful procedure brings and holds together elements to all appearance far removed from one another; the violence done to stable inert sense-elements by connecting them in this way, confers on them merely the semblance of a conceptual unity, and spares itself the trouble of doing what is after all the important thing—expressing the notion itself, the meaning that underlies sense-ideas. All this sort of thing may strike any one who has no experience with admiration and wonder. He may be awed by the profound genius he thinks it displays, and be delighted at the happy ingenuity of such characterisations, since they fill the place of the abstract notion with something tangible and sensuous, and so make it more pleasing; and he may congratulate himself on feeling an instinctive mental affinity for that glorious way of proceeding. The trick of wisdom of that sort is as quickly acquired as it is easy to practise. Its repetition, when once it is familiar, becomes as boring as the repetition of any bit of sleight-of-hand once we see through it. The instrument for producing this monotonous formalism is no more difficult to handle than the palette of a painter, on which lie only two colours, say red and green, the former for colouring the surface when we want a historical piece, the latter when we want a bit of landscape. It would be difficult to settle which is greater in all this, the agreeable ease with which everything in heaven and earth and under the earth is plastered with that botch of colour, or the conceit that prides itself on the excellence of its means for every conceivable purpose; the one lends support to the other. What results from the use of this method of sticking on to everything in heaven and earth, to every kind of shape and form, natural and spiritual, the pair of determinations from the general schema, and filing everything in this manner is no less than an "account as clear as noonday" * of the organised whole of the universe. It is, that is to say, a synoptic index, like a skeleton with tickets stuck all over it, or like rows of pots standing sealed and labelled in a grocer's stall; and is as intelligible as either the one or the other. It has lost hold of the living nature of concrete fact; just as in the former case we have merely dry bones with flesh and blood all gone, and in the latter, what is hidden away in those pots has equally nothing to do with living things. We have already remarked that the final outcome of this style of thinking is, at the same time, to paint entirely in one kind of colour; for it turns with contempt from the distinctions in the schematic table, looks on them as belonging to the activity of mere reflection and lets them drop out of sight in the blankness of the Absolute, and there reinstates pure identity, pure formless whiteness. Such uniformity of colouring in the schema with its lifeless determinations, this absolute identity, and the transition from one to the other— these are one and all alike the expression of inert lifeless understanding, and an external process of knowledge into the bargain.

Not only can what is excellent not escape the fate of becoming thus devitalised and despiritualised, and seeing its skin flayed and paraded about in this way by lifeless knowledge, and the conceit such knowledge engenders; but, further, such a fate lets us see the power the "excellent" exercises over the heart (*Gemüth*), if not over the mind (*Geist*). Moreover, we recognise here, too, that process towards universality and determinateness of form which marks the complete attainment of excellence,

* Expression adopted from Fichte's "Sonnenklarer Bericht an das Publikum über das eigentliche Wesen der neuesten Philosophie."

and which alone makes it possible that this universality can be turned to superficial uses.

Science can become an organic system only by the inherent life of the notion. In science the determinateness, which was taken from the schema and stuck on to existing facts in external fashion, is the self-directing inner soul of the concrete content. The movement of what is partly consists in becoming another to itself, and thus developing explicitly into its own immanent content; partly, again, it takes this evolved content, this existence it assumes, back into itself, i.e. makes *itself* into a moment, and reduces itself to simple determinateness. In the first stage of the process negativity lies in the function of distinguishing and establishing existence; in this latter return into self, negativity consists in the bringing about of determinate simplicity. It is in this way that the content shows its specific characteristic not to be received from something else, and stuck on externally; the content gives itself this determinate characteristic, appoints itself of its own initiative to the rank of a moment and to a place in the whole. The pigeon-holing process of understanding retains for itself the necessity and the notion controlling the content, that which constitutes the concrete element, the actuality and living process of the subject-matter which it labels: or rather, understanding does not retain this for itself, on the contrary, understanding fails to know it. For if it had as much insight as that, it would surely show that it had. It is not even aware of the need for such insight; if it were, it would drop its schematising process, or at least would no longer be satisfied to know by way of a mere table of contents. A table of contents is all that understanding gives, the content itself it does not furnish at all.

If the specific determination (say even one like mag-

netism) is one that in itself is concrete or actual, it all
the same gets degraded into something lifeless and inert,
since it is merely predicated of another existing entity,
and not known as an immanent living principle of this
existence; nor is there any comprehension of how in this
entity its intrinsic and peculiar way of expressing and
producing itself takes effect. This, the very kernel of
the matter, formal understanding leaves to others to
add later on. Instead of making its way into the inherent content of the matter in hand, understanding always takes a survey of the whole, assumes a position
away from the particular existence about which it is
speaking, i.e. it does not see it at all. True scientific
knowledge, on the contrary, demands abandonment to the
very life of the object, or, which means the same thing,
claims to have before it the inner necessity controlling
the object, and to express this only. Steeping itself in
its object, it forgets to take that general survey, which
is merely a turning of knowledge away from the content
back into itself. But being sunk into the material in
hand, and following the course that such material takes,
true knowledge returns back into itself, yet not before
the content in its fullness is taken into itself, is reduced
to the simplicity of being a determinate characteristic,
drops to the level of being one aspect of an existing
entity, and passes over into its higher truth. By this
process the whole as such, taking itself in its entire
sweep, emerges out of the wealth where bare reflection
seemed to get lost.

In general, in virtue of the principle that, as we expressed it before, substance is implicitly and in itself
subject, all content makes its reflection into itself in its
own special way. The subsistence or substance of anything that exists is its self-identity; for its want of
identity, or oneness with itself, would be its dissolution.

But self-identity is pure abstraction; and this is just thinking. When I say Quality, I state simple determinateness; by means of its quality one existence is distinguished from another or is an "existence"; it is for itself, because of this simple characteristic. But by doing so it is essentially Thought.

Here we find contained the principle that Being is Thought: here is exercised that insight which is generally at a discount in the case of the ordinary non-conceptual way of speaking of the identity of thought and being. In virtue, further, of the fact that subsistence on the part of what exists is self-identity or pure abstraction, it is the abstraction of itself from itself, in other words, is itself its own want of identity with itself and dissolution—its own proper inwardness and retraction into self—its process of coming to be.

Owing to the nature which being thus has, and so far as what is has this nature from the point of view of knowledge, this thinking is not an activity which treats the content as something alien and external; it is not reflection into self away from the content. Science is not that kind of Idealism which stepped into the place of the Dogmatism of mere assertion and took the shape of a Dogmatism of mere assurance, the Dogmatism of mere self-certainty. Rather, since knowledge sees the content go back into its own proper inner nature, the activity of knowledge is absorbed in that content—for it (the activity) is the immanent self of the content—and is also at the same time returned into itself, for this activity is pure self-identity in otherness. In this way the knowing activity is the artful device which, pretending to refrain from activity, looks on and watches how specific determinateness, with its concrete life, just where it pretends to be working out its own self-preservation and its own private interest, is, in point of fact, doing the very opposite, is doing what brings about its own dissolution and makes itself a moment in the whole.

While, in the foregoing, the significance of Understanding was stated from the point of view of the self-consciousness of substance; by what has been here stated we can see clearly its significance from the point of view of substance *qua* being. Existence is Quality, self-identical determinateness, or determinate simplicity, determinate thought: this is existence as regards Understanding. On this account it is νους, as Anaxagoras first took reality to be. Those who succeeded him grasped the nature of existence in a more determinate way as ἐῖδος or ἰδέα, i.e. as determinate or specific universality, kind or genus. The term genus or kind seems indeed too ordinary and inadequate to express ideas like beauty, holiness, eternal, which are now the vogue. As a matter of fact, however, idea (ἰδέα) means neither more nor less than kind, genus. But we often find in these days that a term which exactly designates a conception is despised and rejected, and another preferred to it which hides and obscures the conception, and thus sounds more edifying, even though this is merely due to its being expressed in a foreign language.

Precisely for the reason that existence is designated a genus or kind, it is a naked simple thought; νοῦς, simple abstraction, is substance. It is on account of its simplicity, its self-identity, that it appears steady, fixed, and permanent. But this self-identity is likewise negativity; hence that fixed and stable existence carries the process of its own dissolution within itself. The determinateness appears at first to be so solely through its relation to something else; and its process seems imposed and forced upon it externally. But its having its own otherness within itself, and the fact of its being a self-initiated process—these are implied in the very simplicity of thought itself. For this is self-moving thought, thought that distinguishes, is inherent inwardness, the pure notion. Thus, then, it is the very nature of understanding to be a process, and being a process it is Rationality.

In the nature of existence as thus described—to be its own notion and being in one—consists logical necessity in general. This alone is what is rational, the rhythm of the organic whole: it is as much knowledge of content as that content is notion and essential nature. In other words, this alone is the sphere and element of speculative thought. The concrete shape of the content is resolved by its own inherent process into a simple determinate quality. Thereby it is raised to logical form, and its being and essence coincide; its concrete existence is merely this process that takes place, and is *eo ipso* logical existence. It is therefore needless to apply a formal scheme to the concrete content in an external fashion; the content is in its very nature a transition into a formal shape, which, however, ceases to be formalism of an external kind, because the form is the indwelling process of the concrete content itself.

This nature of scientific method, which consists partly in being inseparable from the content, and partly in determining the rhythm of its movement by its own agency, finds, as we mentioned before, its peculiar systematic expression in speculative philosophy. What is here stated describes in effect the essential principle; but cannot stand for more at this stage than an assertion or assurance by way of anticipation. The truth it contains is not to be found in this exposition, which is in part historical in character. And just for that reason, too, it is not in the least refuted if anyone assures us on the contrary that this is not so, that the process in-

stead is here so and so, if ideas we are all used to,
being truths accepted or settled and familiar to everyone, are brought to mind and recounted, or, again, if
something new is served up and guaranteed as coming
from the inner sanctuaries of inspired intuition.

Such a view is bound to meet with opposition. The
first instinctive reaction on the part of knowing, when
offered something that was unfamiliar, is usually to resist it. It seeks by that means to save freedom and native insight, to secure its own inherent authority against
alien authority—for that is the way anything apprehended for the first time appears. This attitude is
adopted, too, in order to do away with the semblance of
a kind of disgrace which would lie in the fact that
something has had to be learnt. In like manner, again,
when the unfamiliar or unknown is received with ap-
plause, the reaction is in the same way an exaltation
of freedom and native authority. It consists in something analogous to ultra-revolutionary declamation and
action.

Hence the important thing for the student of science
is to make himself undergo the strenuous toil of conceptual reflection, of thinking in the form of the notion.
This demands concentrated attention on the notion as
such, on simple and ultimate determinations like being-
in-itself, being-for-itself, self-identity, and so on; for
these are elemental, pure, self-determined functions of
a kind we might call souls, were it not that their conceptual nature denotes something higher than that term
contains. The interruption by conceptual thought of
the habit of always thinking in figurative ideas (*Vorstellungen*) is as annoying and troublesome to this way
of thinking as to that process of formal intelligence
which in its reasoning rambles about with no real
thoughts to reason with. The former, the habit, may be

called materialised thinking, a fortuitous mental state, one that is absorbed in what is material, and hence finds it very distasteful at once to lift its self clear of this matter and be confined to itself alone. The latter, the process of *raisonnement,* is, on the other hand, detachment from all content, and conceited superiority to it. What is wanted here is the effort and struggle to give up this kind of freedom, and instead of being a merely arbitrary principle directing the content anyhow, this freedom should sink into and pervade the content, should get it directed and controlled by its own proper nature, i.e. by the self as its own self, and should see this process taking place. We must abstain from interrupting the immanent rhythm of the movement of conceptual thought; we must refrain from arbitrarily interfering with it, and introducing ideas and reflections that have been obtained elsewhere. Restraint of this sort is itself an essential condition of attending to and getting at the real nature of the notion.

There are the two aspects in the case of that ratiocinative procedure which mark its contrast from conceptual thinking and call for further notice. *Raisonnement,* in the first place, adopts a negative attitude towards the content apprehended; knows how to refute it and reduce it to nothingness. To see what the content is *not* is merely a negative process; it is a dead halt, which does not of itself go beyond itself, and proceed to a new content; it has to get hold of something else from somewhere or other in order to have once more a content. It is reflection upon and into the empty ego, the vanity of its own knowledge. Conceit of this kind brings out not only that this content is vain and empty, but also that to see this is itself fatuity too: for it is negation with no perception of the positive element within it. In that this reflection does not even have its

own negativity as its content, it is not inside actual fact
at all, but for ever away outside it. On that account
it imagines that by asserting mere emptiness it is going
much farther than insight that embraces and reveals a
wealth of content. On the other hand, in the case of
conceptual thinking, as was above indicated, the negative aspect falls within the content itself, and is the
positive substance of that content, as well by being
its inherent character and moving principle as by being
the entirety of what these are. Looked at as a result,
it is determinate specific negation, the negative which
is the outcome of this process, and consequently is a
positive content as well.

In view of the fact that ratiocinative thinking has a
content, whether of images or thoughts or a mixture of
both, there is another side to its process which makes
conceptual comprehension difficult for it. The peculiar
nature of this aspect is closely connected with the essential meaning of the idea (ἰδέα) above described, in fact
expresses the idea in the way this appears as the process
of thinking apprehension. For just as ratiocinative
thinking in its negative reference, which we have been
describing, is nothing but the self into which the content returns; in the same way, on the other hand, in
its positive cognitive process the self is an ideally presented subject to which the content is related as an accident and predicate. This subject constitutes the basis
to which the content is attached and on which the process moves to and fro. Conceptual thinking goes on in
quite a different way. Since the concept or notion is
the very self of the object, manifesting itself as the
development of the object, it is not a quiescent subject,
passively supporting accidents: it is a self-determining
active concept which takes up its determinations and
makes them its own. In the course of this process that

inert passive subject really disappears; it enters into
the different constituents and pervades the content; instead of remaining in inert antithesis to determinateness
of content, it constitutes, in fact, that very specificity,
i.e. the content as differentiated along with the process
of bringing this about. Thus the solid basis, which
ratiocination found in an inert subject, is shaken to its
foundations, and the only object is this very movement
of the subject. The subject supplying the concrete
filling to its own content ceases to be something transcending this content, and cannot have further predicates
or accidents. Conversely, again, the scattered diversity
of the content is brought under the control of the self,
and so bound together; the content is not a universal
that can be detached from the subject, and adapted to
several indifferently. Consequently the content is in
truth no longer predicate of the subject; it is the very
substance, is the inmost reality, and the very principle
of what is being considered. Ideational thinking
(*vorstellen*), since its nature consists in dealing with
accidents or predicates, and in exercising the right to
transcend them because they are nothing more than
predicates and accidents—this way of thinking is checked
in its course, since that which has in the proposition
the form of a predicate is itself the substance of the
statement. It is met by a counter-thrust, as we may
say. Starting from the subject, as if this were a
permanent base on which to proceed, it discovers, by
the predicate being in reality the substance, that the
subject has passed into the predicate, and has thereby
ceased to be subject: and since in this way what seems
to be predicate has become the entire mass of the content, whole and complete, thinking cannot wander and
ramble about at will, but is restrained and controlled
by this weight of content.

Usually the subject is first set down as the fixed and objective self; from this fixed position the necessary process passes on to the multiplicity of determinations or predicates. Here the knowing ego takes the place of that subject and is the function of knitting or combining the predicates one with another, and is the subject holding them fast. But since the former subject enters into the determinate constituents themselves, and is their very life, the subject in the second case—viz. the knowing subject—finds that the former,—which it is supposed to be done with and which it wants to transcend, in order to return into itself,—is still there in the predicate: and instead of being able to be the determining agency in the process of resolving the predicate—reflectively deciding whether this or that predicate should be attached to the former subject—it has really to deal with the self of the content, is not allowed to be something on its own account (*für sich*), but has to exist along with this content.

What has been said can be expressed in a formal manner by saying that the nature of judgment or the proposition in general, which involves the distinction of subject and predicate, is subverted and destroyed by the speculative judgment; and the identical proposition, which the former becomes [by uniting subject and predicate], implies the rejection and repudiation of the above relation between subject and predicate. This conflict between the form of a proposition in general and the unity of the notion which destroys that form, is similar to what we find between metre and accent in the case of rhythm. Rhythm is the result of what hovers between and unites both. So in the case of the speculative or philosophical judgment; the identity of subject and predicate is not intended to destroy their distinction, as expressed in propositional form; their unity is to appear as a harmony of the elements. The form of the judgment is the way the specific sense appears, or is made manifest, it is the accent which differentiates the content of its meaning: that the predicate expresses the substance, and the subject itself falls within the universal, is the unity wherein that accent dies away.

To explain what has been said by examples let us take the proposition God is Being. The predicate is "being": it has substantive significance, and thus absorbs the meaning of the subject within it. Being is meant to be here not predicate but the essential nature. Thereby, God seems to cease to be what he was when the proposition was put forward, viz. a fixed subject. Thinking [i.e. ordinary reflection], instead of getting any farther with the transition from subject to predicate, in reality finds its activity checked through the loss of the subject, and it is thrown back on the thought of the subject because it misses this subject. Or again, since the predicate has itself been pronounced to be a subject, to be *the* being, to be the essential reality, which exhausts the nature of the subject, thinking finds the subject directly present in the predicate too: and now, instead of having, in the predicate, gone into *itself*, and preserved the freedom characteristic of ratiocination, it is absorbed in the content all the while, or, at any rate, is required to be so.

Similarly, when it is said: "the real is the universal," the real, *qua* subject, passes away in its predicate. The universal is not only meant to have the significance of a predicate, as if the proposition stated that the real is universal: the universal is meant to express the essential nature of the real. Thinking therefore loses that fixed objective basis which it had in the subject, just as much as in the predicate it is thrown back on the sub-

ject, and therein returns not into itself but into the
subject underlying the content.

This unaccustomed restraint imposed upon thought is
for the most part the cause of the complaints made regarding the unintelligibility of philosophical writings,
when otherwise the individual has in him the requisite
mental cultivation for understanding them. In what
has been said we see the reason for the definite objection often made against them, that a good deal has to
be read repeatedly before it can be understood—an accusation which is meant to imply something objection-
able in the extreme, and one which if granted to be
sound admits of no further reply. It is obvious from the
above what is the state of the case here. The philosophical proposition, being a proposition, calls up the
accepted view of the usual relation of subject and predicate, and suggests that the idea of the customary procedure which takes place is knowledge. Its philosophical
content destroys this way of proceeding and the ordinary
view taken of this process. The common view discovers
that the statement is intended in another sense than it
is thinking of, and this correction of its opinion compels
knowledge to recur to the proposition and take it now
in some other sense.

There is a difficulty which might well be avoided. It
consists in mixing up the methods of procedure followed by speculation and ratiocination, when what is
said of the subject has at one time the significance of its
conceptual principle, and at another time the meaning
of its predicate or accidental quality. The one mode
of thinking invalidates the other; and only that philosophical exposition can manage to become plastic in
character which resolutely sets aside and has nothing
to do with the ordinary way of relating the parts of a
proposition.

As a matter of fact, non-speculative thinking has its rights too, which are justifiable, but are disregarded in the speculative way of stating a proposition. Abolishing the form of the proposition must not take place merely in an immediate manner, merely through the bare content of the proposition. On the contrary, we must give explicit expression to this cancelling process; it must be not only that internal restraining and confining of thought within its own substance; this turning of the conception back into itself has to be expressly brought out and stated. This process, which constitutes what formerly had to be accomplished by proof, is the internal dialectical movement of the proposition itself. This alone is the concrete speculative element, and only the explicit expression of this is a speculative systematic exposition. *Qua* proposition, the speculative aspect is merely the internal restriction of thought within its own substance where the return of the essential principle into itself is not yet brought out. Hence we often find philosophical expositions referring us to the inner intuition, and thus dispensing with the systematic statement of the dialectical movement of the proposition, which is what we wanted all the while. The proposition ought to express *what* the truth is: in its essential nature the truth is subject: being so, it is merely the dialectical movement, this self-producing course of activity, maintaining its advance by returning back into itself. In the case of knowledge in other spheres this aspect of the articulated internal nature of the content is constituted by proof. When dialectic, however, has been separated from the proof, the idea of philosophical demonstration as a matter of fact vanishes altogether.

On this point it may be mentioned that the dialectical process likewise consists of parts or elements which are propositions. The difficulty indicated seems therefore to recur continually, and seems to be a difficulty inherent in the nature of the case. This is like what happens in the ordinary process of proving anything; the grounds it makes use of themselves need to be based on other grounds again, and so on *ad infinitum*. This manner of furnishing grounds and conditions, however, concerns that type of proof from which the dialectical movement is distinct and hence belongs to the process of external knowledge. As to what this movement is, its element is the bare concept; this furnishes a content which is through and through subject *impliciter* and *per se*. There is to be found, therefore, no sort of content standing in a relation, as it were, to an underlying subject, and getting its significance by being attached to this as a predicate. The proposition as it appears is a mere empty form.

Apart from the sensuously apprehended or ideally presented (*vorgestellten*) self, it is in the main the mere name *qua* name which denotes the subject pure and simple, the empty unit without any conceptual character. For this reason it would e.g. be expedient to avoid the name "God," because this word is not in its primary use a conception as well, but the special name of an underlying subject, its fixed resting-place; while, on the other hand, being or the one, singleness, subject, etc., themselves directly indicate conceptions. Furthermore, if speculative truths are stated about that subject [God], even then their content is devoid of the immanent notion, because that content is merely present in the form of a passive subject, and owing to this the speculative truths easily take on the character of mere edification. From this side, too, the obstacle, arising from the habit of putting the speculative predicate in the form of a proposition, instead of taking it as an inherent essential conception, is capable of being made greater or less by the mere way philosophical truths are put forward. Philosophical exposition, faithfully following its insight into the nature of speculative truth, must retain the dialectical form, and exclude everything which is not grasped conceptually and is a conception.

As in the case of the procedure of ratiocination, the study of philosophy finds obstruction, too, in the unreasoning conceit that builds itself on well-established truths, which the possessor considers he has no need to return upon and reconsider, but rather takes to be fundamental, and thinks he can propound as well as decide and pass sentence by means thereof. In this regard, it is especially needful to make once again a serious business of philosophy. In all spheres of science, art, skill, and handicraft it is never doubted that, in order to master them, a considerable amount of trouble must be spent in learning and in being trained. As regards philosophy, on the contrary, there seems still an assumption prevalent that, though every one with eyes and fingers is not on that account in a position to make shoes if he only gets leather and a last, yet everybody understands how to philosophise straight away, and pass judgment on philosophy, simply because he possesses the criterion for doing so in his natural reason—as if he did not in the same way possess the standard for shoemaking too in his own foot. It seems as if the possession of philosophy lay just in the want of knowledge and study, as if philosophy left off where the latter began. It is commonly held to be a formal kind of knowledge devoid of all substantial content. There is a general failure to perceive that, in the case of any knowledge and any science, what is taken for truth, even as regards content, can only deserve the name of "truth" when philosophy has had a hand in its production.   Let the other sciences try as much as they like to get along by ratiocination or *raisonnement* without philosophy, they are unable to keep alive without it, or to have any spiritual significance and truth in them.

As regards philosophy in its proper and genuine sense, we find put forward without any hesitation, as an entirely sufficient equivalent for the long course of mental discipline—for that profound and fruitful process through which the human spirit attains to knowledge —the direct revelation of the divine and the healthy common sense of mankind, untroubled and undisciplined by any other knowledge or by proper philosophical reflection.   These are held to be a good substitute for real philosophy, much in the way as chicory is lauded as a substitute for coffee.   It is not a very pleasing spectacle, to observe uncultivated ignorance and barbarity of mind, with neither grace nor taste, without the capacity to concentrate its thoughts on an abstract proposition, still less on a connected statement of such propositions, confidently proclaiming itself to be intellectual freedom and toleration, and even the inspiration of genius.   This last used once upon a time, as every one knows, to be all the rage in the case of poetry, as it is now in philosophy.   Instead of poetry, however, the efforts of this form of inspiration, when it had any sense at all, resulted in the production of jejune prose, or, if it got beyond that, it produced raving nonsense. In the same way here in the case of philosophy; philosophising by the light of nature, which thinks itself too good for conceptual thinking, and, because of the want of it, takes itself to have direct intuitive ideas and poetical thoughts,—such philosophising trades in arbitrary combinations of an imagination merely disorganised through thinking—fictitious creations that are neither fish nor flesh, neither poetry nor philosophy.

On the other hand again, when instinctive philosophy follows the more secure course prescribed by healthy common sense, it supplies, at the very best, a rhetorical *mélange* of commonplace truths. When it is charged with the triviality of what it offers, it assures us, in reply, that the fullness and richness of its meaning lie deep down in its own heart, and that others must feel this too, since with such phrases as the "heart's natural innocence," "purity of conscience," and so on, it supposes it has expressed things that are ultimate and final, to which no one can take exception, and about which nothing further can be required. But the very problem in hand was just that the best must not be left behind hidden away in secret, but be brought out of the depths and set forth in the light of day. It could quite well from the start have spared itself this trouble of bringing forward ultimate and final truths of that sort; they were long since to be found, say, in the Catechism, in popular proverbs, etc. It is an easy matter to take such truths in their indefinite and crooked inaccurate form, and in many cases to point out that the mind convinced of them is conscious of the very opposite truths. When it struggles to get itself out of the mental embarrassment thereby produced, it will tumble into further confusion, and possibly burst out with the assertion that in short and in fine the matter is settled, the truth is so and so, and anything else is mere "sophistry"—a password used by plain common sense against cultivated critical reason, like the phrase "visionary dreaming," by which those ignorant of philosophy sum up its character once for all. Since the man of common sense appeals to his feeling, to an oracle within his breast, he is ready to meet any one who does not agree. He has simply to explain that he has no more to say to any one who does not find and feel the same as himself. In other words, he tramples the roots of humanity under foot. For the nature of humanity is to impel men to agree with one another, and its very existence lies simply in the explicit realisation of a community of conscious life. What is anti-human, the condition of mere animals, consists in keeping within the sphere of feeling pure and simple, and in being able to communicate only by way of feeling-states.

When a man asks for a royal road to science, no more convenient and comfortable way can be mentioned to him than to put his trust in "healthy common sense"; and in order, besides, to keep abreast of the times and advance with philosophy, let him read reviews of philosophical works, and even go the length of reading the prefaces and first paragraphs of the works themselves; for the latter give the general principles on which everything turns, while the reviews, besides the historical references, provide over and above the critical judgment and appreciation, which, being a judgment passed on the work, goes farther than the work that is judged. This common way a man can take in his dressing-gown. But spiritual elation in the eternal, the sacred, the infinite, moves along the highway of truth in the robes of the high priest—a road, that, from the first, is itself immediate being in its innermost, the inspiration of profound and original ideas and flashes of elevated thought. All the same, those depths do not yet reveal the well-spring of inner reality; nor, again, do these sky-rockets illumine the empyrean. True thoughts and scientific insight can only be won by the labour of the notion. Conceptions alone can produce universality in the knowing process. This universality is critically developed and completely finished knowledge, and not the common indefiniteness and inadequacy of ordinary intelligence; nor, again, is it that extraordinary kind of universality where the powers and potencies of reason are spoiled and ruined by the indolence and vanity of genius; it is truth successfully arrived at its own inherent native form, and capable of being the property of every self-conscious reason.

Since I have taken the self-development of conceptions or notions to be the medium where science really exists, and since in those respects to which I have drawn attention as well as in others, current ideas about the nature of truth and the shape it assumes deviate from my view, and indeed are quite opposed to my position, it is not likely that the consideration of all this will promise well for a favourable reception of an attempt to expound the system of science in this sense. In the meantime, I may call to mind that while e.g. the supreme merit of Plato's philosophy has sometimes been held to consist in his myths which are scientifically valueless, there have also been times, spoken of even as times of mere sentimentality and emotion, when the Aristotelian philosophy has been respected on account of its speculative depth of insight, and when the *Parmenides* of Plato—perhaps the greatest literary product of ancient dialectic—has been taken to be the positive expression of the divine life, the unveiling and disclosing of its inmost truth. I may reflect, too, that notwithstanding much cloudy obscurity which was the product of ecstasy, this misunderstood ecstasy was in point of fact meant to be nothing else than the activity of the pure notion; furthermore, that what is best in the philosophy of our time takes its value to lie in its scientific character; and even though others take a different view, it is only in virtue of its scientific character that recent philosophy really gets its worth acknowledged and ac-

cepted. Thus, then, I too may hope that this attempt
to vindicate and claim science for conceptual thought,
and systematically to develop and present science in
this its own peculiar medium, will manage to make a
way for itself by the inherent truth of the result accomplished. We may rest assured that it is the nature
of truth to force its way to recognition when its time
comes, and that it only appears when its time has come,
and hence never appears too soon, and never finds a
public that is not ripe to receive it; and, further, we
may be sure that the individual thinker requires this
result to take place, in order to give him confidence in
regard to what is no more as yet than a matter for
himself singly and alone, and in order to find his assurance, which in the first instance merely belongs to a
particular individual, accepted as something universal.
In this connection, however, it is very often necessary
to distinguish the public from those who take upon
themselves to be its representatives and spokesmen.
The public takes up an attitude in many respects quite
different from the latter, indeed, even opposed to them.
Whereas the public good-naturedly and generously will
rather take the blame upon itself when a philosophical
work is not quite acceptable or intelligible to it, these
"representatives," on the contrary, convinced of their
own competence, put all the blame on the authors. The
influence of the work on the public is more silent than
the action of those "representatives," who are like the
dead burying their dead. While the general level of
insight at the present time is in the main more highly
cultivated, its curiosity more quickened and alert, and
its judgment more swiftly made up and pronounced, so
that the feet of those who will carry you out are already
at the door: at the same time we have often to distinguish from all this the slower and more gradual effect

which rectifies the direction of attention caught and compelled by imposing assurances, corrects, too, contemptuous censure, and after a little provides a contemporary audience for one class, while another after a temporary vogue finds no audience with posterity any longer.

For the rest, at a time when the universal nature of spiritual life has become so very much emphasised and strengthened, and the mere individual aspect has become, as it should be, correspondingly a matter of indifference, when, too, that universal aspect holds, by the entire range of its substance, the full measure of the wealth it has built up, and lays claim to it all, the share in the total work of mind that falls to the activity of any particular individual can only be very small. Because this is so, the individual must all the more forget himself, as in fact the very nature of science implies and requires that he should; and he must, moreover, become and do what he can. But all the less must be demanded of him, just as he must expect the less from himself, and ask the less for himself.

II

OUTLINES OF HEGEL'S PHENOM-
ENOLOGY *

Translated by Wm. T. Harris

INTRODUCTION

1. Our ordinary Knowing has before itself only the object which it knows, but does not at first make an object of itself, i.e. of the Knowing. But the whole which is extant in the act of knowing is not the object alone, but also the Ego that knows, and the relation of the Ego and the object to each other, i.e. Consciousness.

2. In Philosophy, the determinations of the Knowing are not considered exclusively in the phase of determinations of things, but likewise as determinations of the Knowing, to which they belong, although in common

* *In 1840, the Editors of Hegel's works published a small volume with the title, Hegel's Philosophical Propaedeutics. The work, which was edited by Karl Rosenkranz, contains substantially the original outline of the Course of Instruction in Philosophy which Hegel gave at the Gymnasium at Nürnberg in 1808-1811, together with sundry additions made from notes taken at the lectures and other sources. We give the entire exposition of the Phenomenology as it occurs in the second year of the course. (The entire course was divided into three years: 1st year, Science of Rights, of Morals, and of Religion; 2nd year, Phenomenology of Spirit and Logic; 3rd year, Science of the Idea and Philosophical Encyclopaedia. The whole is preceded by an admirable preface by the Editor.) —Translator.*

likewise to things.   In other words: they are not taken merely as objective but also as subjective determinations —or rather as definite species of relation of the object and subject to each other.

3. Since things and their determinations are in the Knowing, it is quite possible, on the one hand, to view the same as in and for themselves outside of Consciousness—as given to the latter in the shape of foreign and already existing material for it;—on the other hand, however, for the reason that Consciousness is essential to the Knowing of these, the view is possible that Consciousness itself posits this world, and produces or modifies the determinations of the same, through its mediating relation and its activity, either wholly or in part. The former mode of view is called "Realism," the latter, "Idealism."   Here are to be considered the general determinations of things only as the definite relation of object to the subject.

4. The subject, more definitely seized, is Spirit (the Mind).   It is Phenomenal when essentially relating to an existent object; in so far is it Consciousness.   The Science of Consciousness is, therefore, called The Phenomenology of Spirit (or Mind).

5. But the Mind, according to its self-activity within itself and in relation to itself independent of all relation to others, is considered in the Science of Mind proper, or "Psychology."

6. Consciousness is in general the knowing of an object, whether external or internal, without regard to whether it presents itself without the help of the Mind, or whether it is produced through this. The Mind is to be considered in its activities in so far as the determinations of its consciousness are ascribed to it.

7. Consciousness is the definite relation of the Ego

to an Object.   In so far as one regards it from the objective side, it can be said to vary according to the difference of the Objects which it has.

8. At the same time, however, the Object is essentially determined (modified) through the mediating relation to Consciousness. Its diversity is, therefore, to be considered as conversely dependent upon the development of Consciousness. This reciprocity continues through the Phenomenal sphere of Consciousness and leaves the above-mentioned (3) questions undecided.

9. Consciousness has in general three phases, according to the diversity of the object. It (the object) is namely either the object standing in opposition to the Ego, or it is the Ego itself, or something objective which belongs likewise equally to the Ego: Thought. These determinations are not empirically taken up from without, but are moments of Consciousness itself. Hence it is

(1) Consciousness in general;
(2) Self-Consciousness;
(3) Reason.

FIRST PHASE.

Consciousness in General.

10. Consciousness in general is (1) Sensuous; (2) Perceiving; (3) Understanding.

A.—The Sensuous Consciousness.

11. The simple sensuous Consciousness is the immediate certitude of an external object. The expression for the immediateness of such an object is that "it is," and moreover a "This," a "Now" according to time, and

a "Here" according to space, and different from all other objects and perfectly determined (definite) in itself.

12. This Now and this Here are vanishing somewhats. Now is no more while it is and another Now has entered its place, and this latter Now has likewise vanished. But the Now abides all the same. This abiding Now is the general Now, which is both this and that Now, and is likewise neither of them. This Here which I mean, and point out, has a right and left, an above and a below, a behind and a before, etc., *ad infinitum;* i.e. the Here pointed out is not a simple and hence definite Here, but a unity including many Heres. Therefore, what in truth is extant is not the abstract, sensuous determinateness [the simple "it is"], but the General.

B.—Perception

13. Perception has no longer for object the Sensuous in so far as it is immediate, but in so far as it is general. It is a mingling of sensuous determinations with those of Reflection.

14. The object of this Consciousness is, therefore, the Thing with its Properties. The sensuous properties are (a) *for themselves* immediately in sensation, and likewise determined and mediated through the relation to others; (b) they belong to a thing, and are in this respect, on the one hand, embraced in the individuality of the same; on the other hand, they have generality, according to which they transcend this individual thing, and are at the same time independent of each other.

15. In so far as the Properties are essentially mediated, they have their subsistence in another and are subject to *change.* They are only *accidents.* Things, however, since they subsist in their properties (for the

reason that they are distinguished by means of these),
perish through the change of those properties, and become an alternation of birth and decay.

16. In this change it is not merely the somewhat
that cancels itself and passes over to another, but the
other itself changes. But the other of the other, or the
change of the changeable, is the Becoming of the Abiding—of the in-and-for-itself Subsisting and Internal.

C.—The Understanding

17. The object has now this character: it has (a) a
purely accidental side, and (b) also an essentiality and
an abiding side. Consciousness, for the reason that the
object has for it this character, is the UNDERSTAND-
ING—for which the *"things"* of perception pass for
mere phenomena, and it (the Understanding) contemplates the "Internal of things."

18. The Internal of things is that in them which, on
the one hand, is free from the Phenomenal manifestation—namely, their multiplicity—which constitutes an
External in opposition to it (the Internal); on the other
hand, however, it is that which is related to them through
its comprehension (ideal totality or "definition"). It is
therefore: (1) simple force, which passes over into extantness, its "utterance" (or manifestation).

19. (2) Force remains with this distinction the same
in all the sensuous variations of the Phenomenon. The
Law of the Phenomenon is its quiet, general image. It
is a mediating relation of general abiding determinations whose distinctions are external to the law. The
generality and persistence of this mediating relation lead
to the necessity of the same; yet without the distinction's
being an in-itself-determined or internal one, in which

one of the determinations lies immediately in the comprehension (total definition) of the other.

20. This Comprehension—akin to Consciousness itself—gives another phase thereof. Hitherto it was in
relation to its object as somewhat alien and indifferent.
Since now the distinction in general has become a distinction which at the same time is no distinction, the
previous mode of the distinction of Consciousness from
its object falls away. It has an object and relates to
another, which, however, is at the same time no "other";
in fine, it has itself for object.

21. In other words: the "Internal of things" is the
thought or comprehension thereof. While Consciousness
has the Internal as object, it has thought, or its own
Reflection, or its own form—and, consequently, itself
as object.

Second Phase.

The Self-Consciousness.

22. As Self-Consciousness the Ego intuites itself, and
the expression of the same in its purity is Ego = Ego,
or: I am I.

23. This proposition of self-consciousness is devoid
of all content. The impulse of self-consciousness consists in this: to realize its comprehension ("true nature")
and to become conscious of itself in every respect. It
is therefore: (1) active in cancelling the otherness
(alien-being) of objects, and in positing them like itself; (2) in making itself valid externally, and thus
giving itself, through this, objectivity and extantness.
These two are one and the same activity. The becoming-
determined of self-consciousness is at the same time a

self-determining, and conversely. It produces itself as object.

24. Self-Consciousness has in its culture, or movement, three stages: (1) of Desire in so far as it is related to other things: (2) of the Mediating relation of master and slave (dominion and servitude) in so far as it is related to another self-consciousness not identical with itself; (3) of the general Self-Consciousness which recognizes itself in other self-consciousnesses, and is identical with them as well as self-identical.

A.—Desire.

25. Both sides of self-consciousness, the positing and the cancelling, are thus united with each other immediately. Self-Consciousness posits itself through negation of otherness and is *practical* consciousness. If, therefore, in the real consciousness, which also is called the *theoretical,* the determinations of the same and of the object changed or varied *of themselves, now* it happens that this change occurs through the activity of the Consciousness itself and *for* it. It is conscious that this cancelling activity belongs to it. In the comprehension of self-consciousness the not-yet-realized distinction lies as a characteristic. In so far as this distinction makes its appearance, there arises a feeling of otherness (dependence on others) in consciousness—a feeling of negation in itself, or the feeling of deficiency, a *want.*

26. This feeling of its otherness contradicts its identity with itself. The necessity felt to cancel this opposition is Impulse (or appetite). Negation, or otherness, presents itself to the consciousness as an external thing different from it, which however is determined through the self-consciousness (1) as a somewhat suited to gratify the appetency, and (2) as a somewhat in itself

negative whose subsistence is to be cancelled by the Self and posited in identity with it (i.e. made identical, or assimilated).

27. The activity of desire thus cancels the otherness (alien element) of the object and its subsistence, and unites it with the subject, and by this means the desire is appeased. This is conditioned thus: (1) through an object existing externally or indifferent to it, or through Consciousness; (2) its activity produces the gratification only through destruction of the object. The self-consciousness arrives through this at its feeling of Self.

28. In Desire, Consciousness stands in relation to itself as individual. It relates to an object devoid of self-hood, which is in and for itself another than the self-consciousness. The latter for this reason only attains self-identity as regards the object through destruction of the latter. Desire is in general (1) destructive, (2) in the gratification of its wants, therefore, it comes to the conscious feeling of its for-itself-being as individual—to the undefined Comprehension of the subject as connected with objectivity.

B.—The Relation of Master and Slave.

29. The comprehension of self-consciousness as Subject which is at the same time object, gives the mediating relation: that *another* self-consciousness exists for the self-consciousness.

30. A self-consciousness which is for another is not as a mere object for it, but as its *other self*. The Ego is no abstract generality in which there is no distinction or determination. Since an Ego is thus the object of the Ego, in this respect there is the same for it as object that it is in itself. It intuites itself in another.

31. This self-intuition of one in another is (1) the

abstract moment of self-sameness. (2) Each has, however, also the peculiarity that it manifests itself to the
other as an external object, and in so far as an immediate sensuous and concrete existence. (3) Each is
absolutely for-itself and individual as opposed to the
other, and asserts its right to be such for the other and
to pass for such, and to intuite its own freedom as a for-
itself-existent in the other and to be recognized by it.

32. In order to make itself valid as a free being and
to obtain recognition, self-consciousness must exhibit
itself to another as free from natural existence. This
moment (i.e. the being-for-another) is as necessary as
that of the freedom of self-consciousness *in itself*. The
absolute identity of the Ego with itself is essentially not
an immediate, but such a one as has been achieved
through the cancelling of sensuous immediateness, and
the exhibition of the self to another as free and independent from the Sensuous. Thus it shows itself in
conformity with its comprehension (ideal), and must be
recognized because it gives reality to the Ego.

33. But Independence is freedom not *outside of* and
from the sensuous immediate extant being, but rather
as freedom *in* the same. The one moment is as necessary as the other, but they are not of the same value.
For the reason that non-identity enters—that to one
of two self-consciousnesses freedom passes for the essential in opposition to sensuous extant being, while
with the other the opposite occurs—with the reciprocal
demand for recognition there enters into determined
actuality the mediating relation (of master and slave)
between them; or, in general terms, that of service and
submission, in so far as this diversity of independence is
extant through the immediate agency of nature.

34. Since of two self-consciousnesses opposed to each
other, each must strive to assert and prove itself as an

absolute for-itself-existence against and for the other.
That one enters into a condition of slavery who prefers
life to freedom, and thereby shows that he has not the
capacity to abstract from his sensuous extant being by
his own might for his independence.

35. This pure negative Freedom, which consists in the
abstraction from natural extant being, does not correspond to the definition (comprehension) of Freedom,
for this latter is the self-identity even when involved
with others: partly the intuition of itself in another self,
and partly the freedom (not *from* the existent, but)
in the existent, a freedom which itself has extantness.
The one who serves is devoid of selfhood and has another self in place of his own, so that for his master
he has resigned and cancelled his individual Ego and
now views his essential self in another. The master,
on the contrary, looks upon the servant (the other Ego)
as cancelled and his own individual will as preserved.
(History of Robinson and Friday.)

36. The own individual will of the servant, more
closely regarded, is cancelled in the fear of the master,
and reduced to the internal feeling of its negativity. Its
labor for the service of another is a resignation of its
own will partly in itself, partly it is at the same time,
with the negation of its own desire, the positive transformation of external things through labor; since
through labor the self makes its own determinations
the forms of things, and thus views itself as objective
in its work.   The renunciation of the unessential arbitrary will constitutes the moment of true obedience.
(Pisistratus taught the Athenians to obey. Through this
he made the Code of Solon an actual power; and after
the Athenians had learned this, the dominion of a Ruler
over them was superfluous.)

37. This renunciation of individuality as self is the

moment (phase) through which self-consciousness makes
the transition to the universal will, the transition to
positive freedom.

C.—Universality of Self-Consciousness.

38'. The universal self-consciousness is the intuition of
itself, not as a special existence distinct from others,
but an intuition of the self-existent universal self. Thus
it recognizes itself and the other self-consciousness in
itself, and is in turn recognized by them.

39. Self-consciousness is, according to this its essential universality, only real in so far as it knows its
echo (and reflection) in another (I know that another
knows me as itself), and as pure spiritual universality
(belonging to the family, the native land, &c.) knows
itself as essential self. (This self-consciousness is the
basis of all virtues, of love, honor, friendship, bravery,
all self-sacrifice, all fame, &c.)

THIRD PHASE.

Reason.

40. Reason is the highest union of consciousness and
self-consciousness, or of the knowing of an object and
of the knowing of itself. It is the certitude that its
determinations are just as much objective, i.e. determinations of the essence of things, as they are subjective
thoughts. It (Reason) is just as well the certitude of
itself (subjectivity) as being (or objectivity), and this,
too, in one and the same thinking activity.

41. Or what we see through the insight of Reason,
is: (1) a content which subsists not in our mere subjective notions or thoughts which we make for our-

selves, but which contains the in-and-for-itself-existing essence of objects and possesses objective reality; and (2) which is for the Ego no alien somewhat, no some-what given from without, but throughout penetrated and assimilated by the Ego, and therefore to all intents pro-duced by the Ego.

42. The knowing of Reason is therefore not the mere subjective certitude, but also TRUTH, because Truth consists in the harmony, or rather *unity,* of certitude and Being, or of certitude and objectivity.

III

PHENOMENOLOGY OF THE SPIRIT

Freely translated from the German by Josiah Royce

THE CONTRITE CONSCIOUSNESS *

IN Scepticism Consciousness learns in truth, that it is divided against itself. And from this experience there

* The *Phänomenologie des Geistes,* the first of Hegel's sys-tematic works (1807), is intended as a novel sort of "Intro-duction to Philosophy." It depicts a series of "phases" or *Gestalten* of consciousness which lie between our natural "common sense" view of the real world, and what Hegel re-gards as the truly philosophical view of reality. These phases form a series, whose order Hegel conceives as necessary. Each stage or phase of insight into the truth of things is mean-while illustrated in this book by examples derived from liter-ature, from history, or from the general experience of man-kind. These mere illustrations are freely chosen; and Hegel does not conceive that the special embodiment or clothing

is born a new Type of Consciousness, wherein are linked
the two thoughts which Scepticism had kept asunder.
The thoughtless self-ignorance of Scepticism must pass
away; for in fact the two attitudes of Scepticism express
One Consciousness. This new Type of Consciousness is
therefore explicitly aware of its own doubleness. It
regards itself on the one hand as the Deliverer, changeless and self-possessed; on the other hand it regards itself as the absolutely confounded and contrary; and
it is the awareness of this its own contradiction. In

---

which his choice of the illustrations gives to each phase or
stage of consciousness is part of the necessary development.

The "unhappy" or "contrite" consciousness (*das unglück-
liche Bewusstsein*) is a phase or stage of consciousness which
is subjectively idealistic in its interpretation or reality, but
which is abstract and dualistic in its view of its relations to
truth. It is therefore concerned not with external nature,
but with its own private ideals, and with a search for personal
perfection. It is, in brief, what Professor William James
might call a "variety of religious experience." This experience
is here that of a lonely devotee, whose world consists of his
search for inner spiritual perfection, together with the goal of
this search, namely his far-off "changeless" or divine consciousness. Both the social and the more technically theological aspects of religion play no essential part in the phase of
consciousness here in question. The illustrations are obviously
derived from mediaeval cloister life; but this part of the
setting of the phase in question is accidental. Any lonely
religious experience might present essentially the same features.

The union of theoretical opinions about the nature of
truth, with practical and emotional interpretations of life, is
characteristic of the *Phenomenology*. Any coherent plan of
life embodies a theory of truth and of reality. Any view
about the universe expresses itself in a way of life. Such
is the general notion illustrated by the phases of consciousness
which the *Phenomenology* portrays.—Translator.

Stoicism the Self owns itself in the simplicity of free-dom. In Scepticism it gives itself embodiment, makes naught of other embodied reality, but, in the very act of so doing, renders itself the rather twofold and is now parted in twain. Hereby the same duplication that was formerly shared between two individuals, the Lord and the Slave, has now entered into the nature of one individual. The differentiation of the Self, which is the essential Law of the Spirit, is already present, but not as constituting an organic unity, and the CON-TRITE CONSCIOUSNESS is this awareness of the Self as the Divided Nature, wherein is only conflict.

This Contrite and Broken Consciousness, just be-cause the conflict of its Nature is known as belonging to one person, must forever, in each of its two forms, have the other also present to it. Whenever, in either form, it seems to have come to victory and unity, it finds no rest there, but is forthwith driven over to the other. Its true home-coming, its true reconciliation with itself, will, however, display to us the law of the Spirit, as he will appear when, having come to life, he has entered the world of his manifestation. For it already belongs to the Contrite Consciousness to be one undivided soul in the midst of its doubleness. It is in fact the very gazing of one Self into another; it is both these selves; it has no nature save in so far as it unites the two. But thus far it knows not yet this its own real essence; it has not entered into possession of this unity.

For the first then, the Contrite Consciousness is but the unwon unity of the two selves. To its view the two are not one, but are at war together. And accordingly it regards one of them, viz., the simple, the Changeless Consciousness, as the True Self. The other, the multi-form and fickle, it regards as the False Self. The Con-trite Consciousness finds these two as mutually estranged.

For its own part, because it is the awareness of this
contradiction, it takes sides with the Changeless Consciousness, and calls itself the False Self. But since
it is aware of the Changeless, i.e. of the True Self, its
task must be one of self-deliverance, that is, the task
of delivering itself from the unreality. For on the
one hand it knows itself only as the fickle; and the
changeless is far remote from it. And yet the Contrite Consciousness is in its genuine selfhood one with
the simple and Changeless Consciousness; for therein
lies its own true Self. But yet again it knows that it
is not in possession of this true self. So long as the
Contrite Consciousness assigns to the two selves this
position, they cannot remain indifferent to each other;
or, in other words, the Contrite Consciousness cannot
itself be indifferent to the Changeless. For the Contrite
Consciousness is, as a fact, of both kinds, and knows
the relation of the changeless to the fickle as a relation
of truth to falsehood. The falsehood must be turned
to naught; but since the Contrite Consciousness finds
both the false and the true alike necessary to it, and
contradictory, there remains to it only the contradictory movement, wherein neither of the opposed elements can find repose in going over to its opponent but
must create itself anew in the opponent's very bosom.

To win, then, in this strife against the adversary, is
rather to be vanquished. To attain one goal, is rather
to lose it in its opposite. The whole life, whatever it
be, whatever it do, is aware only of the pain of this
being and doing. For this Consciousness has no object
besides its opposite, the true Self, and its own nothingness. In aspiration it strives hence towards the Changeless. But this aspiration is itself the Contrite Consciousness, and contains forthwith the knowledge of the
opposite, namely of its own individuality. The Change-

less, when it enters consciousness, is sicklied o'er with individuality, is present therewith; instead of being lost in the consciousness of Changeless, individuality arises ever afresh therein.

But one thing the Contrite Consciousness thus learns, namely that individuality is made manifest in the Changeless, and that the Changeless is made manifest in individuality. It finds that in general individuality belongs to the changeless true Self, and that in fact its own individuality also belongs thereto. For the outcome of this process is precisely the unity of this twofold consciousness. This unity, then, comes to light, but for the first only as an unity wherein the diversity of the two aspects plays the chief part. For the Contrite Consciousness there thus result three ways in which individuality and the Changeless are linked. First, it rediscovers itself as again banished into its opposition to the Changeless Self; and it is cast back to the beginning of the strife, which latter still remains the element of the entire relationship. In the second place, the Contrite Consciousness learns that individuality belongs to the very essence of the Changeless, is the incarnation of the Changeless; and the latter hereupon assumes the burden of this whole range of phenomena. In the third place, the Contrite Consciousness discovers itself to be the individual who dwells in the Changeless. In the first stage the Changeless appears to consciousness only as the remote Self, that condemns individuality. In passing through the second stage, consciousness learns that the Changeless is as much an incarnate individual as it is itself; and thus, in the third stage, consciousness reaches the grade of the Spirit, rejoices to find itself in the Spirit, and becomes aware that its individuality is reconciled with the Universal.

What is here set forth as the character and relation-

ship of the Changeless has appeared as the experience
that the divided consciousness obtains in its woe. This
experience is to be sure not its own one-sided process;
for it is itself the Changeless Consciousness, and the
latter is also an individual consciousness; so that the
process is all the while in the Changeless Consciousness,
belonging to the latter quite as much as to the other.
For the Changeless Consciousness passes through the
three stages, being first the changeless as in general
opposed to the individual, then becoming an individual
over against another individual, and finally being united
with the latter. But this observation, in so far as it
is made from our own point of view as observers, is here
premature; for thus far we have come to know the
Changeless only in so far as consciousness has defined
it. Not, as yet, the true Changeless, but the Changeless as modified by the duality of consciousness, has
come to our sight; and so we know not how the developed and self-possessed Changeless will behave.
What has resulted from the foregoing is only this, that
the mentioned characteristics appear, to the consciousness now under consideration, as belonging to the
Changeless.

Consequently the Changeless Consciousness itself also
preserves even in its incarnate form the character and
principle of separation and isolation as against the individual consciousness. From the latter's point of view,
the fact that the Changeless takes on the form of individuality appears as something which somehow *comes*
to *pass*. The opposition to the Changeless is something, moreover, which the individual consciousness
merely finds as a fact. The relation seems to it merely
a result of its natural constitution. As for the final
reconciliation, the individual consciousness looks upon
this as in part its own deed, the result of its own indi-

viduality; but it also regards a part of the unity as
due, both in origin and in existence, to the Changeless.
The element of opposition thus remains even in the
unity.   In fact, in taking on its incarnate form, the
Changeless has not only retained but actually confirmed
its character of remoteness. For although, in assuming
a developed and incarnate individuality, it seems on the
one hand, to have approached the individual, still, on
the other hand, it now stands over against him as an
opaque fact of sense, with all the stubbornness of the
actual about it.   The hope that the individual may become one with the Changeless must remain but hope,
empty and distant; for between hope and fruition stand
now the fatal chance and the lifeless indifference which
have resulted from that very incarnation wherein lies
the foundation of the hope.   Because the Changeless
has thus entered the world of facts, has taken on the
garments of actuality, it follows necessarily that in
the world of time it has vanished, that in space it is
far away, and forever far remains.

If at the outset the mere notion of the divided consciousness demanded that it should undertake the destruction of its individuality, and the growth into the
Changeless, the present result defines the undertaking
thus: That the individual should leave off its relation
with the formless ideal, and should come only into relations with the Changeless as incarnate. For it is now
the fact of the unity of the individual and the Changeless which has become the truth and the object for consciousness, as before, in the mere notion, only the abstract
and disembodied Changeless was the essential object; and
consciousness now finds the total separation of the notion
as the relation which is to be forgotten. The thing which
has now to be reduced to unity is the still external rela-

tion to the embodied Ideal, in so far as the latter is a
foreign actuality.

The process whereby the unreal Self seeks to reach
this unity is once more threefold, since it will be found
to have a threefold relation to its incarnate but remote
Ideal.   In the first place it will appear as the Devout
Consciousness; in the second place, as an individual,
whose relation to the actuality will be one of aspiration
and of service; in the third place it will reach the consciousness of self-possession.   We must now follow these
three states of being, to see how they are involved in
the general relation, and are determined thereby.

Taking the first state, that of the Devout Consciousness, one finds indeed that the incarnate Changeless,
as it appears to this consciousness, seems to be present
in all the completeness of its being.   But as a fact the
fashion of the completed being of the Changeless has
not yet been developed.   Should this completed being
be revealed to consciousness, the revelation would be,
as it were, rather the deed of the Ideal than the work of
the Devout Consciousness; and thus the revelation would
come from one side alone, would be no full and genuine
revelation, but would remain burdened with incompleteness and with duality.

Although the Contrite Consciousness still lacks the
presence of its Ideal, it is nevertheless as we see [also]
beyond the stage of pure thought, whether such thought
were the mere abstract thinking of Stoicism, which forgets all individuality, or the merely restless thinking of
Scepticism, which in fact embodies individuality in its
ignorant contradictions and its ceaseless unrepose.   Both
of these stages the Contrite Consciousness has transcended.   It begins the synthesis of pure thought and of
individuality and persists therein.   But, it has not yet
risen to the thought which is aware of the reconciliation

of the conscious individual with the demands of pure thought. The Contrite Consciousness stands between the two extremes, at the place where pure thought and the individual consciousness meet. It is in fact itself this meeting place; it is the unity of pure thought and individuality. It even knows that pure thought, yes the Changeless itself, is essentially individual. But what it does not know is that this its object, the Changeless, which it regards as having necessarily assumed an incarnate individuality, is identical with its own self, with the very individual as he is in consciousness.

Its attitude then, in this first form, in which it appears as the Devout Consciousness, is not one in which it explicitly thinks about its object. It is implicitly indeed the consciousness of a thinking individual, and its object also is a thinking individual. But the relation between these two is still one that defies pure thought. Consciousness accordingly as it were makes but a feint at thinking, and takes the form of Adoration. Such thought as it has remains the mere formless tinkling of an altar bell, or the wreathing of warm incense smoke—a thinking in music, such as never reaches an organized notion, wherein alone an inner objectivity could be attained. This limitless and devout inner Feeling finds indeed its object, but as something uncomprehended, and so as a stranger. Thus comes to pass the inward activity of the devout soul, which is indeed self-conscious, but only in so far as it possesses the mere feeling of its sorrowful disharmony. This activity is one of ceaseless longing. It possesses the assurance that its true Self is just such a pure soul,—pure thought in fact, taking on the form of individuality,—and that this Being, who is the object of the devotion, since he possessed the thought of his own individuality, recognizes and approves the worshipper.

But at the same time this Being is the unapproachable and remote. As you seize hold upon him he escapes, or rather he has already gone away. He has already gone away; for he is the Ideal giving himself in thought the form of an individual and therefore consciousness gets without hindrance its self-fulfilment in him,—gets self-fulfilment, but only to learn that it is the very opposite of this Ideal. Instead of seizing hold on the true Self, its mere feeling is all. It sinks back into itself. Unable at the moment of union to escape finding itself as the very opposite of the ideal, it has actually seized hold upon its own untruthfulness, not upon the truth. In the true Self it has sought to find its own fulfilment; but *its own* means only its isolated individual reality. For the same reason it cannot get hold upon the true Self in so far as he is at once an individual and a reality. Where one seeks him, the true Self is not to be found; for by definition he is the remote Self, and so is to be found nowhere To seek him in so far as he is an individual is not to look for his universal, his ideal individuality, nor for his presence as the law of life * but merely to seek him as an individual thing, as a fact amongst facts,† as something that sense could touch unhindered. But as such an object the Ideal exists only as a lost object. What consciousness finds is thus only the sepulchre of its true life. But this sepulchre is now the actuality, and, moreover, one that by its nature forbids any abiding possession; and the presence of this tomb means only the strife of a search that must be fruitless. But consciousness thus learns that there is no real sepulchre which can contain its true Lord, the Changeless. As Lord who has been taken away he is not the true Lord. The Changeless will no longer be

* *Begriff*, here paraphrased to suit special context.
† *Wirkliches*, here used as equal to *Seyendes*.

looked for here below, or grasped after as the vanished one. For hereby consciousness learns to look for individuality as a genuine and universal ideal.

In the next place then, the return of the soul to itself is to be defined as its knowledge that in its own individuality it has genuine being. It is the pure heart, which potentially, or from our point of view, has discovered the secret of self-satisfaction. For although in feeling it is sundered from its Ideal, still this feeling is in essence a feeling of self-possession. What has been felt is the Ideal as expressed in terms of pure feeling, and this Ideal is its own very self. It issues from the process then as the feeling of self-possession, and so as an actual and independent being. By this return to itself it has, from our point of view, passed to its second relationship, that of aspiration and service. And in this second stage consciousness confirms itself in the assurance of self-possession (an assurance which we now see it to have attained), by overcoming and feeding upon the true Self, which, in so far as it was an independent thing, was estranged. From the point of view of the Contrite Consciousness, however, all that yet appears is the aspiration and the service. It knows not yet that in finding these it has the assurance of self-possession as the basis of its existence, and that its feeling of the true Self is a self-possessed feeling. Not knowing this, it has still ever within it the fragmentary assurance of itself. Therefore any confirmation which it should receive from the toiling and from communion would still be a fragmentary confirmation. Yes, itself it must destroy even this confirmation also, finding therein indeed a confirmation of something, but only of its isolation and its separation.

The actual world wherein the aspiration and the service find their calling, seems to this consciousness no longer an essentially vain world, that is only to be destroyed and consumed, but rather, like the consciousness itself, a world broken in twain, which is only in one aspect vain, while in another aspect it is a sanctified world, wherein the Changeless is incarnate. For the Changeless has retained the nature of individuality, and being, as changeless, an Universal, its individuality has in general the significance of all actuality.

If consciousness were now aware of its independent personality, and if it regarded the actual world as essentially vain, it would get the feeling of its independence in its service and in its communion, since it would be aware of itself as the victory that overcometh the world. But because the world is regarded by it as an embodiment of the ideal, it may not overcome by its own power. It does indeed attain to conquest over the world and to a feasting thereon, but to this end it is essential that the Changeless should itself give its own body as the food. And in this respect consciousness appears as a mere matter of fact having no part in the deed; but it also appears as inwardly broken in twain, and this doubleness, its division into a Self that stands in a genuine relation to itself and to reality, and a Self whose life is hidden and undeveloped, is now apparent in the contrast between its service and its communion. As in actual relation to the world, consciousness is a doer of works, and knows itself as such, and this side belongs to its individuality. But it has also its undeveloped reality. This is hidden in the true Self, and consists in the talents and virtues of the individual. They are a foreign gift. The Changeless grants them to consciousness that they may be used.

In doing its good works, consciousness is, for the first, parted into a relationship between two extremes. On one side stands the toiler in the world here below;

on the other side stands the passive actuality in whose
midst he toils.   Both are related to each other; both
however are also referred to the Changeless as their
source, and have their being hidden therein.   From
each side, then, there is but a shadowy image let free
to enter into play with the other.   That term of the
relationship which is called the Actuality is overcome by
the other term, the doer of good works.   But the former
term, for its part, can only be overcome because its
own Changeless Nature overcomes it, divides itself in
twain, and gives over the divided part to be the material for deeds.   The power that does the deeds appears
as the might that overcometh the world.   But for this
very reason the present Consciousness, which regards
its true Self as something foreign, must regard this
might also, whereby it works, as a thing remote from itself.   Instead of winning self-possession from its good
works, and becoming thereby sure of itself, Consciousness
relates all this activity back again to the other member
of the relationship, which thus proves itself to be the
pure Universal, the Absolute Might, whence flows every
form of activity, and wherein lies the truth both of the
mutually dissolving terms, as they first appeared, and
of their interchanging of relationship.

The Changeless Consciousness sacrifices its body, and
gives it over to be used.   On the other hand the individual consciousness renders thanks for the gift, forbids itself the satisfaction of a sense of independence,
and refers all its doings to the Changeless.   In these
two aspects of the mutual sacrifice made by both the
members of the relation, Consciousness does indeed win
the sense of its own oneness with the Changeless.   But
at the same time this oneness is still beladen with the
separation, and is divided in itself.   This opposition between the Individual and the Universal comes afresh

to sight. For Consciousness only *seems* to resign selfish
satisfaction. As a fact it gets selfish satisfaction. For
it still remains longing, activity, and fulfilment. As
Consciousnes it has longed, it has acted, it has been
filled. In giving thanks, in acknowledging the Other
as the true Self, in making naught of itself, it has still
been doing its own deed. This deed has repaid the deed
of the Other, has rendered a price for the kindly sacrifice. If the Other has offered its own image as a gift,
consciousness, for its part, has made its return in thanks,
and has herein done actually more than the Other,
since it has offered its All, namely, its good works,
while the Other has but parted with its mere image.
The entire process returns then back to the side of
the individual, and does so not merely in respect of the
actual aspiration, service, and communion, but even in
respect of the very act of giving thanks, an act that was
to attain the opposite result. In giving thanks consciousness is aware of itself as this individual, and refuses to be deceived by its own seeming resignation.
What has resulted is only the twofold reference of the
process to its two terms; and the result is the renewed
division into the conflicting consciousness of the Changeless on the one hand, and, on the other hand, the consciousness of the opposed will, activity, and fulfilment,
and even of the very resignation itself; for these constitute in general the separated individuality.

Herewith begins the third phase of the process of this
consciousness, which follows from the second as a consciousness that in truth, by will and by deed, has proved
its independence. In the first phase it was the mere
notion of a live consciousness, an inner life that had
not yet attained actuality by service and communion.
The second phase was the attainment, as outer activity
and communion. Returned from this outer activity, con-

sciousness has now reached the stage where it has experienced its own actuality and power, where it knows in
truth that it is fully self-possessed. But now the enemy
comes to light in his most genuine form. In the struggle
of the inner life the individual had existence only as an
abstraction, as "passed in music out of sight." In
service and in communion, as the realization of this unreal selfhood, it is able in its immediate experience to
forget itself, and its consciousness of its own merit in
this actual service is turned to humiliation through the
act of thankful acknowledgment. But this humiliation
is in truth a return of consciousness to itself, and to
itself as the possessor of its own actuality.

This third relationship, wherein this genuine actuality
is to be one term, is that relationship of the actuality to
the Universal, wherein the actuality is nevertheless to
appear as an Unreality; and the process of this relationship is still to be considered.

In the first place, as regards the conflicting relationship of consciousness, wherein its own reality appears
to it as an obvious nothingness, the result is that its
actual work seems to it a doing of naught, and its satisfaction is but a sense of its misery. Work and satisfaction thus lose all universal content and meaning; for
if they had any, then they would involve a full self-
possession. Both of them sink to the level of individuality; and consciousness, turning upon this individuality, devotes itself to making naught of it. Consciousness of an actual individual is a consciousness of the
mere animal functions of the body. These latter are
no longer naïvely carried out as something that is altogether of no moment, and that can have no weight
or significance for the spirit; on the contrary, they
become the object of earnest concern, and are of the
very weightiest moment. The enemy arises anew in his

defeat. Consciousness holds him in eye, yet frees itself not from him, but rather dwells upon the sight, and sees constantly its own uncleanness. And because, at the same time, this object of its striving, instead of being significant, is of the most contemptible, instead of being an universal is of the most individual, we therefore behold at this stage only a brooding, unhappy and miserable personality, limited solely to himself and his little deeds.

But all the while this person links both to the sense of his misery and to the worthlessness of his deeds, the consciousness that he is one with the Ideal. For the attempted direct destruction of individuality is determined by the thought of the Ideal, and takes place for the sake of the Ideal. This relation to dependence constitutes the essence of the negative onslaught upon individuality. But the dependence is as such potentially positive, and will bring consciousness to a sense of its own unity.

This determinate dependence is the rational Tie, whereby the individual who at first holds fast by his opposition to the true Self, is still linked to the other term, yet only by means of a third element. This mediating element reveals the true Self to the false Self, which in its turn knows that in the eyes of the true Self it has existence only by virtue of the dependence. It is the dependence then which reveals the two terms of the relationship to one another, and which, as Mediator, takes the part of each one of the terms in presence of the other. The Mediator too is a conscious Being, for its work is the production of this consciousness as such. What it brings to pass is that overcoming of individuality which consciousness is undertaking.

Through the Mediator, then, Consciousness frees itself from regarding its good works and its communion as due

to its private merit. It rejects all claim to independence
of will. It casts upon the Mediator, the intercessor, the
burden of its self-will, its freedom of choice, and its
sins. The Mediator, dwelling in the immediate presence of the Ideal, gives counsel as to what is to be done.
And what is done, being in submission to the will of another, is no longer one's own act. What is still left to
the untrue Self is the objective result of the deed, the
fruit of the toil, the satisfaction. But this too it refuses to accept as its own, and resigns not only its
self-will, but the actual outcome of its service and its
satisfaction. It resigns this outcome, first, because the
latter would involve an attainment of self-conscious truth
and independence (and this consciousness lives in the
thought and the speech of a strange and incomprehensible mystery). Secondly, moreover, it resigns the outcome in so far as the latter consists of worldly goods,
and so it abandons, in a measure, whatever it has earned
by its labor. Thirdly, it resigns all the satisfaction
which has fallen to its lot, forbidding itself such satisfaction through fasting and through penance.

By these characteristics, by the surrender of self-will,
of property, and of satisfaction, and by the further and
positive characteristic of its undertaking of a mysterious
task, consciousness does in truth free itself completely
from any sense of inner or outer freedom, from any
trust in the reality of its independence. It is sure that
it has verily surrendered its Ego, and has reduced its
natural self-consciousnes to a mere thing, to a fact
amongst facts. Only by such a genuine self-surrender
could consciousness prove its own resignation. For only
thus does there vanish the deceit that lies in the inner
offering of thanks with the heart, with the sentiments,
with the lips. Such offering does indeed strip from the
individual all independent might, and ascribes all the

glory to the heavenly Giver. But the individual even
when thus stripped, retains his outer self-will, for he
abandons not his possessions; and he retains his inner
self-will, for he is aware that it is he who undertakes
this self-sacrifice, and who has in himself the virtue involved in such an undertaking,—a virtue which he has
not exchanged for the mysterious grace that cometh from
above.

But in the genuine resignation, when once it has
come to pass, consciousness, in laying aside the burden
of its own deeds, has also, in effect, laid aside the burden
of its grief. Yet that this laying aside has already,
in effect, taken place, is due to the deed of the other
member of the Tie, namely to the essential Self. The
sacrifice of the unreal Self was made not by its own
one-sided act, but involved the working of the Other's
grace. For the resignation of self-will is only in part
negative, and on the other hand involves in its very
notion, or in its beginning, the positive transformation of
the will, and, in particular, its transformation from an
individual into an universal will. Consciousness finds
this positive meaning of the denial of self-will to consist in the will of the Changeless, as this will is done, not
by consciousness itself, but through the counsel of the
Mediator. Consciousness becomes aware, then, that its
will is universal and essential, but it does not regard
itself as identical with this essential nature. Self-
resignation is not seen to be in its very notion identical
with the positive work of the universal will. In the
same way the abandonment of possession and of satisfaction has only the same negative significance, and the
universal that thus comes in sight does not appear to
consciousness as its own deed. The unity of truth and of
self-possession implied in the notion of this activity, an
unity which consciousness accordingly regards as its

essence and its reality, is not recognized as implied in
this very notion.   Nor is the unity recognized by consciousness as its own self-created and immediately possessed object.   Rather does consciousness only hear,
spoken by the mediator's voice, the still fragile assurance that its own grief is, in the yet hidden truth of
the matter, the very reverse, namely the bliss of an
activity which rejoices in its tasks, that its own miserable
deeds are, in the same hidden truth, the perfect work.
And the real meaning of this assurance is that only
what is done by an individual is or can be [*ueberhaupt*]
a deed.   But for consciousness both activity and its own
actual deeds remain miserable.   Its satisfaction is its
sorrow, and the freedom from this sorrow, in a positive joy, it looks for in another world.   But this other
world, where its activity and its being are to become,
even while they remain its own, real activity and being,—what is this world but the image af REASON,—
of the assurance of Consciousness that in its individuality
it is and possesses all Reality?

IV

OUTLINES OF HEGEL'S LOGIC *

Translated by Wm. T. Harris

INTRODUCTION

1. The Science of Logic has for its object the thinking activity and the entire compass of its determinations. "Natural Logic" is a name given to the natural understanding which man possesses by nature, and the immediate use which he makes of it. The Science of Logic, however, is the Knowing of the Thinking in its truth.

Explanatory—Logic considers the province of thought in general. The thinking activity is its peculiar sphere. It is a whole (complete sphere) for and by itself. Logic

* *The following compend of Hegel's Logic is translated from the same volume as the "Outlines of Hegel's Phenomenology." It forms, with the latter, the second year's course of the "Philosophical Propadeutics." It will, we trust, be of good service in familiarizing thinkers with the general features of Hegel's system;—indeed, since it is written by Hegel himself, it is far better adapted for such a purpose than any of those compends given in Cyclopaedias and Histories of Philosophy, which without exception distort its more important features. The Outlines here given close the second year's course of the Propadeutics; the third year commences with a more elaborate exposition of the Comprehension (Begriff), which indeed forms the centre of Hegel's system.—Translator.*

has for its content the determinations peculiar to the thinking activity itself—which have no other ground than the Thinking. The "heteronomical" to it, is what is given to it through representation.* Logic is, therefore, true science. A distinction must, of course, be made between pure thought and reality; but thought has reality in so far as *true actuality* is understood by this term. In so far, however, as sensuous external existence is meant by "the Real," Thought has a far higher reality. The thinking activity has therefore a content (namely, itself) through its autonomy. Through the study of Logic we also learn to think more correctly; for since we think the Thinking of Thinking, the mind increases thereby its power. We learn the nature of the thinking activity, and thus we can trace out the course in which it is liable to be led into error. It is well to know how to give an account of one's deed. Thereby one gains stability, and is not liable to be led astray by others.

2. The thinking activity is, in general, the apprehension and bringing together of the Manifold into unity. The Manifold as such belongs to externality in general —to feeling and sensuous intuition.

Explanatory—The thinking activity consists in bringing the Manifold into unity. When the mind thinks upon things, it brings them into simple forms, which are its pure determinations. The Manifold is, at first, external to the Thinking. In so far as we merely seize the sensuous Manifold, we do not yet "think"; but it is the *relating* of the same that is properly called Thinking.

* *Note by Tr.*—"Representation" (German, *Vorstellung*) with Hegel signifies a mere notion or mental picture which is devoid of universality and necessity—that which should characterize true scientific Thinking.

The immediate seizing of the Manifold we call *feeling* or *sensation*. When I feel, I merely know somewhat; in "intuition" [*Anschauen*], however, I look upon something as external to me in space and time. Feeling becomes "intuition" when it is determined in space and time.

3. The thinking activity is *Abstraction* in so far as intelligence, beginning with concrete intuitions, neglects one of the manifold determinations, selects another, and gives to it the simple form of thought.

Explanatory—If I neglect *all* the determinations of an object, *nothing* remains. If, on the contrary, I neglect *one* and select *another,* the latter is then abstract. The *Ego,* for example, is an abstract determination. I know of the *Ego* only in so far as I exclude all determinations from myself. This is, however, a negative means. I negate the determinations of myself, and leave myself as such, alone by myself. The act of abstraction is the *negative* side of the thinking activity.

4. The *content* of representations [*Vorstellungen* = notions] is taken from experience, but the *form of unity* itself, and its further determinations, have not their source in the Immediate * as such, but in the thinking activity.

Explanatory—The Ego signifies, generally, the thinking activity. If I say: "I think," this is something tautological. The Ego is perfectly simple. The Ego is a thinking activity, and that always. We could not say, however: "I always think." Though *potentially* so, yet what we think is not always *actually* Thought. We could however say, in the sense that we are Ego's:

* *Note by Tr.*—Immediate=direct object. Thus the sensuous world is spoken of as immediate. In general, that which is most simple, most empty, most undeveloped is "immediate."

"We always think," for the Ego is always the simple identity with itself, and this simple identity with itself is Thinking. As Ego, we are the ground of all our determinations. In so far as the object is thought it receives the form of thinking and becomes a thought-object. It is made identical to the Ego, i.e. it is thought.

5. This must not be understood as though this unity was added to the Manifold of objects by the thinking activity, and thereby the act of uniting was done externally; but the unity must be conceived as belonging likewise to the object, and as constituting with its determinations the proper nature thereof.

6. Thoughts are of three kinds: (1) The Categories; (2) Determination of Reflections; (3) Comprehension,* The science of the first two constitutes the objective logic in metaphysics; the science of Comprehensions (concepts or notions) constitutes the proper or subjective logic.

Explanatory—Logic contains the system of pure

---

* *Note by Tr.*—"Comprehension" (German, *Begriff*) signifies the necessary unity of determinations which belong to a whole. "Concept" or "conception" is too subjective, in its ordinary acceptation, to serve as a translation of Hegel's term "*Begriff*." A "concept" may be a mere "representation" (*Vorstellung*), i.e., arbitrary notion, but Hegel's "*Begriff*" is an *organic unity* of Universality, Particularly, and Individuality. "*Bestimmter Begriff*," as Hegel uses it in his Logic, is properly "concept" or "notion." The term "comprehension" has been adopted in this sense by Mr. Brockmeyer in his translation of Hegel's Complete Logic, and though it sounds strangely in some of its connections, it more readily than any other word suggests the *exhaustiveness* of the process in which the Manifold is grasped in unity. *Idea* and *ideal* have also been used to render the sense of *Begriff* in English: "Something is adequate to its *Begriff*," i.e. to its *ideal* or true definition, what it *ought to be.*

Thinking, Being is (1) the Immediate, (2) the Internal; the determinations of Thinking go back again into themselves. The objects of the common system of metaphysics are the *Thing,* the *World, Mind,* and *God,* through which the different metaphysical sciences arise: Ontology, Cosmology, Pneumatology, and Theology. (3) The Comprehension (concept, notion, or idea) presents us with what is *existent* and at the same time *essential.* Being stands in relation to essence as the Immediate to the Mediate. Things *are* in general, but their Being consists in this: that they manifest their Essence. Being goes over into Essence; one can express it thus: "Being presupposes Essence." But although Essence, in comparison with Being, appears as that which is *mediated,* yet Essence is the true Primitive, notwithstanding. Being goes back, in it, into its ground; Being cancels * itself (takes itself up) into Essence. Its Essence is in this form a *Become* or *Produced,* but what appears as "Become" is rather the Original or Primitive.

* *Note by Tr.*—"Cancel"=to annul as an independent something and yet to preserve as a dependent element. (German, *Aufheben.*)   In its mathematical sense "cancel" is used of magnitudes which reduce each other to zero—mutually annual or suppress each other—and therefore become indifferent to the equation.   In its commercial sense, a "cancelled" note or bond has still positive value as a receipt or discharge from the debt.   The term "cancel" in this sense has been adopted by Mr. Brockmeyer in the work before alluded to.   Other equivalents for this word, in various shadings, are these: Annul (Stallo and others), set aside (J. E. Cabot), abrogate (J. D. Sibree), abolish, repeal, transubstantiate, translate, transmute, sublate, (J. H. Sterling), nullify, revoke, neutralize, subordinate, subdue, subjugate, vanquish, transmerge, subvert, destroy, submerge, "take up into," suppress, "do away with," "reduce to moments" (which is its exact signification).   The Greek term is ἀναιρέω.

The Perishable has in Essence its basis, and originates from it. We make comprehensions (i.e. exhaustive concepts). These are somewhats *posited* by us, but they contain also the Reality in and for itself. As compared with the comprehension, Essence in its turn is a "mere posited," but "the posited" in this relation still stands for the true. The comprehension is partly subjective, partly objective. The IDEA * is the union of Subjective and Objective. If we say, "It is a mere conception (*blosser Begriff*)," we mean that it is without reality. The mere Objectivity is devoid of the comprehension. But the Idea is the reality determined through the comprehension. Everything actual is an IDEA.

7. Science presupposes that the separation of itself from Truth is already cancelled, or that the mind is no longer in a phenomenal stage as it was in the *Science of Consciousness* (Phenomenology of Spirit). The certitude of itself comprehends all that is object of consciousness (whether it be an external thing, or a thought produced in the mind), in so far as it does not contain in itself all moments † of the *Being-in-and-for-itself:* (1) to be *in itself,* or simple identity with itself; (2) to have determinate Being or determinateness, Being for others; and (3) to be *for itself,* i.e. in its relation to others to be simple, reflected into itself, and by itself. Science does not *seek* Truth, but is *in* the Truth, and *is* the Truth itself.

* *Note by Tr.*—The Idea = the absolute existing Comprehension of comprehensions; Perfect Being, i.e. Being which is in nowise deficient but whose entire potentiality is realized.

† *Note by Tr.*—"Moment" (German, *Moment*) = "Reciprocally complemental element" (as translated by Seelye from Schwelger's paraphrase of the term). That which is "cancelled" is reduced to a moment, i.e. has lost its immediate and independent first phase, and has sunk into a constituent phase or element—as acid and alkali, e.g., become moments of salt.

PART FIRST.—BEING.

First Division—Quality.

8. Quality is the immediate determinateness, whose change is the transition into a Different.

A.—Being, Naught, Becoming.

9. Being is the simple empty immediateness which has its opposite in *pure Naught,* and whose union therewith is the Becoming: as transition from Naught to Being, it is Beginning; the converse is Ceasing.

(The "sound common sense," as one-sided abstraction often calls itself, will not admit the union of Being and Naught. "Either it is Being, or it is not. There is no third." "What *is,* does not begin; what is not, is *not.*" It asserts, therefore, the impossibility of Beginning.)

B.—Determinate Being *

10. Determinate Being is *become* or *determined* Being, a Being which has a relation to another—hence to its non-being.

* *Note by Tr.*—Determinate Being: (German, *"Daseyn,"* whose literal meaning is to be *present,* to be there or here.) It is equivalent to particular Being. Although it is frequently translated "Existence," and in several respects agrees with that word in signification, yet Hegel uses it to signify mere qualitative determinateness, while "Existence" is generally used in a more concrete sense, and involves quantity and other determinations as well as quality. The proof of the Being of a God (*"Beweis vom Daseyn Gottes,"* as Hegel calls it in his *Philosophy of Religion*) may be called proof of the *existence* of God, or of the "determinate Being" of God. The

11. (a) Determinate Being is, consequently, a somewhat divided in itself: *firstly,* it is *in-itself* (i.e. potential); *secondly,* it is relation to others. Determinate Being, thought with these two determinations is *Reality.*

12. (b) A somewhat which is definite has a relation to another. The "other" is a definite Being as the nonbeing of the somewhat. It has, consequently, a boundary or restraining limit and is finite. What a somewhat ought to be in itself, is called its Destination * (determination).

13. The mode in which a somewhat is for another, or in which it is connected with another, and hence immediately posited through another, is called its *state* or *condition.*†

14. The mode in which a somewhat is *in-itself,* as well for itself as for another, is its *determinateness* or *quality.* The limit is not only the point where the somewhat ceases, but it belongs to the somewhat in itself.

---

loose use of the category of Being in English has allowed it to usurp the whole province of *"Daseyn"*; but for the sake of precision the latter term will be called *determinate* Being in this translation. It is a point worthy of profound consideration that the English, and Southern European nations have used the expression for a concreter mediation = Existence, where the Germans have used a more abstract one = determinate Being.

* *Note by Tr.*—Destination: (German *Bestimmung,* which must be translated "Determination" ordinarily.) It means nearly the "proper sphere" and is also nearly the same as "nature" in the phrase "true nature of a thing."

† *Note by Tr.*—State or condition = (German, *Beschaffenheit*) "the being shaped or fashioned through the action of external influences and relations." "Condition" is rather more concrete and involves more mediation than *Beschaffenheit,* which here is used in the qualitative sense of "fixed state."

15. (c) **Through** its quality, through *what* it is, the somewhat is exposed to CHANGE. It changes in so far as its determinateness comes into connection with another and thereby becomes state or condition [*Beschaffenheit*].

C.—Being For-itself.*

16. Inasmuch as the "state or condition" is cancelled through change, change itself also is cancelled. Being, consequently, with this process, has gone back into itself and excludes otherness from itself. It is FOR ITSELF.

17. It is ONE, and relates only to itself, and stands in a repellent relation towards others.

18. This excluding is at the same time a *bringing-into-relation* to others, and hence it is likewise an *attracting*. No Repulsion without attraction and *vice versa*.

19. Or, with the act of repulsion on the part of the One, many ones are immediately posited. But the many ones are not distinct from each other. Each one is what the other is. Hence their cancelling, i.e. their attraction, is likewise posited.

20. The One is the "Existent-for-itself," which is absolutely distinct from others. But since this distinction (in which Repulsion is cancelled by Attraction) is the distinction posited as cancelled, for that reason it has passed over into another determination—QUANTITY.†

* *Note by Tr.—Being-for-itself*, literal translation of *"Für-sich-seyn"* = Independent Being.

† *Note by Tr.*—Note that Quantity is suggested by the complete grasping (comprehending) of Quality. Quality or "whatness" can only be through the self-determination of a

("Somewhat" without limits has no meaning. If I change the limits of a somewhat, it remains no longer what it is; if I change the limits of a field, it still remains a field as before though somewhat larger or smaller. In this case I have not changed its limits as field, but as a given quantity. To change its qualitative limit as ploughed field means, e.g., to make it a forest.)

Second Division—Quantity.

21. Through quality a somewhat is *what* it is. Through change of quality, there is changed not merely a determination of the somewhat—or of the Finite—but the Finite somewhat, itself changes. Quantity, on the contrary, is the determination which does not constitute the nature of the object itself; it is rather an *"indifferent* distinction," which may be changed, while the object remains the same.

22. Quantity is the cancelled Being-for-itself (or One). It is, therefore, an unbroken CONTINUITY in itself. But since it contains the One, moreover, it possesses also the "moment" of DISCRETENESS.

23. (A) *Magnitude* is either *continuous* or *discrete*. But each of these two kinds of magnitude contains discreteness AND continuity in it; and their difference is this only, that in the discrete magnitude, it is Discreteness which constitutes the main principle, while in the continuous it is Continuity.

24. (B) *Magnitude* or *Quantity* is as limited quantity, a *"Quantum."* Since this limit is nothing fixed in its

somewhat, and such a somewhat is called a Being-for-itself or independent Being. But such determination is not merely the *ceasing* of the somewhat in its other, but likewise its *continuation* into its own externality, and this is Quantity precisely.

nature, it follows that a *"quantum"* [i.e. a given quantity] can be changed indefinitely; it can be increased or decreased at pleasure.

25. The limits of the *"quantum"* in the form of "Being-in-itself" give INTENSIVE quantity; and in the form of externality give EXTENSIVE quantity. But there is no intensive Being which does not likewise at the same time possess the form of extensive Being; and conversely.

26. (C) *"Quantum"* has no in-itself determined limit. There is, hence, no quantum [given quantity] beyond which a larger or smaller cannot be posited. The "quantum" which is, by hypothesis, the *last* one— the one which has no greater or no smaller (as the case may be)—is generally called the infinitely great or the infinitely small [Maximum and Minimum].

27. But in this shape it ceases to be a "quantum" at all, and is by itself = 0. It has then significance only in a RATIO wherein it no longer possesses any magnitude by itself, but only in relation to another. This is the correct comprehension (conception) of the MATHEMATICAL INFINITE.

28. The Infinite in general, when seized in the form of the Infinite Progress, is the process of cancelling the restraining limit whether it be qualitative or quantitative, so that this restraining limit passes for something positive, and continually reappears after its negation. The true Infinite, however, is the NEGATION OF NEGATION, inasmuch as the restraining limit is to be understood as really a negation. In it the progress beyond the Finite does not posit again a new restraining limit, but through the cancelling of the restraining limit, the Being is restored to identity with itself.

29. While the "quantum" cancels itself in the Infinite, in the same process the indifferent, external de-

termination which constitutes the "quantum," is cancelled and becomes an internal, a *qualitative* determination.

Third Division—Measure.*

30. "Measure" is a SPECIFIC QUANTUM in so far as it is not external, but is determined through the nature of the object, through quality.

31. In the change of a "quantum," in its increase or decrease, which goes on within its "measure," there enters likewise a specifying process, in which the indifferent, external movement of magnitude up and down the scale, is determined and modified through the nature of the thing itself.

32. When the "measure" of a thing is changed, the thing itself changes and ceases to be the particular somewhat that it was, through the passing beyond its "measure,"—increasing or decreasing beyond it.

PART SECOND—ESSENCE

33. Essence is Being which has returned from its immediateness and its indifferent relation to others into simple unity with itself.

First Division—The Determinations of Essence in Itself.

34. Essence (*"Wesen"*) appears to itself (*"scheint in sich selbst"*) and determines itself. But its deter-

* *Note by Tr.*—Measure (German *Mass*) is the reciprocal relation of Quality and Quantity. The word "measure" is used here in the sense of "due proportion," "proper extent," "the measure of its capacity.'

minations are in unity. They are only "posited-being,"
i.e. they are not immediately for themselves, but only
such as exist in unity. They are therefore RELA-
TIONS. They are "determinations of Reflection."

35. (1) The first determination is the essential unity
with itself—IDENTITY. Expressed as a proposition
—namely, as a universal determination—it is the proposition "A = A," "everything is identical with itself";
negatively, as the proposition of contradiction: "A cannot be at the same time A and not-A."

36. (2) The second determination is DISTINC-
TION * (a) as the determination of DIFFERENCE—
of Beings indifferent to each other, but distinguished
through some determinateness or other. The proposition which expresses it, reads: "There are no two things
which are perfectly identical with each other"; (b) as
the determination of OPPOSITION (*antithesis*), the
positive against the negative, in which a determinateness
is posited only by means of another determinateness, and
each of these determinatenesses is only in so far as the
other is, but at the same time is only in so far as it is *not*
the other. The proposition through which this is expressed reads: "A is either B or not-B, and there is
no third."

37. (3) The third in which the posited determination
are cancelled in general is Essence, which is, in this
phase, GROUND.† The proposition of Ground reads:
"Every somewhat has its sufficient (reason or) ground."

* *Note by Tr.*—Distinction (German, *"Unterschied"*), which
has also the meaning of "difference" in some instances. In this
translation *"Verschiedenheit"* is translated "difference" in the
sense of "diversity."

† *Note by Tr.*—Ground (German, *Grund*) = cause or reason.
In the expression, "He has reasons for his conduct," "reasons"
are "grounds" in the sense here spoken of.

38. In so far as immediate Being is regarded as a merely "Posited," it has gone back into essence or into its ground. The former (i.e. Being) is here the first—that from which we started. But in this "going back" we retract that position, and recognize the ground rather as the first and essential.

39. The Ground contains that which is grounded through it according to its essential determinations. But the relation of the Ground to the grounded is not a pure transition into the opposite, although the grounded existence has a different shape from its ground, which is likewise an existence, and the chief determination is their common content.

Second Division—Phenomenon.

A.—Thing.

40. The Ground, through its internal determination, posits its Being, a Being which, as proceeding from the Ground, is EXISTENCE.

41. As a totality of its determinations, the existing somewhat is a THING.

42. The properties of a Thing are determinations of its existence which are different from each other, but at the same time independent of each other; and moreover a Thing is, as simple identity with itself (undetermined and) indifferent towards them as determinations.

43. The determinations are through the *thingness* identical with themselves, and the Thing is nothing but this identity of its properties with themselves. Through this circumstance, the Thing dissolves into its properties, as into matters which subsist for and by themselves.

44. Since, however, the "matters" are united in the

unity of a thing, they interpenetrate each other reciprocally and cancel each other. The Thing is consequently this contradiction in itself, or it is posited as a mere self-dissolving, as Phenomenal.

B.—The Phenomenal.

45. Essence has gone out of *Ground* into *Existence*. The Existing posited as not in-and-for-itself, but as grounded in another, is THE PHENOMENAL. Essence *must* manifest itself in so far as it is, as ground, simple immediateness, and hence Being in general.

46. On account of the Identity of the Ground and the Existent, there is nothing in *the Phenomenal* which is not in the Essence, and conversely nothing in the Essence which is not in the Phenomenal.

47. (The identity with itself in the Phenomenal is the Undetermined, the determination a mere CAPACITY—the PASSIVE MATTER. The identity of determinations in their relation to each other, constitutes the ACTIVE, the FORM. Since Matter is determined by Form, the two presuppose each other. There is however, in general, no Matter without Form and no Form without Matter. Matter and form give rise to each other reciprocally.) The essential relation in the determinations of the Phenomenal is the LAW thereof.

48. Since the determinations manifest themselves also in the form of independent existence, the Relation of the same as being determined through each other constitutes the mutual elation [*Verhältniss*].*

* *Note by Tr.*—"*Verhältniss*" is the behavior of one side of a relation as conditioned by the other. "Conduct" is sometimes a good equivalent for it. There is reciprocity in it, and neither side exists except in the relation. In Quantity "*Verhältniss*" is translated by the technical term "*Ratio.*" Here it means

C.—Mutual Relation.

49. The MUTUAL RELATION is a relation to each other of two sides which have partly an indifferent subsistence, but partly each is only through the other and in this unity which determines both.

50. The determinations are posited first in the form of mutual relation, secondly they are only in themselves, and manifest themselves as independent, immediate Existence. They are in this respect presupposed somewhats and internally, already in themselves, contain the totality of form, which can have existence only through that presupposition; or they are in so far conditions, and their mutual relation is a conditional mutual relation.

51. In the conditions and the conditioned mutual relation, the Phenomenal begins to return into Essence and Being-in-itself, but there exists still the difference of the Phenomenal as such, and the former (Essence, &c.) in so far as they are *"in themselves."*

52. (1) The immediately conditioned Mutual Relation is the WHOLE and the PARTS. The parts as existing outside of the Relation, and subsisting for themselves, are mere matters, and, in so far, not parts. As parts they have their determination only in the whole, and the whole is what makes them to be parts, and conversely it is the parts that make it to be the whole.

53. (2) The whole, as internally active Form, is FORCE. It has no external matter as its condition,

---

that close, reciprocal relation which exists between "Whole and Parts," "Force and Manifestation," "Internal and External." "To stand in relation," and "state of relation," seem the best equivalents for *"Verhäiten"* and *"Verhältniss"* in some cases, but here "Mutual Relation" is chosen as the most appropriate term.

but is in the matter itself. Its condition is only an external "occasion" which solicits it. The latter is itself the utterance of a Force and demands in turn a solicitation for its manifestation. It is a reciprocal conditioning and being conditioned, and this is as a Whole, therefore, unconditioned.

54. According to content, Force exhibits in its utterance that which it is in itself, and there is nothing in its utterance which is not in its Internal.

55. (3) The content is consequently, in respect to the distinction of Internal and External, unconditioned. It stands in mutual relation as internal, only to itself as external. The external and internal are therefore the same, only considered from different sides. The internal is the perfection of content-determinations as conditions which themselves have determinate existence. The becoming-external is the reflection of the same or the uniting of the whole, which through this receives existence.

Third Division—Actuality.

A.—Substance.

56. Substance is the unconditioned, in-and-for-itself-subsisting Essence in so far as it has immediate Existence. (*Substantia est—causa sui: id quod par se concipitur sive cujus conceptus involvit existentiam—Spinoza.*)

57. In its existence it has manifold determinations distinct from it = ACCIDENTS. In their Totality they constitute substance, which is the subsistence, and hence the POWER of Accidents.

58. The accidents, in so far as they are contained in the substance, are POTENTIAL.

59. When anything is thought merely in the form of "Being-in-itself," or as not self-contradictory, it is called potential (possible). Everything in so far as it is determined as a Being-in-itself which is only a posited, is called *merely* potential. Such a Possibility, isolated from the Actuality, has an individual content.

60. *Truly* potential is somewhat as a totality of its in-itself-existent determinations. Whatever possesses this internal perfect potentiality is not merely a posited-Being, but in-and-for-itself and immediately *actual*. The potentiality of substance is, therefore, its actuality. (God, e.g., is not only in general but truly potential. His potentiality is a necessary one. He is absolutely Actual.)

61. The combination of accidents in the substance, is their necessity. It is the unity of Possibility and Actuality. Necessity is blind in so far as the combination is merely an internal one, or in so far as the actual is not previously extant as an in-itself-existent unity of its determinations, but results first from the relation of the same.

B.—Cause.

62. Substance manifests itself in the origination and vanishing of its accidents. It is in so far active, or CAUSE.

63. As Cause, substance makes its original content into EFFECT, i.e. into a "posited through another."

64. There is nothing in the effect which is not in the cause, and the cause is cause only in the Effect.

(It is said: the fall of a brick is the cause of the death of a man: the miasma of a region is the cause of fevers. But the former was the cause only of the blow, the latter only of excessive moisture. But the effect in an actual existence which has other determinations, besides, continues to other results.)

65. Cause passes over into effect. Since the cause itself has a definite content and is to be posited as effect, we obtain a regress of causes and effects in an infinite series. Conversely, in so far as that upon which the effect takes place is itself a primitive, it is a cause, and produces an effect in another, through which a progress *ad infinitum* results.

C.—Reciprocal Action.

66. In so far as the effect returns to the cause, it is itself cause. It makes the cause a Posited. It is RE-ACTION. "Action and Reaction are equal."

67. The Reaction takes place against the first cause, which consequently is posited as effect, through which nothing else happens except that it is posited as it is in itself, namely, as a not truly original (primitive) but as a *Transitory*.

68. Reciprocal action consists in this: that which is effect is conversely cause, and that which is cause is conversely effect. Or the reciprocal relation is the mediation of the Thing with itself, in which the Primitive determines itself or makes itself a Posited; and therein reflects itself into itself, and exists first as this reflection into itself, and is therein true Primitiveness.

APPENDIX—THE ANTINOMIES.

69. The categories, the determinations of Being are simple; but the determinations which do not constitute the primitive elements, i.e. the determinations of Essence, are simple only in so far as their antithetical mo-

ments are reduced to simplicity. Whenever such a category is predicated of a subject and is developed through the analysis of those antithetic moments, the two are predicable of the subject, and there arise antithetic propositions, both of which have equal truth.

70. Kant especially has drawn attention to the Antinomies of Reason, although he has not exhausted them, since he has made an exposition of the forms of only a few.

I. The antinomy of the Finitude or Infinitude of the world in regard to Space and Time.

(1) The antinomy in respect to Time.

    (a) THESIS: The world has a beginning in Time.

71. *Proof:* Let one assume that the world has no beginning in respect to time; then, up to any given point of time, an eternity has elapsed, and consequently an infinite series of successive conditions of things in the world. The infinitude of a series consists, however, in this, that it can never be completed by successive synthesis; therefore an infinite series of conditions in the world is impossible; hence a beginning of the same in time is necessitated.

    (b) ANTITHESIS: The world has no beginning in time, and is infinite in respect to time.

72. *Proof:* Let one suppose that it had a beginning, then there would be assumed an empty time before that beginning—a time in which the world was not. In an empty time, however, nothing can originate, for in it there is no condition for existence, since one Being always has another as its condition, i.e. is limited by finite Being only. Therefore the world can have no beginning, but every determinate Being presupposes another, and so on *ad infinitum.*

73. The proof of this antinomy, when reduced to a brief form, becomes the following direct antithesis:

(1) The world is finite in respect to time; i.e. it has a limit. In the proof of the thesis such a limit is assumed, namely, the Now, or some one given point of time.

(2) Determinate Being has a limit, not in determinate non-Being, in empty time, but only in a determinate Being. The self-limiting somewhats are also positively related to each other, and the one has the same determination as the other. Since, therefore, each determinate Being is limited, or each is a finite one, i.e. such a one as must be transcended ["passed beyond" in the act of defining it], it follows that the "Progress into infinity" is posited.

74. The true solution of this antinomy is this: Neither is the mentioned limit something true for itself, nor is the Infinite spoken of, a true somewhat for-itself; for the limit is of such a kind that it must be transcended, and the Infinite spoken of is merely that to which the limit continually arises. The true infinitude is the RE-FLECTION-INTO-ITSELF, and Reason contemplates not the temporal world, but the world in its essence and idea.

(2) The antinomy in respect to space.

(a) THESIS: The world is limited in respect to space.

75. *Proof:* Let one assume that it is unlimited; then it is an infinite given Whole of co-existent things. Such a whole can be viewed as completed only through the synthesis of the parts therein contained. For this completion, however, infinite time is required, which must be assumed as already elapsed, which is impossible. Therefore an infinite aggregate of existing things can-

not be viewed as a co-existent whole. The world is accordingly not infinite in space, but included in limits.

(b) ANTITHESIS: The world is unlimited in respect to space.

76. *Proof:* Let one assume that the world is spatially limited, then it finds itself in an empty unlimited space; it would, therefore, have a relation to this empty space, i.e. a relation to no object. Such a relation, however, as that of the world to empty space is nothing; therefore, the world is spatially infinite.

77. The proofs of these antithetic propositions really rest on direct assertions.

(1) The proof of the thesis refers the completion of the co-existent totality or the spatial world, to the succession of time in which the synthesis must occur and be completed; and this is partly incorrect and partly superfluous, for in the spatial world precisely it is not of *succession* but of *co-existence* that one may speak. Furthermore: when an already elapsed infinite time is assumed, a Now is assumed. Likewise in space a Here is assumed, i.e. a limit in general to space, from which afterwards the impossibility of its illimitableness can be deduced.

(2) Since the limits in space are in general to be transcended, it follows that the negative of the limit is posited; and since it is essentially a negative of the limit, it is conditioned through it [through the limit]. Hence the infinite progress is posited in the same form as in the previous antinomy.

II. The antinomy concerning the simplicity or composite nature of substances.

(a) THESIS: Every composite substance consists of simple parts.

78. *Proof:* Let one assume that composite substances consist *not* of simple parts. If, now, all composition or

combination were annihilated in thought, then there would be no composite part, and, since there is also no simple part, nothing would remain, and accordingly no substance would be given. Consequently it is impossible to annihilate all composition in thought. But the Composite does not consist again of substances, for composition is only an accidental relation of them, and substances must subsist as enduring entities without composition. Therefore the substantial Composite consists of simple parts. It follows hence that things in the world, without exception, are simple entities, and that composition is only an external condition of them.

(b) ANTITHESIS: No composite thing consists of simple parts, and there does not exist anywhere anything simple.

79. *Proof:* Let one assume that a composite thing consists of simple parts. Inasmuch as all external relation, consequently all composition, is possible only in space, then the space which includes it must consist of as many parts as the composite consists of. Now space consists, not of simple parts but of spaces. Therefore every part of the composite must occupy a space. But the absolutely primary parts of all composites are simple. Therefore the simple occupies space. Now since everything real which occupies space contains a manifold whose parts are external to each other and is consequently composite, it follows that the simple is a substantial composite—which is self-contradictory.

80. The proof of the thesis contains the direct assertion that composition is an external relation, or something contingent; hence the Simple is the Essential. The proof of the antithesis rests likewise upon the direct assertion that substances are essentially spatial, and hence composite. In itself this antinomy is the same as the previous one, namely, the positing of a limit and

then the transcending of the same, a process which is
involved in the comprehension of determinate Being.

III. The antinomy concerning the antithesis of
Causality according to natural laws and freedom.

(a) THESIS: Causality according to natural laws
is not the only causality in the phenomena
of the world; there is also a Causality of
Freedom.

81. *Proof:* Let one assume that there is no other
Causality than according to the laws of nature; it follows that everything which happens, presupposes a
previous condition from which it proceeds according to
an invariable rule. Now that previous condition itself
must have happened, since if it always had existed, its
effect must have always existed. Therefore the Causality through which something comes to pass is itself a
something which has come to pass, and which again
presupposes a previous condition and its causality, and
so on *ad infinitum*. There is therefore, at any given
time, only a relative and no first beginning; and hence,
in general, no completeness of series on the part of
the connected causes. The law of nature consists, however, precisely in this: that nothing happens without an
efficient *a priori* cause. Therefore the proposition that
all causality is possible only according to natural laws
refutes itself, and natural laws cannot be assumed as the
only ones.

(b) ANTITHESIS: There is no freedom, but
everything in the world comes to pass
solely according to the laws of nature.

82. *Proof:* Let one assume that there is freedom,
to wit, a power which can absolutely originate a state
or condition, and consequently a series of results thereof,
then not only the series is originated through the spon-

taneity, but the determination of this spontaneity itself
is thus originated in such a manner that nothing can
precede, through which this action is determined according to fixed laws.   Each origination of an act, however,
presupposes a state or condition of the cause which is
not as yet active, and a dynamical first beginning of
the Act presupposes a state which has no causal connexion whatever with the preceding state of the cause,
i.e. which in nowise results from it.   Therefore freedom
is opposed to the laws of causality and such a combination of successive conditions of active causes—according
to which no unity of experience is possible, and which
therefore can never be met with in experience—is an
empty fiction of thought.

83. This antinomy, abstractly considered, rests upon
the antithesis which the causal relation has in itself.
Namely, the cause is: (1) an original cause, a first,
self-moving cause; (2) but it is conditioned through
something upon which it acts, and its activity passes
over into the effect.   In so far, it is to be viewed as
nothing truly original but as a "Posited."   If the first
side is held fast, an absolute causality is assumed, a
causality of freedom; but according to the second side
the cause becomes a something that has happened, and
with it an infinite series of conditions is posited.

84. The true solution of this antinomy is RECI-
PROCITY; a cause which passes over into an effect
has in this again a causal Reaction, by which means the
first cause is reduced in turn to an effect or to a
"Posited."   In this reciprocity, consequently, is involved the fact that neither of the two moments of
causality is for itself and absolute, but that it is only
the *entire circle,* THE TOTALITY, that is in and for
itself.

IV. (a) THESIS: An absolutely necessary Being belongs to the world.

85. *Proof:* The sensuous world, as the sum total of all phenomena, contains at the same time, a series of changes. Every change stands under its condition, under which it is necessary. Now every Conditioned in view of its existence presupposes a perfect series of conditions up to the absolutely Unconditioned, which alone is absolutely necessary. Therefore something absolutely necessary must exist, if change shall exist as its result. This necessary somewhat itself, however, belongs to the sensuous world; for, assume that it exists outside of it, then the series of changes in the world would derive their origin from it, and yet this necessary cause itself would not belong to the sensuous world. Now this is impossible; for since the beginning of a series in time can be determined only through that which precedes it in time, the ultimate condition of the beginning of a series of changes must exist in a time when this series did not as yet exist; hence this ultimate condition belongs to time, and consequently to phenomena or to the sensuous world; therefore there is in the world itself something absolutely necessary.

(b) ANTITHESIS: There exists no absolutely necessary Being, neither in the world nor outside the world, as its cause.

86. *Proof:* Let one assume that the world itself, or something in it, is a necessary entity (Being), then in the series of its changes there would be a beginning which was unconditionally necessary and consequently without cause, and this contradicts the dynamical law of the determination of all phenomena. Or else the series itself would be without a beginning, and though in all its parts contingent and conditioned, yet on the whole absolutely necessary and unconditioned, which is

self-contradictory, for the reason that the existence of an aggregate cannot be a necessary one if no single part of it possesses necessary existence. Furthermore, let one assume that there is an absolutely necessary cause of the world which is outside of the world: then it would begin the existence of the changes in the world and their series; since it must begin to act, its causality would belong to time and hence to the sum total of all phenomena, and hence not be outside of the world. Therefore there is neither in the world nor outside of it any absolutely necessary Being.

87. This antinomy contains, on the whole, the same antithesis as the previous one. With the Conditioned a condition is posited, and indeed a condition *as such,* or an absolute condition, i.e. one which has not its necessity in something else. Since, however, it is in connexion with the Conditioned, or since the Conditioned lies in its comprehension (or complete definition), it belongs itself to the sphere of the Conditioned, or is a Conditioned itself. According to the former side, an absolutely necessary Being is posited, but according to the latter only a *relative* necessity, and hence *contingence.*

PART THIRD—COMPREHENSION.

88. The science of the Comprehension (concepts), or subjective logic, has for its object the Comprehension, and not the Categories, and determinations of Reflection. The Category posits Being in a determinateness as limit; Reflection posits essence in a determination which is mediated through the presupposition of another. The Comprehension [conception?], on the other hand, is the in-and-for-itself Existent, the simple totality out of which all its determinations flow.

89. Subjective logic treats of three chief objects, (1) the Comprehension, (2) the Final Cause, (3) the Idea; namely: (1) the formal Comprehension, or the Comprehension as such; (2) the Comprehension in relation to its realization or its Objectivity (the Final Cause); (3) the Idea as the real or objective Comprehension.

First Division—The Comprehension.

90. Formal Logic contains (1) the comprehension as such, (2) the judgment, and (3) the syllogism.

91. (1) The COMPREHENSION contains the moments of *individuality, particularity,* and *universality.* Individuality is the negative reflection of the comprehension into itself, through which something is in-and-for-itself, and the determinations as moments inhere in it. Universality is the positive, not excluding, unity of the comprehension with itself, which contains the opposite in itself, so that it remains indifferent and undetermined toward it. Particularity is the relation of individuality and universality to each other. It is the Universal reduced to a determination; or, conversely, the individual elevated into universality.

92. As these determinations are distinguished from each other as moments of the Comprehension, so are they distinguished by the different content they may have, as comprehensions of something universal, something particular, and something individual.

93. The Universal subsumes or includes the Particular and Individual under it. The individual has the same, and at the same time several more, determinations than the Particular and Universal. Likewise the same relation exists on the part of the Particular toward the Universal. What, therefore, possesses validity with

regard to the Universal, possesses validity for the Particular and Individual; and what is valid of the Particular is valid of the individual, *but not conversely.*

94. The particular determinations which belong to the same Universal are COÖRDINATED to each other. The same thing applies also to those which belong to the same individual. But these determinations which are coördinated in a Universal cannot be coördinated in one individual.

95. (2) In the JUDGMENT the implicit unity in which the moments are grasped together in the comprehension, is cancelled. It (the judgment) is the *relation* of the determinations of the Comprehension in so far as each is valid by itself as a self-subsisting and consequently as a particular comprehension.

96. The Judgment contains: (1) the subject as the side of individuality or particularity; (2) the predicate as the side of universality, which is at the same time a determined universality, or also particularity; (3) the simple relation (devoid of content) which the subject has to the predicate, is the COPULA.

97. The species of Judgments indicate the different stages in which the external relation of subject and predicate becomes an internal relation of the comprehension. The subject is, *first,* in immediate identity with the predicate—the two are one and the same determination of content; *secondly,* they are distinguished one from the other. The subject is a more complex content than the abstract predicate, and is in regard to form contingent.

98. (3) In the Judgment two determinations of the Comprehension are related immediately to each other. The SYLLOGISM is the Judgment with its ground. The two determinations are connected in the Syllogism by means of a third which is their unity. The Syllogism

ís, therefore, the perfect positing of the Comprehension.

99. According to determined form, the two extremes of the Syllogism are the Individual and the Universal; the Particular, on the contrary, for the reason that in it these two determinations are united, is the middle term of the same. If a determination A belongs to the determination B, and the determination B belongs to a determination C, then the determination A belongs to C.

100. The relation of the two extremes (*termini extremi*) of the syllogism to the middle term is a two-fold one, and forms two judgments (*propositiones praemissae*), each of which contains the moment of particularity—the middle term (*terminus medius*). The one premise contains, moreover, the extreme of universality (*terminus major*) as predicate (*propositio major*); the other contains the extreme of individuality (*terminus minor*) as subject (*propositio minor*); the relation of the two extremes is the third judgment; the inference (*conclusio*), "conclusion," is mediated.

Second Division—The Final Cause, or Teleological Comprehension.

101. In the Final Cause, that which is mediated, or the Inference, is at the same time *immediate, first,* and *ground.* The Produced, or that which is posited through mediation, has the act of producing and its immediate determination for presupposition, and conversely the act of producing happens on account of the result which is the ground, and hence is the first determination of the activity. The teleological act is a syllogism in which the same whole is brought into unity (its objective form with its subjective form, the comprehension with its reality) through the mediation of teleological

activity, and the Comprehension is ground of a reality determined through it.

102. External conformity to end exists in so far as a somewhat possesses the comprehension through which it is determined, not in itself, but is subordinated to it by another subject as an external form or relation.

103. Internal conformity to end is this: an existence possesses its comprehension in itself and is at the same time its own object and means—self-realising and self-realised final cause in itself.

Third Division—The Idea

104. The IDEA is the unity of the Comprehension and Reality, the comprehension in so far as it determines itself and its reality, or the Actuality which is what it ought to be, and contains its comprehension itself.

105. (1) The idea in so far as the comprehension is united with its reality immediately, and does not directly distinguish itself from, and elevate itself out of it, is LIFE. The same exhibited as *physical* and likewise *spiritual* life, and freed from all the conditions and limitations of contingent existence is the BEAUTIFUL.

106. (2) In the Idea of COGNITION and PRACTICAL ACTIVITY is the reality of the Comprehension; or the Subjective is opposed to the Objective and their union is brought about. In *Cognition* Reality lies at the basis as the *first* and as *Essence; Practical Activity,* on the other hand, makes actuality conform to the Comprehension so that the GOOD is produced.

107. (3) The ABSOLUTE IDEA is the content of SCIENCE, namely, the consideration of the universe, as it is in conformity with the Comprehension in-and-for-itself [*"sub specie aeternitatis"*], or the rational Comprehension as it is in-and-for-itself, and as it is in the objective or real world.

V

THE DOCTRINE OF ESSENCE *

SECOND SUB-DIVISION OF LOGIC.

Translated by William Wallace

112. The terms in ESSENCE are always mere pairs of correlatives, and not yet absolutely reflected in themselves: hence in essence the actual unity of the notion is not realised, but only postulated by reflection. Essence,—which is Being coming into mediation with itself through the negativity of itself—is self-relatedness, only in so far as it is relation to an Other,—this Other however coming to view at first not as something which *is*, but as postulated and hypothetised.—Being has not vanished: but, firstly, Essence, as simple self-relation, is Being, and secondly as regards its one-sided characteristic of immediacy, Being is deposed to a mere negative, to a seeming or reflected light—Essence accordingly is Being thus reflecting light into itself.

The Absolute is the Essence. This is the same definition as the previous one that the Absolute is Being, in so far as Being likewise is simple self-relation. But it is at the same time higher, because Essence is Being that has gone into itself: that is to say, the simple self-relation (in Being) is expressly put as negation of the negative, as immanent self-mediation.—Unfortu-

* From *The Encyclopaedia of the Philosophical Sciences*.

nately when the Absolute is defined to be the Essence, the negativity which this implies is often taken only to mean the withdrawal of all determinate predicates. This negative action of withdrawal or abstraction thus falls outside of the Essence—which is thus left as a mere result apart from its premisses,—the *caput mortuum* of abstraction.   But as this negativity, instead of being external to Being, is its own dialectic, the truth of the latter, viz. Essence, will be Being as retired within itself,—immanent Being. That reflection, or light thrown into itself, constitutes the distinction between Essence and immediate Being, and is the peculiar characteristic of Essence itself.

Any mention of Essence implies that we distinguish it from Being: the latter is immediate, and, compared with Essence, we look upon it as mere seeming.   But this seeming is not an utter nonentity and nothing at all, but Being superseded and put by.   The point of view given by the Essence is in general the standpoint of 'Reflection.'   This word 'reflection' is originally applied, when a ray of light in a straight line impinging upon the surface of a mirror is thrown back from it.   In this phenomenon we have two things,—first an immediate fact which is, and secondly the deputed, derivated, or transmitted phase of the same.—Something of this sort takes place when we reflect, or think upon an object; for here we want to know the object, not in its immediacy, but as derivative or mediated.   The problem or aim of philosophy is often represented as the ascertainment of the essence of things: a phrase which only means that things instead of being left in their immediacy, must be shown to be mediated by, or based upon, something else.   The immediate Being of things is thus conceived under the image of a rind or curtain behind which the Essence lies hidden.

Everything, it is said, has an Essence; that is, things really are not what they immediately show themselves. There is therefore something more to be done than merely rove from one quality to another, and merely to advance from qualitative to quantitative, and *vice versa*: there is a permanent in things, and that permanent is in the first instance their Essence. With respect to other meanings and uses of the category of Essence, we may note that in the German auxiliary verb *'sein'* the past tense is expressed by the term for Essence (*Wesen*): we designate past being as *gewesen*. This anomaly of language implies to some extent a correct perception of the relation between Being and Essence. Essence we may certainly regard as past Being, remembering however meanwhile that the past is not utterly denied, but only laid aside and thus at the same time preserved. Thus, to say, Caesar *was* in Gaul, only denies the immediacy of the event, but not his sojourn in Gaul altogether. That sojourn is just what forms the import of the proposition, in which however it is represented as over and gone.—*'Wesen'* in ordinary life frequently means only a collection or aggregate: Zeitungswesen (the Press), Postwesen (the Post-Office), Steuerwesen (the Revenue). All that these terms mean is that the things in question are not to be taken single, in their immediacy, but as a complex, and then, perhaps, in addition, in their various bearings. This usage of the term is not very different in its implication from our own.

People also speak of *finite* Essences, such as man. But the very term Essence implies that we have made a step beyond finitude: and the title as applied to man is so far inexact. It is often added that there is a supreme Essence (Being): by which is meant God. On this two remarks may be made. In the first place the phrase 'there is' suggests a finite only: as when we say, there are so many planets, or, there are plants of such a constitution and plants of such an other. In these cases we are speaking of something which has other things beyond and beside it. But God, the absolutely infinite, is not something outside and beside whom there are other essences. All else outside God, if separated from Him, possesses no essentiality: in its isolation it becomes a mere show or seeming, without stay or essence of its own. But, secondly, it is a poor way of talking to call God the *highest* or supreme Essence. The category of quantity which the phrase employs has its proper place within the compass of the finite. When we call one mountain the highest on the earth, we have a vision of other high mountains beside it. So too when we call any one the richest or most learned in his country. But God, far from being *a* Being, even the highest, is *the* Being. This definition, however, though such a representation of God is an important and necessary stage in the growth of the religious consciousness, does not by any means exhaust the depth of the ordinary Christian idea of God. If we consider God as the Essence only, and nothing more, we know Him only as the universal and irresistible Power; in other words, as the Lord. Now the fear of the Lord is, doubtless, the beginning,— but *only* the beginning, of wisdom. To look at God in this light, as the Lord, and the Lord alone, is especially characteristic of Judaism and also of Mohammedanism. The defect of these religions lies in their scant recognition of the finite, which, be it as natural things or as finite phases of mind, it is characteristic of the heathen and (as they also for that reason are) polytheistic religions to maintain intact. Another not uncommon assertion is that God, as the supreme Being, cannot be known. Such is the view taken by modern 'enlightenment' and abstract understanding, which is content to say, *Il y a un être suprême:* and there lets the matter rest. To speak thus, and treat God merely as the supreme other-world Being, implies that we look upon the world before us in its immediacy as something permanent and positive, and forget that true Being is just the superseding of all that is immediate. If God be the abstract super-sensible Being, outside whom therefore lies all difference and all specific character, He is only a bare name, a mere *caput mortuum* of abstracting understanding. The true knowledge of God begins when we know that things, as they immediately are, have no truth.

In reference also to other subjects besides God the category of Essence is often liable to an abstract use, by which, in the study of anything, its Essence is held to be something unaffected by, and subsisting in independence of, its definite phenomenal embodiment. Thus we say, for example, of people, that the great thing is not what they do or how they behave, but what they are. This is correct, if it means that a man's conduct should be looked at, not in its immediacy, but only as it is explained by his inner self, and as a revelation of that inner self. Still it should be remembered that the only means by which the Essence and the inner self can be verified, is their appearance in outward reality; whereas the appeal which men make to the essential life, as distinct from the material facts of conduct, is generally prompted by a desire to assert their own subjectivity and to elude an absolute and objective judgment.

113. Self-relation in Essence is the form of IDENTITY or of reflection-into-self, which has here taken the place of the immediacy of Being. They are both the same abstraction,—self-relation.

The unintelligence of sense, to take everything lim-

ited and finite, for Being, passes into the obstinacy of
understanding, which views the finite as self-identical,
not inherently self-contradictory.

114. This identity, as it has descended from Being,
appears in the first place only charged with the characteristics of Being, and referred to Being as to something
external. This external Being, if taken in separation
from the true Being (of Essence), is called the UNES-
SENTIAL. But that turns out a mistake. Because
Essence is Being-in-self, it is essential only to the extent that it has in itself its negative, *i.e.* reference to
another, or mediation. Consequently, it has the unessential as its own proper seeming (reflection) in itself.
But in seeming or mediation there is distinction involved:
and since what is distinguished (as distinguished from
the identity out of which it arises, and in which it is not,
or lies as seeming,) receives itself the form of identity,
the semblance is still in the mode of Being, or of self-
related immediacy. The sphere of Essence thus turns
out to be a still imperfect combination of immediacy and
mediation. In it every term is expressly invested with
the character of self-relatedness, while yet at the same
time one is forced beyond it. It has Being,—reflected
being, a being in which another shows, and which shows
in another. And so it is also the sphere in which the
contradiction, still implicit in the sphere of Being, is
made explicit.

As the one notion is the common principle underlying
all logic, there appear in the development of Essence
the same attributes or terms as in the development of
Being, but in a reflex form. Instead of Being and
Nought we have now the forms of Positive and Negative; the former at first as Identity corresponding to
pure and uncontrasted Being, the latter developed
(showing in itself) as Difference. So also, we have Be-

coming represented by the Ground of determinate Being: which itself, when reflected upon the Ground, is Existence.

The theory of Essence is the most difficult branch of Logic. It includes the categories of metaphysic and of the sciences in general. These are products of reflective understanding, which, while it assumes the differences to possess a footing of their own, and at the same time also expressly affirms their relativity, still combines the two statements, side by side, or one after the other, by an 'Also,' without bringing these thoughts into one, or unifying them into the notion.

A.—ESSENCE AS GROUND OF EXISTENCE

(a) *The pure principles or categories of Reflection.*

(a) *Identity.*

115. The Essence lights up *in itself* or is mere reflection: and therefore is only self-relation, not as immediate but as reflected. And that reflex relation is SELF-IDENTITY.

This Identity becomes an Identity in form only, or of the understanding, if it be held hard and fast, quite aloof from difference. Or, rather, abstraction is the imposition of this Identity of form, the transformation of something inherently concrete into this form of elementary simplicity. And this may be done in two ways. Either we may neglect a part of the multiple features which are found in the concrete thing (by what is called analysis) and select only one of them; or, neglecting their variety, we may concentrate the multiple characters into one.

If we associate Identity with the Absolute, making

the Absolute the subject of a proposition, we get: the Absolute is what is identical with itself. However true this proposition may be, it is doubtful whether it be meant in its truth: and therefore it is at least imperfect in the expression. For it is left undecided, whether it means the abstract Identity of understanding,—abstract, that is, because contrasted with the other characteristics of Essence, or the Identity which is inherently concrete. In the latter case, as will be seen, true Identity is first discoverable in the Ground, and, with a higher truth, in the Notion.—Even the word Absolute is often used to mean no more than 'abstract.' Absolute space and absolute time, for example, is another way of saying abstract space and abstract time.

When the principles of Essence are taken as essential principles of thought they become predicates of a presupposed subject, which, because they are essential, is 'Everything.' The propositions thus arising have been stated as universal Laws of Thought. Thus the first of them, the maxim of Identity, reads: Everything is identical with itself, $A = A$: and, negatively, A cannot at the same time be A and not A.—This maxim, instead of being a true law of thought, is nothing but the law of abstract understanding. The propositional form itself contradicts it: for a proposition always promises a distinction between subject and predicate; while the present one does not fulfil what its form requires. But the Law is particularly set aside by the following so-called Laws of Thought, which make laws out of its opposite.—It is asserted that the maxim of Identity, though it cannot be proved, regulates the procedure of every consciousness, and that experience shows it to be accepted as soon as its terms are apprehended. To this alleged experience of the logic-books may be opposed the universal experience that no mind thinks or forms conceptions or speaks, in accordance with this law, and that no existence of any kind whatever conforms to it. Utterances after the fashion of this pretended law (A planet is—a planet; Magnetism is—magnetism; Mind is—mind) are, as they deserve to be, reputed silly. That is certainly matter of general experience. The logic which seriously propounds such laws and the scholastic world in which alone they are valid have long been discredited with practical common sense as well as with the philosophy of reason.

Identity is, in the first place, the repetition of what we had earlier as Being, but as *become,* through supersession of its character of immediateness. It is therefore Being as Ideality.—It is important to come to a proper understanding on the true meaning of Identity: and, for that purpose, we must especially guard against taking it as abstract Identity, to the exclusion of all Difference. That is the touch-stone for distinguishing all bad philosophy from what alone deserves the name philosophy. Identity in its truth, as an Ideality of what immediately is, is a high category for our religious modes of mind as well as all other forms of thought and mental activity. The true knowledge of God, it may be said, begins when we know Him as identity,—as absolute identity. To know so much is to see that all the power and glory of the world sinks into nothing in God's presence, and subsists only as the reflection of His power and His glory. In the same way, Identity, as self-consciousness, is what distinguishes man from nature, particularly from the brutes which never reach the point of comprehending themselves as 'I,' that is, pure self-contained unity. So again, in connexion with thought, the main thing is not to confuse the true identity, which contains Being and its characteristics ideally transfigured in it, with an abstract Identity, identity of bare form. All the charges of narrowness, hardness, meaninglessness, which are so often directed against thought from the quarter of feeling and immediate perception, rest on the perverse assumption that thought acts only as a faculty of abstract Identification. The Formal Logic itself confirms this assumption by laying down the supreme law of thought (so-called) which has been discussed above. If thinking were no more than an abstract Identity, we could not but own it to be a most futile and tedious business. No doubt the notion, and the idea too, are identical with themselves: but identical only in so far as they at the same time involve distinction.

(β) Difference.

116. Essence is mere Identity and reflection in itself only as it is self-relating negativity, and in that way self-repulsion. It contains therefore essentially the characteristic of DIFFERENCE.

Other-being is here no longer qualitative, taking the shape of the character or limit. It is now in Essence, in self-relating essence, and therefore the negation is at the same time a relation,—is, in short, Distinction, Relativity, Mediation.

To ask, 'How Identity comes to Difference,' assumes that Identity as mere abstract Identity is something of itself, and Difference also something else equally independent. This supposition renders an answer to the question impossible. If Identity is viewed as diverse from Difference, all that we have in this way is but Difference; and hence we cannot demonstrate the advance to difference, because the person who asks for the How of the progress thereby implies that for him the starting point is non-existent. The question then when put to the test has obviously no meaning, and its proposer may be met with the question what he means by Identity; whereupon we should soon see that he attaches no idea to it at all, and that Identity is for him an empty name. As we have seen, besides, Identity is undoubtedly a negative,—not however an abstract empty Nought, but the negation of Being and its characteristics. Being so, Identity is at the same time self-relation, and, what is more, negative self-relation; in other words, it draws a distinction between it and itself.

117. Difference is, first of all, (1) immediate difference, *i.e.* DIVERSITY or variety. In Diversity the different things are each individually what they are, and unaffected by the relation in which they stand to each other. This relation is therefore external to them. In consequence of the various things being thus indifferent to the difference between them, it falls outside them into a third thing, the agent of Comparison. This external difference, as an identity of the objects related, is Likeness; as a non-identity of them, is Unlikeness.

The gap which understanding allows to divide these characteristics, is so great, that although comparison has one and the same substratum for likeness and unlikeness, which are explained to be different aspects and points of view in it, still likeness by itself is the first of the elements alone, viz. identity, and unlikeness by itself is difference.

Diversity has, like Identity, been transformed into a maxim: 'Everything is various or different': or, 'There are no two things completely like each other.' Here Everything is put under a predicate, which is the reverse of the identity attributed to it in the first maxim; and therefore under a law contradicting the first. However there is an explanation. As the diversity is supposed due only to external comparison, anything taken *per se* is expected and understood always to be identical with

itself, so that the second law need not interfere with the
first.   But, in that case, variety does not belong to the
something or everything in question: it constitutes no
intrinsic characteristic of the subject: and the second
maxim on this showing does not admit of being stated
at all.   If, on the other hand, the something *itself* is as
the maxim says diverse, it must be in virtue of its own
proper character: but in this case the specific difference,
and not variety as such, is what is intended.   And
this is the meaning of the maxim of Leibnitz.

When understanding sets itself to study Identity, it
has already passed beyond it, and is looking at Difference in the shape of bare Variety. ʻIf we follow the so-
called law of Identity, and say,—The sea is the sea,
The air is the air, The moon is the moon, these objects
pass for having no bearing on one another.   What we
have before us therefore is not Identity, but Difference.
We do not stop at this point however, or regard things
merely as different.   We compare them one with another,
and thus discover the features of likeness and unlikeness.
The work of the finite sciences lies to a great extent in
the application of these categories, and the phrase ʻsci-
entific treatment' generally means no more than the
method which has for its aim comparison of the objects
under examination.   This method has undoubtedly led
to some important results;—we may particularly mention the great advance of modern times in the provinces
of comparative anatomy and comparative linguistics.
But it is going too far to suppose that the comparative
method can be employed with equal success in all
branches of knowledge.   Nor—and this must be emphasised—can mere comparison ever ultimately satisfy the
requirements of science.   Its results are indeed indispensable, but they are still labours only preliminary to
truly intelligent cognition.

If it be the office of comparison to reduce existing differences to Identity, the science, which most perfectly fulfils that end, is mathematics. The reason of that is, that quantitative difference is only the difference which is quite external. Thus, in geometry, a triangle and a quadrangle, figures qualitatively different, have this qualitative difference discounted by abstraction, and are equalised to one another in magnitude. It follows from what has been formerly said about the mere Identity of understanding that, as has also been pointed out, neither philosophy nor the empirical sciences need envy this superiority of Mathematics.

The story is told that, when Leibnitz propounded the maxim of Variety, the cavaliers and ladies of the court, as they walked round the garden, made efforts to discover two leaves indistinguishable from each other, in order to confute the law stated by the philosopher. Their device was unquestionably a convenient method of dealing with metaphysics,—one which has not ceased to be fashionable. All the same, as regards the principle of Leibnitz, difference must be understood to mean not an external and indifferent diversity merely, but difference essential. Hence the very nature of things implies that they must be different.

118. LIKENESS is an Identity only of those things which are not the same, not identical with each other: and UNLIKENESS is a relation of things unlike. The two therefore do not fall on different aspects or points of view in the thing, without any mutual affinity: but one throws light into the other. Variety thus comes to be reflexive difference, or difference (distinction) implicit and essential, DETERMINATE or SPECIFIC DIFFERENCE.

While things merely various show themselves unaffected by each other, likeness and unlikeness on the contrary are a pair of characteristics which are in completely reciprocal relation. The one of them cannot be thought without the other. This advance from simple variety to opposition appears in our common acts of thought, when we allow that comparison has a meaning only upon the hypothesis of an existing difference, and that on the other hand we can distinguish only on the hypothesis of existing similarity. Hence, if the problem be the discovery of a difference, we attribute no great cleverness to the man who only distinguishes those objects, of which the difference is palpable, *e.g.* a pen and a camel: and similarly, it implies no very advanced faculty of comparison, when the objects compared, *e.g.* a beech and an oak, a temple and a church, are near akin. In the case of difference, in short, we like to see identity, and in the case of identity we like to see difference. Within the range of the empirical sciences however, the one of these two categories is often allowed to put the other out of sight and mind. Thus the scientific problem at one time is to reduce existing differences to identity; on another occasion, with equal one-sidedness, to discover new differences. We see this especially in physical science. There the problem consists, in the first place, in the continual search for new 'elements,' new forces, new genera, and species. Or, in another direction, it seeks to show that all bodies hitherto believed to be simple are compound: and modern physicists and chemists smile at the ancients, who were satisfied with four elements, and these not simple. Secondly, and on the other hand, mere identity is made the chief question. Thus electricity and chemical affinity are regarded as the same, and even the organic processes of digestion and assimilation are looked upon as a mere chemical operation. Modern philosophy has often been nicknamed the Philosophy of Identity. But,

as was already remarked, it is precisely philosophy, and
in particular speculative logic, which lays bare the
nothingness of the abstract, undifferentiated identity,
known to understanding; though it also undoubtedly
urges its disciples not to rest at mere diversity, but to
ascertain the inner unity of all existence.

119. Difference implicit is essential difference, the
POSITIVE and the NEGATIVE: and that is this way.
The Positive is the identical self-relation in such a way
as not to be the Negative, and the Negative is the different by itself so as not to be the Positive. Thus either has
an existence of its own in proportion as it is not the
other. The one is made visible in the other, and is only
in so far as that other is. Essential difference is therefore Opposition; according to which the different is
not confronted by *any* other but by *its* other. That is,
either of these two (Positive and Negative) is stamped
with a characteristic of its own only in its relation to
the other: the one is only reflected into itself as it is
reflected into the other. And so with the other. Either
in this way is the other's *own* other.

Difference implicit or essential gives the maxim,
Everything is essentially distinct; or, as it has also
been expressed, Of two opposite predicates the one only
can be assigned to anything, and there is no third possible. This maxim of Contrast or Opposition most expressly controverts the maxim of Identity: the one says
a thing should be only self-relation, the other says that
it must be an opposite, a relation to its other. The
native unintelligence of abstraction betrays itself by
setting in juxtaposition two contrary maxims, like these,
as laws, without even so much as comparing them.—
The Maxim of Excluded Middle is the maxim of the
definite understanding, which would fain avoid contradiction, but in so doing falls into it. A must be either

$+$ A or $-$ A, it says. It virtually declares in these words a third A which is neither $+$ nor $-$, and which at the same time is yet invested with $+$ and $-$ characters. If $+$ W means 6 miles to the West, and $-$ W mean 6 miles to the East, and if the $+$ and $-$ cancel each other, the 6 miles of way or space remain what they were with and without the contrast. Even the mere *plus* and *minus* of number or abstract direction have, if we like, zero, for their third: but it need not be denied that the empty contrast, which understanding institutes between *plus* and *minus,* is not without its value in such abstractions as number, direction, &c.

In the doctrine of contradictory concepts, the one notion is, say, blue (for in this doctrine even the sensuous generalised image of a colour is called a notion) and the other not-blue. This other then would not be an affirmative, say, yellow, but would merely be kept at the abstract negative.—That the Negative in its own nature is quite as much Positive (see next §), is implied in saying that what is opposite to another is *its* other. The inanity of the opposition between what are called contradictory notions is fully exhibited in what we may called the grandiose formula of a general law, that Everything has the one and not the other of *all* predicates which are in such opposition. In this way, mind is either white or not-white, yellow or not-yellow, &c., *ad infinitum.*

It was forgotten that Identity and Opposition are themselves opposed, and the maxim of Opposition was taken even for that of Identity, in the shape of the principle of Contradiction. A notion, which possesses neither or both of two mutually contradictory marks, *e.g.* a quadrangular circle, is held to be logically false. Now though a multangular circle and a rectilineal arc no less contradict this maxim, geometers never hesitate to treat the circle as a polygon with rectilineal sides. But anything like a circle (that is to say its mere character or nominal definition) is still no notion. In the notion of a circle, centre and circumference are equally essential; both marks belong to it: and yet centre and circumference are opposite and contradictory to each other.

The conception of Polarity, which is so dominant in physics, contains by implication the more correct definition of Opposition. But physics for its theory of the laws of thought adheres to the ordinary logic; it might therefore well be horrified in case it should ever work out the conception of Polarity, and get at the thoughts which are implied in it.

(1) With the positive we return to identity, but in its higher truth as identical self-relation, and at the same time with the note that it is not the negative. The negative *per se* is the same as difference itself. The identical as such is primarily the yet uncharacterised: the positive on the other hand is what is self-identical, but with the mark of antithesis to an other. And the negative is difference as such, characterised as not identity. This is the difference of difference within its own self.

Positive and negative are supposed to express an absolute difference. The two however are at bottom the same: the name of either might be transferred to the other. Thus, for example, debts and assets are not two particular, self-subsisting species of property. What is negative to the debtor, is positive to the creditor. A way to the east is also a way to the west. Positive and negative are therefore intrinsically conditioned by one another, and are only in relation to each other. The north pole of the magnet cannot be without the south pole, and *vice versa*. If we cut a magnet in two, we

have not a north pole in one piece, and a south pole in
the other. Similarly, in electricity, the positive and the
negative are not two diverse and independent fluids. In
opposition, the different is not confronted by any other,
but by *its* other. Usually we regard different things as
unaffected by each other. Thus we say: I am a human
being, and around me are air, water, animals, and all
sorts of things. Everything is thus put outside of every
other. But the aim of philosophy is to banish indifference, and to ascertain the necessity of things. By that
means the other is seen to stand over against *its* other.
Thus, for example, inorganic nature is not to be considered merely something else than organic nature, but the
necessary antithesis of it. Both are in essential relation
to one another; and the one of the two is, only in so
far as it excludes the other from it, and thus relates
itself thereto. Nature in like manner is not without
mind, nor mind without nature. An important step has
been taken, when we cease in thinking to use phrases
like: Of course something else is also possible. While
we so speak, we are still tainted with contingency: and
all true thinking, we have already said, is a thinking of
necessity.

In modern physical science the opposition, first observed to exist in magnetism as polarity, has come to be
regarded as a universal law pervading the whole of
nature. This would be a real scientific advance, if care
were at the same time taken not to let mere variety
revert without explanation, as a valid category, side by
side with opposition. Thus at one time the colours are
regarded as in polar opposition to one another, and
called complementary colours: at another time they are
looked at in their indifferent and merely quantitative
difference of red, yellow, green, &c.

(2) Instead of speaking by the maxim of Excluded

Middle (which is the maxim of abstract understanding) we should rather say: Everything is opposite. Neither in heaven nor in earth, neither in the world of mind nor of nature, is there anywhere such an abstract 'Either—or' as the understanding maintains. Whatever exists is concrete, with difference and opposition in itself. The finitude of things will then lie in the want of correspondence between their immediate being, and what they essentially are. Thus, in inorganic nature, the acid is implicitly at the same time the base: in other words, its only being consists in its relation to its other. Hence also the acid is not something that persists quietly in the contrast: it is always in effort to realise what it potentially is. Contradiction is the very moving principle of the world: and it is ridiculous to say that contradiction is unthinkable. The only thing correct in that statement is that contradiction is not the end of the matter, but cancels itself. But contradiction, when cancelled, does not leave abstract identity; for that is itself only one side of the contrariety. The proximate result of opposition (when realised as contradiction) is the Ground, which contains identity as well as difference superseded and deposed to elements in the completer notion.

120. Contrariety then has two forms. The Positive in the aforesaid various (different) which is understood to be independent, and yet at the same not to be unaffected by its relation to its other. The Negative is to be, no less independently, negative self-relating, self-subsistent, and yet at the same time as Negative must on every point have this its self-relation, *i.e.* its Positive, only in the other. Both Positive and Negative are therefore explicit contradiction; both are potentially the same. Both are so actually also; since either is the abrogation of the other and of itself. Thus they fall to the Ground.—

Or as is plain, the essential difference, as a difference, is only the difference of it from itself, and thus contains the identical: so that to essential and actual difference there belongs itself as well as identity. As self-relating difference it is likewise virtually enunciated as the self-identical. And the opposite is in general that which includes the one and its other, itself and its opposite. The immanence of essence thus defined is the Ground.

(γ) *The Ground*

121. The GROUND is the unity of identity and difference, the truth of what difference and identity have turned out to be,—the reflection-into-self, which is equally a reflection-into-an-other, and *vice versa*. It is essence put explicitly as a totality.

The maxim of the Ground runs thus: Everything has its Sufficient Ground: that is, the true essentiality of any thing is not the predication of it as identical with itself, or as different (various), or merely positive, or merely negative, but as having its Being in an other, which, being its self-same, is its essence. And to this extent the essence is not abstract reflection into self, but into an other. The Ground is the essence in its own inwardness; the essence is intrinsically a ground; and it is a ground only when it is a ground of somewhat, of an other.

We must be careful, when we say that the ground is the unity of identity and difference, not to understand by this unity an abstract identity. Otherwise we only change the name, while we still think the identity (of understanding) already seen to be false. To avoid this misconception we may say that the ground, besides being the unity, is also the difference of identity and

difference. In that case in the ground, which promised
at first to supersede contradiction, a new contradiction
seems to arise. It is however a contradiction which, so
far from persisting quietly in itself, is rather the ex-
pulsion of it from itself. The ground is a ground only
to the extent that it affords ground: but the result
which thus issued from the ground is only itself. In
this lies its formalism. The ground and what is
grounded are one and the same content: the difference
between the two is the mere difference of form which
separates simple self-relation, on the one hand, from
mediation or derivativeness on the other. Inquiry into
the grounds of things goes with the point of view which,
as already noted, is adopted by Reflection. We wish, as
it were, to see the matter double, first in its immediacy,
and secondly in its ground, where it is no longer immediate. This is the plain meaning of the law of sufficient
ground, as it is called; it asserts that things should
essentially be viewed as mediated. The manner in which
Formal Logic establishes this law of thought, sets a bad
example to other sciences. Formal Logic asks these
sciences not to accept their subject-matter as it is immediately given; and yet herself lays down a law of
thought without deducing it,—in other words, without
exhibiting its mediation. With the same justice as the
logician maintains our faculty of thought to be so constituted that we must ask for the ground of everything,
might the physicist, when asked why a man who falls
into water is drowned, reply that man happens to be
so organized that he cannot live under water; or the
jurist, when asked why a criminal is punished, reply
that civil society happens to be so constituted that crimes
cannot be left unpunished.

Yet even if logic be excused the duty of giving a
ground for the law of the sufficient ground, it might at

least explain what is to be understood by a ground. The common explanation, which described the ground as what has a consequence, seems at the first glance more lucid and intelligible than the preceding definition in logical terms. If you ask however what the consequence is, you are told that it is what has a ground; and it becomes obvious that the explanation is intelligible only because it assumes what in our case has been reached as the termination of an antecedent movement of thought. And this is the true business of logic: to show that those thoughts, which as usually employed merely float before consciousness neither understood nor demonstrated, are really grades in the self-determination of thought. It is by this means that they are understood and demonstrated.

In common life, and it is the same in the finite sciences, this reflective form is often employed as a key to the secret of the real condition of the objects under investigation. So long as we deal with what may be termed the household needs of knowledge, nothing can be urged against this method of study. But it can never afford definitive satisfaction, either in theory or practice. And the reason why it fails is that the ground is yet without a definite content of its own; so that to regard anything as resting upon a ground merely gives the formal difference of mediation in place of immediacy. We see an electrical phenomenon, for example, and we ask for its ground (or reason): we are told that electricity is the ground of this phenomenon. What is this but the same content as we had immediately before us, only translated into the form of inwardness?

The ground however is not merely simple self-identity, but also different: hence various grounds may be alleged for the same sum of fact. This variety of grounds, again, following the logic of difference, culminates in opposition of grounds *pro* and *contra*. In any action, such as a theft, there is a sum of fact in which several aspects may be distinguished. The theft has violated the right of property: it has given the means of satisfying his wants to the needy thief: possibly too the man, from whom the theft was made, misused his property. The violation of property is unquestionably the decisive point of view before which the others must give way: but the bare law of the ground cannot settle that question. Usually indeed the law is interpreted to speak of a sufficient ground, not of any ground whatever: and it might be supposed therefore, in the action referred to, that, although other points of view besides the violation of property might be held as grounds, yet they would not be sufficient grounds. But here comes a dilemma. If we use the phrase 'sufficient ground,' the epithet is either otiose, or of such a kind as to carry us past the mere category of ground. The Predicate is otiose and tautological, if it only states the capability of giving a ground or reason: for the ground is a ground, only in so far as it has this capability. If a soldier runs away from battle to save his life, his conduct is certainly a violation of duty: but it cannot be held that the ground which led him so to act was insufficient, otherwise he would have remained at his post. Besides, there is this also to be said. On the one hand any ground suffices: on the other no ground suffices as mere ground; because, as already said, it is yet void of a content objectively and intrinsically determined, and is therefore not self-acting and productive. A content thus objectively and intrinsically determined, and hence self-acting, will hereafter come before us as the notion: and it is the notion which Leibnitz had in his eye when he spoke of sufficient ground, and urged the study of things under its point of view. His remarks were originally directed against that merely mechanical method of conceiving things so much in vogue even now; a method which he justly pronounces insufficient. We may see an instance of this mechanical theory of investigation, when the organic process of the circulation of the blood is traced back merely to the contraction of the heart; or when certain theories of criminal law explain the purpose of punishment to lie in deterring people from crime, in rendering the criminal harmless, or in other extraneous grounds of the same kind. It is unfair to Leibnitz to suppose that he was content with anything so poor as this formal law of the ground. The method of investigation which he inaugurated is the very reverse of a formalism which acquiesces in mere grounds, where a full and concrete knowledge is sought. Considerations to this effect led Leibnitz to contrast *causae efficientes* and *causae finales,* and to insist on the place of final causes as the conception to which the efficient were to lead up. If we adopt this distinction, light, heat, and moisture would be the *causae efficientes,* not the *causa finalis* of the growth of plants; the *causa finalis* is the notion of the plant itself.

To get no further than mere grounds, especially on questions of law and morality, is the position and principle of the Sophists. Sophistry, as we ordinarily conceive it, is a method of investigation which aims at distorting what is just and true, and exhibiting things in a false light. Such however is not the proper or primary tendency of Sophistry: the standpoint of which is no other than that of 'Raisonnement.' The Sophists came on the scene at a time when the Greeks had begun to grow dissatisfied with mere authority and tradition and felt the need of intellectual justification for what they

were to accept as obligatory. That desideratum the
Sophists supplied by teaching their countrymen to
seek for the various points of view under which things
may be considered: which points of view are the same
as grounds. But the ground, as we have seen, has no
essential and objective principles of its own, and it is
as easy to discover grounds for what is wrong and immoral as for what is moral and right. Upon the observer
therefore it depends to decide what points are to have
most weight. The decision in such circumstances is
prompted by his individual views and sentiments. Thus
the objective foundation of what ought to have been of
absolute and essential obligation, accepted by all, was
undermined: and Sophistry by this destructive action
deservedly brought upon itself the bad name previously
mentioned. Socrates, as we all know, met the Sophists
at every point, not by a bare re-assertion of authority
and tradition against their argumentations, but by showing dialectically how untenable the mere grounds were,
and by vindicating the obligation of justice and goodness,—by reinstating the universal or notion of the will.
In the present day such a method of argumentation is
not quite out of fashion. Nor is that the case only in
the discussion of secular matters. It occurs even in
sermons, such as those where every possible ground of
gratitude to God is propounded. To such pleading Socrates and Plato would not have scrupled to apply the
name of Sophistry. For Sophistry has nothing to do
with what is taught:—that may very possibly be true.
Sophistry lies in the formal circumstance of teaching it
by grounds which are as available for attack as for
defence. In a time so rich in reflection and so devoted
to *raisonnement* as our own, he must be a poor creature
who cannot advance a good ground for everything, even

for what is worst and most depraved. Everything in
the world that has become corrupt has had good ground
for its corruption. An appeal to grounds at first makes
the hearer think of beating a retreat: but when experience has taught him the real state of these matters, he
closes his ears against them, and refuses to be imposed
upon any more.

122. As it first comes, the chief feature of Essence is
shown in itself and intermediation in itself. But when it
has completed the circle of intermediation, its unity with
itself is explicitly put as the self-annulling of difference, and therefore of intermediation. Once more then
we come back to immediacy or Being,—but Being in so
far as it is intermediated by annulling the intermediation. And that Being is EXISTENCE.

The ground is not yet determined by objective principles of its own, nor is it an end or final cause: hence
it is not active, nor productive. An Existence only *proceeds from* the ground. The determinate ground is
therefore a formal matter: that is to say, any point will
do, so long as it is expressly put as self-relation, as
affirmation, in correlation with the immediate existence
depending on it. If it be a ground at all, it is a good
ground: for the term 'good' is employed abstractly
as equivalent to affirmative; and any point (or feature)
is good which can in any way be enunciated as confessedly affirmative. So it happens that a ground can
be found and adduced for everything: and a good ground
(for example, a good motive for action) may effect
something or may not, it may have a consequence or it
may not. It becomes a motive (strictly so called) and
effects something, *e.g.* through its reception into a will;
there and there only it becomes active and is made a
cause.

(b) *Existence.*

123. Existence is the immediate unity of reflection-into-self and reflection-into-another. It follows from this that existence is the indefinite multitude of existence as reflected-into-themselves, which at the same time equally throw light upon one another,—which, in short, are co-relative, and form a world of reciprocal dependence and of infinite interconnexion between grounds and consequents. The grounds are themselves existences: and the existents in like manner are in many directions grounds as well as consequents.

The phrase 'Existence' (derived from *existere*) suggests the fact of having proceeded from something. Existence is Being which has proceeded from the ground, and been reinstated by annulling its intermediation. The Essence, as Being set aside and absorbed, originally came before us as shining or showing in self, and the categories of this reflection are identity, difference and ground. The last is the unity of identity and difference; and because it unifies them it has at the same time to distinguish itself from itself. But that which is in this way distinguished from the ground is as little mere difference, as the ground itself is abstract sameness. The ground works its own suspension: and when suspended, the result of its negation is existence. Having issued from the ground, existence contains the ground in it: the ground does not remain, as it were, behind existence, but by its very nature supersedes itself and translates itself into existence. This is exemplified even in our ordinary mode of thinking, when we look upon the ground of a thing, not as something abstractly inward, but as itself also an existent. For example, the lightning-flash which has set a house on fire would be considered the ground of the conflagration: or the manners of a nation and the condition of its life would be regarded as the ground of its constitution. Such indeed is the ordinary aspect in which the existent world originally appears to reflection,—an indefinite crowd of things existent, which being simultaneously reflected on themselves and on one another are related reciprocally as ground and consequence. In this motley play of the world, if we may so call the sum of existents, there is nowhere a firm footing to be found: everything bears an aspect of relativity, conditioned by and conditioning something else. The reflective understanding makes it its business to elicit and trace these connexions running out in every direction; but the question touching an ultimate design is so far left unanswered, and therefore the craving of the reason after knowledge passes with the further development of the logical idea beyond this position of mere relativity.

124. The reflection-on-another of the existent is however inseparable from the reflection-on-self: the ground is their unity, from which existence has issued. The existent therefore includes relativity, and has on its own part its multiple interconnexions with other existents: it is reflected on itself as its ground. The existent is, when so described, a THING.

The 'thing-by-itself' (or thing in the abstract), so famous in the philosophy of Kant, shows itself here in its genesis. It is seen to be the abstract reflection-on-self, which is clung to, to the exclusion of reflection-on-other-things and of all prediction of difference. The thing-by-itself therefore is the empty substratum for these predicates of relation.

If to know means to comprehend an object in its concrete character, then the thing-by-itself, which is nothing but the quite abstract and indeterminate thing in general, must certainly be as unknowable as it is alleged to be. With as much reason however as we speak of the thing-by-itself, we might speak of quality-by-itself or quantity-by-itself, and of any other category. The expression would then serve to signify that these categories are taken in their abstract immediacy, apart from their development and inward character. It is no better than a whim of the understanding, therefore, if we attach the qualificatory 'in or by-itself' to the *thing* only. But this 'in or by-itself' is also applied to the facts of the mental as well as the natural world: as we speak of electricity or of a plant in itself, so we speak of man or the state in itself. By this 'in-itself' in these objects we are meant to understand what they strictly and properly are. This usage is liable to the same criticism as the phrase 'thing in itself!' For if we stick to the mere 'in-itself' of an object, we apprehend it not in its truth, but in the inadequate form of mere abstraction. Thus the man, by or in himself, is the child. And what the child has to do is to rise out of this abstract and undeveloped 'in-himself,' and become 'for himself' that he is at first only 'in-himself,'—a free and reasonable being. Similarly, the state-in-itself is the yet immature and patriarchal state, where the various political functions, latent in the notion of the state, have not received the full logical constitution which the logic of political principles demands. In the same sense, the germ may be called the plant-in-itself. These examples may show the mistake of supposing that the 'thing-in-itself' or the 'in-itself' of things is something inaccessible to our cognition. All things are originally in-themselves, but that is not the end of the matter. As the germ, being the plant-in-itself, means self-development, so the thing in general passes beyond its in-itself, (the abstract reflection on self,) to manifest itself further as a reflection on other things.   It is in this sense that it has properties.

(c) *The Thing.*

125. (*a*) The Thing is the totality—the development in explicit unity—of the categories of the ground and of existence. On the side of one of its factors, viz. reflection-on-other-things, it has in it the differences, in virtue of which it is a characterised and concrete thing. These characteristics are different from one another; they have their reflection-into-self not on their own part, but on the part of the thing. They are PROPERTIES of the thing: and their relation to the thing is expressed by the word 'have.'

As a term of relation, 'to have' takes the place of 'to be.' True, somewhat has qualities on its part too: but this transference of 'Having' into the sphere of Being is inexact, because the character as quality is directly one with the somewhat, and the somewhat ceases to be when it loses its quality. But the thing is reflection-into-self: for it is an identity which is also distinct from the difference, *i.e.* from its attributes.—In many languages 'have' is employed to denote past time. And with reason: for the past is absorbed or suspended being, and the mind is its reflection-into-self; in the mind only it continues to subsist,—the mind however distinguishing from itself this being in it which has been absorbed or suspended.

In the Thing all the characteristics of reflection recur as existent. Thus the thing, in its initial aspect, as the thing-by-itself, is the self-same or identical. But identity, it was proved, is not found without difference: so the properties, which the thing has, are the existent difference in the form of diversity. In the case of

diversity or variety each diverse member exhibited an
indifference to every other, and they had no other relation to each other, save what was given by a comparison external to them. But now in the thing we have
a bond which keeps the various properties in union.
Property, besides, should not be confused with quality.
No doubt, we also say, a thing has qualities. But the
phraseology is a misplaced one: 'having' hints at an
independence, foreign to the 'Somewhat,' which is still
directly identical with its quality. Somewhat is what
it is only by its quality: whereas, though the thing indeed exists only as it has its properties, it is not confined
to this or that definite property, and can therefore lose
it, without ceasing to be what it is.

126. (β) Even in the ground, however, the reflection-
on-something-else is directly convertible with reflection-
on-self. And hence the properties are not merely different from each other; they are also self-identical,
independent, and relieved from their attachment to the
thing. Still, as they are the characters of the thing distinguished from one another (as reflected-into-self), they
are not themselves things, if things be concrete; but
only existences reflected into themselves as abstract
characters. They are what are called MATTERS.

Nor is the name 'things' given to Matters, such as
magnetic and electric matters. They are qualities
proper, a reflected Being,—one with their Being,— they
are the character that has reached immediacy, existence:
they are 'entities.'

To elevate the properties, which the Thing has, to
the independent position of matters, or materials of
which it consists, is a proceeding based upon the notion
of a Thing: and for that reason is also found in experience. Thought and experience however alike protest
against concluding from the fact that certain proper-

ties of a thing, such as colour, or smell, may be represented as particular colouring or odorific matters, that we are then at the end of the inquiry, and that nothing more is needed to penetrate to the true secret of things than a disintegration of them into their component materials. This disintegration into independent matters is properly restricted to inorganic nature only. The chemist is in the right therefore when, for example, he analyses common salt or gypsum into its elements, and finds that the former consists of muriatic acid and soda, the latter of sulphuric acid and calcium. So too the geologist does well to regard granite as a compound of quartz, felspar, and mica. These matters, again, of which the thing consists, are themselves partly things, which in that way may be once more reduced to more abstract matters. Sulphuric acid, for example, is a compound of sulphur and oxygen. Such matters or bodies can as a matter of fact be exhibited as subsisting by themselves: but frequently we find other properties of things, entirely wanting this self-subsistence, also regarded as particular matters. Thus we hear caloric, and electrical or magnetic matters spoken of. Such matters are at the best figments of understanding. And we see here the usual procedure of the abstract reflection of understanding. Capriciously adopting single categories, whose value entirely depends on their place in the gradual evolution of the logical idea, it employs them in the pretended interests of explanation, but in the face of plain, unprejudiced perception and experience, so as to trace back to them every object investigated. Nor is this all. The theory, which makes things consist of independent matters, is frequently applied in a region where it has neither meaning nor force. For within the limits of nature even, wherever there is organic life, this category is obviously inadequate. An animal may be said

to consist of bones, muscles, nerves, &c.: but evidently
we are here using the term 'consist' in a very different
sense from its use when we spoke of the piece of granite
as consisting of the above-mentioned elements.   The elements of granite are utterly indifferent to their combination: they could subsist as well without it.   The
different parts and members of an organic body on the
contrary subsist only in their union: they cease to exist
as such, when they are separated from each other.

127. Thus Matter is the mere abstract or indeterminate reflection-into-something-else, or reflection-into-self
at the same time as determinate; it is consequently
Thinghood which then and there is,—the subsistence of
the thing.   By this means the thing has on the part of
the matters its reflection-into-self (the reverse of § 125);
It subsists not on its own part, but consists of the matters, and is only a superficial association between them,
an external combination of them.

128. (γ) Matter, being the immediate unity of existence with itself, is also indifferent towards specific
character.   Hence the numerous diverse matters coalesce
into the one MATTER, or into existence under the
reflective characteristic of identity.   In contrast to this
one Matter these distinct properties and their external
relation which they have to one another in the thing,
constitute the FORM,—the reflective category of difference, but a difference which exists and is a totality.

This one featureless Matter is also the same as the
Thing-by-itself was: only the latter is intrinsically
quite abstract, while the former essentially implies relation to something else, and in the first place to the
Form.

The various matters of which the thing consists are
potentially the same as one another.   Thus we get one
Matter in general to which the difference is expressly

attached externally and as a bare form. This theory which holds things all round to have one and the same matter at bottom, and merely to differ externally in respect to form, is much in vogue with the reflective understanding. Matter in that case counts for naturally indeterminate, but susceptible of any determination; while at the same time it is perfectly permanent, and continues the same amid all change and alteration. And in finite things at least this disregard of matter for any determinate form is certainly exhibited. For example, it matters not to a block of marble, whether it receive the form of this or that statue or even the form of a pillar. Be it noted however that a block of marble can disregard form only relatively, that is, in reference to the sculptor: it is by no means purely formless. And so the mineralogist considers the relatively formless marble as a special formation of rock, differing from other equally special formations, such as sandstone or porphyry. Therefore we say it is an abstraction of the understanding which isolates matter into a certain natural formlessness. For properly speaking the thought of matter includes the principle of form throughout, and no formless matter therefore appears anywhere even in experience as existing. Still the conception of matter as original and pre-existent, and as naturally formless, is a very ancient one; it meets us even among the Greeks, at first in the mythical shape of Chaos, which is supposed to represent the unformed substratum of the existing world. Such a conception must of necessity tend to make God not the Creator of the world, but a mere world-moulder or demiurge. A deeper insight into nature reveals God as creating the world out of nothing. And that teaches two things. On the one hand it enunciates that matter, as such, has no independent subsistence, and on the other that the form does not super-

vene upon matter from without, but as a totality involves
the principle of matter in itself. This free and infinite
form will hereafter come before us as the notion.

129. Thus the Thing suffers a disruption into Matter
and Form. Each of these is the totality of thinghood and
subsists for itself. But Matter, which is meant to be
the positive and indeterminate existence, contains, as an
existence, reflection-on-another, every whit as much as
it contains self-enclosed being. Accordingly as uniting
these characteristics, it is itself the totality of Form.
But Form, being a complete whole of characteristics,
ipso facto involves reflection-into-self; in other words,
as self-relating Form it has the very function attributed
to Matter. Both are at bottom the same. Invest them
with this unity, and you have the relation of Matter and
Form, which are also no less distinct.

130. The Thing, being this totality, is a contradiction.
On the side of its negative unity it is Form in which Matter is determined and deposed to the rank of properties.
At the same time it consists of Matters, which in the
reflection-of-the-thing-into-itself are as much independent as they are at the same time negatived. Thus the
thing is the essential existence, in such a way as to
be an existence that suspends or absorbs itself in itself.
In other words, the thing is an Appearance or
Phenomenon.

The negation of the several matters, which is insisted
on in the thing no less than their independent existence,
occurs in Physics as *porosity*. Each of the several
matters (colouring matter, odorific matter, and if we
believe some people, even sound-matter,—not excluding
caloric, electric matter, &c.) is also negated: and in
this negation of theirs, or as interpenetrating their pores,
we find the numerous other independent matters, which,
being similarly porous, make room in turn for the ex-

istence of the rest. Pores are not empirical facts; they
are figments of the understanding, which uses them to
represent the element of negation in independent matters. The further working-out of the contradictions is
concealed by the nebulous inbroglio in which all matters
are independent and all no less negated in each other.—
If the faculties or activities are similarly hypostatised
in the mind, their living unity similarly turns to the im-
broglio of an action of the one on the others.

These pores (meaning thereby not the pores in an organic body, such as the pores of wood or of the skin,
but those in the so-called 'matters,' such as colouring
matter, caloric, or metals, crystals, &c.) cannot be verified by observation. In the same way matter itself,—
furthermore form which is separated from matter,—
whether that be the thing as consisting of matters, or
the view that the thing itself subsists and only has
properties,—is all a product of the reflective understanding which, while it observes and professes to record only
what it observes, is rather creating a metaphysic,
bristling with contradictions of which it is unconscious.

B.—APPEARANCE.

131. The essence must appear or shine forth. Its
shining or reflection in it is the suspension and translation
of it to immediacy, which, whilst as reflection-on-self it is
matter or subsistence, is also form, reflection-on-some-
thing-else, a subsistence which sets itself aside. To
show or shine is the characteristic by which essence is
distinguished from being,—by which it is essence; and
it is this show which, when it is developed, shows itself,
and is Appearance. Essence accordingly is not something beyond or behind appearance, but just because it

is the essence which exists—the existence is APPEAR-
ANCE (Forth-shining).

Existence stated explicitly in its contradictions is Appearance. But appearance (forth-shining) is not to be
confused with a mere show (shining). Show is the
proximate truth of Being or immediacy. The immediate, instead of being, as we suppose, something independent, resting on its own self, is a mere show, and as such
it is packed or summed up under the simplicity of the
immanent essence. The essence is, in the first place,
the sum total of the showing itself, shining in itself (inwardly); but, far from abiding in this inwardness, it
comes as a ground forward into existence; and this existence being grounded not in itself, but on something
else, is just appearance. In our imagination we ordinarily combine with the term appearance or phenomenon the conception of an indefinite congeries of things
existing, the being of which is purely relative, and which
consequently do not rest on a foundation of their own,
but are esteemed only as passing stages. But in this
conception it is no less implied that essence does not
linger behind or beyond appearance. Rather it is, we
may say, the infinite kindness which lets its own show
freely issue into immediacy, and graciously allows it
the joy of existence. The appearance which is thus
created does not stand on its own feet, and has its being
not in itself but in something else. God who is the essence, when He lends existence to the passing stages of
His own show in Himself, may be described as the
goodness that creates a world: but He is also the power
above it, and the righteousness, which manifests the
merely phenomenal character of the content of this existing world, whenever it tries to exist in independence.

Appearance is in every way a very important grade
of the logical idea. It may be said to be the distinction

of philosophy from ordinary consciousness that it sees the merely phenomenal character of what the latter supposes to have a self-subsistent being. The significance of appearance however must be properly grasped, or mistakes will arise. To say that anything is a *mere* appearance may be misinterpreted to mean that, as compared with what is merely phenomenal, there is greater truth in the immediate, in that which *is*. Now in strict fact, the case is precisely the reverse. Appearance is higher than mere Being,—a richer category because it holds in combination the two elements of reflection-into-self and reflection-into-another: whereas Being (or immediacy) is still mere relationslessness, and apparently rests upon itself alone. Still, to say that anything is *only* an appearance suggests a real flaw, which consists in this, that Appearance is still divided against itself and without intrinsic stability. Beyond and above mere appearance comes in the first place Actuality, the third grade of Essence, of which we shall afterwards speak.

In the history of Modern Philosophy, Kant has the merit of first rehabilitating this distinction between the common and the philosophic modes of thought. He stopped half-way however, when he attached to Appearance a subjective meaning only, and put the abstract essence immovable outside it as the thing-in-itself beyond the reach of our cognition. For it is the very nature of the world of immediate objects to be appearance only. Knowing it to be so, we know at the same time the essence, which, far from staying behind or beyond the appearance, rather manifests its own essentiality by deposing the world to a mere appearance. One can hardly quarrel with the plain man who, in his desire for totality, cannot acquiesce in the doctrine of subjective idealism, that we are solely concerned with phenomena. The plain man, however, in his desire to save the objectivity of knowledge, may very naturally return to abstract immediacy, and maintain that immediacy to be true and actual. In a little work published under the title, '*A Report, clear as day, to the larger Public touching the proper nature of the Latest Philosophy: an Attempt to force the reader to understand,*' Fichte examined the opposition between subjective idealism and immediate consciousness in a popular form, under the shape of a dialogue between the author and the reader, and tried hard to prove that the subjective idealist's point of view was right. In this dialogue the reader complains to the author that he has completely failed to place himself in the idealist's position, and is inconsolable at the thought that things around him are no real things but mere appearances. The affliction of the reader can scarcely be blamed when he is expected to consider himself hemmed in by an impervious circle of purely subjective conceptions. Apart from this subjective view of Appearance, however, we have all reason to rejoice that the things which environ us are appearances and not steadfast and independent existences; since in that case we should soon perish of hunger, both bodily and mental.

(a) *The World of Appearance.*

132. The Apparent or Phenomenal exists in such a way, that its subsistence is *ipso facto* thrown into abeyance, or suspended and is only one stage in the form itself. The form embraces in it the matter or subsistence as one of its characteristics. In this way the phenomenal has its ground in this (form) as its essence, its reflection-into-self in contrast with its immediacy, but, in so doing, has it only in another aspect of the form. This

ground of it is no less phenomenal than itself, and the phenomenon accordingly goes on to an endless mediation of subsistence by means of form, and thus equally by non-subsistence. This endless inter-mediation is at the same time a unity of self-relation; and existence is developed into a totality, into a world of phenomena,—of reflected finitude.

(b) *Content and Form.*

133. Outside one another as the phenomena in this phenomenal world are, they form a totality, and are wholly contained in their self-relatedness. In this way the self-relation of the phenomenon is completely specified, it has the FORM in itself: and because it is in this identity, has it as essential subsistence. So it comes about that the form is CONTENT: and in its mature phase is the LAW OF THE PHENOMENON. When the form, on the contrary, is not reflected into self, it is equivalent to the negative of the phenomenon, to the non-independent and changeable: and that sort of form is the indifferent or External Form.

The essential point to keep in mind about the opposition of Form and Content is that the content is not formless, but has the form in its own self, quite as much as the form is external to it. There is thus a doubling of form. At one time it is reflected into itself; and then is identical with the content. At another time it is not reflected into itself, and then is the external existence, which does not at all affect the content. We are here in presence, implicitly, of the absolute correlation of content and form: viz. their reciprocal revulsion, so that content is nothing but the revulsion of form into content, and form nothing but the revulsion of content into form. This mutual revulsion

is one of the most important laws of thought. But it is
not explicitly brought out before the Relations of Substance and Causality.

Form and content are a pair of terms frequently employed by the reflective understanding, especially with
a habit of looking on the content as the essential and
independent, the form on the contrary as the unessential
and dependent. Against this it is to be noted that both
are in fact equally essential; and that, while a formless
content can be as little found as a formless *matter,* the
two (content and matter) are distinguished by this circumstance, that matter, though implicitly not without
form, still in its existence manifests a disregard of form,
whereas the content, as such, is what it is only because
the matured form is included in it.   Still the form
comes before us sometimes as an existence indifferent
and external to content, and does so for the reason that
the whole range of Appearance still suffers from externality.   In a book, for instance, it certainly has no
bearing upon the content, whether it be written or
printed, bound in paper or in leather.   That however
does not in the least imply that apart from such an
indifference and external form, the content of the book
is itself formless.   There are undoubtedly books enough
which even in reference to their content may well be
styled formless: but want of form in this case is the
same as bad form, and means the defect of the right
form, not the absence of all form whatever.   So far is
this right form from being unaffected by the content that
it is rather the content itself.   A work of art that wants
the right form is for that very reason no right or true
work of art: and it is a bad way of excusing an artist,
to say that the content of his works is good and even
excellent, though they want the right form.   Real
works of art are those where content and form exhibit

a thorough identity.   The content of the Iliad, it may
be said, is the Trojan war, and especially the wrath
of Achilles.   In that we have everything, and yet very
little after all; for the Iliad is made an Iliad by the
poetic form, in which that content is moulded.   The
content of Romeo and Juliet may similarly be said to
be the ruin of two lovers through the discord between
their families: but something more is needed to make
Shakespeare's immortal tragedy.

   In reference to the relation of form and content in
the field of science, we should recollect the difference
between philosophy and the rest of the sciences.   The
latter are finite, because their mode of thought, as a
merely formal act, derives its content from without.
Their content therefore is not known as moulded from
within through the thoughts which lie at the ground of
it, and form and content do not thoroughly interpenetrate each other.   This partition disappears in philosophy, and thus justifies its title of infinite knowledge.
Yet even philosophic thought is often held to be a
merely formal act; and that logic, which confessedly
deals only with thoughts *quä* thoughts, is merely formal,
is especially a foregone conclusion.   And if content
means no more than what is palpable and obvious to
the senses, all philosophy and logic in particular must be
at once acknowledged to be void of content, that is to
say, of content perceptible to the senses.   Even ordinary forms of thought however, and the common usage
of language, do not in the least restrict the appella-
tion of content to what is perceived by the senses, or
to what has a being in place and time.   A book without
content is, as every one knows, not a book with empty
leaves, but one of which the content is as good as none.
We shall find as the last result on closer analysis, that
by what is called content an educated mind means noth-

ing but the presence and power of thought. But this
is to admit that thoughts are not empty forms without
affinity to their content, and that in other spheres as
well as in art the truth and the sterling value of the content essentially depend on the content showing itself
identical with the form.

134. But immediate existence is a character of the
subsistence itself as well as of the form: it is consequently external to the character of the content; but
in an equal degree this externality, which the content
has through the factor of its subsistence, is essential to
it. When thus explicitly stated, the phenomenon is relativity or correlation: where one and the same thing, viz.
the content or the developed form, is seen as the externality and antithesis of independent existences, and as
their reduction to a relation of identity, in which identification alone the two things distinguished are what
they are.

(c) *Relation or Correlation.*

135. (a) The immediate relation is that of the
WHOLE and the PARTS. The content is the whole,
and consists of the parts (the form), its counterpart.
The parts are diverse one from another. It is they that
possess independent being. But they are parts, only
when they are identified by being related to one another; or, in so far as they make up the whole, when
taken together. But this 'Together' is the counterpart
and negation of the part.

Essential correlation is the specific and completely universal phase in which things appear. Everything that
exists stands in correlation, and this correlation is the
veritable nature of every existence. The existent thing
in this way has no being of its own, but only in some-

thing else: in this other however it is self-relation; and correlation is the unity of the self-relation and relation-to-others.

The relation of the whole and the parts is untrue to this extent, that the notion and the reality of the relation are not in harmony. The notion of the whole is to contain parts; but if the whole is taken and made what its notion implies, *i.e.* if it is divided, it at once ceases to be a whole. Things there are, no doubt, which correspond to this relation: but for that very reason they are low and untrue existences. We must remember however what 'untrue' signifies. When it occurs in a philosophical discussion, the term 'untrue' does not signify that the thing to which it is applied is non-existent. A bad state or a sickly body may exist all the same; but these things are untrue, because their notion and their reality are out of harmony.

The relation of whole and parts, being the immediate relation, comes easy to reflective understanding; and for that reason it often satisfies when the question really turns on profounder ties. The limbs and organs, for instance, of an organic body are not merely parts of it: it is only in their unity that they are what they are, and they are unquestionably affected by that unity, as they also in turn affect it. These limbs and organs become mere parts, only when they pass under the hands of the anatomist, whose occupation, be it remembered, is not with the living body but with the corpse. Not that such analysis is illegitimate: we only mean that the external and mechanical relation of whole and parts is not sufficient for us, if we want to study organic life in its truth. And if this be so in organic life, it is the case to a much greater extent when we apply this relation to the mind and the formations of the spiritual world.

Psychologists may not expressly speak of parts of the soul or mind, but the mode in which this subject is treated by the analytic understanding is largely founded on the analogy of this finite relation. At least that is so, when the different forms of mental activity are enumerated and described merely in their isolation one after another, as so-called special powers and faculties.

136. (β) The one-and-same of this correlation (the self-relation found in it) is thus immediately a negative self-relation. The correlation is in short the mediating process whereby one and the same is first unaffected towards difference, and secondly is the negative self-relation, which repels itself as reflection-into-self to difference, and invests itself (as reflection-into-something-else) with existence, whilst it conversely leads back this reflection-into-other to self relation and indifference. This gives the correlation of FORCE and its EXPRESSION.

The relationship of whole and part is the immediate and therefore unintelligent (mechanical) relation,—a revulsion of self-identity into mere variety. Thus we pass from the whole to the parts, and from the parts to the whole: in the one we forget its opposition to the other, while each on its own account, at one time the whole, at another the parts, is taken to be an independent existence. In other words, when the parts are declared to subsist in the whole, and the whole consist of the parts, we have either member of the relation at different times taken to be permanently subsistent, while the other is non-essential. In its superficial form the mechanical nexus consists in the parts being independent of each other and of the whole.

This relation may be adopted for the progression *ad infinitum,* in the case of the divisibility of matter: and then it becomes an unintelligent alternation with the two

sides.   A thing at one time is taken as a whole: then
we go on to specify the parts: this specifying is forgotten, and what was a part is regarded as a whole:
then the specifying of the part comes up again, and so
on for ever.   But if this infinity be taken as the negative
which it is, it is the *negative* self-relating element in the
correlation,—Force, the self-identical whole, or immanency; which yet supersedes this immanency and gives
itself expression;—and conversely the expression which
vanishes and returns into Force.

Force, notwithstanding this infinity, is also finite:
for the content, or the one and the same of the Force
and its out-putting, is this identity at first only for
the observer: the two sides of the relation are not yet,
each on its own account, the concrete identity of that
one and same, not yet the totality.   For one another
they are therefore different, and the relationship is a
finite one.   Force consequently requires solicitation from
without: it works blindly: and on account of this defectiveness of form, the content is also limited and accidental.   It is not yet genuinely identical with the form:
not yet is it *as* a notion and an end; that is to say, it
is not intrinsically and actually determinate.   This difference is most vital, but not easy to apprehend: it will
assume a clearer formulation when we reach Design.
If it be overlooked, it leads to the confusion of conceiving God as Force, a confusion from which Herder's
God especially suffers.

It is often said that the nature of Force itself is unknown and only its manifestation apprehended.   But, in
the first place, it may be replied, every article in the
import of Force is the same as what is specified in the
Exertion: and the explanation of a phenomenon by a
Force is to that extent a mere tautology.   What is supposed to remain unknown, therefore, is really nothing but

the empty form of reflection-into-self, by which alone
the Force is distinguished from the Exertion,—and that
form too is something familiar.   It is a form that does
not make the slightest addition to the content and to
the law, which have to be discovered from the phenomenon alone.   Another assurance always given is
that to speak of forces implies no theory as to their
nature: and that being so, it is impossible to see why the
form of Force has been introduced into the sciences at all.
In the second place the nature of Force is undoubtedly
unknown: we are still without any necessity binding
and connecting its content together in itself, as we are
without necessity in the content, in so far as it is expressly limited and hence has its character by means of
another thing outside it.

(1) Compared with the immediate relation of whole
and parts, the relation between force and its putting-
forth may be considered infinite.   In it that identity of
the two sides is realised, which in the former relation
only existed for the observer.   The whole, though we
can see that it consists of parts, ceases to be a whole
when it is divided: whereas force is only shown to be
force when it exerts itself, and in its exercise only comes
back to itself.   The exercise is only force once more.
Yet, on further examination even this relation will appear finite, and finite in virtue of this mediation: just
as, conversely, the relation of whole and parts is obviously finite in virtue of its immediacy.   The first
and simplest evidence for the finitude of the mediated relation of force and its exercise is, that each and every
force is conditioned and requires something else than itself for its subsistence.   For instance, a special vehicle
of magnetic force, as is well known, is iron, the other
properties of which, such as its colour, specific weight,
or relation to acids, are independent of this connexion

with magnetism. The same thing is seen in all other forces, which from one end to the other are found to be conditioned and mediated by something else than themselves. Another proof of the finite nature of force is that it requires solicitation before it can put itself forth. That through which the force is solicited, is itself another exertion of force, which cannot put itself forth without similar solicitation. This brings us either to a repetition of the infinite progression, or to a reciprocity of soliciting and being solicited. In either case we have no absolute beginning of motion. Force is not as yet, like the final cause, inherently self-determining: the content is given to it as determined, and force, when it exerts itself, is, according to the phrase, blind in its working. That phrase implies the distinction between abstract force-manifestation and teleological action.

(2) The oft-repeated statement, that the exercise of the force and not the force itself admits of being known, must be rejected as groundless. It is the very essence of force to manifest itself, and thus in the totality of manifestation, conceived as a law, we at the same time discover the force itself. And yet this assertion that force in its own self is unknowable betrays a well-grounded presentiment that this relation is finite. The several manifestations of a force at first meet us in indefinite multiplicity, and in their isolation seem accidental: but, reducing this multiplicity to its inner unity, which we term force, we see that the apparently contingent is necessary, by recognising the law that rules it. But the different forces themselves are a multiplicity again, and in their mere juxtaposition seem to be contingent. Hence in empirical physics, we speak of the forces of gravity, magnetism, electricity, &c., and in empirical psychology of the forces of memory, imagina-

tion, will, and all the other faculties. All this multiplicity again excites a craving to know these different forces
as a single whole, nor would this craving be appeased
even if the several forces were traced back to one common primary force. Such a primary force would be
really no more than an empty abstraction, with as little
content as the abstract thing-in-itself. And besides this,
the correlation of force and manifestation is essentially
a mediated correlation (of reciprocal dependence), and
it must therefore contradict the notion of force to view
it as primary or resting on itself.

Such being the case with the nature of force, though
we may consent to let the world be called a manifestation of divine forces, we should object to have God
Himself viewed as a mere force. For force is after all
a subordinate and finite category. At the so-called
renascence of the sciences, when steps were taken to
trace the single phenomena of nature back to underlying
forces, the Church branded the enterprise as impious.
The argument of the Church was as follows: If it be
the forces of gravitation, of vegetation, &c. which occasion the movements of the heavenly bodies, the growth
of plants, &c., there is nothing left for divine providence,
and God sinks to the level of a leisurely onlooker, sur-
veying this play of forces. The students of nature, it
is true, and Newton more than others, when they employed the reflective category of force to explain natural
phenomena, have expressly pleaded that the honour of
God as the Creator and Governor of the world, would
not thereby be impaired. Still the logical issue of this
explanation by means of forces is that the inferential
understanding proceeds to fix each of these forces, and
to maintain them in their finitude as ultimate. And
contrasted with this deinfinitised world of independent
forces and matters, the only terms in which it is possible

still to describe God will present Him in the abstract infinity of an unknowable. supreme Being in some other world far away. This is precisely the position of materialism, and of modern 'free-thinking,' whose theology ignores what God is and restricts itself to the mere fact *that* He is. In this dispute therefore the Church and the religious mind have to a certain extent the right on their side. The finite forms of understanding certainly fail to fulfill the conditions for a knowledge either of Nature or of the formations in the world of Mind as they truly are. Yet on the other side it is impossible to overlook the formal right which, in the first place, entitles the empirical sciences to vindicate the right of thought to know the existent world in all the speciality of its content, and to seek something further than the bare statement of mere abstract faith that God creates and governs the world. When our religious consciousness, resting upon the authority of the Church, teaches us that God created the world by His almighty will, that He guides the stars in their courses, and vouchsafes to all His creatures their existence and their well-being, the question Why? is still left to answer. Now it is the answer to this question which forms the common task of empirical science and of philosophy. When religion refuses to recognise this problem, or the right to put it, and appeals to the unsearchableness of the decrees of God, it is taking up the same agnostic ground as is taken by the mere Enlightenment of understanding. Such an appeal is no better than an arbitrary dogmatism, which contravenes the express command of Christianity, to know God in spirit and in truth, and is prompted by a humility which is not Christian, but born of ostentatious bigotry.

137. Force is a whole, which is in its own self negative self-relation; and as such a whole it continually

pushes itself off from itself and puts itself forth. But since this reflection-into-another (corresponding to the distinction between the Parts of the Whole) is equally a reflection-into-self, this out-putting is the way and means by which Force that returns back into itself is as a Force. The very act of out-putting accordingly sets in abeyance the diversity of the two sides which is found in this correlation, and expressly states the identity which virtually constitutes their content. The truth of Force and utterance therefore is that relation, in which the two sides are distinguished only as Outward and Inward.

138. (γ) The INWARD (Interior) is the ground, when it stands as the mere form of the one side of the Appearance and the Correlation,—the empty form of reflection-into-self. As a counterpart to it stands the OUTWARD (Exterior),—Existence, also as the form of the other side of the correlation, with the empty characteristic of reflection-into-something-else. But Inward and Outward are identified: and their identity is identity brought to fulness in the content, that unity of reflection-into-self and reflection-into-other which was forced to appear in the movement of force. Both are the same one totality, and this unity makes them the content.

139. In the first place then, Exterior is the same content as Interior. What is inwardly is also found outwardly, and *vice versa*. The appearance shows nothing that is not in the essence, and in the essence there is nothing but what is manifested.

140. In the second place, Inward and Outward, as formal terms, are also reciprocally opposed, and that thoroughly. The one is the abstraction of identity with self; the other, of mere multiplicity or reality. But as stages of the one form, they are essentially identical:

so that whatever is at first explicitly put only in the
one abstraction, is also as plainly and at one step only in
the other.   Therefore what is only internal is also
only external: and what is only external, is so far only
at first internal.

It is the customary mistake of reflection to take the
essence to be merely the interior. If it be so taken,
even this way of looking at it is purely external, and
that sort of essence is the empty external abstraction.

> *Jns Jnnere der Natur*
> *Dringt kein erschaffner Geist,*
> *Zu glücklich wenn er nur*
> *Die äussere Schaale weist.**

It ought rather to have been said that, if the essence of
nature is ever described as the inner part, the person
who so describes it only knows its outer shell.   In
Being as a whole, or even in mere sense-perception, the
notion is at first only an inward, and for that very reason is something external to Being, a subjective thinking
and being, devoid of truth.—In Nature as well as in
Mind, so long as the notion, design, or law are at first
the inner capacity, mere possibilities, they are first only
an external, inorganic nature, the knowledge of a third
person, alien force, and the like.   As a man is outwardly, that is to say in his actions (not of course in his
merely bodily outwardness), so is he inwardly: and if
his virtue, morality, &c. are only inwardly his,—that is
if they exist only in his intentions and sentiments, and

* Compare Goethe's indignant outcry—'To Natural Science,'
vol. *i.* pt. 3:

> Das hör ich sechzig Jahre wiederholen,
> Und fluche drauf, aber verstohlen, ——
> Natur hat weder Kern noch Schaale,
> Alles ist sie mit einem Male.

his outward acts are not identical with them, the one half of him is as hollow and empty as the other.

The relation of Outward and Inward unites the two relations that precede, and at the same time sets in abeyance mere relativity and phenomenality in general. Yet so long as understanding keeps the Inward and Outward fixed in their separation, they are empty forms, the one as null as the other. Not only in the study of nature, but also of the spiritual world, much depends on a just appreciation of the relation of inward and outward, and especially on avoiding the misconception that the former only is the essential point on which everything turns, while the latter is unessential and trivial. We find this mistake made when, as is often done, the difference between nature and mind is traced back to the abstract difference between inner and outer. As for nature, it certainly is in the gross external, not merely to the mind, but even on its own part. But to call it external 'in the gross' is not to imply an abstract externality—for there is no such thing. It means rather that the idea which forms the common content of nature and minds, is found in nature as outward only, and for that very reason only inward. The abstract understanding, with its 'Either—or,' may struggle against this conception of nature. It is none the less obviously found in our other modes of consciousness, particularly in religion. It is the lesson of religion that nature, no less than the spiritual world, is a revelation of God: but with this distinction, that while nature never gets so far as to be conscious of its divine essence, that consciousness is the express problem of the mind, which in the matter of that problem is as yet finite. Those who look upon the essence of nature as mere inwardness, and therefore inaccessible to us, take up the same line as that ancient creed which regarded God as envious and jealous; a creed which both Plato and Aristotle pronounced against long ago. All that God is, He imparts and reveals; and He does so, at first, in and through nature.

Any object indeed is faulty and imperfect when it is only inward, and thus at the same time only outward, or (which is the same thing) when it is only an outward and thus only an inward. For instance, a child, taken in the gross as human being, is no doubt a rational creature; but the reason of the child as child is at first a mere inward, in the shape of his natural ability or vocation, &c. This mere inward, at the same time, has for the child the form of a more outward, in the shape of the will of his parents, the attainments of his teachers, and the whole world of reason that environs him. The education and instruction of a child aim at making him actually and for himself what he is at first potentially and therefore for others, viz. for his grown-up friends. The reason, which at first exists in the child only as an inner possibility, is actualised through education: and conversely, the child by these means becomes conscious that the goodness, religion, and science which he had at first looked upon as an outward authority, are his own and inward nature. As with the child so it is in this matter with the adult, when, in opposition to his true destiny, his intellect and will remain in the bondage of the natural man. Thus, the criminal sees the punishment to which he has to submit as an act of violence from without: whereas in fact the penalty is only the manifestation of his own criminal will.

From what has now been said, we may learn what to think of a man who, when blamed for his shortcomings, it may be, his discreditable acts, appeals to the (professedly) excellent intentions and sentiments of the inner self he distinguishes therefrom. There certainly may be individual cases, where the malice of outward circumstances frustrates well-meant designs, and disturbs the execution of the bestlaid plans. But in general even here the essential unity between inward and outward is maintained. We are thus justified in saying that a man is what he does; and the lying vanity which consoles itself with the feeling of inward excellence, may be confronted with the words of the gospel: 'By their fruits ye shall know them!' That grand saying applies primarily in a moral and religious aspect, but it also holds good in reference to performances in art and science. The keen eye of a teacher who perceives in his pupil decided evidences of talent, may lead him to state his opinion that a Raphael or a Mozart lies hidden in the boy: and the result will show how far such an opinion was well-founded. But if a daub of a painter, or a poetaster, soothe themselves by the conceit that their head is full of high ideals, their consolation is a poor one; and if they insist on being judged not by their actual works but by their projects, we may safely reject their pretensions as unfounded and unmeaning. The converse case however also occurs. In passing judgment on men who have accomplished something great and good, we often make use of the false distinction between inward and outward. All that they have accomplished, we say, is outward merely; inwardly they were acting from some very different motive, such as a desire to gratify their vanity or other unworthy passion. This is the spirit of envy. Incapable of any great action of its own, envy tries hard to depreciate greatness and to bring it down to its own level. Let us, rather, recall the fine expression of Goethe, that there is no remedy but Love against great superiorities of others. We may seek to rob men's great actions of their grandeur, by the insinuation of hypocrisy; but, though it is possi-

ble that men in an instance now and then may dissemble
and disguise a good deal, they cannot conceal the whole
of their inner self, which infallibly betrays itself in the
decursus vitae. Even here it is true that a man is nothing but the series of his actions.

What is called the 'pragmatic' writing of history has
in modern times frequently sinned in its treatment of
great historical characters, and defaced and tarnished
the true conception of them by this fallacious separation
of the outward from the inward. Not content with
telling the unvarnished tale of the great acts which have
been wrought by the heroes of the world's history, and
with acknowledging that their inward being corresponds
with the import of their acts, the pragmatic historian
fancies himself justified and even obliged to trace the
supposed secret motives that lie behind the open facts
of the record. The historian, in that case, is supposed to
write with more depth in proportion as he succeeds in
tearing away the aureole from all that has been hereto-
fore held grand and glorious, and in depressing it, so
far as its origin and proper significance are concerned,
to the level of vulgar mediocrity. To make these pragmatical researches in history easier, it is usual to recom-
mend the study of psychology, which is supposed to
make us acquainted with the real motives of human
actions. The psychology in question however is only
that petty knowledge of men, which looks away from the
essential and permanent in human nature to fasten its
glance on the casual and private features shown in
isolated instincts and passions.

A pragmatical psychology ought at least to leave the
historian, who investigates the motives at the ground of
great actions, a choice between the 'substantial' interests
of patriotism, justice, religious truth and the like, on
the one hand, and the subjective and 'formal' interests of

vanity, ambition, avarice and the like, on the other. The
latter however are the motives which must be viewed by
the pragmatists as really efficient, otherwise the assumption of a contrast between the inward (the disposition of the agent) and the outward (the import of
the action) would fall to the ground. But inward and
outward have in truth the same content; and the right
doctrine is the very reverse of this pedantic judiciality.
If the heroes of history had been actuated by subjective
and formal interests alone, they would never have accomplished what they have. And if we have due regard to the unity between the inner and the outer, we
must own that great men willed what they did, and did
what they willed.

141. The empty abstractions, by means of which the
one identical content perforce continues in the two cor
relatives, suspend themselves in the immediate transition, the one in the other. The content is itself nothing
but their identity: and these abstractions are the seeming of essence, put as seeming. By the manifestation of
force the inward is put into existence: but this putting
is the mediation by empty abstractions. In its own self
the intermediating process vanishes to the immediacy,
in which the inward and the outward are absolutely identical and their difference is distinctly no more than assumed and imposed. This identity is Actuality.

C.—ACTUALITY.

142. ACTUALITY is the unity, become immediate,
of essence with existence, or of inward with outward.
The utterance of the actual is the actual itself: so that in
this utterance it remains just as essential, and only
is essential, in so far as it is in immediate external
existence.

We have ere this met Being and Existence as forms
of the immediate. Being is, in general, unreflected immediacy and transition into another. Existence is immediate unity of being and reflection; hence appearance;
it comes from the ground, and falls to the ground. In
actuality this unity is explicitly put, and the two sides
of the relation identified. Hence the actual is exempted
from transition, and its externality is its energising.
In that energising it is reflected into itself: its existence
is only the manifestation of itself, not of an other.

Actuality and thought (or Idea) are often absurdly
opposed. How commonly we hear people saying that,
though no objection can be urged against the truth and
correctness of a certain thought, there is nothing of
the kind to be seen in actuality, or it cannot be actually
carried out! People who use such language only prove
that they have not properly apprehended the nature
either of thought or of actuality. Thought in such
a case is, on one hand, the synonym for a subjective
conception, plan, intention or the like, just as actuality,
on the other, is made synonymous with external and
sensible existence. This is all very well in common
life, where great laxity is allowed in the categories and
the names given to them: and it may of course happen
that *e.g.* the plan, or so-called idea, say of a certain
method of taxation, is good and advisable in the abstract,
but that nothing of the sort is found in so-called actuality, or could possibly be carried out under the given conditions. But when the abstract understanding gets hold
of these categories and exaggerates the distinction they
imply into a hard and fast line of contrast, when it
tells us that in this actual world we must knock ideas
out of our heads, it is necessary energetically to protest against these doctrines, alike in the name of science
and of sound reason. For on the one hand Ideas are

THE DOCTRINE OF ESSENCE 187

not confined to our heads merely, nor is the Idea, upon the whole, so feeble as to leave the question of its actualisation or non-actualisation dependent on our will. The Idea is rather the absolutely active as well as actual. And on the other hand actuality is not so bad and irrational, as purblind or wrong-headed and muddle-brained would-be reformers imagine. So far is actuality, as distinguished from mere appearance, and primarily presenting a unity of inward and outward, from being in contrariety with reason, that it is rather thoroughly reasonable, and everything which is not reasonable must on that very ground cease to be held actual. The same view may be traced in the usages of educated speech, which declines to give the name of real poet or real statesman to a poet or a statesman who can do nothing really meritorious or reasonable.

In that vulgar conception of actuality which mistakes for it what is palpable and directly obvious to the senses, we must seek the ground of a wide-spread prejudice about the relation of the philosophy of Aristotle to that of Plato. Popular opinion makes the difference to be as follows. While Plato recognises the idea and only the idea as the truth, Aristotle, rejecting the idea, keeps to what is actual, and is on that account to be considered the founder and chief of empiricism. On this it may be remarked: that although actuality certainly is the principle of the Aristotelian philosophy, it is not the vulgar actuality of what is immediately at hand, but the idea as actuality. Where then lies the controversy of Aristotle against Plato? It lies in this, Aristotle calls the Platonic idea a mere δύναμις, and establishes in opposition to Plato that the idea, which both equally recognise to be the only truth, is essentially to be viewed as an ἐνέργεια, in other words, as the inward which is quite to the fore, or as the unity of inner and outer, or as actuality, in the emphatic sense here given to the word.

143. Such a concrete category as Actuality includes the characteristics aforesaid and their difference, and is therefore also the development of them, in such a way that, as it has them, they are at the same time plainly understood to be a show, to be assumed or imposed.

(a) Viewed as an identity in general, Actuality is first of all POSSIBILITY—the reflection-into-self which, as in contrast with the concrete unity of the actual, is taken and made an abstract and unessential essentiality. Possibility is what is essential to reality, but in such a way that it is at the same time only a possibility.

It was probably the import of Possibility which induced Kant to regard it along with necessity and actuality as Modalities, 'since these categories do not in the least increase the notion as object, but only express its relation to the faculty of knowledge.' For Possibility is really the bare abstraction of reflection-into-self,— what was formerly called the Inward, only that it is now taken to mean the external inward, lifted out of reality and with the being of a mere supposition, and is thus, sure enough, supposed only as a bare modality, an abstraction which comes short, and, in more concrete terms, belongs only to subjective thought. It is otherwise with Actuality and Necessity. They are anything but a mere sort and mode for something else: in fact the very reverse of that. If they are supposed, it is as the concrete, not merely supposititious, but intrinsically complete.

As Possibility is, in the first instance, the mere form of identity-with-self (as compared with the concrete which is actual), the rule for it merely is that a thing must not be self-contradictory. Thus everything is possible; for an act of abstraction can give any content this form of identity. Everything however is as impossible as it is possible. In every content,—which is and must be concrete,—the speciality of its nature may be viewed as a specialised contrariety and in that way as a contradiction. Nothing therefore can be more meaningless than to speak of such possibility and impossibility. In philosophy, in particular, there should never be a word said of showing that 'It is possible,' or 'There is still another possibility,' or, to adopt another phraseology, 'It is conceivable.' The same consideration should warn the writer of history against employing a category which has now been explained to be on its own merits untrue: but the subtlety of the empty understanding finds its chief pleasure in the fantastic ingenuity of suggesting possibilities and lots of possibilities.

Our picture-thought is at first disposed to see in possibility the richer and more comprehensive, in actuality the poorer and narrower category. Everything, it is said, is possible, but everything which is possible is not on that account actual. In real truth, however, if we deal with them as thoughts, actuality is the more comprehensive, because it is the concrete thought which includes possibility as an abstract element. And that superiority is to some extent expressed in our ordinary mode of thought when we speak of the possible, in distinction from the actual, as *only* possible. Possibility is often said to consist in a thing's being thinkable. 'Think,' however, in this use of the word, only means to conceive any content under the form of an abstract identity. Now every content can be brought under this form, since nothing is required except to separate it from the relations in which it stands. Hence any content, however absurd and nonsensical, can be viewed as possible. It is possible that the moon might fall upon the earth tonight; for the moon is a body separate from the earth,—and may as well fall down upon it as a stone thrown into the air does. It is possible that the Sultan may become Pope; for, being a man, he may be converted to the Christian faith, may become a Catholic priest, and so on. In language like this about possibilities, it is chiefly the law of the sufficient ground or reason which is manipulated in the style already explained. Everything, it is said, is possible, for which you can state some ground. The less education a man has, or, in other words, the less he knows of the specific connexions of the objects to which he directs his observations, the greater is his tendency to launch out into all sorts of empty possibilities. An instance of this habit in the political sphere is seen in the pot-house politician. In practical life too it is no uncommon thing to see ill-will and indolence slink behind the category of possibility, in order to escape definite obligations. To such conduct the same remarks apply as were made in connexion with the law of sufficient ground. Reasonable and practical men refuse to be imposed upon by the possible, for the simple ground that it is possible only. They stick to the actual (not meaning by that word merely whatever immediately is now and here). Many of the proverbs of common life express the same contempt for what is abstractly possible. 'A bird in the hand is worth two in the bush.'

After all there is as good reason for taking everything to be impossible, as to be possible: for every content (a content is always concrete) includes not only diverse but even opposite characteristics. Nothing is so impossible, for instance, as this, that I am: for 'I' is at the same time simple self-relation and, as undoubtedly, relation to something else. The same may be seen in every other fact in the natural or spiritual world.

Matter, it may be said, is impossible: for it is the unity
of attraction and repulsion.   The same is true of life,
law, freedom, and above all, of God Himself, as the true,
i.e. the triune God,—a notion of God, which the abstract
'Enlightenment' of Understanding, in conformity with
its canons, rejected on the allegation that it was contradictory in thought.   Generally speaking, it is the
empty understanding which haunts these empty forms:
and the business of philosophy in the matter is to show
how null and meaningless they are.   Whether a thing is
possible or impossible, depends altogether on the subject-matter: that is, on the sum total of the elements in
actuality, which, as it opens itself out, discloses itself
to be necessity.

144. (β) But the Actual in its distinction from possibility (which is reflection into self) is itself only the
outward concrete, the unessential immediate.   In other
words, to such extent as the actual is primarily the simple merely immediate unity of Inward and Outward, it
is obviously made an unessential outward, and thus at
the same time it is merely inward, the abstraction of
reflection-into-self.   Hence it is itself characterised as a
merely possible.   When thus valued at the rate of a mere
possibility, the actual is a CONTINGENT or Accidental, and, conversely, possibility is mere Accident itself or
CHANCE.

145. Possibility and Contingency are the two factors
of Actuality,—Inward and Outward, put as mere forms
which constitute the externality of the actual.   They have
their reflection-into-self on the body of actual fact, or
content, with its intrinsic definiteness which gives the
essential ground of their characterisation.   The finitude
of the contingent and the possible lies, therefore, as we
now see, in the distinction of the form-determination
from the content: and, therefore, it depends on the

content alone whether anything is contingent and possible.

As possibility is the mere *inside* of actuality, it is for that reason a mere *outside* actuality, in other words, Contingency. The contingent, roughly speaking, is what has the ground of its being not in itself but in somewhat else. Such is the aspect under which actuality first comes before consciousness, and which is often mistaken for actuality itself. But the contingent is only one side of the actual,—the side, namely, of reflection on somewhat else. It is the actual, in the signification of something merely possible. Accordingly we consider the contingent to be what may or may not be, what may be in one way or in another, whose being or not-being, and whose being on this wise or otherwise, depends not upon itself but on something else. To overcome this contingency is, roughly speaking, the problem of science on the one hand; as in the range of practice, on the other, the end of action is to rise above the contingency of the will, or above caprice. It has however often happened, most of all in modern times, that contingency has been unwarrantably elevated, and had a value attached to it, both in nature and the world of mind, to which it has no just claim. Frequently Nature—to take it first,—has been chiefly admired for the richness and variety of its structures. Apart, however, from what disclosure it contains of the Idea, this richness gratifies none of the higher interests of reason, and in its vast variety of structures, organic and inorganic, affords us only the spectacle of a contingency losing itself in vagueness. At any rate, the chequered scene presented by the several varieties of animals and plants, conditioned as it is by outward circumstances,—the complex changes in the figuration and grouping of clouds, and the like, ought not to be ranked higher than the equally casual fancies of the mind which surrenders itself to its own caprices. The wonderment with which such phenomena are welcomed is a most abstract frame of mind, from which one should advance to a closer insight into the inner harmony and uniformity of nature.

Of contingency in respect of the Will it is especially important to form a proper estimate. The Freedom of the Will is an expression that often means mere free-choice, or the will in the form of contingency. Freedom of choice, or the capacity of determining ourselves towards one thing or another, is undoubtedly a vital element in the will (which in its very notion is free); but instead of being freedom itself, it is only in the first instance a freedom in form. The genuinely free will, which includes free choice as suspended, is conscious to itself that its content is intrinsically firm and fast, and knows it at the same time to be thoroughly its own. A will, on the contrary, which remains standing on the grade of option, even supposing it does decide in favour of what is in import right and true, is always haunted by the conceit that it might, if it had so pleased, have decided in favour of the reverse course. When more narrowly examined, free choice is seen to be a contra-diction, to this extent that its form and content stand in antithesis. The matter of choice is given, and known as a content dependent not on the will itself, but on outward circumstances. In reference to such a given content, freedom lies only in the form of choosing, which, as it is only a freedom in form, may consequently be regarded as freedom only in supposition. On an ultimate analysis it will be seen that the same outwardness of circumstances, on which is founded the content that the will finds to its hand, can alone account for the will giving its decision for the one and not the other of the two alternatives.

Although contingency, as it has thus been shown, is
only one aspect in the whole of actuality, and therefore
not to be mistaken for actuality itself, it has no less
than the rest of the forms of the idea its due office in the
world of objects. This is, in the first place, seen in
Nature. On the surface of Nature, so to speak, Chance
ranges unchecked, and that contingency must simply be
recognised, without the pretension sometimes erroneously
ascribed to philosophy, of seeking to find in it a could-
only-be-so-and-not-otherwise. Nor is contingency less
visible in the world of Mind. The will, as we have
already remarked, includes contingency under the shape
of option or free-choice, but only as a vanishing and
abrogated element. In respect of Mind and its works,
just as in the case of Nature, we must guard against
being so far misled by a well-meant endeavour after
rational knowledge, as to try to exhibit the necessity of
phenomena which are marked by a decided contingency,
or, as the phrase is, to construe them *a priori*. Thus in
language (although it be, as it were, the body of
thought) Chance still unquestionably plays a decided
part; and the same is true of the creations of law, of
art, &c. The problem of science, and especially of
philosophy, undoubtedly consists in eliciting the necessity concealed under the semblance of contingency. That
however is far from meaning that the contingent belongs
to our subjective conception alone, and must therefore
be simply set aside, if we wish to get at the truth. All
scientific researches which pursue this tendency exclusively, lay themselves fairly open to the charge of
mere jugglery and an over-strained precisianism.

146. When more closely examined, what the aforesaid outward side of actuality implies is this. Contingency, which is actuality in its immediacy, is the self-
identical, essentially only as a supposition which is **no**

sooner made than it is revoked and leaves an existent
externality. In this way, the external contingency is
something pre-supposed, the immediate existence of
which is at the same time a possibility, and has the vocation to be suspended, to be the possibility of something else. Now this possibility is the CONDITION.

The Contingent, as the immediate actuality, is at the
same time the possibility of somewhat else,—no longer
however that abstract possibility which we had at first,
but the possibility which *is*. And a possibility existent
is a Condition. By the Condition of a thing we mean
first, an existence, in short an immediate, and secondly
the vocation of this immediate to be suspended and sub-
serve the actualising of something else.—Immediate actuality is in general as such never what it ought to be;
it is a finite actuality with an inherent flaw, and its
vocation is to be consumed. But the other aspect of
actuality is its essentiality. This is primarily the inside, which as a mere possibility is no less destined to be
suspended. Possibility thus suspended is the issuing
of a new actuality, of which the first immediate actuality
was the pre-supposition. Here we see the alternation
which is involved in the notion of a Condition. The
Conditions of a thing seem at first sight to involve no
bias any way. Really however an immediate actuality
of this kind includes in it the germ of something else
altogether. At first this something else is only a possibility: but the form of possibility is soon suspended
and translated into actuality. This new actuality thus
issuing is the very inside of the immediate actuality
which it uses up. Thus there comes into being quite
an other shape of things, and yet it is not an other: for
the first actuality is only put as what it in essence was.
The conditions which are sacrificed, which fall to the
ground and are spent, only unite with themselves in

the other actuality. Such in general is the nature of
the process of actuality. The actual is no mere case of
immediate Being, but, as essential Being, a suspension
of its own immediacy, and thereby mediating itself with
itself.

147. (γ) When this externality (of actuality) is thus
developed into a circle of the two categories of possibility and immediate actuality, showing the intermediation
of the one by the other, it is what is called REAL POS-
SIBILITY. Being such a circle, further, it is the totality, and thus the content, the actual fact or affair in its
all-round definiteness. Whilst in like manner, if we
look at the distinction between the two characteristics
in this unity, it realises the concrete totality of the
form, the immediate self-translation of inner into outer,
and of outer into inner. This self-movement of the
form is ACTIVITY, carrying into effect the fact or
affair as a *real* ground which is self-suspended to actuality, and carrying into effect the contingent actuality,
the conditions; *i.e.* it is their reflection-in-self, and their
self-suspension to an other actuality, the actuality of
the actual fact. If all the conditions are at hand, the
fact (event) *must* be actual; and the fact itself is one
of the conditions: for being in the first place only inner,
it is at first itself only pre-supposed. Developed actuality, as the coincident alternation of inner and outer,
the alternation of their opposite motions combined into
a single motion, is NECESSITY.

Necessity has been defined, and rightly so, as the
union of possibility and actuality. This mode of expression, however, gives a superficial and therefore
unintelligible description of the very difficult notion of
necessity. It is difficult because it is the notion itself,
only that its stages or factors are still as actualities,
which are yet at the same time to be viewed as forms

only, collapsing and transient. In the two following paragraphs therefore an exposition of the factors which constitute necessity must be given at greater length.

When anything is said to be necessary, the first question we ask is, Why? Anything necessary accordingly comes before us as something due to a supposition, the result of certain antecedents. If we go no further than mere derivation from antecedents however, we have not gained a complete notion of what necessity means. What is merely derivative, is what it is, not through itself, but through something else; and in this way it too is merely contingent. What is necessary, on the other hand, we would have be what it is through itself; and thus, although derivative, it must still contain the antecedent whence it is derived as a vanishing element in itself. Hence we say of what is necessary, 'It is.' We thus hold it to be simple self-relation, in which all dependence on something else is removed.

Necessity is often said to be blind. If that means that in the process of necessity the End or final cause is not explicitly and overtly present, the statement is correct. The process of necessity begins with the existence of scattered circumstances which appear to have no inter-connexion and no concern one with another. These circumstances are an immediate actuality which collapses, and out of this negation a new actuality proceeds. Here we have a content which in point of form is doubled, once as content of the final realised fact, and once as content of the scattered circumstances which appear as if they were positive, and make themselves at first felt in that character. The latter content is in itself nought and is accordingly inverted into its negative, thus becoming content of the realised fact. The immediate circumstances fall to the ground as conditions, but are at the same time retained as content of the ultimate reality. From such circumstances and conditions there has, as we say, proceeded quite another thing, and it is for that reason that we call this process of necessity blind. If on the contrary we consider teleological action, we have in the end of action a content which is already fore-known. This activity therefore is not blind but seeing. To say that the world is ruled by Providence implies that design, as what has been absolutely pre-determined, is the active principle, so that the issue corresponds to what has been fore-known and fore-willed.

The theory however which regards the world as determined through necessity and the belief in a divine providence are by no means mutually excluding points of view. The intellectual principle underlying the idea of divine providence will hereafter be shown to be the notion. But the notion is the truth of necessity, which it contains in suspension in itself; just as, conversely, necessity is the notion implicit. Necessity is blind only so long as it is not understood. There is nothing therefore more mistaken than the charge of blind fatalism made against the Philosophy of History, when it takes for its problem to understand the necessity of every event. The philosophy of history rightly understood takes the rank of a Théodicée; and those, who fancy they honour Divine Providence by excluding necessity from it, are really degrading it by this exclusiveness to a blind and irrational caprice. In the simple language of the religious mind which speaks of God's eternal and immutable decrees, there is implied an express recognition that necessity forms part of the essence of God. In his difference from God, man, with his own private opinion and will, follows the call of caprice and arbitrary humour, and thus often finds his acts turn out something quite different from what he had meant and

willed. But God knows what He wills, is determined
in His eternal will neither by accident from within nor
from without, and what He wills He also accomplishes,
irresistibly.

Necessity gives a point of view which has important
bearings upon our sentiments and behaviour. When we
look upon events as necessary, our situation seems at
first sight to lack freedom completely. In the creed
of the ancients, as we know, necessity figured as Destiny. The modern point of view, on the contrary, is
that of Consolation. And Consolation means that, if
we renounce our aims and interests, we do so only in
prospect of receiving compensation. Destiny, on the
contrary, leaves no room for Consolation. But a close
examination of the ancient feeling about destiny, will
not by any means reveal a sense of bondage to its
power. Rather the reverse. This will clearly appear,
if we remember, that the sense of bondage springs from
inability to surmount the antithesis, and from looking
at what *is,* and what happens, as contradictory to what
ought to be and happen. In the ancient mind the feeling
was more of the following kind: Because such a thing
is, it is, and as it is, so ought it to be. Here there is no
contrast to be seen, and therefore no sense of bondage,
no pain, and no sorrow. True, indeed, as already remarked, this attitude towards destiny is void of consolation. But then, on the other hand, it is a frame of
mind which does not need consolation, so long as personal subjectivity has not acquired its infinite significance. It is this point on which special stress should be
laid in comparing the ancient sentiment with that of
the modern and Christian world.

By Subjectivity, however, we may understand, in the
first place, only the natural and finite subjectivity, with
its contingent and arbitrary content of private interests

and inclinations,—all, in short, that we call person as
distinguished from thing: taking 'thing' in the emphatic
sense of the word (in which we use the (correct) expression that it is a question of *things* and not of *persons*). In this sense of subjectivity we cannot help
admiring the tranquil resignation of the ancients to
destiny, and feeling that it is a much higher and worthier
mood than that of the moderns who obstinately pursue
their subjective aims, and when they find themselves
constrained to resign the hope of reaching them, console
themselves with the prospect of a reward in some other
shape. But the term subjectivity is not to be confined
merely to the bad and finite kind of it which is contrasted
with the thing (fact). In its truth subjectivity is immanent in the fact, and as a subjectivity thus infinite
is the very truth of the fact. Thus regarded, the doctrine of consolation receives a newer and a higher significance. It is in this sense that the Christian religion
is to be regarded as the religion of consolation, and even
of absolute consolation. Christianity, we know, teaches
that God wishes all men to be saved. That teaching
declares that subjectivity has an infinite value. And that
consoling power of Christianity just lies in the fact that
God Himself is in it known as the absolute subjectivity,
so that, inasmuch as subjectivity involves the element
of particularity, *our* particular personality too is recognised not merely as something to be solely and simply
nullified, but as at the same time something to be preserved. The gods of the ancient world were also, it is
true, looked upon as personal; but the personality of
a Zeus and an Apollo is not a real personality: it is only
a figure in the mind. In other words, these gods are
mere personifications, which, being such, do not know
themselves, and are only known. An evidence of this
defect and this powerlessness of the old gods is found

even in the religious beliefs of antiquity. In the ancient creeds not only men, but even gods, were represented as subject to destiny (πεπρωμένυν or sίμαρμένη), a destiny which we must conceive as necessity not unveiled, and thus as something wholly impersonal, selfless, and blind. On the other hand, the Christian God is God not known merely, but also self-knowing; He is a personality not merely figured in our minds, but rather absolutely actual.

We must refer to the Philosophy of Religion for a further discussion of the points here touched. But we may note in passing how important it is for any man to meet everything that befalls him with the spirit of the old proverb which describes each man as the architect of his own fortune. That means that it is only himself after all of which a man has the usufruct. The other way would be to lay the blame of whatever we experience upon other men, upon unfavourable circumstances, and the like. And this is a fresh example of the language of unfreedom, and at the same time the spring of discontent. If man saw, on the contrary, that whatever happens to him is only the outcome of himself, and that he only bears his own guilt, he would stand free, and in everything that came upon him would have the consciousness that he suffered no wrong. A man who lives in dispeace with himself and his lot, commits much that is perverse and amiss, for no other reason than because of the false opinion that he is wronged by others. No doubt too there is a great deal of chance in what befalls us. But the chance has its root in the 'natural' man. So long however as a man is otherwise conscious that he is free, his harmony of soul and peace of mind will not be destroyed by the disagreeables that befall him. It is their view of necessity, therefore, which is at the root of the content and discontent of men, and which in that way determines their destiny itself.

148. Among the three elements in the process of necessity—the Condition, the Fact, and the Activity—

a. The Condition is (a) what is pre-supposed or ante-stated, *i.e.* it is not only supposed or stated, and so only a correlative to the fact, but also prior, and so independent, a contingent and external circumstance which exists without respect to the fact. While thus contingent, however, this pre-supposed or ante-stated term, in respect withal of the fact, which is the totality, is a complete circle of conditions. (β) The conditions are passive, are used as materials for the fact, into the content of which they thus enter. They are likewise intrinsically conformable to this content, and already contain its whole characteristic.

b. The Fact is also (a) something pre-supposed or ante-stated, *i.e.* it is at first. and as supposed, only inner and possible, and also, being prior, an independent content by itself. (β) By using up the conditions, it receives its external existence, the realisation of the articles of its content, which reciprocally correspond to the conditions, so that whilst it presents itself out of these as the fact, it also proceeds from them.

c. The Activity similarly has (a) an independent existence of its own (as a man, a character), and at the same time it is possible only where the conditions are and the fact. (β) It is the movement which translates the conditions into fact, and the latter into the former as the side of existence, or rather the movement which educes the fact from the conditions in which it is potentially present, and which gives existence to the fact by abolishing the existence possessed by the conditions.

In so far as these three elements stand to each other

in the shape of independent existences, this process has the aspect of an outward necessity. Outward necessity has a limited content for its fact. For the fact is this whole, in phase of singleness. But since in its form this whole is external to itself, it is self-externalised even in its own self and in its content, and this externality, attaching to the fact, is a limit of its content.

149. Necessity, then is potentially the one essence, self-same but now full of content, in the reflected light of which its distinctions take the form of independent realities. This self-sameness is at the same time, as absolute form, the activity which reduces into dependency and mediates into immediacy.—Whatever is necessary is through an other, which is broken up into the mediating ground (the Fact and the Activity) and an immediate actuality or accidental circumstance, which is at the same time a Condition. The necessary, being through an other, is not in and for itself: hypothetical, it is a mere result of assumption. But this intermediation is just as immediately however the abrogation of itself. The ground and contingent condition is translated into immediacy, by which that dependency is now lifted up into actuality, and the fact has closed with itself. In this return to itself the necessary simply and positively *is*, as unconditioned actuality. The necessary is so, mediated through a circle of circumstances: it is so, because the circumstances are so, and at the same time it is so, unmediated: it is so, because it is.

(a) *Relationship of Substantiality.*

150. The necessary is in itself an absolute correlation of elements, i.e. the process developed (in the preceding paragraphs), in which the correlation also suspends itself to absolute identity.

In its immediate form it is the relationship of Substance and Accident. The absolute self-identity of this
relationship is Substance as such, which as necessity
gives the negative to this form of inwardness, and thus
invests itself with actuality, but which also gives the
negative to this outward thing. In this negativity, the
actual, as immediate, is only an accidental which through
this bare possibility passes over into another actuality.
This transition is the identity of substance, regarded as
form-activity.

151. SUBSTANCE is accordingly the totality of the
ACCIDENTS, revealing itself in them as their absolute
negativity, (that is to say, as absolute power,) and at
the same time as the wealth of all content. This content however is nothing but that very revelation, since
the character (being reflected in itself to make content)
is only a passing stage of the form which passes away
in the power of substance. Substantiality is the absolute form-activity and the power of necessity: all content is but a vanishing element which merely belongs to
this process, where there is an absolute revulsion of
form and content into one another.

In the history of philosophy we meet with Substance
as the principle of Spinoza's system. On the import
and value of that much-praised and no less decried
philosophy there has been great misunderstanding and
a deal of talking since the days of Spinoza. The atheism
and, as a further charge, the pantheism of the system
has formed the commonest ground of accusation. These
cries arise because of Spinoza's conception of God as
substance, and substance only. What we are to think
of this charge follows, in the first instance, from the
place which substance takes in the system of the logical
idea. Though an essential stage in the evolution of the
idea, substance is not the same with absolute Idea, but

the idea under the still limited form of necessity. It is
true that God is necessity, or, as we may also put it,
that He is the absolute Thing: He is however no less
the absolute Person. That he is the absolute Person
however is a point which the philosophy of Spinoza
never reached: and on that side it falls short of the true
notion of God which forms the content of religious
consciousness in Christianity. Spinoza was by descent
a Jew; and it is upon the whole the Oriental way of
seeing things, according to which the nature of the finite
world seems frail and transient, that has found its intellectual expression in his system. This Oriental view of
the unity of substance certainly gives the basis for all
real further development. Still it is not the final idea.
It is marked by the absence of the principle of the
Western World, the principle of individuality, which
first appeared under a philosophic shape, contemporaneously with Spinoza, in the Monadology of Leibnitz.

From this point we glance back to the alleged atheism
of Spinoza. The charge will be seen to be unfounded
if we remember that his system, instead of denying God,
rather recognises that He alone really is. Nor can it
be maintained that the God of Spinoza, although he is
described as alone true, is not the true God, and therefore as good as no God. If that were a just charge, it
would only prove that all other systems, where speculation has not gone beyond a subordinate stage of the
idea,—that the Jews and Mohammedans who know God
only as the Lord,—and that even the many Christians
for whom God is merely the most high, unknowable, and
transcendent being, are as much atheists as Spinoza.
The so-called atheism of Spinoza is merely an exaggeration of the fact that he defrauds the principle of difference or finitude of its due. Hence his system, as it
holds that there is properly speaking no world, at any

rate that the world has no positive being, should rather be styled Acosmism. These considerations will also show what is to be said of the charge of Pantheism. If Pantheism means, as it often does, the doctrine which takes finite things in their finitude and in the complex of them to be God, we must acquit the system of Spinoza of the crime of Pantheism. For in that system, finite things and the world as a whole are denied all truth. On the other hand, the philosophy which is Acosmism is for that reason certainly pantheistic.

The shortcoming thus acknowledged to attach to the content turns out at the same time to be a shortcoming in respect of form. Spinoza puts substance at the head of his system, and defines it to be the unity of thought and extension, without demonstrating how he gets to this distinction, or how he traces it back to the unity of substance. The further treatment of the subject proceeds in what is called the mathematical method. Definitions and axioms are first laid down: after them comes a series of theorems, which are proved by an analytical reduction of them to these unproved postulates. Although the system of Spinoza, and that even by those who altogether reject its contents and results, is praised for the strict sequence of its method, such unqualified praise of the form is as little justified as an unqualified rejection of the content. The defect of the content is that the form is not known as immanent in it, and therefore only approaches it as an outer and subjective form. As intuitively accepted by Spinoza without a previous mediation by dialectic, Substance, as the universal negative power, is as it were a dark shapeless abyss which engulfs all definite content as radically null, and produces from itself nothing that has a positive subsistence of its own.

152. At the stage, where substance, as absolute power,

is the self-relating power (itself a merely inner possibility) which thus determines itself to accidentality,—from which power the externality it thereby creates is distinguished—necessity is a correlation strictly so called, just as in the first form of necessity, it is substance. This is the correlation of Causality.

(b) *Relationship and Causality.*

153. Substance is CAUSE, in so far as substance reflects into self as against its passage into accidentality and so stands as the *primary* fact, but again no less suspends this reflection-into-self (its bare possibility), lays itself down as the negative of itself, and thus produces an EFFECT, an actuality, which, though so far only assumed as a sequence, is through the process that effectuates it at the same time necessary.

As primary fact, the cause is qualified as having absolute independence and a subsistence maintained in face of the effect: but in the necessity, whose identity constitutes that primariness itself, it is wholly passed into the effect. So far again as we can speak of a definite content, there is no content in the effect that is not in the cause. That identity in fact is the absolute content itself: but it is no less also the form-characteristic. The primariness of the cause is suspended in the effect in which the cause makes itself a dependent being. The cause however does not for that reason vanish and leave the effect to be alone actual. For this dependency is in like manner directly suspended, and is rather the reflection of the cause in itself, its primariness: in short, it is in the effect that the cause first becomes actual and a cause. The cause consequently is in its full truth *causa sui.*—Jacobi, sticking to the partial conception of mediation (in his Letters on Spinoza, second edit. p. 416), has treated the *causa sui* (and the *effectus sui* is the same), which is the absolute truth of the cause, as a mere formalism. He has also made the remark that God ought to be defined not as the ground of things, but essentially as cause. A more thorough consideration of the nature of cause would have shown that Jacobi did not by this means gain what he intended. Even in the finite cause and its conception we can see this identity between cause and effect in point of content. The rain (the cause) and the wet (the effect) are the self-same existing water. In point of form the cause (rain) is dissipated or lost in the effect (wet): but in that case the result can no longer be described as effect; for without the cause it is nothing, and we should have only the unrelated wet left.

In the common acceptation of the causal relation the cause is finite, to such extent as its content is so (as is also the case with finite substance), and so far as cause and effect are conceived as two several independent existences: which they are, however, only when we leave the causal relation out of sight. In the finite sphere we never get over the difference of the form-characteristics in their relation: and hence we turn the matter round and define the cause also as something dependent or as an effect. This again has another cause, and thus there grows up a progress from effects to causes *ad infinitum.* There is a descending progress too: the effect, looked at in its identity with the cause, is itself defined as a cause, and at the same time as another cause, which again has other effects, and so on for ever.

The way understanding bristles up against the idea of substance is equalled by its readiness to use the relation of cause and effect. Whenever it is proposed to view any sum of fact as necessary, it is especially the relation of causality to which the reflective understanding makes a point of tracing it back. Now, although this relation does undoubtedly belong to necessity, it forms only one aspect in the process of that category. That process equally requires the suspension of the mediation involved in causality and the exhibition of it as simple self-relation. If we stick to causality as such, we have it not in its truth. Such a causality is merely finite, and its finitude lies in retaining the distinction between cause and effect unassimilated. But these two terms, if they are distinct, are also identical. Even in ordinary consciousness that identity may be found. We say that a cause is a cause, only when it has an effect, and *vice versa*. Both cause and effect are thus one and the same content: and the distinction between them is primarily only that the one lays down and the other is laid down. This formal difference however again suspends itself, because the cause is not only a cause of something else, but also a cause of itself; while the effect is not only an effect of something else, but also an effect of itself. The finitude of things consists accordingly in this. While cause and effect are in their notion identical, the two forms present themselves severed so that, though the cause is also an effect, and the effect also a cause, the cause is not an effect in the same connexion as it is a cause, nor the effect a cause in the same connexion as it is an effect. This again gives the infinite progress, in the shape of an endless series of causes, which shows itself at the same time as an endless series of effects.

154. The effect is different from the cause. The former as such has a being dependent on the latter. But such a dependence is likewise reflection-into-self and immediacy: and the action of the cause, as it constitutes the effect, is at the same time the pre-constitution of the effect, so long as effect is kept separate from cause.

There is thus already in existence another substance on which the effect takes place. As immediate, this substance is not a self-related negativity and *active,* but *passive.* Yet it is a substance, and it is therefore active also: it therefore suspends the immediacy it was originally put forward with, and the effect which was put into it: it reacts, *i.e.* suspends the activity of the first substance. But this first substance also in the same way sets aside its own immediacy, or the effect which is put into it; it thus suspends the activity of the other substance and reacts. In this manner causality passes into the relation of ACTION AND REACTION, or RECIPROCITY.

The Reciprocity, although causality is not yet invested with its true characteristic, the rectilinear movement out from causes to effects, and from effects to causes, is bent round and back into itself, and thus the progress *ad infinitum* of causes and effects is, as a progress, really and truly suspended. This bend, which transforms the infinite progression into a self-contained relationship, is here as always the plain reflection that in the above meaningless repetition there is only one and the same thing, viz. one cause and another, and their connexion with one another. Reciprocity—which is the development of this relation—itself however only distinguishes turn and turn about (—not causes), but factors of causation, in each of which—just because they are inseparable (on the principle of the identity that the cause is cause in the effect, and *vice versa*)—the other factor is also equally supposed.

(c) *Reciprocity or Action and Reaction.*

155. The characteristics which in Reciprocal Action are retained as distinct are (*a*) potentially the same.

The one side is a cause, is primary, active, passive, &c., just as the other is. Similarly the pre-supposition of another side and the action upon it, the immediate primariness and the dependence produced by the alternation, are one and the same on both sides. The cause assumed to be first is on account of its immediacy passive, a dependent being, and an effect. The distinction of the causes spoken of as two is accordingly void: and properly speaking there is only one cause, which, while it suspends itself (as substance) in its effect, also rises in this operation only to independent existence as a cause.

156. But this unity of the double cause is also (β) actual. All this alternation is properly the cause in act of constituting itself and in such constitution lies its being. The nullity of the distinctions is not only potential, or a reflection of ours. Reciprocal action just means that each characteristic we impose is also to be suspended and inverted into its opposite, and that in this way the essential nullity of the 'moments' is explicitly stated. An effect is introduced into the primariness; in other words, the primariness is abolished: the action of a cause becomes reaction, and so on.

Reciprocal action realises the causal relation in its complete development. It is this relation, therefore, in which reflection usually takes shelter when the conviction grows that things can no longer be studied satisfactorily from a causal point of view, on account of the infinite progress already spoken of. Thus in historical research the question may be raised in a first form, whether the character and manners of a nation are the cause of its constitution and its laws, or if they are not rather the effect. Then, as the second step, the character and manners on one side and the constitution and laws on the other are conceived on the principles of reciprocity; and in that case the cause in the same connexion as it is a cause will at the same time be an effect, and *vice versa*. The same thing is done in the study of Nature, and especially of living organisms. There the several organs and functions are similarly seen to stand to each other in the relation of reciprocity. Reciprocity is undoubtedly the proximate truth of the relation of cause and effect, and stands, so to say, on the threshold of the notion; but on that very ground, supposing that our aim is a thoroughly comprehensive idea, we should not rest content with applying this relation. If we get no further than studying a given content under the point of view of reciprocity, we are taking up an attitude which leaves matter utterly incomprehensible. We are left with a mere dry fact; and the call for mediation, which is the chief motive in applying the relation of causality, is still unanswered. And if we look more narrowly into the dissatisfaction felt in applying the relation of reciprocity, we shall see that it consists in the circumstance, that this relation, instead of being treated as an equivalent for the notion, ought, first of all, to be known and understood in its own nature. And to understand the relation of action and reaction we must not let the two sides rest in their state of mere given facts, but recognise them, as has been shown in the two paragraphs preceding, for factors of a third and higher, which is the notion and nothing else. To make, for example, the manners of the Spartans the cause of their constitution and their constitution conversely the cause of their manners, may no doubt be in a way correct. But, as we have comprehended neither the manners nor the constitution of the nation, the result of such reflections can never be final or satisfactory. The satisfactory point will be reached only when these two, as well as all other, special aspects of Spartan life and Spartan history are seen to be founded in this notion.

157. This pure self-reciprocation is therefore Necessity unveiled or realised. The link of necessity *qua* necessity is identity, as still inward and concealed, because it is the identity of what are esteemed actual things, although their very self-subsistence is bound to be necessity. The circulation of substance through causality and reciprocity therefore only expressly makes out or states that self-subsistence is the infinite negative self-relation—a relation *negative,* in general, for in it the act of distinguishing and intermediating becomes a primariness of actual things independent one against the other,—and *infinite self-relation,* because their independence only lies in their identity.

158. This truth of necessity, therefore, is *Freedom:* and the truth of substance is the Notion,—an independence which, though self-repulsive into distinct independent elements, yet in that repulsion is self-identical, and in the movement of reciprocity still at home and conversant only with itself.

Necessity is often called hard, and rightly so, if we keep only to necessity as such, *i.e.* to its immediate shape. Here we have, first of all, some state or, generally speaking, fact, possessing an independent subsistence: and necessity primarily implies that there falls upon such a fact something else by which it is brought low. This is what is hard and sad in necessity immediate or abstract. The identity of the two things, which necessity presents as bound to each other and thus bereft of their independence, as at first only inward, and therefore has no existence for those under the yoke of necessity. Freedom too from this point of view is only abstract, and is preserved only by renouncing all that we immediately are and have. But, as we have seen already, the process of necessity is so directed that it overcomes the rigid externality which it first had and reveals its inward nature. It then appears that the members, linked to one another, are not really foreign to each other, but only elements of one whole, each of them, in its connexion with the other, being, as it were, at home, and combining with itself. In this way necessity is transfigured into freedom,—not the freedom that consists in abstract negation, but freedom concrete and positive. From which we may learn what a mistake it is to regard freedom and necessity as mutually exclusive. Necessity indeed *qua* necessity is far from being freedom: yet freedom pre-supposes necessity, and contains it as an unsubstantial element in itself. A good man is aware that the tenor of his conduct is essentially obligatory and necessary. But this consciousness is so far from making any abatement from this freedom, that without it real and reasonable freedom could not be distinguished from arbitrary choice,—a freedom which has no reality and is merely potential. A criminal, when punished, may look upon his punishment as a restriction of his freedom. Really the punishment is not foreign constraint to which he is subjected, but the manifestation of his own act: and if he recognises this, he comports himself as a free man. In short, man is most independent when he knows himself to be determined by the absolute idea throughout. It was this phase of mind and conduct which Spinoza called *Amor intellectualis Dei*.

159. Thus the Notion is the truth of Being and Essence, inasmuch as the shining or show of self-reflection is itself at the same time independent immediacy, and this being of a different actuality is immediately only a shining or show on itself.

The Notion has exhibited itself as the truth of Being

and Essence, as the ground to which the regress of both leads.   Conversely it has been developed out of being as its ground.   The former aspect of the advance may be regarded as a concentration of being into its depth, thereby disclosing its inner nature: the latter aspect as an issuing of the more perfect from the less perfect.   When such development is viewed on the latter side only, it does prejudice to the method of philosophy. The special meaning which these superficial thoughts of more imperfect and more perfect have in this place is to indicate the distinction of being, as an immediate unity with itself, from the notion, as free mediation with itself.   Since being has shown that it is an element in the notion, the latter has thus exhibited itself as the truth of being.   As this is reflection in itself and as an absorption of the mediation, the notion is the pre-supposition of the immediate—a pre-supposition which is identical with the return to self; and in this identity lie freedom and the notion.   If the partial element therefore be called the imperfect, then the notion, or the perfect, is certainly a development from the imperfect; since its very nature is thus to suspend its pre-supposition.   At the same time it is the notion alone which, in the act of supposing itself, makes its pre-supposition; as has been made apparent in causality in general and especially in reciprocal action.

Thus in reference to Being and Essence the Notion is defined as Essence reverted to the simple immediacy of Being,—the shining or show of Essence thereby having actuality, and its actuality being at the same time a free shining or show in itself.   In this manner the notion has being as its simple self-relation, or as the immediacy of its immanent unity.   Being is so poor a category that it is the least thing which can be shown to be found in the notion.

The passage from necessity to freedom, or from actuality into the notion, is the very hardest, because it proposes that independent actuality shall be thought as having all its substantiality in the passing over and identity with the other independent actuality. The notion, too, is extremely hard, because it is itself just this very identity. But the actual substance as such, the cause, which in its exclusiveness resists all invasion, is *ipso facto* subjected to necessity or the destiny of passing into dependency: and it is this subjection rather where the chief hardness lies. To think necessity, on the contrary, rather tends to melt that hardness. For thinking means that, in the other, one meets with one's self.—It means a liberation, which is not the flight of abstraction, but consists in that which is actual having itself not as something else, but as its own being and creation, in the other actuality with which it is bound up by the force of necessity. As existing in an individual form, this liberation is called I: as developed to its totality, it is free Spirit; as feeling, it is Love; and as enjoyment, it is Blessedness.—The great vision of substance in Spinoza is only a potential liberation from finite exclusiveness and egoism: but the notion itself realises for its own both the power of necessity and actual freedom.

When, as now, the notion is called the truth of Being and Essence, we must expect to be asked, why we do not begin with the notion? The answer is that, where knowledge by thought is our aim, we cannot begin with the truth, because the truth, when it forms the beginning, must rest on mere assertion. The truth when it is thought must as such verify itself to thought. If the notion were put at the head of Logic, and defined, quite correctly in point of content, as the unity of Being and Essence, the following question would come up: What are we to think under the terms 'Being' and 'Essence,' and how do they come to be embraced in the unity of the Notion? But if we answered these questions, then our beginning with the notion would be merely nominal. The real start would be made with Being, as we have here done: with this difference, that the characteristics of Being as well as those of Essence would have to be accepted uncritically from figurate conception, whereas we have observed Being and Essence in their own dialectical development and learnt how they lose themselves in the unity of the notion.

VI

THE PHILOSOPHY OF MIND *

SECTION II

Mind Objective.

Translated by William Wallace

483. THE objective Mind is the absolute Idea, but only existing *in posse:* and as it is thus on the territory of finitude, its actual rationality retains the aspect of external apparency. The free will finds itself immediately confronted by differences which arise from the circumstance that freedom is its *inward* function and aim, and is in relation to an external and already subsisting objectivity, which splits up into different heads: viz. anthropological data (i.e. private and personal needs), external things of nature which exist for consciousness, and the ties of relation between individual wills which are conscious of their own diversity and particularity. These aspects constitute the external material for the embodiment of the will.

484. But the purposive action of this will is to realise its concept, Liberty, in these externally-objective aspects, making the latter a world moulded by the former, which in it is thus at home with itself, locked together with it: the concept accordingly perfected to the Idea. Liberty, shaped into the actuality of a world, receives the *form of Necessity* the deeper substantial nexus of

* From *The Encyclopaedia of the Philosophical Sciences.*

which is the system or organisation of the principles of liberty, whilst its phenomenal nexus is power or authority, and the sentiment of obedience awakened in consciousness.

485. This unity of the rational will with the single will (this being the peculiar and immediate medium in which the former is actualised) constitutes the simple actuality of liberty. As it (and its content) belongs to thought, and is the virtual *universal,* the content has its right and true character only in the form of universality. When invested with this character for the intelligent consciousness, or instituted as an authoritative power, it is a *Law.*[1]   When, on the other hand, the content is freed from the mixedness and fortuitousness, attaching to it in the practical feeling and in impulse, and is set and grafted in the individual will, not in the form of impulse, but in its universality, so as to become its habit, temper and character, it exists as manner and custom, or *Usage.*[2]

486. This 'reality,' in general, where free will has *existence,* is the *Law* (Right),—the term being taken in a comprehensive sense not merely as the limited juristic law, but as the actual body of all the conditions of freedom.   These conditions, in relation to the *subjective* will, where they, being universal, ought to have and can only have their existence, are its *Duties;* whereas as its temper and habit they are *Manners.*   What is a right is also a duty, and what is a duty, is also a right.   For a mode of existence is a right, only as a consequence of the free substantial will: and the same content of fact, when referred to the will distinguished as subjective and individual, is a duty.   It is the same content which the subjective consciousness recognises as a duty, and brings

[1] Gesetz.

[2] Sitte.

into existence in these several wills. The finitude of the objective will thus creates the semblance of a distinction between rights and duties.

In the phenomenal range right and duty are *correlata,* at least in the sense that to a right on my part corresponds a duty in some one else. But, in the light of the concept, my right to a thing is not merely possession, but as possession by a *person* it is *property,* or legal possession, and it is a *duty* to possess things as *property,* i.e. to be as a person. Translated into the phenomenal relationship, viz. relation to another person—this grows into the duty of some one *else* to respect *my* right. In the morality of the conscience, duty in general is in me— a free subject—at the same time a right of my subjective will or disposition. But in this individualist moral sphere, there arises the division between what is only inward purpose (disposition or intention), which only has its being in me and is merely subjective duty, and the actualisation of that purpose: and with this division a contingency and imperfection which makes the inadequacy of mere individualistic morality. In social ethics these two parts have reached their truth, their absolute unity; although even right and duty return to one another and combine by means of certain adjustments and under the guise of necessity. The rights of the father of the family over its members are equally duties toward them; just as the children's duty of obedience is their right to be educated to the liberty of manhood. The penal judicature of a government, its rights of administration, &c., are no less its duties to punish, to administer, &c.; as the services of the members of the State in dues, military service, &c., are duties and yet their right to the protection of their private property and of the general substantial life in which they have their root. All the aims of society and the State are the private aim of the individuals.   But the set of adjustments, by which their duties come back to them as the exercise and enjoyment of right, produces an appearance of diversity: and this diversity is increased by the variety of shapes which value assumes in the course of exchange, though it remains intrinsically the same. Still it holds fundamentally good that he who has no rights has no duties and *vice versa.*

Distribution

487. The free will is

A. itself at first immediate, and hence as a single being—the *person:* the existence which the person gives to its liberty is *property.*   The *Right as* right (law) is *formal, abstract right.*

B. When the will is reflected into self, so as to have its existence inside it, and to be thus at the same time characterised as a *particular,* it is the right of the *subjective* will, *morality* of the individual conscience.

C. When the free will is the substantial will, made actual in the subject and conformable to its concept and rendered a totality of necessity,—it is the ethics of actual life in family, civil society, and state.

SUB-SECTION A.

LAW *

(a) PROPERTY.

488. MIND, in the immediacy of its self-secured liberty, is an individual, but one that knows its individuality as an absolutely free will: it is a *person,* in whom

* Das Recht.

the inward sense of this freedom, as in itself still abstract and empty, has its particularity and fulfilment not yet on its own part, but on an external *thing*. This thing, as something devoid of will, has no rights against the subjectivity of intelligence and volition, and is by that subjectivity made adjectival to it, the external sphere of its liberty;—*possession*.

489. By the judgment of possession, at first in the outward appropriation, the thing acquires the predicate of 'mine.' But this predicate, on its own account merely 'practical,' has here the signification that I import my personal will into the thing. As so characterised, possession is *property*, which as possession is a *means*, but as existence of the personality is an *end*.

490. In his property the person is brought into union with itself. But the thing is an abstractly external thing, and the I in it is abstractly external. The concrete return of me into me in the externality is that I, the infinite self-relation, am as a person the repulsion of me from myself, and have the existence of my personality in the *being of other persons,* in my relation to them and in my recognition by them, which is thus mutual.

491. The thing is the *mean* by which the extremes meet in one. These extremes are the persons who, in the knowledge of their identity as free, are simultaneously mutually independent. For them my will has its *definite recognisable existence* in the thing by the immediate bodily act of taking possession, or by the formation of the thing or, it may be, by mere designation of it.

492. The casual aspect of property is that I place my will in *this* thing: so far as my will is *arbitrary,* I can just as well put it in it as not,—just as well withdraw it as not. But so far as my will lies in a thing, it is only I who can withdraw it: it is only with my will that the

thing can pass to another, whose property it similarly becomes only with his will:—*Contract.*

(b) CONTRACT.

493. The two wills and their agreement in the contract are as an *internal* state of mind different from its realisation in the *performance.* The comparatively 'ideal' utterance (of contract) in the *stipulation* contains the actual surrender of a property by the one, its changing hands, and its acceptance by the other will. The contract is thus thoroughly binding: it does not need the performance of the one or the other to become so— otherwise we should have an infinite regress or infinite division of thing, labour, and time. The utterance in the stipulation is complete and exhaustive. The inwardness of the will which surrenders and the will which accepts the property is in the realm of ideation, and in that realm the word is deed and thing—the full and complete deed, since here the conscientiousness of the will does not come under consideration (as to whether the thing is meant in earnest or is a deception), and the will refers only to the external thing.

494. Thus in the stipulation we have the *substantial* being of the contract standing out in distinction from its real utterance in the performance, which is brought down to a mere sequel. In this way there is put into the thing or performance a distinction between its immediate specific *quality* and its substantial being or *value,* meaning by value the quantitative terms into which that qualitative feature has been translated. One piece of property is thus made comparable with another, and may be made equivalent to a thing which is (in quality) wholly heterogeneous. It is thus treated in general as an abstract, universal thing or commodity.

495. The contract, as an agreement which has a voluntary origin and deals with a casual commodity, involves at the same time the giving to this 'accidental' will a positive fixity. This will may just as well not be conformable to law (right), and, in that case, produces a *wrong:* by which however the absolute law (right) is not superseded, but only a relationship originated of right to wrong.

(c) RIGHT *versus* WRONG.

496. Law (right) considered as the realisation of liberty in externals, breaks up into a multiplicity of relations to this external sphere and to other persons. In this way there are (1) several titles or grounds at law, of which (seeing that property both on the personal and the real side is exclusively individual) only one is the right, but which, because they face each other, each and all are invested with a *show* of right, against which the former is defined as the intrinsically right.

497. Now so long as (compared against this show) the one intrinsically right, still presumed identical with the several titles, is affirmed, willed, and recognised, the only diversity lies in this, that the special thing is subsumed under the one law or right by the *particular* will of *these* several persons. This is naïve, non-malicious wrong. Such wrong in the several claimants is a simple *negative judgment,* expressing the *civil suit.* To settle it there is required a third judgment, which, as the judgment of the intrinsically right, is disinterested, and a power of giving the one right existence as against that semblance.

498. But (2) if the semblance of right is willed as such *against* right intrinsical by the particular will, which thus becomes *wicked,* then the external *recognition*

of right is separated from the right's true value; and while the former only is respected, the latter is violated. This gives the wrong of *fraud*—the infinite judgment as identical,—where the nominal relation is retained, but the sterling value is let slip.

499. (3) Finally, the particular will sets itself in opposition to the intrinsic right by negating that right itself as well as its recognition or semblance. [Here there is a negatively infinite judgment in which there is denied the class as a whole, and not merely the particular mode—in this case the apparent recognition.] Thus the will is violently wicked, and commits a *crime*.

500. As an outrage on right, such an action is essentially and actually null. In it the agent, as a volitional and intelligent being, sets up a law—a law however which is nominal and recognised by him only—a universal which holds good *for him,* and under which he has at the same time subsumed himself by his action. To display the nullity of such an act, to carry out simultaneously this nominal law and the intrinsic right, in the first instance by means of a subjective individual will, is the work of *Revenge.* But, revenge, starting from the interest of an immediate particular personality, is at the same time only a new outrage; and so on without end. This progression, like the last, abolishes itself in a third judgment, which is disinterested—*punishment.*

501. The instrumentality by which authority is given to intrinsic right is (a) that a particular will, that of the judge, being conformable to the right, has an interest to turn against the crime (—which in the first instance, in revenge, is a matter of chance), and (β) that an executive power (also in the first instance casual) negates the negation of right that was created by the criminal. This negation of right has its existence in the will of the criminal; and consequently revenge or

punishment directs itself against the person or property of the criminal and exercises *coercion* upon him. It is in this legal sphere that coercion in general has possible scope,—compulsion against the thing, in seizing and maintaining it against another's seizure: for in this sphere the will has its existence immediately in externals as such, or in corporeity, and can be seized only in this quarter. But more than *possible* compulsion is not, so long as I can withdraw myself as free from every mode of existence, even from the range of all existence, i.e. from life. It is legal only as abolishing a first and original compulsion.

502. A distinction has thus emerged between the law (right) and the subjective will. The 'reality' of right, which the personal will in the first instance gives itself in immediate wise, is seen to be due to the instrumentality of the subjective will,—whose influence as on one hand it gives existence to the essential right, so may on the other cut itself off from and oppose itself to it. Conversely, the claim of the subjective will to be in this abstraction a power over the law of right is null and empty of itself: it gets truth and reality essentially only so far as that will in itself realises the reasonable will. As such it is *morality* [1] proper.

The phrase 'Law of Nature,' or Natural Right,[2] in use for the philosophy of law involves the ambiguity that it may mean either right or something existing ready-formed in nature, or right as governed by the nature of things, i.e. by the notion. The former used to be the common meaning, accompanied with the fiction of a *state of nature,* in which the law of nature should hold sway; whereas the social and political state rather required and implied a restriction of liberty and a sac-

[1] Moralität.
[2] Naturrecht.

rifice of natural rights. The real fact is that the whole
law and its every article are based on free personality
alone,—on self-determination or autonomy, which is the
very contrary of determination by nature. The law of
nature—strictly so called—is for that reason the predominance of the strong and the reign of force, and a
state of nature a state of violence and wrong, of which
nothing truer can be said than that one ought to depart
from it. The social state, on the other hand, is the
condition in which alone right has its actuality: what is
to be restricted and sacrificed is just the wilfulness and
violence of the state of nature.

SUB-SECTION B.

THE MORALITY OF CONSCIENCE.*

503. The free individual, who, in mere law, counts
only as a *person,* is now characterised as a *subject,*—a
will reflected into itself so that, be its affection what it
may, it is distinguished (as existing in it) as *its own*
from the existence of freedom in an external thing. Because the affection of the will is thus inwardised, the
will is at the same time made a particular, and there
arise further particularisations of it and relations of
these to one another. This affection is partly the essential and implicit will, the reason of the will, the essential
basis of law and moral life: partly it is the existent
volition, which is before us and throws itself into actual
deeds, and thus comes into relationship with the former.
The subjective will is *morally* free, so far as these features are its inward institution, its own, and willed by it.
Its utterance in deed with this freedom is an *action,* in
the externality of which it only admits as its own, and
* Moralität.

allows to be imputed to it, so much as it has consciously willed.

This subjective or 'moral' freedom is what a European especially calls freedom. In virtue of the right thereto a man must possess a personal knowledge of the distinction between good and evil in general: ethical and religious principles shall not merely lay their claim on him as external laws and precepts of authority to be obeyed, but have their assent, recognition, or even justification in his heart, sentiment, conscience, intelligence, &c. The subjectivity of the will in itself is its supreme aim and absolutely essential to it.

The 'moral' must be taken in the wider sense in which it does not signify the morally good merely. In French *le moral* is opposed to *le physique,* and means the mental or intellectual in general. But here the moral signifies volitional mode, so far as it is in the interior of the will in general; it thus includes purpose and intention,—and also moral wickedness.

a. PURPOSE.*

504. So far as the action comes into immediate touch with *existence, my part* in it is to this extent formal, that external existence is also *independent* of the agent. This externality can pervert his action and bring to light something else than lay in it. Now, though any alteration as such, which is set on foot by the subject's action, is its *deed,*† still the subject does not for that reason recognise it as its *action,*‡ but only admits as its own that existence in the deed which lay in its knowledge

* Der Vorsatz.
† Handlung.
‡ That.

and will, which was its *purpose*. Only for that does it hold itself responsible.

b. INTENTION AND WELFARE.*

505. As regards its empirically concrete *content* (1) the action has a variety of particular aspects and connexions.   In point of *form,* the agent must have known and willed the action in its essential feature, embracing these individual points.   This is the right of *intention.* While *purpose* affects only the immediate fact of existence, *intention* regards the underlying essence and aim thereof.   (2) The agent has no less the right to see that the particularity of content in the action, in point of its matter, is not something external to him, but is a particularity of his own,—that it contains his needs, interests, and aims.   These aims, when similarly comprehended in a single aim, as in happiness, constitute his *well-being*.   This is the right to well-being. Happiness (good fortune) is distinguished from well-being only in this, that happiness implies no more than some sort of immediate existence, whereas well-being regards it as also justified as regards morality.

506. But the essentiality of the intention is in the first instance the abstract form of generality.   Reflection can put in this form this and that particular aspect in the empirically-concrete action, thus making it essential to the intention or restricting the intention to it.   In this way the supposed essentiality of the intention and the real essentiality of the action may be brought into the greatest contradiction—e.g. a good intention in case of a crime.   Similarly well-being is abstract and may be set on this or that: as appertaining to this single agent, it is always something particular.

* Die Absicht und das Wohl.

c. GOODNESS AND WICKEDNESS.*

507. The truth of these particularities and the concrete unity of their formalism is the content of the universal, essential and actual, will,—the law and underlying essence of every phase of volition, the essential and
actual good. It is thus the absolute final aim of the
world, and *duty* for the agent who *ought* to have *insight*
into the *good*, make it his *intention* and bring it about
by his activity.

508. But though the good is the universal of will—a
universal determined in itself,—and thus including in it
particularity,—still so far as this particularity is in the
first instance still abstract, there is no principle at hand
to determine it. Such determination therefore starts
up also outside that universal; and as heteronomy or
determinance of a will which is free and has rights of
its own, there awakes here the deepest contradiction.
(*a*) In consequence of the indeterminate determinism of
the good, there are always *several sorts* of good and
many kinds of duties, the variety of which is a dialectic
of one against another and brings them into *collision.*
At the same time because good is one, they *ought* to
stand in harmony; and yet each of them, though it is
a particular duty, is as good and as duty absolute. It
falls upon the agent to be the dialectic which, superseding this absolute claim of each, concludes such a
combination of them as excludes the rest.

509. (*β*) To the agent, who in his existent sphere of
liberty is essentially as a *particular,* his *interest and
welfare* must, on account of that existent sphere of liberty, be essentially an aim and therefore a duty. But at
the same time in aiming at the good, which is the not-

* Das Gute und das Böse.

particular but only universal of the will, the particular
interest *ought* not to be a constituent motive.   On account of this independency of the two principles of
action, it is likewise an accident whether they harmonise.
And yet they *ought* to harmonise, because the agent, as
individual and universal, is always fundamentally one
identity.

(γ) But the agent is not only a mere particular in
his existence; it is also a form of his existence to be
an abstract self-certainty, an abstract reflection of freedom into himself.   He is thus distinct from the reason
in the will, and capable of making the universal itself
a particular and in that way a semblance.   The good
is thus reduced to the level of a mere 'may happen' for
the agent, who can therefore resolve itself to somewhat
opposite to the good, can be wicked.

510. (δ) The external objectivity, following the distinction which has arisen in the subjective will, constitutes a peculiar world of its own,—another extreme
which stands in no rapport with the internal will-deter-
mination.   It is thus a matter of chance, whether it har-
monises with the subjective aims, whether the good is
realised, and the wicked, an aim essentially and actually
null, nullified in it: it is no less matter of chance
whether the agent finds in it his well-being, and more
precisely whether in the world the good agent is happy
and the wicked unhappy.   But at the same time the
world *ought* to allow the good action, the essential
thing, to be carried out in it; it *ought* to grant the good
agent the satisfaction of his particular interest, and
refuse it to the wicked; just as it *ought* also to make
the wicked itself null and void.

511. The all-round contradiction, expressed by this
repeated *ought,* with its absoluteness which yet at the
same time is *not*—contains the most abstract 'analysis'

of the mind in itself, its deepest descent into itself. The
only relation the self-contradictory principles have to
one another is in the abstract certainty of self; and for
this infinitude of subjectivity the universal will, good,
right, and duty, no more exist than not. The subjectivity alone is aware of itself as choosing and deciding.
This pure self-certitude, rising to its pitch, appears in
the two directly interchanging forms—of *Conscience*
and *Wickedness*. The former is the will of goodness;
but a goodness which to this pure subjectivity is the *non-
objective*, non-universal, the unutterable; and over which
the agent is conscious that *he* in his *individuality* has
the decision. Wickedness is the same awareness that
the single self possesses the decision, so far as the
single self does not merely remain in this abstraction,
but takes up the content of a subjective interest contrary to the good.

512. This supreme pitch of the *'phenomenon'* of will,
—sublimating itself to this absolute vanity—to a goodness, which has no objectivity, but is only sure of itself,
and a self-assurance which involves the nullification of
the universal—collapses by its own force. Wickedness,
as the most intimate reflection of subjectivity itself, in
opposition to the objective and universal, (which it
treats as mere sham,) is the same as the good sentiment
of abstract goodness, which reserves to the subjectivity
the determination thereof:—the utterly abstract semblance, the bare perversion and annihilation of itself.
The result, the truth of this semblance, is, on its negative
side, the absolute nullity of this volition which would
fain hold its own against the good, and of the good,
which would only be abstract. On the affirmative side,
in the notion, this semblance thus collapsing is the same
simple universality of the will, which is the good. The
subjectivity, in this its *identity* with the good, is only

the infinite form, which actualises and developes it.   In this way the standpoint of bare reciprocity between two independent sides,—the standpoint of the *ought,* is abandoned, and we have passed into the field of ethical life.

SUB-SECTION C.

THE MORAL LIFE, OR SOCIAL ETHICS.*

513. The moral life is the perfection of spirit objective—the truth of the subjective and objective spirit itself.   The failure of the latter consists—partly in having its freedom *immediately* in reality, in something external therefore, in a thing,—partly in the abstract universality of its goodness.   The failure of spirit subjective similarly consists in this, that it is, as against the universal, abstractly self-determinant in its inward individuality.   When these two imperfections are suppressed, subjective *freedom* exists as the covertly and overtly *universal* rational will, which is sensible of itself and actively disposed in the consciousness of the individual subject, whilst its practical operation and immediate universal *actuality* at the same time exist as moral usage, manner and custom,—where self-conscious *liberty* has become *nature.*

514. The consciously free substance, in which the absolute 'ought' is no less an 'is,' has actuality as the spirit of a nation.   The abstract disruption of this spirit singles it out into *persons,* whose independence it however controls and entirely dominates from within.   But the person, as an intelligent being, feels that underlying essence to be his own very being—ceases when so minded to be mere accident of it—looks upon it as his absolute

* Die Sittlichkeit.

final aim. In its actuality he sees not less an achieved present, than somewhat he brings it about by his action, —yet somewhat which without all question *is*. Thus, without any selective reflection, the person performs its duty as *his own* and as something which *is;* and in this necessity he has himself and his actual freedom.

515. Because the substance is the absolute unity of individuality and universality of freedom, it follows that the actuality and action of each individual to keep and to take care of his own being, while it is on one hand conditioned by the pre-supposed total in whose complex alone he exists, is on the other a transition into a universal product.—The social disposition of the individuals is their sense of the substance, and of the identity of all their interests with the total; and that the other individuals mutually know each other and are actual only in this identity, is confidence (trust)—the genuine ethical temper.

516. The relations between individuals in the several situations to which the substance is particularised form their *ethical duties*. The ethical personality, i.e. the subjectivity which is permeated by the substantial life, is *virtue*. In relation to the bare facts of external being, to *destiny,* virtue does not treat them as a mere negation, and is thus a quiet repose in itself: in relation to substantial objectivity, to the total of ethical actuality, it exists as confidence, as deliberate work for the community, and the capacity of sacrificing self thereto; whilst in relation to the incidental relations of social circumstance, it is in the first instance justice and then benevolence. In the latter sphere, and in its attitude to its own visible being and corporeity, the individuality expresses its special character, temperament, &c. as personal *virtues*.

517. The ethical substance is

AA. as 'immediate' or *natural* mind,—the *Family*.

BB. The 'relative' totality of the 'relative' relations of the individuals as independent persons to one another in a formal universality—*Civil Society*.

CC. The self-conscious substance, as the mind developed to an organic actuality—the *Political Constitution*.

AA. THE FAMILY.

518. The ethical spirit, in its *immediacy,* contains the natural factor that the individual has its substantial existence in its natural universal, i.e. in its kind. This is the sexual tie, elevated however to a spiritual significance,—the unanimity of love and the temper of trust. In the shape of the family, mind appears as feeling.

519. (1) The physical difference of sex thus appears at the same time as a difference of intellectual and moral type. With their exclusive individualities these personalities combine to form a *single person:* the subjective union of hearts, becoming a 'substantial' unity, makes this union an ethical tie—*Marriage*. The 'substantial' union of hearts makes marriage an indivisible personal bond—monogamic marriage: the bodily conjunction is a sequel to the moral attachment. A further sequel is community of personal and private interests.

520. (2) By the community in which the various members constituting the family stand in reference to property, the property of the one person (representing the family) acquires an ethical interest, as do also its industry, labour, and care for the future.

521. The ethical principle which is conjoined with the natural generation of the children, and which was as-

sumed to have primary importance in first forming the marriage union, is actually realised in the second or spiritual birth of the children,—in educating them to independent personality.

522. (3) The children, thus invested with independence, leave the concrete life and action of the family to which they primarily belong, acquire an existence of their own, destined however to found anew such an actual family. Marriage is of course broken up by the *natural* element contained in it, the death of husband and wife: but even their union of hearts, as it is a mere 'substantiality' of feeling, contains the germ of liability to chance and decay. In virtue of such fortuitousness, the members of the family take up to each other the status of persons; and it is thus that the family finds introduced into it for the first time the element, originally foreign to it, of *legal* regulation.

BB. CIVIL SOCIETY.*

523. As the substance, being an intelligent substance, particularises itself abstractly into many persons (the family is only a single person), into families or individuals, who exist independent and free, as private persons, it loses its ethical character: for these persons as such have in their consciousness and as their aim not the absolute unity, but their own petty selves and particular interests. Thus arises the system of *atomistic:* by which the substance is reduced to a general system of adjustments to connect self-subsisting extremes and their particular interests. The developed totality of this connective system is the state as civil society, or *state external.*

* Die bürgerliche Gesellschaft.

a. The System of Wants.*

524. (a) The particularity of the persons includes in the first instance their wants. The possibility of satisfying these wants is here laid on the social fabric, the general stock from which all derive their satisfaction. In the condition of things in which this method of satisfaction by indirect adjustment is realised, immediate seizure of external objects as means thereto exists barely or not at all: the objects are already property. To acquire them is only possible by the intervention, on one hand, of the possessors' will, which as particular has in view the satisfaction of their variously defined interests; while on the other hand it is conditioned by the ever continued production of fresh means of exchange by the exchangers' own labour. This instrument, by which the labour of all facilitates satisfaction of wants, constitutes the general stock.

525. (β) The glimmer of universal principle in this particularity of wants is found in the way intellect creates differences in them, and thus causes an indefinite multiplication both of wants and of means for their different phases. Both are thus rendered more and more abstract. This 'morcellement' of their content by abstraction gives rise to the *division of labour*. The habit of this abstraction in enjoyment, information, feeling and demeanour, constitutes training in this sphere, or nominal culture in general.

526. The labour which thus becomes more abstract tends on one hand by its uniformity to make labour easier and to increase production,—on another to limit each person to a single kind of technical skill, and thus produce more unconditional dependence on the social sys-

* Das System der Bedürfnisse.

tem.   The skill itself becomes in this way mechanical, and gets the capability of letting the machine take the place of human labour.

527. (γ) But the concrete division of the general stock—which is also a general business (of the whole society)—into particular masses determined by the factors of the notion,—masses each of which possesses its own basis of subsistence, and a corresponding mode of labour, of needs, and of means for satisfying them, besides of aims and interests, as well as of mental culture and habit—constitutes the difference of Estates (orders or ranks).   Individuals apportion themselves to these according to natural talent, skill, option and accident. As belonging to such a definite and stable sphere, they have their actual existence, which as existence is essentially a particular; and in it they have their social morality, which is *honesty,* their recognition and their *honour.*

Where civil society, and with it the State, exists, there arise the several estates in their difference: for the universal substance, as vital, exists only so far as it organically *particularises* itself.   The history of constitutions is the history of the growth of these estates, of the legal relationships of individuals to them, and of these estates to one another and to their centre.

528. To the 'substantial,' natural estate the fruitful soil and ground supply a natural and stable capital; its action gets direction and content through natural features, and its moral life is founded on faith and trust. The second, the 'reflected' estate has as its allotment the social capital, the medium created by the action of middlemen, of mere agents, and an ensemble of contingencies, where the individual has to depend on his subjective skill, talent, intelligence and industry.   The third, 'thinking' estate has for its business the general

interests; like the second it has a subsistence procured
by means of its own skill, and like the first a certain subsistence, certain however because guaranteed through
the whole society.

b. Administration of Justice.*

529. When matured through the operation of natural
need and free option into a system of universal relationships and a regular course of external necessity, the
principle of casual particularity gets that stable articulation which liberty requires in the shape of *formal
right*. (1) The actualisation which right gets in this
sphere of mere practical intelligence is that it be
brought to consciousness as the stable universal, that
it be known and stated in its specificality with the voice
of authority—the *Law*.†

The *positive* element in laws concerns only their form
of *publicity* and *authority*—which makes it possible for
them to be known by all in a customary and external
way. Their content *per se* may be reasonable—or it
may be unreasonable and so wrong. But when right,
in the course of definite manifestation, is developed in
detail, and its content analyses itself to gain definiteness,
this analysis, because of the finitude of its materials,
falls into the falsely infinite progress: the *final* definiteness, which is absolutely essential and causes a break in
this progress of unreality, can in this sphere of finitude
be attained only in a way that savours of contingency
and arbitrariness. Thus whether three years, ten tha-
lers, or only $2\frac{1}{2}$, $2\frac{3}{4}$, $2\frac{4}{5}$ years, and so on *ad infinitum,* be the right and just thing, can by no means be

* Die Rechtspflege.
† Gesetz.

decided on intelligible principles,—and yet it should be decided. Hence, though of course only at the final points of deciding, on the side of external existence, the 'positive' principle naturally enters law as contingency and arbitrariness. This happens and has from of old happened in all legislations: the only thing wanted is clearly to be aware of it, and not be misled by the talk and the pretence as if the ideal of law were, or could be, to be, at *every* point, determined through reason or legal intelligence, on purely reasonable and intelligent grounds. It is a futile perfectionism to have such expectations and to make such requirements in the sphere of the finite.

There are some who look upon laws as an evil and a profanity, and who regard governing and being governed from natural love, hereditary divinity or nobility, by faith and trust, as the genuine order of life, while the reign of law is held an order of corruption and injustice. These people forget that the stars—and the cattle too—are governed and well governed too by laws;—laws however which are only internally in these objects, not for *them,* not as laws *set to* them:—whereas it is man's privilege to *know* his law. They forget therefore that he can truly obey only such known law,—even as his law can only be a just law, as it is a *known* law;—though in other respects it must be in its essential content contingency and caprice, or at least be mixed and polluted with such elements.

The same empty requirement of perfection is employed for an opposite thesis—viz. to support the opinion that a code is impossible or impracticable. In this case there comes in the additional absurdity of putting essential and universal provisions in one class with the particular detail. The finite material is definable on

and on to the false infinite: but this advance is not, as
in the mental images of space, a generation of new
spatial characteristics of the same quality as those
preceding them, but an advance into greater and ever
greater speciality by the acumen of the analytic intellect, which discovers new distinctions, which again make
new decisions necessary. To provisions of this sort
one may give the name of *new* decisions or *new* laws;
but in proportion to the gradual advance in specialisa-
tion the interest and value of these provisions declines.
They fall within the already subsisting 'substantial,'
general laws, like improvements on a floor or a door,
within the house—which though something *new,* are not
a new *house.* But there is a contrary case. If the
legislation of a rude age began with single provisos,
which go on by their very nature always increasing
their number, there arises, with the advance in multitude, the need of a simpler code,—the need i.e. of embracing that lot of singulars in their general features.
To find and be able to express these principles well
beseems an intelligent and civilised nation. Such a
gathering up of single rules into general forms, first
really deserving the name of laws, has lately been begun
in some directions by the English Minister Peel, who
has by so doing gained the gratitude, even the admiration, of his countrymen.

530. (2) The positive form of Laws—to be *pro-*
mulgated and made known as laws—is a condition of
the *external obligation* to obey them; inasmuch as, being
laws of strict right, they touch only the abstract will,—
itself at bottom external—not the moral or ethical will.
The subjectivity to which the will has in this direction
a right is here only publicity. This subjective existence
is as existence of the essential and developed truth in

this sphere of Right at the same time an externally objective existence, as universal authority and necessity.

The legality of property and of private transactions concerned therewith—in consideration of the principle that all law must be promulgated, recognised, and thus become authoritative—gets its universal guarantee through *formalities*.

531. (3) Legal forms get the necessity, to which objective existence determines itself, in the *judicial system*. Abstract right has to exhibit itself to the *court* —to the individualised right—as *proven:*—a process in which there may be a difference between what is abstractly right and what is provably right. The court takes cognisance and action in the interest of right as such, deprives the existence of right of its contingency, and in particular transforms this existence,—as this exists as revenge—into *punishment*.

The comparison of the two species, or rather two elements in the judicial conviction, bearing on the actual state of the case in relation to the accused,—(1) according as that conviction is based on mere circumstances and other people's witness alone,—or (2) in addition requires the confession of the accused, constitutes the main point in the question of the so-called jury-courts. It is an essential point that the two ingredients of a judicial cognisance, the judgment as to the state of the fact, and the judgment as application of the law to it, should, as at bottom different sides, be exercised as *different functions*. By the said institution they are allotted even to bodies differently qualified,—from the one of which individuals belonging to the official judiciary are expressly excluded. To carry this separation of functions up to this separation in the courts rests rather on extra-essential considerations:

the main point remains only the separate performance of these essentially different functions.—It is a more important point whether the confession of the accused is or is not to be made a condition of penal judgment. The institution of the jury-court loses sight of this condition. The point is that on this ground certainty is completely inseparable from truth: but the confession is to be regarded as the very acme of certainty-giving which in its nature is subjective. The final decision therefore lies with the confession. To this therefore the accused has an absolute right, if the proof is to be made final and the judges to be convinced. No doubt this factor is incomplete, because it is only one factor; but still more incomplete is the other when no less abstractly taken,—viz. mere circumstantial evidence. The jurors are essentially judges and pronounce a judgment. In so far, then, as all they have to go on are such objective proofs, whilst at the same time their defect of certainty (incomplete in so far as it is only *in them*) is admitted, the jury-court shows traces of its barbaric origin in a confusion and admixture between objective proofs and subjective or so-called 'moral' conviction.—It is easy to call *extraordinary* punishments an absurdity; but the fault lies rather with the shallowness which takes offence at a mere name. Materially the principle involves the difference of objective probation according as it goes with or without the factor of absolute certification which lies in confession.

532. The function of judicial administration is only to actualise to necessity the abstract side of personal liberty in civil society. But this actualisation rests at first on the particular subjectivity of the judge, since here as yet there is not found the necessary unity of it with right in the abstract. Conversely, the blind neces-

sity of the system of wants is not lifted up into the consciousness of the universal, and worked from that period of view.

C. *Police and Corporation.**

533. Judicial administration naturally has no concern with such part of actions and interests as belongs only to particularity, and leaves to chance not only the occurrence of crimes but also the care for public weal. In civil society the sole end is to satisfy want—and that, because it is man's want, in a uniform general way, so as to *secure* this satisfaction. But the machinery of social necessity leaves in many ways a casualness about this satisfaction. This is due to the variability of the wants themselves, in which opinion and subjective good-pleasure play a great part. It results also from circumstances of locality, from the connexions between nation and nation, from errors and deceptions which can be foisted upon single members of the social circulation and are capable of creating disorder in it,—as also and especially from the unequal capacity of individuals to take advantage of that general stock. The onward march of this necessity also sacrifices the very particularities by which it is brought about, and does not itself contain the affirmative aim of securing the satisfaction of individuals. So far as concerns them, it *may* be far from beneficial: yet here the individuals are the morally-justifiable end.

534. To keep in view this general end, to ascertain the way in which the powers composing that social necessity act, and their variable ingredients, and to maintain that end in them and against them, is the work

* Die Polizei und die Corporation.

of an institution which assumes on *one* hand, to the concrete of civil society, the position of an external universality. Such an order acts with the power of an external state, which, in so far as it is rooted in the higher or substantial state, appears as state-'police.' On the *other* hand, in this sphere of particularity the only recognition of the aim of substantial universality and the only carrying of it out is restricted to the business of particular branches and interests. Thus we have the *corporation,* in which the particular citizen in his private capacity finds the securing of his stock, whilst at the same time he in it emerges from his single private interest, and has a conscious activity for a comparatively universal end, just as in his legal and professional duties he has his social morality.

CC. THE STATE.

535. The State is the *self-conscious* ethical substance, the unification of the family principle with that of civil society. The same unity, which is the family as a feeling of love, is its essence, receiving however at the same time through the second principle of conscious and spontaneously active volition the *form* of conscious universality. The universal principle, with all its evolution in detail, is the absolute aim and content of the knowing subject, which thus identifies itself in its volition with the system of reasonableness.

536. The state is (a) its inward structure as a self-relating development—constitutional (inner-state) law: (β) a particular individual, and therefore in connexion with other particular individuals,—international (outer-state) law; (γ) but these particular minds are only stages in the general development of mind in its actuality: universal history.

*a. Constitutional Law.**

537. The essence of the state is the universal, self-originated and self-developed,—the reasonable spirit of will; but, as self-knowing and self-actualising, sheer subjectivity, and—as an actuality—one individual. Its *work* generally—in relation to the extreme of individuality as the multitude of individuals—consists in a double function. First it maintains them as persons, thus making right a necessary actuality, then it promotes their welfare, which each originally takes care of for himself, but which has a thoroughly general side; it protects the family and guides civil society. Secondly, it carries back both, and the whole disposition and action of the individual—whose tendency is to become a centre of his own—into the life of the universal substance; and, in this direction, as a free power it interferes with those subordinate spheres and retains them in substantial immanence.

538. The laws express the special provisions for objective freedom. First, to the immediate agent, his independent self-will and particular interest, they are restrictions. But, secondly, they are an absolute final end and the universal work: hence they are a product of the 'functions' of the various orders which parcel themselves more and more out of the general particularising, and are a fruit of all the acts and private concerns of individuals. Thirdly, they are the substance of the volition of individuals—which volition is thereby free—and of their disposition: being as such exhibited as current usage.

539. As a living mind, the state only is as an organised whole, differentiated into particular agencies, which, proceeding from the one notion (though not known as

* Inneres Staatsrecht.

notion) of the reasonable will, continually produce it as their result. The *constitution* is this articulation or organisation of state-power. It provides for the reasonable will,—in so far as it is in the individuals only *implicitly* the universal will,—coming to a consciousness and an understanding of itself and being *found;* also for that will being put in actuality, through the action of the government and its several branches, and not left to perish, but protected both against *their* casual subjectivity and against that of the individuals. The constitution is existent *justice,*—the actuality of liberty in the development of all its reasonable provisions.

Liberty and Equality are the simple rubrics into which is frequently concentrated what should form the fundamental principle, the final aim and result of the constitution. However true this is, the defect of these terms is their utter abstractness: if stuck to in this abstract form, they are principles which either prevent the rise of the concreteness of the state, i.e. its articulation into a constitution and a government in general, or destroy them. With the state there arises inequality, the difference of governing powers and of governed, magistracies, authorities, directories, &c. The principle of equality, logically carried out, rejects all differences, and thus allows no sort of political condition to exist. Liberty and equality are indeed the foundation of the state, but as the most abstract also the most superficial, and for that very reason naturally the most familiar. It is important therefore to study them closer.

As regards, first, Equality, the familiar proposition, All men are by nature equal, blunders by confusing the 'natural' with the 'notion.' It ought rather to read: *By nature* men are only unequal. But the notion of liberty, as it exists as such, without further specification and development, is abstract subjectivity, as a person capable of property. This single abstract feature of personality constitutes the actual *equality* of human beings. But that this freedom should exist, that it should be *man* (and not as in Greece, Rome, &c. *some* men) that is recognised and legally regarded as a person, is so little *by nature,* that it is rather only a result and product of the consciousness of the deepest principle of mind, and of the universality and expansion of this consciousness. That the citizens are equal before the law contains a great truth, but which so expressed is a tautology: it only states that the legal status in general exists, that the laws rule. But, as regards the concrete, the citizens—besides their personality—are equal before the law only in these points when they are otherwise equal *outside the law.* Only that equality which (in whatever way it be) they, as it happens, otherwise have in property, age, physical strength, talent, skill, &c.—or even in crime, can and ought to make them deserve equal treatment before the law:—only it can make them—as regards taxation, military service, eligibility to office, &c.—punishment, &c.—equal in the concrete. The laws themselves, except in so far as they concern that narrow circle of personality, presuppose unequal conditions, and provide for the unequal legal duties and appurtenances resulting therefrom.

As regards Liberty, it is originally taken partly in a negative sense against arbitrary intolerance and lawless treatment, partly in the affirmative sense of subjective freedom; but this freedom is allowed great latitude both as regards the agent's self-will and action for his particular ends, and as regards his claim to have a personal intelligence and a personal share in general affairs. Formerly the legally defined rights, private as well as public rights of a nation, town, &c. were called its 'liberties.' Really, every genuine law is a liberty:

it contains a reasonable principle of objective mind; in other words, it embodies a liberty. Nothing has become, on the contrary, more familiar than the idea that each must *restrict* his liberty in relation to the liberty of others: that the state is a condition of such reciprocal restriction, and that the laws are restrictions. To such habits of mind liberty is viewed as only casual good-pleasure and self-will. Hence it has also been said that 'modern' nations are only susceptible of equality, or of equality more than liberty: and that for no other reason than that, with an assumed definition of liberty (chiefly the participation of all in political affairs and actions), it was impossible to make ends meet in actuality—which is at once more reasonable and more powerful than abstract presuppositions. On the contrary, it should be said that it is just the great development and maturity of form in modern states which produces the supreme concrete inequality of individuals in actuality: while, through the deeper reasonableness of laws and the greater stability of the legal state, it gives rise to greater and more stable liberty, which it can without incompatibility allow. Even the superficial distinction of the words liberty and equality points to the fact that the former tends to inequality: whereas, on the contrary, the current notions of liberty only carry us back to equality. But the more we fortify liberty,—as security of property, as possibility for each to develop and make the best of his talents and good qualities, the more it gets taken for granted: and then the sense and appreciation of liberty especially turns in a *subjective* direction. By this is meant the liberty to attempt action on every side, and to throw oneself at pleasure in action for particular and for general intellectual interests, the removal of all checks on the individual particularity, as well as the inward liberty in which the subject has

principles, has an insight and conviction of his own, and
thus gains moral independence. But this liberty itself
on one hand implies the supreme differentiation in which
men are unequal and make themselves more unequal by
education; and on another it only grows up under conditions of that objective liberty, and is and could grow
to such height only in modern states. If, with this
development of particularity, there be simultaneous and
endless increase of the number of wants, and of the
difficulty of satisfying them, of the lust of argument
and the fancy of detecting faults, with its insatiate
vanity, it is all but part of that indiscriminating relaxation of individuality in this sphere which generates all
possible complications, and must deal with them as it
can. Such a sphere is of course also the field of restrictions, because liberty is there under the taint of
natural self-will and self-pleasing, and has therefore
to restrict itself: and that, not merely with regard to
the naturalness, self-will and self-conceit, of others, but
especially and essentially with regard to reasonable
liberty.

The term political liberty, however, is often used to
mean formal participation in the public affairs of state
by the will and action even of those individuals who
otherwise find their chief function in the particular aims
and business of civil society. And it has in part become usual to give the title constitution only to the side
of the state which concerns such participation of these
individuals in general affairs, and to regard a state, in
which this is not formally done, as a state without a
constitution. On this use of the term, the only thing
to remark is that by constitution must be understood the
determination of rights, i.e. of liberties in general, and
the organisation of the actualisation of them; and that
political freedom in the above sense can in any case

only constitute a part of it.   Of it the following paragraphs will speak.

540. The guarantee of a constitution (i.e. the necessity that the laws be reasonable, and their actualisation
secured) lies in the collective spirit of the nation,—especially in the specific way in which it is itself conscious
of its reason.   (Religion is that consciousness in its
absolute substantiality.)   But the guarantee lies also at
the same time in the actual organisation or development
of that principle in suitable institutions.   The constitution presupposes that consciousness of the collective
spirit, and conversely that spirit presupposes the constitution: for the actual spirit only has a definite consciousness of its principles, in so far as it has them
actually existent before it.

The question—To whom (to what authority and how
organised) belongs the power to make a constitution?
is the same as the question, Who has to make the spirit
of a nation?   Separate our idea of a constitution from
that of the collective spirit, as if the latter exists or has
existed without a constitution, and your fancy only
proves how superficially you have apprehended the nexus
between the spirit in its self-consciousness and in its
actuality.   What is thus called 'making' a 'constitution,'
is—just because of this inseparability—a thing that has
never happened in history, just as little as the making of
a code of laws.   A constitution only develops from the
national spirit identically with that spirit's own development, and runs through at the same time with it the
grades of formation and the alterations required by its
concept.   It is the indwelling spirit and the history of
the nation (and, be it added, the history is only that
spirit's history) by which constitutions have been and
are made.

541. The really living totality,—that which preserves,

in other words continually produces the state in general
and its constitution, is the *government*. The organisation which natural necessity gives is seen in the rise
of the family and of the 'estates' of civil society. The
government is the *universal* part of the constitution, i.e.
the part which intentionally aims at preserving those
parts, but at the same time gets hold of and carries
out those general aims of the whole which rise above
the function of the family and of civil society. The
organisation of the government is likewise its differentiation into powers, as their peculiarities have a basis in
principle; yet without that difference losing touch with
the *actual unity* they have in the nation's subjectivity.

As the most obvious categories of the notion are those
of *universality* and *individuality,* and their relationship
that of *subsumption* of individual under universal, it
has come about that in the state the legislative and executive power have been so distinguished as to make
the former *exist* apart as the absolute superior, and to
subdivide the latter again into administrative (government) power and judicial power, according as the laws
are applied to public or private affairs. The *division*
of these powers has been treated as *the* condition of
political equilibrium, meaning by division their independence one of another in existence,—subject always
however to the above-mentioned subsumption of the
powers of the individual under the power of the general. The theory of such 'division' unmistakably implies the elements of the notion, but so combined by
'understanding' as to result in an absurd collocation, instead of the self-redintegration of the living spirit. The
one essential canon to make liberty deep and real is
to give every business belonging to the general interests
of the state a separate organisation wherever they are
essentially distinct. Such real division must be: for

liberty is only deep when it is differentiated in all its fullness and these differences manifested in existence. But to make the business of legislation an independent power—to make it the first power, with the further proviso that all citizens shall have part therein, and the government be merely executive and dependent, presupposes ignorance that the true idea, and therefore the living and spiritual actuality, is the self-redintegrating notion, in other words, the subjectivity which contains in it universality as only one of its moments. (A mistake still greater, if it goes with the fancy that the constitution and the fundamental laws were still one day to make,—in a state of society, which includes an already existing development of differences.) Individuality is the first and supreme principle *which* makes itself fall through the state's organisation. Only through the government, and by its embracing in itself the particular businesses (including the abstract legislative business, which taken apart is also particular), is the state *one*. These, as always, are the terms on which the different elements essentially and alone truly stand towards each other in the logic of 'reason,' as opposed to the external footing they stand on in 'understanding,' which never gets beyond subsuming the individual and particular under the universal. What disorganises the unity of logical reason, equally disorganises actuality.

542. In the government—regarded as organic totality —the sovereign power (principate) is (*a*) *subjectivity* as the infinite self-unity of the notion in its development;—the all-sustaining, all-decreeing will of the state, its highest peak and all-pervasive unity. In the perfect form of the state, in which each and every element of the notion has reached free existence, this subjectivity is not a so-called 'moral person,' or a decree issuing from a majority (forms in which the unity of the decreeing will

has not an *actual* existence), but an actual individual,—
the will of a decreeing individual,—*monarchy*.   The
monarchical constitution is therefore the constitution of
developed reason: all other constitutions belong to lower
grades of the development and realisation of reason.

The unification of all concrete state-powers into one
existence, as in the patriarchal society,—or, as in a
democratic constitution, the participation of all in all
affairs—impugns the principle of the division of powers,
i.e. the developed liberty of the constituent factors of
the Idea.   But no whit less must the division (the working out of these factors each to free totality) be reduced
to 'ideal' unity, i.e. to *subjectivity*.   The mature differentiation or realisation of the Idea means, essentially,
that this subjectivity should grow to be a *real* 'moment,'
an *actual* existence; and this actuality is not otherwise
than as the individuality of the monarch—the subjectivity of abstract and final decision existent in *one* person.   All those forms of collective decreeing and willing,
—a common will which shall be the sum and the resultant (on aristocratical or democratical principles) of
the atomistic of single wills, have on them the mark of
the unreality of an abstraction.   Two points only are
all-important, first to see the necessity of each of the
notional factors, and secondly the form in which it is
actualised.   It is only the nature of the speculative
notion which can really give light on the matter.   That
subjectivity—being the 'moment' which emphasises the
need of abstract deciding in general—partly leads on
to the proviso that the name of the monarch appear as
the bond and sanction under which everything is done
in the government;—partly, being simple self-relation,
has attached to it the characteristic of *immediacy,* and
then of *nature*—whereby the destination of individuals

for the dignity of the princely power is fixed by inheritance.

543. (*b*) In the *particular* government-power there emerges, first, the devision of state-business into its branches (otherwise defined), legislative power, administration of justice or judicial power, administration and police, and its consequent distribution between particular boards or offices, which having their business appointed by law, to that end and for that reason, possess independence of action, without at the same time ceasing to stand under higher supervision. Secondly, too, there arises the participation of *several* in state-business, who together constitute the 'general order' in so far as they take on themselves the charge of universal ends as the essential function of their particular life;—the further condition for being able to take individually part in this business being a certain training, aptitude, and skill for such ends.

544. The estates-collegium or provincial council is an institution by which all such as belong to civil society in general, and are to that degree private persons, participate in the governmental power, especially in legislation—viz. such legislation as concerns the universal scope of those interests which do not, like peace and war, involve the, as it were, personal interference and action of the State as one man, and therefore do not belong specially to the province of the sovereign power. By virtue of this participation subjective liberty and conceit, with their general opinion, can show themselves palpably efficacious and enjoy the satisfaction of feeling themselves to count for something.

The division of constitutions into democracy, aristocracy and monarchy, is still the most definite statement of their difference in relation to sovereignty. They must at the same time be regarded necessary structures in the path of development,—in short, in the history of the State. Hence it is superficial and absurd to represent them as an object of *choice*. The pure forms—necessary to the process of evolution—are, in so far as they are finite and in course of change, conjoined both the forms of their degeneration,—such as ochlocracy, &c., and with earlier transition-forms. These two forms are not to be confused with those legitimate structures. Thus, it may be—if we look only to the fact that the will of one individual stands at the head of the state—oriental despotism is included under the vague name monarchy,—as also feudal monarchy, to which indeed even the favourite name of 'constitutional monarchy' cannot be refused. The true difference of these forms from genuine monarchy depends on the true value of those principles of right which are in vogue and have their actuality and guarantee in the state-power. These principles are those expounded earlier, liberty of property, and above all personal liberty, civil society, with its industry and its communities, and the regulated efficiency of the particular bureaux in subordination to the laws.

The question which is most discussed is in what sense we are to understand the participation of private persons in state affairs. For it is as private persons that the members of bodies of estates are primarily to be taken, be they treated as mere individuals, or as representatives of a number of people or of the nation. The aggregate of private persons is often spoken of as the *nation:* but as such an aggregate it is *vulgus,* not *populus:* and in this direction, it is the one sole aim of the state that a nation should *not* come to existence, to power and action, *as such an aggregate.* Such a condition of a nation is a condition of lawlessness, demoralisation, brutishness: in it the nation would only be a shape-

less, wild, blind force, like that of the stormy, elemental
sea, which however is not self-destructive, as the nation
—a spiritual element—would be. Yet such a condition
may be often heard described as that of true freedom.
If there is to be any sense in embarking upon the question of the participation of private persons in public
affairs, it is not a brutish mass, but an already organised
nation—one in which a governmental power exists—
which should be presupposed. The desirability of such
participation however is not to be put in the superiority
of particular intelligence, which private persons are supposed to have over state officials—the contrary may be
the case—nor in the superiority of their good will for
the general best. The members of civil society as such
are rather people who find their nearest duty in their
private interest and (as especially in the feudal society)
in the interest of their privileged corporation. Take the
case of *England* which, because private persons have a
predominant share in public affairs, has been regarded as
having the freest of all constitutions. Experience shows
that that country—as compared with the other civilised
states of Europe—is the most backward in civil and
criminal legislation, in the law and liberty of property,
in arrangements for art and science, and that objective freedom or rational right is rather *sacrificed* to
formal right and particular private interest; and that
this happens even in the institutions and possessions
supposed to be dedicated to religion. The desirability of
private persons taking part in public affairs is partly
to be put in their concrete, and therefore more urgent,
sense of general wants. But the true motive is the right
of the collective spirit to appear as an *externally universal* will, acting with orderly and express efficacy for
the public concerns. By this satisfaction of this right
it gets its own life quickened, and at the same time

breathes fresh life in the administrative officials; who thus have it brought home to them that not merely have they to enforce duties but also to have regard to rights. Private citizens are in the state the incomparably greater number, and form the multitude of such as are recognised as persons. Hence the will-reason exhibits its existence in them as a preponderating majority of freemen, or in its 'reflectional' universality, which has its actuality vouchsafed it as a participation in the sovereignty. But it has already been noted as a 'moment' of civil society that the individuals rise from external into substantial universality, and form a *particular* kind, —the Estates: and it is not in the inorganic form of mere individuals as such (after the *democratic* fashion of election), but as organic factors, as estates, that they enter upon that participation. In the state a power or agency must never appear and act as a formless, inorganic shape, i.e. basing itself on the principle of multeity and mere numbers.

Assemblies of Estates have been wrongly designated as the *legislative power,* so far as they form only one branch of that power,—a branch in which the special government-officials have an *ex officio* share, while the sovereign power has the privilege of final decision. In a civilised state moreover legislation can only be a further modification of existing laws, and so-called new laws can only deal with minutiae of detail and particularities, the main drift of which has been already prepared or preliminarily settled by the practice of the law-courts. The so-called *financial law,* in so far as requires the assent of the estates, is really a government affair: it is only improperly called a law, in the general sense of embracing a wide, indeed the whole, range of the external means of government. The finances deal

with what in their nature are only particular needs,
ever newly recurring, even if they touch on the sum
total of such needs. If the main part of the requirement were—as it very likely is—regarded as permanent, the provision for it would have more the nature
of a law: but to be a law, it would have to be made
once for all, and not be made yearly, or every few
years, afresh. The part which varies according to
time and circumstances concerns in reality the smallest
part of the amount, and the provisions with regard to
it have even less the character of a law: and yet it is
and may be only this slight variable part which is
matter of dispute, and can be subjected to a varying
yearly estimate. It is this last then which falsely bears
the high-sounding name of the 'Grant' of the Budget,
i.e. of the whole of the finances. A law for one year
and made each year has even to the plain man something palpably absurd: for he distinguishes the essential and developed universal, as content of a true law,
from the reflectional universality which only externally
embraces what in its nature is many. To give the
name of a law to the annual fixing of financial requirements only serves—with the presupposed separation of
legislative from executive—to keep up the illusion of
that separation having real existence, and to conceal the
fact that the legislative power, when it makes a decree
about finance, is really engaged with strict executive
business. But the importance attached to the power of
from time to time granting 'supply,' on the ground that
the assembly of estates possesses in it a *check* on the
government, and thus a guarantee against injustice and
violence,—this importance is in one way rather plausible than real. The financial measures necessary for the
state's subsistence cannot be made conditional on any

other circumstances, nor can the state's subsistence be
put yearly in doubt. It would be a parallel absurdity if
the government were e.g. to grant and arrange the
judicial institutions always for a limited time merely;
and thus, by the threat of suspending the activity of
such an institution and the fear of a consequent state of
brigandage, reserve for itself a means of coercing private
individuals. Then again, the pictures of a condition of
affairs, in which it might be useful and necessary to have
in hand means of compulsion, are partly based on the
false conception of a contract between rulers and ruled,
and partly presuppose the possibility of such a divergence in spirit between these two parties as would make
constitution and government quite out of the question.
If we suppose the empty possibility of getting *help* by
such compulsive means brought into existence, such help
would rather be the derangement and dissolution of the
state, in which there would no longer be a government,
but only parties, and the violence and oppression of one
party would only be helped away by the other. To fit
together the several parts of the state into a constitution after the fashion of mere understanding—i.e. to
adjust within it the machinery of a balance of powers
external to each other—is to contravene the fundamental
idea of what a state is.

545. The final aspect of the state is to appear in immediate actuality as a single nation marked by physical
conditions. As a single individual it is exclusive against
other like individuals. In their mutual relations, waywardness and chance have a place; for each person
in the aggregate is autonomous: the universal of law
is only postulated between them, and not actually ex
istent. This independence of a central authority reduces disputes between them to terms of mutual

violence, a *state of war,* to meet which the general estate in the community assumes the particular function of maintaining the state's independence against other states, and becomes the estate of bravery.

546. This state of war shows the omnipotence of the state in its individuality—an individuality that goes even to abstract negativity. Country and fatherland then appear as the power by which the particular independence of individuals and their absorption in the external existence of possession and in natural life is convicted of its own nullity,—as the power which procures the maintenance of the general substance by the patriotic sacrifice on the part of these individuals of this natural and particular existence,—so making nugatory the nugatoriness that confronts it.

β. *Eternal Public Law.**

547. In the game of war the independence of States is at stake. In one case the result may be the mutual recognition of free national individualities: and by peace-conventions supposed to be for ever, both this general recognition, and the special claims of nations on one another, are settled and fixed. External state-rights rest partly on these positive treaties, but to that extent contain only rights falling short of true actuality: partly on so-called *international* law, the general principle of which is its presupposed recognition by the several States. It thus restricts their otherwise unchecked action against one another in such a way that the possibility of peace is left; and distinguishes individuals as private persons (non-belligerents) from the state. In general, international law rests on social usage.

* Das aüssere Staatsrecht.

γ. *Universal History.**

548. As the mind of a special nation is actual and its liberty is under natural conditions, it admits on this nature-side the influence of geographical and climatic qualities. It is in time; and as regards its range and scope, has essentially a *particular* principle on the lines of which it must run through a development of its consciousness and its actuality. It has, in short, a history of its own. But as a restricted mind its independence is something secondary; it passes into universal world-history, the events of which exhibit the dialectic of the several national minds,—the judgment of the world.

549. This movement is the path of liberation for the spiritual substance, the deed by which the absolute final aim of the world is realised in it, and the merely implicit mind achieves consciousness and self-consciousness. It is thus the revelation and actuality of its essential and completed essence, whereby it becomes to the outward eye a universal spirit—a world-mind. As this development is in time and in real existence, as it is a history, its several stages and steps are the national minds, each of which, as single and endued by nature with a specific character, is appointed to occupy only one grade, and accomplish one task in the whole deed.

The presupposition that history has an essential and actual end, from the principles of which certain characteristic results logically flow, is called an *a priori* view of it, and philosophy is reproached with *a priori* history-writing. On this point, and on history-writing in general, this note must go into further detail. That history, and above all universal history, is founded on an essential and actual aim, which actually is and

* Die Weltgeschichte.

will be realised in it—the plan of Providence; that, in short, there is Reason in history, must be decided on strictly philosophical ground, and thus shown to be essentially and in fact necessary. To presuppose such aim is blameworthy only when the assumed conceptions or thoughts are arbitrarily adopted, and when a determined attempt is made to force events and actions into conformity with such conceptions. For such *a priori* methods of treatment at the present day, however, those are chiefly to blame who profess to be purely historical, and who at the same time take opportunity expressly to raise their voice against the habit of philosophising, first in general, and then in history. Philosophy is to them a troublesome neighbour: for it is an enemy of all arbitrariness and hasty suggestions. Such *a priori* history-writing has sometimes burst out in quarters where one would least have expected it, especially on the philological side, and in Germany more than in France and England, where the art of historical writing has gone through a process of purification to a firmer and maturer character. Fictions, like that of a primitive age and its primitive people, possessed from the first of the true knowledge of God and all the sciences,—of sacerdotal races,—and, when we come to minutiae, of a Roman epic, supposed to be the source of the legends which pass current for the history of ancient Rome, &c., have taken the place of the pragmatising which detected psychological motives and associations. There is a wide circle of persons who seem to consider it incumbent on a *learned* and *ingenious* historian drawing from the original sources to concoct such baseless fancies, and form bold combinations of them from a learned rubbish-heap of out-of-the-way and trivial facts, in defiance of the best-accredited history.

Setting aside this subjective treatment of history, we

find what is properly the opposite view forbidding us to import into history an *objective purpose*. This is after all synonymous with what *seems* to be the still more legitimate demand that the historian should proceed with *impartiality*. This is a requirement often and especially made on the *history of philosophy:* where it is insisted there should be no prepossession in favour of an idea or opinion, just as a judge should have no special sympathy for one of the contending parties. In the case of the judge it is at the same time assumed that he would administer his office ill and foolishly, if he had not an interest, and an exclusive interest in justice, if he had not that for his aim and one sole aim, or if he declined to judge at all. This requirement which we may make upon the judge may be called *partiality* for justice; and there is no difficulty here in distinguishing it from *subjective* partiality. But in speaking of the impartiality required from the historian, this self-satisfied insipid chatter lets the distinction disappear, and rejects both kinds of interest. It demands that the historian shall bring with him no definite aim and view by which he may sort out, state and criticise events, but shall narrate them exactly in the casual mode he finds them, in their incoherent and unintelligent particularity. Now it is at least admitted that a history must have an object, e.g. Rome and its fortunes, or the Decline of the grandeur of the Roman empire. But little reflection is needed to discover that this is the presupposed end which lies at the basis of the events themselves, as of the critical examination into their comparative importance, i.e. their nearer or more remote relation to it. A history without such aim and such criticism would be only an imbecile mental divagation, not as good as a fairy tale, for even children expect a *motif* in their stories, a pur-

pose at least dimly surmisable with which events and
actions are put in relation.

In the existence of a *nation* the substantial aim is to
be a state and preserve itself as such. A nation with no
state formation, (*a mere nation*), has strictly speaking
no history,— like the nations which existed before the
rise of states and others which still exist in a condition
of savagery. What happens to a nation, and takes place
with it, has its essential significance in relation to the
state: whereas the mere particularities of individuals are
at the greatest distance from the true object of history.
It is true that the general spirit of an age leaves its
imprint in the character of its celebrated individuals,
and even their particularities are but the very distant
and the dim media through which the collective light
still plays in fainter colours. Ay, even such singularities as a petty occurrence, a word, express not a subjective particularity, but an age, a nation, a civilisation,
in striking portraiture and brevity; and to select such
trifles shows the hand of a historian of genius. But, on
the other hand, the main mass of singularities is a futile
and useless mass, by the painstaking accumulation of
which the objects of real historical value are overwhelmed and obscured. The essential characteristic of
the spirit and its age is always contained in the great
events. It was a correct instinct which sought to banish
such portraiture of the particular and the gleaning of
insignificant traits, into the *Novel* (as in the celebrated
romances of Walter Scott, &c.). Where the picture
presents an unessential aspect of life it is certainly in
good taste to conjoin it with an unessential material,
such as the romance takes from private events and subjective passions. But to take the individual pettiness
of an age and of the persons in it, and, in the interest
of so-called truth, weave them into the picture of gen-

eral interests, is not only against taste and judgment, but violates the principles of objective truth. The only truth for mind is the substantial and underlying essence, and not the trivialities of external existence and contingency. It is therefore completely indifferent whether such insignificancies are duly vouched for by documents, or, as in the romance, invented to suit the character and ascribed to this or that name and circumstances.

The point of interest of *Biography*—to say a word on that here—appears to run directly counter to any universal scope and aim. But biography too has for its background the historical world, with which the individual is intimately bound up: even purely personal originality, the freak of humour, &c. suggests by allusion that central reality and has its interest heightened by the suggestion. The mere play of sentiment, on the contrary, has another ground and interest than history.

The requirement of impartiality addressed to the history of philosophy (and also, we may add, to the history of religion, first in general, and secondly, to church history) generally implies an even more decided bar against presupposition of any objective aim. As the State was already called the point to which in political history criticism had to refer all events, so here the 'Truth' must be the object to which the several deeds and events of the spirit would have to be referred. What is actually done is rather to make the contrary presupposition. Histories with such an object as religion or philosophy are understood to have only subjective aims for their theme, i.e. only opinions and mere ideas, not an essential and realised object like the truth. And that with the mere excuse that there is no truth. On this assumption the sympathy with truth appears

as only a partiality of the usual sort, a partiality for
opinion and mere ideas, which all alike have no stuff
in them, and are all treated as indifferent. In that way
historical truth means but correctness—an accurate report of externals, without critical treatment save as regards this correctness—admitting, in this case, only
qualitative and quantitative judgments, no judgments of
necessity or notion. But, really, if Rome or the German
empire, &c. are an actual and genine object of political
history, and the aim to which the phenomena are to be
related and by which they are to be judged; then in universal history the genuine spirit, the consciousness of it
and of its essence, is even in a higher degree a true and
actual object and theme, and an aim to which all other
phenomena are essentially and actually subservient.
Only therefore through their relationship to it, i.e.
through the judgment in which they are subsumed under
it, while it inheres in them, have they their value and
even their existence. It is the spirit which not merely
broods *over* history as over the waters, but lives in it and
is alone its principle of movement: and in the path of
that spirit, liberty, i.e. a development determined by the
notion of spirit, is the guiding principle and only its notion its final aim, i.e. truth. For Spirit is consciousness.
Such a doctrine—or in other words that Reason is in
history—will be partly at least a plausible faith, partly
it is a cognition of philosophy.

550. This liberation of mind, in which it proceeds to
come to itself and to realise its truth, and the business
of so doing, is the supreme right, the absolute Law. The
self-consciousness of a particular nation is a vehicle for
the contemporary development of the collective spirit
in its actual existence: it is the objective actuality in
which that spirit for the time invests its will. Against
this absolute will the other particular natural minds

have no rights: *that* nation dominates the world: but yet the universal will steps onward over its property for the time being, as over a special grade, and then delivers it over to its chance and doom.

551. To such extent as this business of actuality appears as an action, and therefore as a work of *individuals*, these individuals, as regards the substantial issue of their labour, are *instruments*, and their subjectivity, which is what is peculiar to them, is the empty form of activity. What they personally have gained therefore through the individual share they took in the substantial business (prepared and appointed independently of them) is a formal universality or subjective mental idea —*Fame*, which is their reward.

552. The national spirit contains nature-necessity, and stands in external existence: the ethical substance, potentially infinite, is actually a particular and limited substance; on its subjective side it labours under contingency, in the shape of its unreflective natural usages, and its content is presented to it as something *existing* in time and tied to an external nature and external world. The spirit, however, (which *thinks* in this moral organism) over-rides and absorbs within itself the finitude attaching to it as national spirit in its state and the state's temporal interests, in the system of laws and usages. It rises to apprehend itself in its essentiality. Such apprehension, however, still has the immanent limitedness of the national spirit. But the spirit which thinks in universal history, stripping off at the same time those limitations of the several national minds and its own temporal restrictions, lays hold of its concrete universality, and rises to apprehend the absolute mind, as the eternally actual truth in which the contemplative reason enjoys freedom, while the necessity

of nature and the necessity of history are only minis-
trant to its revelation and the vessels of its honour.

The strictly technical aspects of the Mind's elevation
to God have been spoken of in the Introduction to the
Logic. As regards the starting-point of that elevation,
Kant has on the whole adopted the most correct, when
he treats belief in God as proceeding from the practical Reason. For that starting-point contains the material or content which constitutes the content of the
notion of God. But the true concrete material is neither
Being (as in the cosmological) nor mere action by design (as in the physico-theological proof) but the Mind,
the absolute characteristic and function of which is effective reason, i.e. the self determining and self-realising notion itself,—Liberty. That the elevation of subjective mind to God which these considerations give is
by Kant again deposed to a *postulate*—a mere 'ought'—
is the peculiar perversity, formerly noticed, of calmly
and simply reinstating as true and valid that very antithesis of finitude, the supersession of which into truth
is the essence of that elevation.

As regards the 'mediation' which, as it has been already shown, that elevation to God really involves, the
point specially calling for note is the 'moment' of negation through which the essential content of the starting-
point is purged of its finitude so as to come forth free.
This factor, abstract in the formal treatment of logic,
now gets its most concrete interpretation. The finite,
from which the start is now made, is the real ethical
self-consciousness. The negation through which that
consciousness raises its spirit to its truth, is the purification, *actually* accomplished in the ethical world, whereby
its conscience is purged of subjective opinion and its
will freed from the selfishness of desire. Genuine religion and genuine religiosity only issue from the moral

life: religion is that life rising to think, i.e. becoming aware of the free universality of its concrete essence. Only from the moral life and by the moral life is the Idea of God seen to be free spirit: outside the ethical spirit therefore it is vain to seek for true religion and religiosity.

But—as is the case with all speculative process—this development of one thing out of another means that what appears as sequel and derivative is rather the absolute *prius* of what it appears to be mediated by, and what is here in mind known as its truth.

Here then is the place to go more deeply into the reciprocal relations between the state and religion, and in doing so to elucidate the terminology which is familiar and current on the topic. It is evident and apparent from what has preceded that moral life is the state retracted into its inner heart and substance, while the state is the organisation and actualisation of moral life; and religion is the very substance of the moral life itself and of the state. At this rate, the state rests on the ethical sentiment, and that on the religious. If religion then is the consciousness of '*absolute*' *truth,* then whatever is to rank as right and justice, as law and duty, i.e. as *true* in the world of free will, can be so esteemed only as it is participant in that truth, as it is subsumed under it and is its sequel. But if the truly moral life is to be a sequel of religion, then perforce religion must have the *genuine* content; i.e. the idea of God it knows must be the true and real. The ethical life is the divine spirit as indwelling in self-consciousness, as it is actually present in a nation and its individual members. This self-consciousness retiring upon itself out of its empirical actuality and bringing its truth to consciousness, has in its *faith* and in its *conscience* only what it has consciously secured in its spiritual actuality. The two are inseparable: there cannot be two kinds of conscience, one religious and another ethical, differing from the former in body and value of truth. But in point of form, i.e. for thought and knowledge—(and religion and ethical life belong to the intelligence and are a thinking and knowing)—the body of religious truth, as the pure self-subsisting and therefore supreme truth, exercises a sanction over the moral life which lies in empirical actuality. Thus for self-consciousness religion is the 'basis' of moral life and of the state. It has been the monstrous blunder of our times to try to look upon these inseparables as separable from one another, and even as mutually indifferent. The view taken of the relationship of religion and the state has been that, whereas the state had an independent existence of its own, springing from some force and power, religion was a later addition, something desirable perhaps for strengthening the political bulwarks, but purely subjective in individuals:—or it may be, religion is treated as something without effect on the moral life of the state, i.e. its reasonable law and constitution which are based on a ground of their own.

As the inseparability of the two sides has been indicated, it may be worth while to note the separation as it appears on the side of religion. It is primarily a point of form: the attitude which self-consciousness takes to the body of truth. So long as this body of truth is the very substance or indwelling spirit of self-consciousness in its actuality, then self-consciousness in this content has the certainty of itself and is free. But if this present self-consciousness is lacking, then there may be created, in point of form, a condition of spiritual slavery, even though the *implicit* content of religion is absolute spirit. This great difference (to cite a specific case) comes out within the Christian religion itself, even though here it is not the nature-element in which the idea of God is embodied, and though nothing of the sort even enters as a factor into its central dogma and sole theme of a God who is known in spirit and in truth. And yet in Catholicism this spirit of all truth is in actuality set in rigid opposition to the self-conscious spirit. And, first of all, God is in the 'host' presented to religious adoration as an *external thing*. (In the Lutheran Church, on the contrary, the host as such is not at first consecrated, but in the moment of enjoyment, i.e. in the annihilation of its externality, and in the act of faith, i.e. in the free self-certain spirit: only then is it consecrated and exalted to be present God.) From that first and supreme status of externalisation flows every other phase of externality,—of bondage, non-spirituality, and superstition. It leads to a laity, receiving its knowledge of divine truth, as well as the direction of its will and conscience from without and from another order—which order again does not get possession of that knowledge in a spiritual way only, but to that end essentially requires an external consecration. It leads to the non-spiritual style of praying —partly as mere moving of the lips, partly in the way that the subject foregoes his right of directly addressing God, and prays others to pray—addressing his devotion to miracle-working images, even to bones, and expecting miracles from them. It leads, generally, to justification by external works, a merit which is supposed to be gained by acts, and even to be capable of being transferred to others. All this binds the spirit under an externalism by which the very meaning of spirit is perverted and misconceived at its source, and law and justice, morality and conscience, responsibility and duty are corrupted at their root.

Along with this principle of spiritual bondage, and

these applications of it in the religious life, there can only go in the legislative and constitutional system a legal and moral bondage, and a state of lawlessness and immorality in political life. Catholicism has been loudly praised and is still often praised—logically enough—as the one religion which secures the stability of governments. But in reality this applies only to governments which are bound up with institutions founded on the bondage of the spirit (of that spirit which should have legal and moral liberty), i.e. with institutions that embody injustice and with a morally corrupt and barbaric state of society. But these governments are not aware that in fanaticism they have a terrible power, which does not rise in hostility against them, only so long as and only on condition that they remain sunk in the thraldom of injustice and immorality. But in mind there is a very different power available against that externalism and dismemberment induced by a false religion. Mind collects itself into its inward free actuality. Philosophy awakes in the spirit of governments and nations the wisdom to discern what is essentially and actually right and reasonable in the real world. It was well to call these products of thought, and in a special sense Philosophy, the wisdom of the world; * for thought makes the spirit's truth an actual present, leads it into the real world, and thus liberates it in its actuality and in its own self.

Thus set free, the content of religion assumes quite another shape. So long as the form, i.e. our consciousness and subjectivity, lacked liberty, it followed necessarily that self-consciousness was conceived as not immanent in the ethical principles which religion embodies, and these principles were set at such a distance as to seem to have true being only as negative to actual self-

* Weltweisheit.

consciousness. In this unreality ethical content gets the name of *Holiness*. But once the divine spirit introduces itself into actuality, and actuality emancipates itself to spirit, then what in the world was a postulate of holiness is supplanted by the actuality of *moral* life. Instead of the vow of chastity, *marriage* now ranks as the ethical relation; and, therefore, as the highest on this side of humanity stands the family. Instead of the vow of poverty (muddled up into a contradiction of assigning merit to whosoever gives away goods to the poor, i.e. whosoever enriches them) is the precept of action to acquire goods through one's own intelligence and industry,—of honesty in commercial dealing, and in the use of property,—in short moral life in the socio-economic sphere. And instead of the vow of obedience, true religion sanctions obedience to the law and the legal arrangements of the state—an obedience which is itself the true freedom, because the state is a self-possessed, self-realising reason—in short, moral life in the state. Thus, and thus only, can law and morality exist. The precept of religion, 'Give to Caesar what is Caesar's and to God what is God's' is not enough: the question is to settle what is Caesar's, what belongs to the secular authority: and it is sufficiently notorious that the secular no less than the ecclesiastical authority have claimed almost everything as their own. The divine spirit must interpenetrate the entire secular life: whereby wisdom is concrete within it, and it carries the terms of its own justification. But that concrete indwelling is only the aforesaid ethical organisations. It is the morality of marriage as against the sanctity of a celibate order;— the morality of economic and industrial action against the sanctity of poverty and its indolence;—the morality of an obedience dedicated to the law of the state as against the sanctity of an obedience from which law and duty are absent and where conscience is enslaved. With the growing need for law and morality and the sense of the spirit's essential liberty, there sets in a conflict of spirit with the religion of unfreedom. It is no use to organise political laws and arrangements on principles of equity and reason, so long as in religion the principle of unfreedom is not abandoned. A free state and a slavish religion are incompatible. It is silly to suppose that we may try to allot them separate spheres, under the impression that their diverse natures will maintain an attitude of tranquillity one to another and not break out in contradiction and battle. Principles of civil freedom can be but abstract and superficial, and political institutions deduced from them must be, if taken alone, untenable, so long as those principles in their wisdom mistake religion so much as not to know that the maxims of the reason in actuality have their last and supreme sanction in the religious conscience in subsumption under the consciousness of 'absolute' truth. Let us suppose even that, no matter how, a code of law should arise, so to speak *a priori*, founded on principles of reason, but in contradiction with an established religion based on principles of spiritual unfreedom; still, as the duty of carrying out the laws lies in the hands of individual members of the government, and of the various classes of the administrative *personnel*, it is vain to delude ourselves with the abstract and empty assumption that the individuals will act only according to the letter or meaning of the law, and not in the spirit of their religion where their inmost conscience and supreme obligation lies. Opposed to what religion pronounces holy, the laws appear something made by human hands: even though backed by penalties and externally introduced, they could offer no lasting resistance to the contradiction and attacks of the religious spirit. Such laws, however sound their provisions may be, thus founder on the conscience, whose spirit is different from the spirit of the laws and refuses to sanction them. It is nothing but a modern folly to try to alter a corrupt moral organisation by altering its political constitution and code of laws without changing the religion,—to make a revolution without having made a reformation, to suppose that a political constitution opposed to the old religion could live in peace and harmony with it and its sanctities, and that stability could be procured for the laws by external guarantees, e.g. so-called 'chambers,' and the power given them to fix the budget, &c. At best it is only a temporary expedient—when it is obviously too great a task to descend into the depths of the religious spirit and to raise that same spirit to its truth— to seek to separate law and justice from religion. Those guarantees are but rotten bulwarks against the consciences of the persons charged with administering the laws—among which laws these guarantees are included. It is indeed the height and profanity of contradiction to seek to bind and subject to the secular code the religious conscience to which mere human law is a thing profane.

The perception had dawned upon Plato with great clearness of the gulf which in his day had commenced to divide the established religion and the political constitution, on one hand, from those deeper requirements which, on the other hand, were made upon religion and politics by liberty which had learnt to recognise its inner life. Plato gets hold of the thought that a genuine constitution and a sound political life have their deeper foundation on the Idea,—on the essentially and actually universal and genuine principles of eternal righteousness. Now to see and ascertain what these are is certainly the function and the business of *philosophy*. It

is from this point of view that Plato breaks out into
the celebrated or notorious passage where he makes
Socrates emphatically state that philosophy and political power must coincide, that the Idea must be regent,
if the distress of nations is to see its end. What Plato
thus definitely set before his mind was that the Idea—
which implicitly indeed is the free self-determining
thought—could not get into consciousness save only
in the form of a thought; that the substance of the
thought could only be true when set forth as a universal,
and as such brought to consciousness under its most abstract form.

To compare the Platonic standpoint in all its definiteness with the point of view from which the relationship
of state and religion is here regarded, the notional differences on which everything turns must be recalled to
mind. The first of these is that in natural things their
substance or genus is different from their existence
in which that substance is as subject: further that this
subjective existence of the genus is distinct from that
which it gets, when specially set in relief as genus, or,
to put it simply, as the universal in a mental concept
or idea. This additional 'individuality'—the soil on
which the universal and underlying principle *freely* and
expressly exists,—is the intellectual and thinking *self*.
In the case of *natural* things their truth and reality
does not get the form of universality and essentiality
through themselves, and their 'individuality' is not itself the form: the form is only found in subjective thinking, which in philosophy gives that universal truth and
reality an existence of its own. In man's case it is otherwise: his truth and reality is the free mind itself, and
it comes to existence in his self-consciousness. This
absolute nucleus of man—mind intrinsically concrete—

is just this—to have the form (to have thinking) itself
for a content. To the height of the thinking consciousness of this principle Aristotle ascended in his notion
of the entelechy of thought, (which is νόησις τῆς νοήσεως),
thus surmounting the Platonic Idea (the genus,
or essential being). But thought always—and that
on account of this very principle—contains the immediate self-subsistence of subjectivity no less than it
contains universality; the genuine Idea of the intrinsically concrete mind is just as essentially under the one
of its terms (subjective consciousness) as under the
other (universality): and in the one as in the other it
is the same substantial content. Under the subjective
form, however, fall feeling, intuition, pictorial representation; and it is in fact necessary that in point of time
the consciousness of the absolute Idea should be first
reached and apprehended in this form: in other words,
it must exist in its immediate reality as religion, earlier
than it does as philosophy. Philosophy is a later development from this basis (just as Greek philosophy
itself is later than Greek religion), and in fact reaches
its completion by catching and comprehending in all
its definite essentiality that principle of spirit which
first manifests itself in religion. But Greek philosophy could set itself up only in opposition to Greek
religion: the unity of thought and the substantiality of
the Idea could take up none but a hostile attitude to an
imaginative polytheism, and to the gladsome and frivo-
lous humours of its poetic creations. The *form* in its infinite truth, the *subjectivity* of mind, broke forth at first
only as a subjective free *thinking,* which was not yet
identical with the *substantiality* itself,—and thus this
underlying principle was not yet apprehended as
absolute mind. Thus religion might appear as first purified only through philosophy,—through pure self-ex-

istent thought: but the form pervading this underlying principle—the form which philosophy attacked—was that creative imagination.

Political power, which is developed similarly, but earlier than philosophy, from religion, exhibits the one-sidedness, which in the actual world may infect its *implicitly* true Idea, as demoralisation. Plato, in common with all his thinking contemporaries, perceived this demoralisation of democracy and the defectiveness even of its principle; he set in relief accordingly the underlying principle of the state, but could not work into his idea of it the infinite form of subjectivity, which still escaped his intelligence. His state is therefore, on its own showing, wanting in subjective liberty. The truth which should be immanent in the state, should knit it together and control it, he, for these reasons, got hold of only the form of thought-out truth, of philosophy; and hence he makes that utterance that 'so long as philosophers do not rule in the states, or those who are now called kings and rulers do not soundly and comprehensively philosophise, so long neither the state nor the race of men can be liberated from evils,—so long will the idea of the political constitution fall short of possibility and not see the light of the sun.' It was not vouchsafed to Plato to go on so far as to say that as long as true religion did not spring up in the world and hold sway in political life, so long the genuine principle of the state had not come into actuality. But so long too this principle could not emerge even in thought, nor could thought lay hold of the genuine idea of the state, —the idea of the substantial moral life, with which is identical the liberty of an independent self-consciousness. Only in the principle of mind, which is aware of its own essence, is implicitly in absolute liberty, and has its actuality in the act of self-liberation, does the absolute possibility and necessity exist for political power, religion, and the principles of philosophy coinciding in one, and for accomplishing the reconciliation of actuality in general with the mind, of the state with the religious conscience as well as with the philosophical consciousness. Self-realising subjectivity is in this case absolutely identical with substantial universality. Hence religion as such, and the state as such,—both as forms in which the principle exists—each contain the absolute truth: so that the truth, in its philosophic phase, is after all only in one of its forms. But even religion, as it grows and expands, lets other aspects of the Idea of humanity grow and expand also. As it is left therefore behind, in its first immediate, and so also one-sided phase, Religion may, or rather *must,* appear in its existence degraded to sensuous externality, and thus in the sequel become an influence to oppress liberty of spirit and to deprave political life. Still the principle has in it the infinite 'elasticity' of the 'absolute' form, so as to overcome this depraving of the form-determination (and of the content by these means), and to bring about the reconciliation of the spirit in itself. Thus ultimately, in the Protestant conscience the principles of the religious and of the ethical conscience come to be one and the same: the free spirit learning to see itself in its reasonableness and truth. In the Protestant state the constitution and the code, as well as their several applications, embody the principle and the development of the moral life, which proceeds and can only proceed from the truth of religion, when reinstated in its original principle and in that way as such first become actual. The moral life of the state and the religious spirituality of the state are thus reciprocal guarantees of strength.

VII

THE PHILOSOPHY OF MIND *

SECTION III

Absolute Mind.†

Translated by William Wallace

553. THE *notion* of mind has its *reality* in the mind. If this reality in identity with that notion is to exist as the consciousness of the absolute Idea, then the necessary aspect is that the *implicitly free intelligence* be in its actuality liberated to its notion, if that actuality is to be a vehicle worthy of it. The subjective and the objective spirit are to be looked on as the road on which this aspect of *reality* or existence rises to maturity.

554. The absolute mind, while it is self-centered *identity,* is always also identity returning and ever returned into itself: if it is the one and universal *substance* it is so as a spirit, discerning itself into a self and a consciousness, for which it is as substance. *Religion,* as this supreme sphere may be in general designated, if it has on one hand to be studied as issuing from the subject and having its home in the subject, must no less be regarded as objectively issuing from the absolute spirit which as spirit is in its community.

That here, as always, belief or faith is not opposite to consciousness or knowledge, but rather to a sort of knowledge, and that belief is only a particular form of

* From *The Encyclopaedia of the Philosophical Sciences.*
† Der absolute Geist.

the latter, has been remarked already. If nowadays
there is so little consciousness of God, and his objective
essence is so little dwelt upon, while people speak so
much more of the subjective side of religion, i.e. of
God's indwelling in us, and if that and not the truth
as such is called for,—in this there is at least the correct principle that God must be apprehended as spirit
in his community.

555. The subjective consciousness of the absolute
spirit is essentially and intrinsically a process, the immediate and substantial unity of which is the *Belief* in
the witness of the spirit as the *certainty* of objective
truth. Belief, at once this immediate unity and containing it as a reciprocal dependence of these different
terms, has a *devotion*—the implicit or more explicit act
of worship (*cultus*)—passed over into the process of
superseding the contrast till it becomes spiritual liberation, the process of authenticating that first certainty by
this intermediation, and of gaining its concrete determination, viz. reconciliation, the actuality of the spirit.

SUB-SECTION A.

ART.

556. As this consciousness of the Absolute first takes
shape, its immediacy produces the factor of finitude in
Art. On one hand that is, it breaks up into a work of
external common existence, into the subjective which
produces that work, and the subject which contemplates
and worships it. But, on the other hand, it is the concrete *contemplation* and mental picture of implicitly absolute spirit as the *Ideal*. In this ideal, or the concrete
shape born of the subjective spirit, its natural immediacy, which is only a *sign* of the Idea, is so transfigured

by the informing spirit in order to express the Idea, that the figure shows it and it alone:—the shape or form of *Beauty*.

557. The sensuous externality attaching to the beautiful,—the *form of immediacy* as such,—at the same time *qualifies* what *embodies*: and the God (of art) has with his spirituality at the same time the stamp upon him of a natural medium or natural phase of existence —He contains the so-called *unity* of nature and spirit— i.e. the immediate unity in sensuously intuitional form —hence not the spiritual unity, in which the natural would be put only as 'ideal,' as superseded in spirit, and the spiritual content would be only in self-relation.   It is not the absolute spirit which enters this consciousness. On the subjective side the community has of course an ethical life, aware, as it is, of the spirituality of its essence: and its self-consciousness and actuality are in it elevated to substantial liberty.   But with the stigma of immediacy upon it, the subject's liberty is only a *manner of life,* without the infinite self-reflection and the subjective inwardness of *conscience.*   These considerations govern in their further developments the devotion and the worship in the religion of fine art.

558. For the objects of contemplation it has to produce, Art requires not only an external given material —(under which are also included subjective images and ideas), but—for the expression of spiritual truth—must use the given forms of nature with a significance which art must divine and possess.   Of all such forms the human is the highest and the true, because only in it can the spirit have its corporeity and thus its visible expression.

This disposes of the principle of the *imitation of nature* in art: a point cn which it is impossible to come to an understanding while a distinction is left thus ab-

stract,—in other words, so long as the natural is only
taken in its externality, not as the 'characteristic' mean-
ingful nature-form which is significant of spirit.

559. In such single shapes the 'absolute' mind cannot
be made explicit: in and to art therefore the spirit is a
limited natural spirit whose implicit universality, when
steps are taken to specify its fullness in detail, breaks
up into an indeterminate polytheism. With the essential restrictedness of its content, Beauty in general goes
no further than a penetration of the vision or image by
the spiritual principle,—something formal, so that the
thought embodied, or the idea, can, like the material
which it uses to work in, be of the most diverse and
unessential kind, and still the work be something beautiful and a work of art.

560. The one-sidedness of *immediacy* on the part of
the Ideal involves the opposite one-sidedness that it is
something *made* by the artist. The subject or agent
is the mere technical activity: and the work of art is
only then an expression of the God, when there is no
sign of subjective particularity in it, and the net power
of the indwelling spirit is conceived and born into the
world, without admixture and unspotted from its contingency. But as liberty only goes as far as there is
thought, the action inspired with the fullness of this
indwelling power, the artist's *enthusiasm,* is like a foreign force under which he is bound and passive; the
artistic *production* has on its part the form of natural immediacy, it belongs to the *genius* or particular endow-
ment of the artist,—and is at the same time a labour
concerned with technical cleverness and mechanical ex-
ternalities. The work of art therefore is just as much
a work due to free option, and the artist is the master of
the God.

561. In work so inspired the reconciliation appears so

obvious in its initial stage that it is without more ado accomplished in the subjective self-consciousness, which is thus self-confident and of good cheer, without the depth and without the sense of its antithesis to the absolute essence. On the further side of the perfection (which is reached in such reconciliation, in the beauty of *classical art*) lies the art of sublimity,—*symbolic art*, in which the figuration suitable to the Idea is not yet found, and the thought as going forth and wrestling with the figure is exhibited as a negative attitude to it, and yet all the while toiling to work itself into it. The meaning or theme thus shows it has not yet reached the infinite form, is not yet known, not yet conscious of itself, as free spirit. The artist's theme only is as the abstract God of pure thought, or an effort towards him, —a restless and unappeased effort which throws itself into shape after shape as it vainly tries to find its goal.

562. In another way the Idea and the sensuous figure it appears in are incompatible; and that is where the infinite form, subjectivity, is not as in the first extreme a mere superficial personality, but its inmost depth, and God is known not as only seeking his form or satisfying himself in an external form, but as only finding himself in himself, and thus giving himself his adequate figure in the spiritual world alone. *Romantic art* gives up the task of showing him as such in external form and by means of beauty: it presents him as only condescending to appearance, and the divine as the heart of hearts in an externality from which it always disengages itself. Thus the external can here appear as contingent toward its significance.

The Philosophy of Religion has to discover the logical necessity in the progress by which the Being, known as the Absolute, assumes fuller and firmer features; it has to note to what particular feature the kind of cultus corresponds,—and then to see how the secular self-consciousness, the consciousness of what is the supreme vocation of man,—in short how the nature of a nation's moral life, the principle of its law, of its actual liberty, and of its constitution, as well as of its art and science, corresponds to the principle which constitutes the substance of a religion. That all these elements of a nation's actuality constitute one systematic totality, that one spirit creates and informs them, is a truth on which follows the further truth that the history of religions coincides with the world-history.

As regards the close connexion of art with the various religions it may be specially noted that *beautiful* art can only belong to those religions in which the spiritual principle, though concrete and intrinsically free, is not yet absolute. In religions where the Idea has not yet been revealed and known in its free character, though the craving for art is felt in order to bring in imaginative visibility to consciousness the idea of the supreme being, and though art is the sole organ in which the abstract and radically indistinct content,—a mixture from natural and spiritual sources,—can try to bring itself to consciousness;—still this art is defective; its form is defective because its subject-matter and theme is so,— for the defect in subject-matter comes from the form not being immanent in it. The representations of this symbolic art keep a certain tastelessness and stolidity—for the principle it embodies is itself stolid and dull, and hence has not the power freely to transmute the external to significance and shape. Beautiful art, on the contrary, has for its condition the self-consciousness of the free spirit,—the consciousness that compared with it the natural and sensuous has no standing of its own: it makes the natural wholly into the mere expression of spirit, which is thus the inner form that gives utterance to itself alone.

But with a further and deeper study, we see that the advent of art, in a religion still in the bonds of sensuous externality, shows that such religion is on the decline. At the very time it seems to give religion the supreme glorification, expression and brilliancy, it has lifted the religion away over its limitation. In the sublime divinity to which the work of art succeeds in giving expression the artistic genius and the spectator find themselves at home, with their personal sense and feeling, satisfied and liberated: to them the vision and the consciousness of free spirit has been vouchsafed and attained. Beautiful art, from its side, has thus performed the same service as philosophy: it has purified the spirit from its thraldom. The older religion in which the need of fine art, and just for that reason, is first generated, looks up in its principle to an other-world which is sensuous and unmeaning: the images adored by its devotees are hideous idols regarded as wonder-working talismans, which point to the unspiritual objectivity of that other world,—and bones perform a similar or even a better service than such images. But even fine art is only a grade of liberation, not the supreme liberation itself.—The genuine objectivity which is only in the medium of thought,—the medium in which alone the pure spirit is for the spirit, and where the liberation is accompanied with reverence,—is still absent in the sensuous beauty of the work of art, still more in that external, unbeautiful sensuousness.

563. Beautiful Art, like the religion peculiar to it, has its future in true religion. The restricted value of the Idea passes utterly and naturally into the universality identical with the infinite form;—the vision in which consciousness has to depend upon the senses

passes into self-mediating knowledge, into an existence which is itself knowledge,—into *revelation*. Thus the principle which gives the Idea its content is that it embody free intelligence, and as 'absolute' *spirit it is for the spirit*.

Sub-Section B.

REVEALED RELIGION.*

564. It lies essentially in the notion of religion,—the religion i.e. whose content is absolute mind—that it be *revealed,* and, what is more, revealed *by God*. Knowledge (the principle by which the substance is mind) is a self-determining principle, as infinite self-realising form,—it therefore is manifestation out and out. The spirit is only spirit in so far as it is for the spirit, and in the absolute religion it is the absolute spirit which manifests no longer abstract elements of its being but itself.

The old conception—due to a one-sided survey of human life—of Nemesis, which made the divinity and its action in the world only a levelling power, dashing to pieces everything high and great,—was confronted by Plato and Aristotle with the doctrine that God is not *envious*. The same answer may be given to the modern assertions that man cannot ascertain God. These assertions (and more than assertions they are not) are the more illogical, because made within a religion which is expressly called the revealed; for according to them it would rather be the religion in which nothing of God was revealed, in which he had not revealed himself, and those belonging to it would be the heathen 'who know not God.' If the word of God is taken in

* Die geoffenbarte Religion.

earnest in religion at all, it is from Him, the theme and
centre of religion, that the method of divine knowledge
may and must begin: and if self-revelation is refused
Him, then the only thing left to constitute His nature
would be to ascribe envy to Him.   But clearly if the
word Mind is to have a meaning, it implies the revelation of Him.

If we recollect how intricate is the knowledge of the
divine Mind for those who are not content with the
homely pictures of faith but proceed to thought,—at
first only 'rationalising' reflection, but afterwards, as in
duty bound, to speculative comprehension, it may almost
create surprise that so many, and especially theologians
whose vocation it is to deal with these Ideas, have tried
to get off their task by gladly accepting anything offered
them for this behoof.   And nothing serves better to shirk
it than to adopt the conclusion that man knows nothing
of God.   To know what God as spirit is—to apprehend
this accurately and distinctly in thoughts—requires careful and thorough speculation.   It includes, in its fore-
front, the propositions: God is God only so far as he
knows himself: his self-knowledge is, further, his self-
consciousness in man, and man's knowledge *of* God,
which proceed to man's self-knowledge in God.—See
the profound elucidation of these propositions in the
work from which they are taken: *Aphorisms on Knowing and Not-knowing,* &c., by C. F. G—l.: Berlin 1829.

565. When the immediacy and sensuousness of shape
and knowledge is superseded, God is, in point of content, the essential and actual spirit of nature and spirit,
while in point of form he is, first of all, presented to
consciousness as a mental representation.   This quasi-
pictorial representation gives to the elements of his content, on one hand, a separate being, making them pre-

suppositions towards each other, and phenomena which succeed each other; their relationship it makes a series of events according to finite reflective categories. But, on the other hand, such a form of finite representationalism is also overcome and superseded in the faith which realises one spirit and in the devotion of worship.

566. In this separating, the form parts from the content: and in the form the different functions of the notion part off into special spheres or media, in each of which the absolute spirit exhibits itself; (*a*) as eternal content, abiding self-centred, even in its manifestation; (*β*) as distinction of the eternal essence from its manifestation, which difference becomes the phenomenal world into which the content enters; (*γ*) as infinite return, and reconciliation with the eternal being, of the world it gave away—the withdrawal of the eternal from the phenomenal into the unity of its fullness.

567. (*a*) Under the 'moment' of *Universality*,—the sphere of pure thought or the abstract medium of essence,—it is therefore the absolute spirit, which is at first the presupposed principle, not however staying aloof and inert, but (as underlying and essential power under the reflective category of causality) creator of heaven and earth: but yet in this eternal sphere rather only begetting himself as his *son*, with whom, though different, he still remains in original identity,—just as, again, this differentiation of him from the universal essence eternally supersedes itself, and, though this mediating of a self-superseding mediation, the first substance is essentially as *concrete individuality* and subjectivity, —is the *Spirit*.

568. (*β*) Under the 'moment' of *particularity*, or of judgment, it is this concrete eternal being which is presupposed: its movement is the creation of the phenomenal world. The eternal 'moment' of mediation—of

the only Son—divides itself to become the antithesis of two separate worlds. On one hand is heaven and earth, the elemental and the concrete nature,—on the other hand, standing in action and reaction with such nature, the spirit, which therefore is finite. That spirit, as the extreme of inherent negativity, completes its independence till it becomes wickedness, and is that extreme through its connexion with the confronting nature and through its own naturalness thereby investing it. Yet, amid that naturalness, it is, when it thinks, directed towards the Eternal, though, for that reason, only standing to it in an external connexion.

569. (γ) Under the 'moment' of *individuality* as such, —of subjectivity and the notion itself, in which the contrast of universal and particular has sunk to its identical ground, the place of presupposition (1) is taken by the *universal* substance, as actualised out of its abstraction into an *individual* self-consciousness. This individual, who as such is identified with the essence,—(in the Eternal sphere he is called the Son)—is transplanted into the world of time, and in him wickedness is implicitly overcome. Further, this immediate, and thus sensuous, existence of the absolutely concrete is represented as putting himself in judgment and expiring in the pain of *negativity,* in which he, as infinite subjectivity, keeps himself unchanged, and thus, as absolute return from that negativity and as universal unity of universal and individual essentiality, has realised his being as the Idea of the spirit, eternal, but alive and present in the world.

570. (2) This objective totality of the divine man who is the Idea of the spirit is the implicit presupposition for the *finite* immediacy of the single subject. For such subject therefore it is at first an Other, an object of contemplating vision,—but the vision of implicit truth, through which witness of the spirit in him, he, on

account of his immediate nature, at first characterised himself as nought and wicked. But, secondly, after the example of his truth, by means of the faith on the unity (in that example implicitly accomplished) of universal and individual essence, he is also the movement to throw off his immediacy, his natural man and self-will, to close himself in unity with that example (who is his implicit life) in the pain of negativity, and thus to know himself made one with the essential Being. Thus the Being of Beings (3) through this mediation brings about his own indwelling in self-consciousness, and is the actual presence of the essential and self-subsisting spirit who is all in all.

571. These three syllogisms, constituting the one syllogism of the absolute self-mediation of spirit, are the revelation of that spirit whose life is set out as a cycle of concrete shapes in pictorial thought. From this its separation into parts, with a temporal and external sequence, the unfolding of the mediation contracts itself in the result,—where the spirit closes in unity with itself,—not merely to the simplicity of faith and devotional feeling, but even to thought. In the immanent simplicity of thought the unfolding still has its expansion, yet is all the while known as an indivisible coherence of the universal, simple, and eternal spirit in itself. In this form of truth, truth is the object of *philosophy*.

If the result—the realised Spirit in which all mediation has superseded itself—is taken in a merely formal, contentless sense, so that the spirit is not also at the same time known as *implicitly* existent and objectively self-unfolding;—then that infinite subjectivity is the merely formal self-consciousness, knowing itself in itself as absolute,—Irony. Irony, which can make every objective reality nought and vain, is itself the emptiness and vanity, which from itself, and therefore by chance and its own good pleasure, gives itself direction and content, remains master over it, is not bound by it,—and, with the assertion that it stands on the very summit of religion and philosophy, falls rather back into the vanity of wilfulness. It is only in proportion as the pure infinite form, the self-centred manifestation, throws off the one-sidedness of subjectivity in which it is the vanity of thought, that it is the free thought which has its infinite characteristic at the same time as essential and actual content, and has that content as an object in which it is also free. Thinking, so far, is only the formal aspect of the absolute content.

SUB-SECTION C.

PHILOSOPHY.

572. This science is the unity of Art and Religion. Whereas the vision-method of Art, external in point of form, is but subjective production and shivers the substantial content into many separate shapes, and whereas Religion, with its separation into parts, opens it out in mental picture, and mediates what is thus opened out; Philosophy not merely keeps them together to make a total, but even unifies them into the simple spiritual vision, and then in that raises them to self-conscious thought. Such consciousness is thus the intelligible unity (cognised by thought) of art and religion, in which the diverse elements in the content are cognised as necessary, and this necessary as free.

573. Philosophy thus characterises itself as a cognition of the necessity in the content of the absolute picture-idea, as also of the necessity in the two forms—on one hand, immediate vision and its poetry, and the objective and external revelation presupposed by repre-

sentation,—on the other hand, first the subjective retreat inwards, then the subjective movement of faith and its final identification with the presupposed object. This cognition is thus the *recognition* of this content and its form; it is the liberation from the one-sidedness of the forms, elevation of them into the absolute form, which determines itself to content, remains identical with it, and is in that the cognition of that essential and actual necessity. This movement, which philosophy is, finds itself already accomplished, when at the close it seizes its own notion,—i.e. only *looks back* on its knowledge.

Here might seem to be the place to treat in a definite exposition of the reciprocal relations of philosophy and religion. The whole question turns entirely on the difference of the forms of speculative thought from the forms of mental representation and 'reflecting' intellect. But it is the whole cycle of philosophy, and of logic in particular, which has not merely taught and made known this difference, but also criticised it, or rather has let its nature develop and judge itself by these very categories. It is only by an insight into the value of these forms that the true and needful conviction can be gained, that the content of religion and philosophy is the same,— leaving out, of course, the further details of external nature and finite mind which fall outside the range of religion. But religion is the truth *for all men:* faith rests on the witness of the spirit, which as witnessing is the spirit in man. This witness—the underlying essence in all humanity—takes, when driven to expound itself, its first definite form under those acquired habits of thought which his secular consciousness and intellect otherwise employs. In this way the truth becomes liable to the terms and conditions of finitude in general. This does not prevent the spirit, even in employing sensuous ideas and finite categories of thought, from retaining its content (which as religion is essentially speculative,) with a tenacity which does violence to them, and acts *inconsistently* towards them. By this inconsistency it corrects their defects. Nothing easier therefore for the 'Rationalist' than to point out contradictions in the exposition of the faith, and then to prepare triumphs for its principle of formal identity. If the spirit yields to this finite reflection, which has usurped the title of reason and philosophy—('Rationalism')—it strips religious truth of its infinity and makes it in reality nought. Religion in that case is completely in the right in guarding herself against such reason and philosophy and treating them as enemies. But it is another thing when religion sets herself against comprehending reason, and against philosophy in general, and specially against a philosophy of which the doctrine is speculative, and so religious. Such an opposition proceeds from failure to appreciate the difference indicated and the value of spiritual form in general, and particularly of the logical form; or, to more precise still, from failure to note the distinction of the content—which may be in both the same—from these forms. It is on the ground of form that philosophy has been reproached and accused by the religious party; just as conversely its speculative content has brought the same charges upon it from a self-styled philosophy—and from a pithless orthodoxy. It had too little of God in it for the former; too much for the latter.

The charge of *Atheism*, which used often to be brought against philosophy (that it has *too little* of God), has grown rare: the more wide-spread grows the charge of Pantheism, that it has *too much* of him:—so much so, that it is treated not so much as an imputation, but as a proved fact, or a sheer fact which needs no proof. Piety, in particular, which with its pious airs of superi-

ority fancies itself free to dispense with proof, goes
hand in hand with empty rationalism—(which means to
be so much opposed to it, though both repose really on
the same habit of mind)—in the wanton assertion, almost as if it merely mentioned a notorious fact, that
Philosophy is the All-one doctrine, or Pantheism. It
must be said that it was more to the credit of piety and
theology when they accused a philosophical system (e.g.
Spinozism) of Atheism than of Pantheism, though the
former imputation at the first glance looks more cruel
and insidious. The imputation of Atheism presupposes
a definite idea of a full and real God, and arises because
the popular idea does not detect in the philosophical
notion the peculiar form to which it is attached. Philosophy indeed can recognise its own forms in the
categories of religious consciousness, and even its own
teaching in the doctrine of religion—which therefore it
does not disparage. But the converse is not true: the
religious consciousness does not apply the criticism of
thought to itself, does not comprehend itself, and is
therefore, as it stands, exclusive. To impute Pantheism instead of Atheism to Philosophy is part of the
modern habit of mind—of the new piety and new theology. For them philosophy has too much of God:—so
much so, that, if we believe them, it asserts that God
is everything and everything is God. This new theology,
which makes religion only a subjective feeling and denies
the knowledge of the divine nature, thus retains nothing
more than a God in general without objective characteristics. Without interest of his own for the concrete,
fulfilled notion of God, it treats it only as an interest
which *others* once had, and hence treats what belongs to
the doctrine of God's concrete nature as something
merely historical. The indeterminate God is to be found
in all religions; every kind of piety—that of the Hindoo

to asses, cows,—or to dalailamas,—that of the Egyptians to the ox—is always adoration of an object which, with all its absurdities, also contains the generic abstract, God in General. If this theory needs no more than such a God, so as to find God in everything called religion, it must at least find such a God recognised even in philosophy, and can no longer accuse it of Atheism. The mitigation of the reproach of Atheism into that of Pantheism has its ground therefore in the superficial idea to which this mildness has attenuated and emptied God. As that popular idea clings to its abstract universality, from which all definite quality is excluded, all such definiteness is only the non-divine, the secularity of things, thus left standing in fixed undisturbed substantiality. On such a presupposition, even after philosophy has maintained God's absolute universality, and the consequent untruth of being of external things, the hearer clings as he did before to his belief that secular things still keep their being, and form all that is definite in the divine universality. He thus changes that universality into what he calls the pantheistic:—*Everything is* —(empirical things, without distinction, whether higher or lower in the scale, *are*)—all possess substantiality; and so—thus he understands philosophy—each and every secular thing is God. It is only his own stupidity, and the falsifications due to such misconception, which generate the imagination and the allegation of such pantheism.

But if those who give out that a certain philosophy is Pantheism, are unable and unwilling to see this—for it is just to see the notion that they refuse—they should before everything have verified the alleged fact that *any one philosopher, or any one man,* had really ascribed substantial or objective and inherent reality to *all* things and regarded them as God:—that such an idea had ever come into the hand of any body but themselves. This allegation I will further elucidate in this exoteric discussion: and the only way to do so is to set down the evidence. If we want to take so-called Pantheism in its most poetical, most sublime, or if you will its grossest shape, we must, as is well known, consult the oriental poets: and the most copious delineations of it are found in Hindoo literature. Amongst the abundant resources open to our disposal on this topic, I select—as the most authentic statement accessible—the Bhagavat-Gita, and amongst its effusions, prolix and reiterative *ad nauseam,* some of the most telling passages. In the 10th Lesson (in Schlegel, p. 162) Krishna says of himself *:—'I am the self, seated in the hearts of all beings. I am the beginning and the middle and the end also of all beings . . . I am the beaming sun amongst the shining ones, and the moon among the lunar mansions. . . . Amongst the Vedas I am the Sama-Veda: I am mind amongst the senses: I am consciousness in living beings. And I am Sankara (Siva) among the Rudras, . . . Meru among the high-topped mountains, . . . the Himalaya among the firmly-fixed (mountains) . . . Among beasts I am the lord of beasts . . . Among letters I am the letter A . . . I am the spring among the seasons . . . I am also that which is the seed of all things: there is nothing moveable or immoveable which can exist without me.'

Even in these totally sensuous delineations, Krishna (and we must not suppose there is, besides Krishna, still God, or a God besides; as he said before he was Siva, or Indra, so it is afterwards said that Brahma too is in him) makes himself out to be—not everything, but only—the most excellent of everything. Every-

* [The citation given by Hegel from Schlegel's translation is here replaced by the version (in one or two points different) in the *Sacred Books of the East,* vol. viii.]

where there is a distinction drawn between external, unessential existences, and one essential amongst them, which he is. Even when, at the beginning of the passage, he is said to be the beginning, middle, and end of living things, this totality is distinguished from the living things themselves as single existences. Even such a picture which extends deity far and wide in its existence cannot be called pantheism: we must rather say that in the infinitely multiple empirical world, everything is reduced to a limited number of essential existences, to a polytheism. But even what has been quoted shows that these very substantialities of the externally-existent do not retain the independence entitling them to be named Gods; even Siva, Indra, &c. melt into the one Krishna.

This reduction is more expressly made in the following scene (7th Lesson, p. 7 sqq.). Krishna says: 'I am the producer and the destroyer of the whole universe. There is nothing else higher than myself; all this is woven upon me, like number of pearls upon a thread. I am the taste in water; . . . I am the light of the sun and the moon; I am "Om" in all the Vedas. . . . I am life in all beings. . . . I am the discernment of the discerning ones. . . . I am also the strength of the strong.' Then he adds: 'The whole universe deluded by these three states of mind developed from the qualities [sc. goodness, passion, darkness] does not know me who am beyond them and inexhaustible: for this delusion of mine,' [even the Maya is *his*, nothing independent], 'developed from the qualities is divine and difficult to transcend. Those cross beyond this delusion who resort to me alone.' Then the picture gathers itself up in a simple expression: 'At the end of many lives, the man possessed of knowledge approaches me, (believing) that Vasudeva is everything. Such a high-souled mind is very hard to find. Those who are deprived of knowledge by various desires approach other divinities . . . Whichever form of deity one worships with faith, from it he obtains the beneficial things he desires really given by me. But the fruit thus obtained by those of little judgment is perishable. . . . The undiscerning ones, not knowing my transcendent and inexhaustible essence, than which there is nothing higher, think me who am unperceived to have become perceptible.'

This 'All,' which Krishna calls himself, is not, any more than the Eleatic One, and the Spinozan Substance, the Every-thing. This every-thing, rather, the infinitely-manifold sensuous manifold of the finite is in all these pictures, but defined as the 'accidental,' without essential being of its very own, but having its truth in the substance, the One which, as different from that accidental, is alone the divine and God. Hindooism however has the higher conception of Brahma, the pure unity of thought in itself, where the empirical everything of the world, as also those proximate substantialities, called Gods, vanish. On that account Colebrooke and many others have described the Hindoo religion as at bottom a Monotheism. That this description is not incorrect is clear from these short citations. But so little concrete is this divine unity—spiritual as its idea of God is—so powerless its grip, so to speak—that Hindooism, with a monstrous inconsistency, is also the maddest of polytheisms. But the idolatry of the wretched Hindoo, when he adores the ape, or other creature, is still a long way from that wretched fancy of a Pantheism, to which everything is God, and God everything. Hindoo monotheism moreover is itself an example how little comes of mere monotheism, if the Idea of God is not deeply determinate in itself. For that unity, if it be intrinsically abstract and therefore empty,

tends of itself to let whatever is concrete, outside it—
be it as a lot of Gods or as a secular, empirical individuals—keep its independence.   That pantheism indeed—on the shallow conception of it—might with a
show of logic as well be called a monotheism; for if
God, as it says, is identical with the world, then as there
is only one world there would be in that pantheism only
one God.   Perhaps the empty numerical unity must be
predicated of the world: but such abstract predication of
it has no further special interest; on the contrary, a
mere numerical unity just means that its *content* is an
infinite multeity and variety of finitudes.   But it is
that delusion with the empty unity, which alone makes
possible and induces the wrong idea of pantheism.   It
is only the picture—floating in the indefinite blue—of
the world as *one thing, the all,* that could ever be considered capable of combining with God: only on that
assumption could philosophy be supposed to teach that
God is the world: for if the world were taken as it is,
as everything, as the endless lot of empirical existence,
then it would hardly have been even held possible to
suppose a pantheism which asserted of such stuff that
it is God.

But to go back again to the question of fact.   If we
want to see the consciousness of the One—not as with
the Hindoos split between the featureless unity of abstract thought, on one hand, and on the other, the long-
winded weary story of its particular detail, but—in its
finest purity and sublimity, we must consult the Mohammedans.   If e.g. in the excellent Jelaleddin-Rumi in
particular, we find the unity of the soul with the One
set forth, and that unity described as love, this spiritual
unity is an exaltation above the finite and vulgar, a
transfiguration of the natural and the spiritual, in which
the externalism and transitoriness of immediate nature,

and of empirical secular spirit, is discarded and absorbed.*

* In order to give a clearer impression of it, I cannot refrain from quoting a few passages, which may at the same time give some indication of the marvellous skill of Rückert, from whom they are taken, as a translator. [For Rückert's verses a version is here substituted in which I have been kindly helped by Miss May Kendall.]

III.

I saw but One through all heaven's starry spaces gleaming:
  I saw but One in all sea billows wildly streaming.
I looked into the heart, a waste of worlds, a sea, ——
  I saw a thousand dreams,—yet One amid all dreaming.
And earth, air, water, fire, when thy decree is given,
  Are molten into One: against thee none hath striven.
There is no living heart but beats unfailingly
  In the one song of praise to thee, from earth and heaven.

V.

As one ray of thy light appears the noonday sun,
But yet thy light and mine eternally are one.
As dust beneath thy feet the heaven that rolls on high:
Yet only one, and one for ever, thou and I.
The dust may turn to heaven, and heaven to dust decay;
Yet art thou one with me, and shalt be one for aye.
How may the words of life that fill heaven's utmost part
Rest in the narrow casket of one poor human heart?
How can the sun's own rays, a fairer glean to fling,
Hide in a lowly husk, the jewel's covering?
How may the rose-grove all its glorious bloom unfold,
Drinking in mire and slime, and feeding on the mould?
How can the darksome shell that sips the salt sea stream
Fashion a shining pearl, the sunlight's joyous beam?
Oh, heart! should warm winds fan thee, should'st thou floods
    endure,
One element are wind and flood; but be thou pure.

I refrain from accumulating further examples of the religious and poetic conceptions which it is customary to call pantheistic. Of the philosophies to which that name is given, the Eleatic, or Spinozist, it has been remarked earlier that so far are they from identifying

IX.

I'll tell thee how from out the dust God moulded man, ——
Because the breath of Love He breathed into his clay:
I'll tell thee why the spheres their whirling paths began, ——
They mirror to God's throne Love's glory day by day:
I'll tell thee why the morning winds blow o'er the grove, ——
It is to bid Love's roses bloom abundantly:
I'll tell thee why the night broods deep the earth above, ——
Love's bridal tent to deck with sacred canopy:
All riddles of the earth dost thou desire to prove? ——
To every earthly riddle is Love alone the key.

XV.

Life shrinks from Death in woe and fear,
    Though Death ends well Life's bitter need:
So shrinks the heart when Love draws near,
    As though 'twere Death in very deed:
For wheresoever Love finds room,
    There Self, the sullen tyrant, dies.
So let him perish in the bloom, ——
    Thou to the dawn of freedom rise.

In this poetry, which soars over all that is external and sensuous, who would recognise the prosaic ideas current about so-called pantheism—ideas which let the divine sink to the external and the sensuous? The copious extracts which Tholuck, in his work *Anthology from the Eastern Mystics*, gives us from the poems of Jelaleddin and others, are made from the very point of view now under discussion. In his Introduction, Herr Tholuck proves how profoundly his soul has caught the note of mysticism; and there, too, he points out

God with the world and making him finite, that in these systems this 'everything' has no truth, and that we should rather call them monotheistic, or, in relation to the popular idea of the world, acosmical. They are most accurately called systems which apprehend the Absolute only as substance. Of the oriental, especially the Mohammedan, modes of envisaging God, we may rather say that they represent the Absolute as the utterly universal genus which dwells in the species or existences, but dwells so potently that these existences have no actual reality. The fault of all these modes of thought and systems is that they stop short of defining substance as subject and as mind.

These systems and modes of pictorial conception originate from the one need common to all philosophies and all religions of getting an idea of God, and, secondly, of the relationship of God and the world. (In philosophy it is specially made out that the determination of God's nature determines his relations with the world.) The 'reflective' understanding begins by rejecting all

the characteristic traits of its oriental phase, in distinction from that of the West and Christendom. With all their divergence, however, they have in common the mystical character. The conjunction of Mysticism with so-called Pantheism, as he says (p. 53), implies that inward quickening of soul and spirit which inevitably tends to annihilate that external *Everything,* which Pantheism is usually held to adore. But beyond that, Herr Tholuck leaves matters standing at the usual indistinct conception of Pantheism; a profounder discussion of it would have had, for the author's emotional Christianity, no direct interest; but we see that personally he is carried away by remarkable enthusiasm for a mysticism which, in the ordinary phrase, entirely deserves the epithet Pantheistic. Where, however, he tries philosophising (p. 12), he does not get beyond the standpoint of the 'rationalist' metaphysic with its uncritical categories.

systems and modes of conception, which, whether they
spring from heart, imagination or speculation, express
the inter-connexion of God and the world: and in order
to have God pure in faith or consciousness, he is as
essence parted from appearance, as infinite from the
finite.   But, after this partition, the conviction arises
also that the appearance has a relation to the essence,
the finite to the infinite, and so on: and thus arises the
question of reflection as to the nature of this relation.
It is in the reflective form that the whole difficulty of
the affair lies, and that causes this relation to be called
incomprehensible by the agnostic.   The close of philosophy is not the place, even in a general exoteric discussion, to waste a word on what a 'notion' means.   But
as the view taken of this relation is closely connected
with the view taken of philosophy generally and with all
imputations against it, we may still add the remark that
though philosophy certainly has to do with unity in
general, it is not however with abstract unity, mere
identity, and the empty absolute, but with concrete
unity (the notion), and that in its whole course it has
to do with nothing else;—that each step in its advance
is a peculiar term or phase of this concrete unity, and
that the deepest and last expression of unity is the
unity of absolute mind itself.   Would-be judges and
critics of philosophy might be recommended to familiar-
ise themselves with these phases of unity and to take
the trouble to get acquainted with them, at least to
know so much that of these terms there are a great many,
and that amongst them there is great variety.   But they
show so little acquaintance with them—and still less
take trouble about it—that, when they hear of unity—
and relation *ipso facto* implies unity—they rather stick
fast at quite abstract indeterminate unity, and lose sight
of the chief point of interest—the special mode in which

the unity is qualified. Hence all they can say about
philosophy is that dry identity is its principle and result,
and that it is the system of identity. Sticking fast to
the undigested thought of identity, they have laid hands
on, not the concrete unity, the notion and content of
philosophy, but rather its reverse. In the philosophical
field they proceed, as in the physical field the physicist;
who also is well aware that he has before him a variety
of sensuous properties and matters—or usually matters
alone, (for the properties get transformed into matters
also for the physicist)—and that these matters (elements) *also* stand in *relation* to one another. But the
question is, Of what kind is this relation? Every peculiarity and the whole difference of natural things, inorganic and living, depend solely on the different modes
of this unity. But instead of ascertaining these different modes, the ordinary physicist (chemist included)
takes up only one, the most external and the worst, viz.
composition, applies only it in the whole range of
natural structures, which he thus renders for ever inexplicable.

The aforesaid shallow pantheism is an equally obvious
inference from this shallow identity. All that those who
employ this invention of their own to accuse philosophy
gather from the study of God's *relation* to the world is
that the one, but only the one factor of this category of
relation—and that the factor of indeterminateness—is
identity. Thereupon they stick fast in this half-per-
ception, and assert—falsely as a fact—that philosophy
teaches the identity of God and the world. And as in
their judgment either of the two,—the world as much as
God—has the same solid substantiality as the other,
they infer that in the philosophic Idea God is *composed*
of God and the world. Such then is the idea they form
of pantheism, and which they ascribe to philosophy.

Unaccustomed in their own thinking and apprehending of thoughts to go beyond such categories, they import them into philosophy, where they are utterly unknown; they thus infect it with the disease against which they subsequently raise an outcry.   If any difficulty emerge in comprehending God's relation to the world, they at once and very easily escape it by admitting that this relation contains for them an inexplicable contradiction; and that hence, they must stop at the vague conception of such relation, perhaps under the more familiar names of, e.g. omnipresence, providence, &c.   Faith in their use of the term means no more than a refusal to define the conception, or to enter on a closer discussion of the problem.   That men and classes of untrained intellect are satisfied with such indefiniteness, is what one expects; but when a trained intellect and an interest for reflective study is satisfied, in matters admitted to be of superior, if not even of supreme interest, with indefinite ideas, it is hard to decide whether the thinker is really in earnest with the subject.   But if those who cling to this crude 'rationalism' were in earnest, e.g. with God's omnipresence, so far as to realise their faith thereon in a definite mental idea, in what difficulties would they be involved by their belief in the true reality of the things of sense!   They would hardly like, as Epicurus does, to let God dwell in the interspaces of things, i.e. in the pores of the physicists,—said pores being the negative, something supposed to exist *beside* the material reality.   This very 'Beside' would give their pantheism its spatiality,—their everything, conceived as the mutual exclusion of parts in space.   But in ascribing to God, in his relation to the world, an action on and in the space thus filled on the world and in it, they would endlessly split up the divine actuality into infinite materiality.   They would really thus have the misconception they call pantheism or all-one-doctrine, only as the necessary sequel of their misconceptions of God and the world. But to put that sort of thing, this stale gossip of oneness or identity, on the shoulders of philosophy, shows such recklessness about justice and truth that it can only be explained through the difficulty of getting into the head thoughts of notions, i.e. not abstract unity, but the many-shaped modes specified. If statements as to facts are put forward, and the facts in question are thoughts and notions, it is indispensable to get hold of their meaning. But even the fulfilment of this requirement has been rendered superfluous, now that it has long been a foregone conclusion that philosophy is pantheism, a system of identity, an all-one-doctrine, and that the person therefore who might be unaware of this fact is treated either as merely unaware of a matter of common notoriety, or as prevaricating for a purpose. On account of this chorus of assertions, then, I have believed myself obliged to speak at more length and exoterically on the outward and inward untruth of this alleged fact: for exoteric discussion is the only method available in dealing with the external apprehension of notions as mere facts,—by which notions are perverted into their opposite. The esoteric study of God and identity, as of cognitions and notions, is philosophy itself.

574. This notion of philosophy is the self-thinking Idea, the truth aware of itself,—the logical system, but with the signification that it is universality approved and certified in concrete content as in its actuality. In this way the science has gone back to its beginning: its result is the logical system but as a spiritual principle: out of the presupposing judgment, in which the notion was only implicit and the beginning an immediate,— and thus out of the *appearance* which it had there—it

has risen into its pure principle and thus also into its proper medium.

575. It is this appearing which originally gives the motive of the further development. The first appearance is formed by the syllogism, which is based on the Logical system as starting-point, with Nature for the middle term which couples the Mind with it. The Logical principle turns to Nature and Nature to Mind. Nature, standing between the Mind and its essence, sunders itself, not indeed to extremes of finite abstraction, nor itself to something away from them and independent,—which, as other than they, only serves as a link between them: for the syllogism is *in the Idea* and Nature is essentially defined as a transition-point and negative factor, and as implicitly the Idea. Still the mediation of the notion has the external form of *transition,* and the science of Nature presents itself as the course of necessity, so that it is only in the one extreme that the liberty of the notion is explicit as a self-amalgamation.

576. In the second syllogism this appearance is so far superseded, that that syllogism is the standpoint of the Mind itself, which—as the mediating agent in the process—presupposes Nature and couples it with the Logical principle. It is the syllogism where Mind reflects on itself in the Idea: philosophy appears as a subjective cognition, of which liberty is the aim, and which is itself the way to produce it.

577. The third syllogism is the Idea of philosophy, which has self-knowing reason, the absolutely-universal, for its middle term: a middle, which divides itself into Mind and Nature, making the former its presupposition, as process of the Idea's subjective activity, and the latter its universal extreme, as process of the objectively and implicitly existing Idea. The self-judging of the

Idea into its two appearances characterises both as its
(the self-knowing reason's) manifestations: and in it
there is a unification of the two aspects:—it is the nature
of the fact, the notion, which causes the movement and
development, yet this same movement is equally the
action of cognition. The eternal Idea, in full fruition
of its essence, eternally sets itself to work, engenders
and enjoys itself as absolute Mind.

VIII

INTRODUCTION TO THE PHI-LOSOPHY OF ART *

Selected and translated by J. Loewenberg

THE MEANING OF ART

THE appropriate expression for our subject is the Philosophy of Art, or, more precisely, the Philosophy of Fine Arts. By this expression we wish to exclude the beauty of nature. In common life we are in the habit of speaking of beautiful color, a beautiful sky, a beautiful river, beautiful flowers, beautiful animals, and beautiful human beings. But quite aside from the question, which we wish not to discuss here, how far beauty may be predicated of such objects, or how far natural beauty may be placed side by side with artistic beauty, we must begin by maintaining that artistic beauty is higher than the beauty of nature. For the beauty of art is beauty born—and born again—of the spirit. And as spirit and its products stand higher than nature and its phenomena, by so much the beauty that resides in art is superior to the beauty of nature.

To say that spirit and artistic beauty stand higher than natural beauty, is to say very little, for 'higher' is a very indefinite expression, which states the difference between them as quantitative and external. The 'higher' quality of spirit and of artistic beauty does not at all stand in a merely relative position to nature. Spirit only is the true essence and content of the world,

* From Hegel's Preface to *Vorlesungen über die Aesthetik*.

so that whatever is beautiful is truly beautiful only when it partakes of this higher essence and is produced by it. In this sense natural beauty appears only as a reflection of the beauty that belongs to spirit; it is an imperfect and incomplete expression .of the spiritual substance.

Confining ourselves to artistic beauty, we must first consider certain difficulties. The first that suggests itself is the question whether art is at all worthy of a philosophic treatment. To be sure, art and beauty pervade, like a kindly genius, all the affairs of life, and joyously adorn all its inner and outer phases, softening the gravity and the burden of actual existence, furnishing pleasure for idle moments, and, where it can accomplish nothing positive, driving evil away by occupying its place. Yet, although art wins its way everywhere with its pleasing forms, from the crude adornment of the savages to the splendour of the temple with its marvellous wealth of decoration, art itself appears to fall outside the real aims of life. And though the creations of art cannot be said to be directly disadvantageous to the serious purposes of life, nay, on occasion actually further them by holding evil at bay, on the whole, art belongs to the relaxation and leisure of the mind, while the substantial interests of life demand its exertion. At any rate, such a view renders art a superfluity, though the tender and emotional influence which is wrought upon the mind by occupation with art is not thought necessarily detrimental, because effeminate.

There are others, again, who, though acknowledging art to be a luxury, have thought it necessary to defend it by pointing to the practical necessities of the fine arts and to the relation they bear to morality and piety. Very serious aims have been ascribed to art. Art has been recommended as a mediator between reason and sensuousness, between inclination and duty, as the reconcilor of all these elements constantly warring with one another.   But it must be said that, by making art serve two masters, it is not rendered thereby more worthy of a philosophic treatment.   Instead of being an end in itself, art is degraded into a means of appealing to higher aims, on the one hand, and to frivolity and idleness on the other.

Art considered as means offers another difficulty which springs from its form.   Granting that art can be subordinated to serious aims and that the results which it thus produces will be significant, still the means used by art is deception, for beauty is appearance, its form is its life; and one must admit that a true and real purpose should not be achieved through deception.   Even if a good end is thus, now and then, attained by art its success is rather limited, and even then deception cannot be recommended as a worthy means; for the means should be adequate to the dignity of the end, and truth can be produced by truth alone and not by deception and semblance.

It may thus appear as if art were not worthy of philosophic consideration because it is supposed to be merely a pleasing pastime; even when it pursues more serious aims it does not correspond with their nature. On the whole, it is conceived to serve both grave and light interests, achieving its results by means of deception and semblance.

As for the worthiness of art to be philosophically considered, it is indeed true that art can be used as a casual amusement, furnishing enjoyment and pleasure, decorating our surroundings, lending grace to the external conditions of life, and giving prominence to other objects through ornamentation.   Art thus employed is indeed not an independent or free, but rather a subservient art. That art might serve other purposes and still retain its pleasure-giving function, is a relation which it has in common with thought. For science, too, in the hands of the servile understanding is used for finite ends and accidental means, and is thus not self-sufficient, but is determined by outer objects and circumstances. On the other hand, science can emancipate itself from such service and can rise in free independence to the pursuit of truth, in which the realization of its own aims is its proper function.

Art is not genuine art until it has thus liberated itself. It fulfils its highest task when it has joined the same sphere with religion and philosophy and has become a certain mode of bringing to consciousness and expression the divine meaning of things, the deepest interests of mankind, and the most universal truths of the spirit. Into works of art the nations have wrought their most profound ideas and aspirations. Fine Art often constitutes the key, and with many nations it is the only key, to an understanding of their wisdom and religion. This character art has in common with religion and philosophy. Art's peculiar feature, however, consists in its ability to represent in *sensuous form* even the highest ideas, bringing them thus nearer to the character of natural phenomena, to the senses, and to feeling. It is the height of a supra-sensuous world into which *thought* reaches, but it always appears to immediate consciousness and to present experience as an alien *beyond*. Through the power of philosophic thinking we are able to soar above what is merely *here*, above sensuous and finite experience. But spirit can heal the breach between the supra-sensuous and the sensuous brought on by its own advance; it produces out of itself the world of fine art as the first reconciling medium between what is merely external, sensuous, and transient, and the world of pure thought, between nature with its finite reality and the infinite freedom of philosophic reason.

Concerning the unworthiness of art because of its character as appearance and deception, it must be admitted that such criticism would not be without justice, if appearance could be said to be equivalent to falsehood and thus to something that ought not to be. Appearance is essential to reality; truth could not be, did it not shine through appearance. Therefore not appearance in general can be objected to, but merely the particular kind of appearance through which art seeks to portray truth. To charge the appearance in which art chooses to embody its ideas as deception, receives meaning only by comparison with the external world of phenomena and its immediate materiality, as well as with the inner world of sensations and feelings. To these two worlds we are wont, in our empirical work-a-day life, to attribute the value of actuality, reality, and truth, in contrast to art, which is supposed to be lacking such reality and truth. But, in fact, it is just the whole sphere of the empirical inner and outer world that is not the world of true reality; indeed it may be called a mere show and a cruel deception in a far stricter sense than in the case of art. Only beyond the immediacy of sense and of external objects is genuine reality to be found. Truly real is but the fundamental essence and the underlying substance of nature and of spirit, and the universal element in nature and in spirit is precisely what art accentuates and makes visible. This essence of reality appears also in the common outer and inner world, but it appears in the form of a chaos of contingencies, distorted by the immediateness of sense perception, and by the capriciousness and conditions, events, characters, etc. Art frees the true meaning of

appearances from the show and deception of this bad
and transient world, and invests it with a higher reality
and a more genuine being than the things of ordinary
life.

THE CONTENT AND IDEAL OF ART

The content of art is spiritual, and its form is sensuous; both sides art has to reconcile into a united whole.
The first requirement is that the content, which art is
to represent, must be worthy of artistic representation;
otherwise we obtain only a bad unity, since a content
not capable of artistic treatment is made to take on an
artistic form, and a matter prosaic in itself is forced
into a form quite opposed to its inherent nature.

The second requirement demands of the content of
art that it shall be no abstraction. By this is not meant
that it must be concrete, as the sensuous is alleged to
be concrete in contrast to everything spiritual and intellectual. For everything that is genuinely true, in
the realm of thought as well as in the domain of
nature, is concrete, and has, in spite of universality,
nevertheless, a particular and subjective character. By
saying, for example, that God is simply One, the
Supreme Being as such, we express thereby nothing
but a lifeless abstraction of an understanding devoid of
reason. Such a God, as indeed he is not conceived in
his concrete truth, can furnish no content for art, least
of all for plastic art. Thus the Jews and the Turks
have not been able to represent their God, who is still
more abstract, in the positive manner in which the Christians have represented theirs. For in Christianity God
is conceived in his truth, and therefore concrete, as a
person, as a subject, and, more precisely still, as Spirit.
What he is as spirit appears to the religious conscious-

ness as a Trinity of persons, which at the same time is One. Here the essence of God is the reconciled unity of universality and particularity, such unity alone being concrete. Hence, as a content in order to be true must be concrete in this sense, art demands the same concreteness; because a mere abstract idea, or an abstract universal, cannot manifest itself in a particular and sensuous unified form.

If a true and therefore concrete content is to have its adequate sensuous form and shape, this sensuous form must—this being the third requirement—also be something individual, completely concrete, and one. The nature of concreteness belonging to both the content and the representation of art, is precisely the point in which both can coincide and correspond to each other. The natural shape of the human body, for example, is a sensuous concrete object, which is perfectly adequate to represent the spiritual in its concreteness; the view should therefore be abandoned that an existing object from the external world is accidentally chosen by art to express a spiritual idea. Art does not seize upon this or that form either because it simply finds it or because it can find no other, but the concrete spiritual content itself carries with it the element of external, real, yes, even sensuous, representation. And this is the reason why a sensuous concrete object, which bears the impress of an essentially spiritual content, addresses itself to the inner eye; the outward shape whereby the content is rendered visible and imaginable aims at an existence only in our heart and mind. For this reason alone are content and artistic shape harmoniously wrought. The mere sensuously concrete external nature as such has not this purpose for its only origin. The gay and variegated plumage of the birds shines unseen, and their song dies away unheard; the torch-thistle which blossoms only for a night withers without having been admired in the wilds of southern forests; and these forests, groves of the most beautiful and luxuriant vegetation, with the most odorous and fragrant perfumes, perish and waste, no more enjoyed. The work of art is not so unconsciously self-immersed, but it is essentially a question, an address to the responsive soul, an appeal to the heart and to the mind.

Although the sensuous form in which art clothes its content is not accidental, yet it is not the highest form whereby the spiritually concrete may be grasped. A higher mode than representation through a sensuous form, is thought. True and rational thinking, though in a relative sense abstract, must not be one-sided, but concrete. How far a definite content can be adequately treated by art and how far it needs, according to its nature, a higher and more spiritual form, is a distinction which we see at once, if, for example, the Greek gods are compared with God as conceived in accordance with Christian notions. The Greek god is not abstract but individual, closely related to the natural human form. The Christian God is also a concrete personality, but he is purely spiritual, and can be known only as spirit and in spirit. His sphere of existence is therefore essentially inner knowledge, and not the outer natural shape through which he can be represented but imperfectly and not in the whole depth of his essence.

But the task of art is to represent a spiritual idea to direct contemplation in sensuous form, and not in the form of thought or of pure spirituality. The value and dignity of such representation lies in the correspondence and unity of the two sides, of the spiritual content and its sensuous embodiment, so that the perfection and excellency of art must depend upon the grade of inner

harmony and union with which the spiritual idea and the
sensuous form interpenetrate.

The requirement of the conformity of spiritual idea
and sensuous form might at first be interpreted as meaning that any idea whatever would suffice, so long as the
concrete form represented this idea and no other.   Such
a view, however, would confound the ideal of art with
mere correctness, which consists in the expression of
any meaning in its appropriate form.   The artistic ideal
is not to be thus understood.   For any content whatever
is capable, according to the standard of its own nature,
of adequate representation, but yet it does not for that
reason lay claim to artistic beauty in the ideal sense.
Judged by the standard of ideal beauty, even such correct representation will be defective.   In this connection
we may remark that the defects of a work of art are not
to be considered simply as always due to the incapacity
of the artist; defectiveness of form has also its root in
defectiveness of content.   Thus, for instance, the Chinese, Indians, Egyptians, in their artistic objects, their
representations of the gods, and their idols, adhered to
formlessness, or to a vague and inarticulate form, and
were not able to arrive at genuine beauty, because their
mythological ideas, the content and conception of their
works of art, were as yet vague and obscure.   The more
perfect in form works of art are, the more profound is
the inner truth of their content and thought.   And it is
not merely a question of the greater or lesser skill with
which the objects of external nature are studied and
copied, for, in certain stages of artistic consciousness and
artistic activity, the misrepresentation and distortion of
natural objects are not unintentional technical inexpert-
ness and incapacity, but conscious alteration, which depends upon the content that is in consciousness, and is,
in fact, demanded by it.   We may thus speak of im-

perfect art, which, in its own proper sphere, may be quite perfect both technically and in other respects. When compared with the highest idea and ideal of art, it is indeed defective. In the highest art alone are the idea and its representation in perfect congruity, because the sensuous form of the idea is in itself the adequate form, and because the content, which that form embodies, is itself a genuine content.

The higher truth of art consists, then, in the spiritual having attained a sensuous form adequate to its essence. And this also furnishes the principle of division for the philosophy of art. For the Spirit, before it wins the true notion or meaning of its absolute essence, has to develop through a series of stages which constitute its very life. To this universal evolution there corresponds a development of the phases of art, under the form of which the Spirit—as artist—attains to a comprehension of its own meaning.

This evolution within the spirit of art has two sides. The development is, in the first place, a spiritual and universal one, in so far as a gradual series of definite conceptions of the universe—of nature, man, and God— finds artistic representation. In the second place, this universal development of art, embodying itself in sensuous form, determines definite modes of artistic expression and a totality of necessary distinctions within the sphere of art. These constitute the particular arts.

We have now to consider three definite relations of the spiritual idea to its sensuous expression.

SYMBOLIC ART

Art begins when the spiritual idea, being itself still indefinite and obscure and ill-comprehended, is made the content of artistic forms. As indefinite, it does not yet

have that individuality which the artistic ideal demands;
its abstractness and one-sidedness thus render its shape
defective and whimsical.   The first form of art is therefore rather a mere search after plasticity than a capacity
of true representation.   The spiritual idea has not yet
found its adequate form, but is still engaged in striving
and struggling after it.   This form we may, in general,
call the *symbolic* form of art; in such form the abstract
idea assumes a shape in natural sensuous matter which
is foreign to it; with this foreign matter the artistic
creation begins, from which, however, it seems unable
to free itself.   The objects of external nature are repro-
duced unchanged, but at the same time the meaning of
the spiritual idea is attached to them.   They thus receive
the vocation of expressing it, and must be interpreted as
if the spiritual idea were actually present in them.   It
is indeed true that natural objects possess an aspect
which makes them capable of representing a universal
meaning, but in symbolic art a complete correspondence
is not yet possible.   In it the correspondence is confined to an abstract quality, as when, for example, a
lion is meant to stand for strength.

This abstract relation brings also to consciousness the
foreignness of the spiritual idea to natural phenomena.
And the spiritual idea, having no other reality to express
its essence, expatiates in all these natural shapes, seeks
itself in their unrest and disproportion, but finds them
inadequate to it.   It then exaggerates these natural phenomena and shapes them into the huge and the boundless.
The spiritual idea revels in them, as it were, seethes and
ferments in them, does violence to them, distorts and
disfigures them into grotesque shapes, and endeavors by
the diversity, hugeness, and splendor of such forms to
raise the natural phenomena to the spiritual level.   For
here it is the spiritual idea which is more or less vague

and non-plastic, while the objects of nature have a thoroughly definite form.

The incongruity of the two elements to each other makes the relation of the spiritual idea to objective reality a negative one. The spiritual as a wholly inner element and as the universal substance of all things, is conceived unsatisfied with all externality, and in its *sublimity* it triumphs over the abundance of unsuitable forms. In this conception of sublimity the natural objects and the human shapes are accepted and left unaltered, but at the same time recognized as inadequate to their own inner meaning; it is this inner meaning which is glorified far and above every worldly content.

These elements constitute, in general, the character of the primitive artistic pantheism of the Orient, which either invests even the lowest objects with absolute significance, or forces all phenomena with violence to assume the expression of its world-view. This art becomes therefore bizarre, grotesque, and without taste, or it represents the infinite substance in its abstract freedom turning away with disdain from the illusory and perishing mass of appearances. Thus the meaning can never be completely molded into the expression, and, notwithstanding all the aspiration and effort, the incongruity between the spiritual idea and the sensuous form remains insuperable. This is, then, the first form of art—symbolic art with its endless quest, its inner struggle, its sphinx-like mystery, and its sublimity.

CLASSICAL ART

In the second form of art, which we wish to designate as the *classical*, the double defect of symbolic art is removed. The symbolic form is imperfect, because the spiritual meaning which it seeks to convey enters into consciousness in but an abstract and vague manner, and thus the congruity between meaning and form must always remain defective and therefore abstract. This double aspect disappears in the classical type of art; in it we find the free and adequate embodiment of the spiritual idea in the form most suitable to it, and with it meaning and expression are in perfect accord. It is classical art, therefore, which first affords the creation and contemplation of the completed ideal, realizing it as a real fact in the world.

But the congruity of idea and reality in classical art must not be taken in the formal sense of the agreement of a content with its external form; otherwise every photograph of nature, every picture of a countenance, landscape, flower, scene, etc., which constitutes the aim of a representation, would, through the conformity of content and form, be at once classical. The peculiarity of classical art, on the contrary, consists in its content being itself a concrete idea, and, as such, a concrete spiritual idea, for only the spiritual is a truly classical content. For a worthy object of such a content, Nature must be consulted as to whether she contains anything to which a spiritual attribute really belongs. It must be the World-Spirit itself that *invented* the proper form for the concrete spiritual ideal; the subjective mind— in this case the spirit of art—has only *found* it, and given it natural plastic existence in accordance with free individual spirituality. The form in which the idea, as spiritual and individual, clothes itself when revealed as a temporal phenomenon, is *the human form*. To be sure, personification and anthropomorphism have frequently been decried as a degradation of the spiritual; but art, in so far as its task is to bring before direct contemplation the spiritual in sensuous form, must advance to such anthropomorphism, for only in its body can mind appear in an adequately sensuous fashion. The migration of souls is, in this respect, an abstract notion, and physiology should make it one of its fundamental principles that life has necessarily, in its evolution, to advance to the human shape as the only sensuous phenomenon appropriate to the mind.

The human body as portrayed by classical art is not represented in its mere physical existence, but solely as the natural and sensuous form and garb of mind; it is therefore divested of all the defects that belong to the merely sensuous and of all the finite contingencies that appertain to the phenomenal. But if the form must be thus purified in order to express the appropriate content, and, furthermore, if the conformity of meaning and expression is to be complete, the content which is the spiritual idea must be perfectly capable of being expressed through the bodily form of man, without projecting into another sphere beyond the physical and sensuous representation. The result is that Spirit is characterized as a particular form of mind, namely, as human mind, and not as simply absolute and eternal; but the absolute and eternal Spirit must be able to reveal and express itself in a manner far more spiritual.

This latter point brings to light the defect of classical art, which demands its dissolution and its transition to a third and higher form, to wit, the *romantic* form of art.

ROMANTIC ART

The romantic form of art destroys the unity of the spiritual idea and its sensuous form, and goes back, though on a higher level, to the difference and opposition of the two, which symbolic art left unreconciled. The classical form of art attained, indeed, the highest degree of perfection which the sensuous process of art was capable of realizing; and, if it shows any defects, the defects are those of art itself, due to the limitation of its sphere. This limitation has its root in the general attempt of art to represent in sensuous concrete form the infinite and universal Spirit, and in the attempt of the classical type of art to blend so completely spiritual and sensuous existence that the two appear in mutual conformity. But in such a fusion of the spiritual and sensuous aspects Spirit cannot be portrayed according to its true essence, for the true essence of Spirit is its infinite subjectivity; and its absolute internal meaning does not lend itself to a full and free expression in the confinement of the bodily form as its only appropriate existence.

Now, romantic art dissolves the inseparable unity which is the ideal of the classical type, because it has won a content which goes beyond the classical form of art and its mode of expression. This content—if familiar ideas may be recalled—coincides with what Christianity declares to be true of God as Spirit, in distinction to the Greek belief in gods which constitutes the essential and appropriate subject for classical art. The concrete content of Hellenic art implies the unity of the human and divine nature, a unity which, just because it is merely *implied* and *immediate,* permits of a representation in an immediately visible and sensuous mold. The Greek god is the object of naïve contemplation and sensuous imagination; his shape is, therefore, the bodily shape of man; the circle of his power and his essence is individual and confined. To man the Greek god appears as a being and a power with whom he may *feel* a kinship and unity, but this kinship and unity, are not reflected upon or raised into definite knowledge. The higher stage is the *knowledge* of this unconscious unity, which underlies the classical form of art and which it has rendered capable of complete plastic embodiment. The elevation of what is unconscious and implied into self-conscious knowledge brings about an enormous difference; it is the infinite difference which, for example, separates man from the animal. Man is an animal, but, even in his animal functions, does not rest satisfied with the potential and the unconscious as the animal does, but becomes conscious of them, reflects upon them, and raises them—as, for instance, the process of digestion—into self-conscious science. And it is thus that man breaks through the boundary of his merely immediate and unconscious existence, so that, just because he knows himself to be animal, he ceases in virtue of such knowledge to be animal, and, through such self-knowledge only, can characterize himself as mind or spirit.

If in the manner just described the unity of the human and divine nature is raised from an *immediate* to a *conscious* unity, the true mold for the reality of this content is no longer the sensuous, immediate existence of the spiritual, the bodily frame of man, but self-conscious and internal contemplation. For this reason Christianity, in depicting God as Spirit—not as particularized individual mind, but as absolute and universal Spirit—retires from the sensuousness of imagination into the sphere of inner being, and makes this, and not the bodily form, the material and mold of its content; and thus the unity of the human and divine nature is a conscious unity, capable of realization only by spiritual knowledge. The new content, won by this unity, is not dependent upon sensuous representation; it is now exempt from such immediate existence. In this way, however, romantic art becomes art which transcends itself, carrying on this process of self-transcendence within its own artistic sphere and artistic form.

Briefly stated, the essence of romantic art consists in the artistic object being the free, concrete, spiritual idea itself, which is revealed in its spirituality to the inner, and not the outer, eye. In conformity with such a content, art can, in a sense, not work for sensuous perception, but must aim at the inner mood, which completely fuses with its object, at the most subjective inner shrine, at the heart, the feeling, which, as spiritual feeling, longs for freedom within itself and seeks and finds reconciliation only within the inner recesses of the spirit. This *inner* world is the content of romantic art, and as such an inner life, or as its reflection, it must seek embodiment. The inner life thus triumphs over the outer world—indeed, so triumphs over it that the outer world itself is made to proclaim its victory, through which the sensuous appearance sinks into worthlessness.

On the other hand, the romantic type of art, like every other, needs an external mode of expression. But the spiritual has now retired from the outer mode into itself, and the sensuous externality of form assumes again, as it did in symbolic art, an insignificant and transient character. The subjective, finite mind and will, the peculiarity and caprice of the individual, of character, action or of incident and plot, assume likewise the character they had in symbolic art. The external side of things is surrendered to accident and committed to the excesses of the imagination, whose caprice now mirrors existence as it is, now chooses to distort the objects of the outer world into a bizarre and grotesque medley, for the external form no longer possesses a meaning and significance, as in classical art, on its own account and for its own sake. Feeling is now everything. It finds its artistic reflection, not in the world of external things and their forms, but in its own expression; and in every incident and accident of life, in every misfortune, grief, and even crime, feeling preserves or regains its healing power of reconciliation.

Hence, the indifference, incongruity, and antagonism of spiritual idea and sensuous form, the characteristics of symbolic art, reappear in the romantic type, but with this essential difference. In the romantic realm, the spiritual idea, to whose defectiveness was due the defective forms of symbolic art, now reveals itself in its perfection within mind and feeling. It is by virtue of the higher perfection of the idea that it shuns any adequate union with an external form, since it can seek and attain its true reality and expression best within itself.

This, in general terms, is the character of the symbolic, classical, and romantic forms of art, which stand for the three relations of the spiritual idea to its expression in the realm of art. They consist in the aspiration after, and the attainment and transcendence of, the ideal as the true idea of beauty.

THE PARTICULAR ARTS

But, now, there inhere in the idea of beauty different motifications which art translates into sensuous forms. And we find a fundamental principle by which the several particular arts may be arranged and defined— that is, the species of art contain in themselves the same essential differences which we have found in the three general types of art. External objectivity, moreover, into which these types are molded by means of a sensuous and particular material, renders them independent and separate means of realizing different artistic functions, as far as each type finds its definite character in some one definite external material whose mode of portrayal determines its adequate realization. Furthermore, the general types of art correspond to the several particular arts, so that they (the particular arts) belong each of them *specifically* to *one* of the general types of art. It is these particular arts which give adequate and artistic external being to the general types.

ARCHITECTURE

The first of the particular arts with which, according to their fundamental principle, we have to begin, is architecture. Its task consists in so shaping external inorganic nature that it becomes homogeneous with mind, as an artistic outer world. The material of architecture is matter itself in its immediate externality as a heavy mass subject to mechanical laws, and its forms remain the forms of inorganic nature, but are merely arranged and ordered in accordance with the abstract rules of the understanding, the rules of symmetry. But in such material and in such forms the ideal as concrete spirituality cannot be realized; the reality which is represented in them remains, therefore, alien to the spiritual idea, as something external which it has not penetrated or with which it has but a remote and abstract relation. Hence the fundamental type of architecture is the *symbolical* form of art. For it is architecture that paves the way, as it were, for the adequate realization of the God, toiling and wrestling in his service with external nature, and seeking to extricate it from the chaos of

finitude, and the abortiveness of chance. By this means
it levels a space for the God, frames his external surroundings, and builds him his temple as the place for
inner contemplation and for reflection upon the eternal
objects of the spirit. It raises an inclosure around those
gathered together, as a defense against the threatening
of the wind, against rain, the thunder-storm, and wild
beasts, and reveals the will to assemble, though
externally, yet in accordance with the artistic form. A
meaning such as this, the art of architecture is able to
mold into its material and its forms with more or less
success, according as the determinate nature of the
content which it seeks to embody is more significant or
more trivial, more concrete or more abstract, more
deeply rooted within its inner being or more dim and
superficial. Indeed, it may even advance so far as to
endeavor to create for such meaning an adequate artistic
expression with its material and forms, but in such an
attempt it has already overstepped the bounds of its
own sphere, and inclines towards sculpture, the higher
phase of art. For the limit of architecture lies precisely in this, that it refers to the spiritual as an internal
essence in contrast with the external forms of its art,
and thus whatever is endowed with mind and spirit must
be indicated as something other than itself.

SCULPTURE

Architecture, however, has purified the inorganic external world, has given it symmetric order, has impressed
upon it the seal of mind, and the temple of the God,
the house of his community, stands ready. Into this
temple now enters the God himself. The lightning-flash
of individuality strikes the inert mass, permeates it, and

a form no longer merely symmetrical, but infinite and spiritual, concentrates and molds its adequate bodily shape. This is the task of sculpture. Inasmuch as in it the inner spiritual element, which architecture can no more than hint at, completely abides with the sensuous form and its external matter, and as both sides are so merged into each other that neither predominates, sculpture has the *classical* form of art as its fundamental type. In fact, the sensuous realm itself can command no expression which could not be that of the spiritual sphere, just as, conversely, no spiritual content can attain perfect plasticity in sculpture which is incapable of being adequately presented to perception in bodily form. It is sculpture which arrests for our vision the spirit in its bodily frame, in immediate unity with it, and in an attitude of peace and repose; and the form in turn is animated by the content of spiritual individuality. Therefore the external sensuous matter is here not wrought, either according to its mechanical quality alone, as heavy mass, or in forms peculiar to inorganic nature, or as indifferent to color, etc., but in ideal forms of the human shape, and in the whole of the spatial dimensions. In this last respect sculpture should be credited with having first revealed the inner and spiritual essence in its eternal repose and essential self-possession. To such repose and unity with itself corresponds only that external element which itself persists in unity and repose. Such an element is the form taken in its abstract spatiality. The spirit which sculpture represents is that which is solid in itself, not variously broken up in the play of contingencies and passions; nor does its external form admit of the portrayal of such a manifold play, but it holds to this one side only, to the abstraction of space in the totality of its dimensions.

THE DEVELOPMENT OF THE ROMANTIC
ARTS

After architecture has built the temple and the hand
of sculpture has placed inside it the statue of the God,
then this sensuously visible God faces in the spacious
halls of his house the *community*. The community is
the spiritual, self-reflecting element in this sensuous
realm, it is the animating subjectivity and inner life.
A new principle of art begins with it. Both the content
of art and the medium which embodies it in outward
form now demand particularization, individualization,
and the subjective mode of expressing these. The solid
unity which the God possesses in sculpture breaks up
into the plurality of inner individual lives, whose unity is
not sensuous, but essentially ideal.

And now God comes to assume the aspect which makes
him truly spiritual. As a hither-and-thither, as an alteration between the unity within himself and his realization in subjective knowledge and individual consciousness, as well as in the common and unified life of the
man individuals, he is genuinely Spirit—the Spirit in
his community. In his community God is released from
the abstractness of a mysterious self-identity, as well
as from the naïve imprisonment in a bodily shape, in
which he is represented by sculpture. Here he is exalted into spirituality, subjectivity, and knowledge. For
this reason the higher content of art is now this spirituality in its absolute form. But since what chiefly reveals
itself in this stage is not the serene repose of God in
himself, but rather his appearance, his being, and his
manifestation to others, the objects of artistic representation are now the most varied subjective expressions
of life and activity for their own sake, as human pas-

sions, deeds, events, and, in general, the wide range of human feeling, will, and resignation. In accordance with this content, the sensuous element must differentiate and show itself adequate to the expression of subjective feeling. Such different media are furnished by color, by the musical sound, and finally by the sound as the mere indication of inner intuitions and ideas; and thus as different forms of realizing the spiritual content of art by means of these media we obtain painting, music, and poetry. The sensuous media employed in these arts being individualized and in their essence recognized as ideal, they correspond most effectively to the spiritual content of art, and the union between spiritual meaning and sensuous expression develops, therefore, into greater intimacy than was possible in the case of architecture and sculpture. This intimate unity, however, is due wholly to the subjective side.

Leaving, then, the symbolic spirit of architecture and the classical ideal of sculpture behind, these new arts in which form and content are raised to an ideal level borrow their type from the *romantic* form of art, whose mode of expression they are most eminently fitted to voice. They form, however, a totality of arts, because the romantic type is the most concrete in itself.

PAINTING

The first art in this totality, which is akin to sculpture, is painting. The material which it uses for its content and for the sensuous expression of that content is visibility as such, in so far as it is individualized, viz. specified as color. To be sure, the media employed in architecture and sculpture are also visible and colored, but they are not, as in painting, visibility as such, not the simple light which contrasts itself with darkness and in combination with it becomes color. This visibility as a subjective and ideal attribute, requires neither, like architecture, the abstract mechanical form of mass which we find in heavy matter, nor, like sculpture, the three dimensions of sensuous space, even though in concentrated and organic plasticity, but the visibility which appertains to painting has its differences on a more ideal level, in the particular kind of color; and thus painting frees art from the sensuous completeness in space peculiar to material things only, by confining itself to a plane surface.

On the other hand, the content also gains in varied particularization. Whatever can find room in the human heart, as emotion, idea, and purpose, whatever it is able to frame into a deed, all this variety of material can constitute the many-colored content of painting. The whole range of particular existence, from the highest aspirations of the mind down to the most isolated objects of nature, can obtain a place in this art. For even finite nature, in its particular scenes and aspects, can here appear, if only some allusion to a spiritual element makes it akin to thought and feeling.

MUSIC

The second art in which the romantic form finds realization, on still a higher level than in painting, is music. Its material, though still sensuous, advances to a deeper subjectivity and greater specification. The idealization of the sensuous, music brings about by negating space. In music the indifferent extension of space whose appearance painting admits and consciously imitates is concentrated and idealized into a single point. But in the form of a motion and tremor of the material body within itself, this single point becomes a concrete

and active process within the idealization of matter.
Such an incipient ideality of matter which no longer
appears under the spatial form, but as temporal ideality,
is sound—the sensuous acknowledged as ideal, whose abstract visibility is transformed into audibility. Sound,
as it were, exempts the ideal from its absorption in
matter.

This earliest animation and inspiration of matter
furnishes the medium for the inner and intimate life of
the spirit, as yet on an indefinite level; it is through the
tones of music that the heart pours out its whole scale
of feelings and passions. Thus as sculpture constitutes
the central point between architecture and the arts of
romantic subjectivity, so music forms the centre of the
romantic arts, and represents the point of transition between abstract spatial sensuousness, which belongs to
painting, and the abstract spirituality of poetry. Within
itself music has, like architecture, an abstract quantitative relation, as a contrast to its inward and emotional
quality; it also has as its basis a permanent law to which
the tones with their combinations and successions must
conform.

POETRY

For the third and most spiritual expression of the
romantic form of art, we must look to poetry. Its
characteristic peculiarity lies in the power with which
it subjugates to the mind and to its ideas the sensuous
element from which music and painting began to set
art free. For sound, the one external medium of which
poetry avails itself, is in it no longer a feeling of the
tone itself, but is a sign which is, by itself, meaningless. This sign, moreover, is a sign of an idea which
has become concrete, and not merely of indefinite feel-

ing and of its *nuances* and grades. By this means the tone becomes the *word,* an articulate voice, whose function it is to indicate thoughts and ideas. The negative point to which music had advanced now reveals itself in poetry as the completely concrete point, as the spirit or the self-consciousness of the individual, which spontaneously unites the infinite space of its ideas with the time-element of sound. But this sensuous element which, in music, was still in immediate union with inner feelings and moods, is, in poetry, divorced from the content of consciousness, for in poetry the mind determines this content on its own account and for the sake of its ideas, and while it employs sound to express them, yet sound itself is reduced to a symbol without value or meaning. From this point of view sound may just as well be considered a mere letter, for the audible, like the visible, is now relegated to a mere suggestion of mind. Thus the genuine mode of poetic representation is the inner perception and the poetic imagination itself. And since all types of art share in this mode, poetry runs through them all, and develops itself independently in each. Poetry, then, is the universal art of the spirit which has attained inner freedom, and which does not depend for its realization upon external sensuous matter, but expatiates only in the inner space and inner time of the ideas and feelings. But just in this, its highest phase, art oversteps the bounds of its own sphere by abandoning the harmoniously sensuous mode of portraying the spirit and by passing from the poetry of imagination into the prose of thought.

SUMMARY

Such, then, is the organic totality of the several arts; the external art of architecture, the objective art of sculpture, and the subjective arts of painting, music, and poetry. The higher principle from which these are derived we have found in the types of art, the symbolic, the classical, and the romantic, which form the universal phases of the idea of beauty itself. Thus symbolic art finds its most adequate reality and most perfect application in architecture, in which it is self-complete, and is not yet reduced, so to speak, to the inorganic medium for another art. The classical form of art, on the other hand, attains its most complete realization in sculpture, while it accepts architecture only as forming an inclosure round its products and is as yet not capable of developing painting and music as absolute expressions of its meaning. The romantic type of art, finally, seizes upon painting, music, and poetry as its essential and adequate modes of expression. Poetry, however, is in conformity with all types of the beautiful and extends over them all, because its characteristic element is the aesthetic imagination, and imagination is necessary for every product of art, to whatever type it may belong.

Thus what the particular arts realize in individual artistic creations are, according to the philosophic conception, simply the universal types of the self-unfolding idea of beauty. Out of the external realization of this idea arises the wide Pantheon of art, whose architect and builder is the self-developing spirit of beauty, for the completion of which, however, the history of the world will require its evolution of countless ages.

IX

INTRODUCTION TO THE PHI-
LOSOPHY OF HISTORY

Translated by J. Sibree.

THE subject of this course of Lectures is the Philosophical History of the World. And by this must be
understood, not a collection of general observations respecting it, suggested by the study of its records, and
proposed to be illustrated by its facts, but Universal
History itself.* To gain a clear idea at the outset, of
the nature of our task, it seems necessary to begin with
an examination of the other methods of treating History. The various methods may be ranged under three
heads:

I. Original History.

II. Reflective History.

III. Philosophical History.

I. Of the first kind, the mention of one or two distinguished names will furnish a definite type. To this
category belong *Herodotus, Thucydides,* and other historians of the same order, whose descriptions are for the
most part limited to deeds, events, and states of society,

* I cannot mention any work that will serve as a compendium
of the course, but I may remark that in my "Outlines of the
Philosophy of Law," §§. 341-360, I have already given a definition of such a Universal History as it is proposed to develop,
and a syllabus of the chief elements or periods into which it
naturally divides itself.

which they had before their eyes, and whose spirit they shared. They simply transferred what was passing in the world around them, to the realm of representative intellect. An external phenomenon is thus translated into an internal conception. In the same way the *poet* operates upon the material supplied him by his emotions, projecting it into an image for the conceptive faculty. These original historians did, it is true, find statements and narratives of other men ready to hand. One person cannot be an eye and ear witness of everything. But they make use of such aids only as the poet does of that heritage of an already-formed language, to which he owes so much; merely as an ingredient. Historiographers bind together the fleeting elements of story, and treasure them up for immortality in the Temple of Mnemosyne. Legends, Ballad-stories, Traditions must be excluded from such original history. These are but dim and hazy forms of historical apprehension, and therefore belong to nations whose intelligence is but half awakened. Here, on the contrary, we have to do with people fully conscious of what they were and what they were about. The domain of reality—actually seen, or capable of being so—affords a very different basis in point of firmness from that fugitive and shadowy element, in which were engendered those legends and poetic dreams whose historical prestige vanishes, as soon as nations have attained a mature individuality.

Such original historians, then, change the events, the deeds and the states of society with which they are conversant, into an object for the conceptive faculty. The narratives they leave us cannot, therefore, be very comprehensive in their range. Herodotus, Thucydides, Guicciardini, may be taken as fair samples of the class in this respect. What is present and living in their environment, is their proper material. The influences

that have formed the writer are identical with those
which have moulded the events that constitute the matter
of his story. The author's spirit, and that of the actions
he narrates, is one and the same. He describes scenes
in which he himself has been an actor, or at any
rate an interested spectator. It is short periods of time,
individual shapes of persons and occurrences, single unreflected traits, of which he makes his picture. And his
aim is nothing more than the presentation to posterity
of an image of events as clear as that which he himself
possessed in virtue of personal observation, or life-like
descriptions. Reflections are none of his business, for
he lives in the spirit of his subject; he has not attained
an elevation above it. If, as in Caesar's case, he belongs
to the exalted rank of generals or statesmen, it is the
prosecution of *his own aims* that constitutes the history.

Such speeches as we find in Thucydides (for example)
of which we can positively assert that they are not *bona
fide* reports, would seem to make against our statement
that a historian of his class presents us no reflected picture; that persons and people appear in his works in
propriâ personâ. Speeches, it must be allowed, are
veritable transactions in the human commonwealth; in
fact, very gravely influential transactions. It is, indeed,
often said, "Such and such things are only talk"; by way
of demonstrating their harmlessness. That for which
this excuse is brought, may be mere "talk"; and talk enjoys the important privilege of being harmless. But
addresses of peoples to peoples, or orations directed to
nations and to princes, are integrant constituents of history. Granted that such orations as those of Pericles—
that most profoundly accomplished, genuine, noble statesman—were elaborated by Thucydides; it must yet be
maintained that they were not foreign to the character of
the speaker. In the orations in question, these men

proclaim the maxims adopted by their countrymen, and which formed their own character; they record their views of their political relations, and of their moral and spiritual nature; and the principle of their designs and conduct. What the historian puts into their mouths is no supposititious system of ideas, but an uncorrupted transcript of their intellectual and moral habitudes.

Of these historians, whom we must make thoroughly our own, with whom we must linger long, if we would live with their respective nations, and enter deeply into their spirit: of these historians, to whose pages we may turn not for the purpose of erudition merely, but with a view to deep and genuine enjoyment, there are fewer than might be imagined. Herodotus the *Father,* i.e. the *Founder* of History, and Thucydides have been already mentioned Xenophon's *Retreat of the Ten Thousand* is a work equally original. Caesar's *Commentaries* are the simple masterpiece of a mighty spirit. Among the ancients, these annalists were necessarily great captains and statesmen. In the Middle Ages, if we except the Bishops, who were placed in the very centre of the political world, the Monks monopolize this category as naïve chroniclers who were as decidedly *isolated* from active life as those elder annalists had been connected with it. In modern times the relations are entirely altered. Our culture is essentially comprehensive, and immediately changes all events into historical representations. Belonging to the class in question, we have vivid, simple, clear narrations—especially of military transactions—which might fairly take their place with those of Caesar. In richness of matter and fulness of detail as regards strategic appliances, and attendant circumstances, they are even more instructive. The French "Memoires" also fall under this category. In many cases these are written by men of mark, though

relating to affairs of little note. They not unfrequently
contain a large proportion of anecdotical matter, so
that the ground they occupy is narrow and trivial. Yet
they are often veritable masterpieces in history; as those
of Cardinal Retz, which in fact trench on a larger historical field. In Germany such masters are rare. Fred-
erick the Great ("Histoire de mon temps") is an illustrious exception. Writers of this order must occupy an
elevated position. Only from such a position is it
possible to take an extensive view of affairs—to see
everything. This is out of the question for him, who
from below merely gets a glimpse of the great world
through a miserable cranny.

II. The second kind of history we may call the *reflective*. It is history whose mode of representation is
not really confined by the limits of the time to which it
relates, but whose spirit transcends the present. In this
second order strongly marked variety of species may
be distinguished.

1. It is the aim of the investigator to gain a view of
the entire history of a people or a country, or of the
world, in short, what we call *Universal History*. In
this case the working up of the historical material is the
main point. The workman approaches his task with *his
own* spirit; a spirit distinct from that of the element he
is to manipulate. Here a very important consideration
will be the principles to which the author refers, the
bearing and motives of the actions and events which he
describes, and those which determine the form of his
narrative. Among us Germans this reflective treatment
and the display of ingenuity which it occasions, assume
a manifold variety of phases. Every writer of history
proposes to himself an original method. The English
and French confess to general principles of historical
composition. Their stand-point is more that of cosmo-

politan or of national culture.   Among us each labours
to invent a purely individual point of view.   Instead of
writing history, we are always beating our brains to
discover how history ought to be written.   This first
kind of Reflective History is most nearly akin to the
preceding, when it has no farther aim than to present
the annals of a country complete.   Such compilations
(among which may be reckoned the works of Livy, Dio-
dorus Siculus, Johannes von Müller's History of Switzerland) are, if well performed, highly meritorious.
Among the best of the kind may be reckoned such annalists as approach those of the first class; who give so
vivid a transcript of events that the reader may well
fancy himself listening to contemporaries and eye wit-
nesses.   But it often happens that the individuality of
tone which must characterize a writer belonging to a
different culture, is not modified in accordance with the
periods such a record must traverse.   The spirit of the
writer is quite other than that of the times of which he
treats.   Thus Livy puts into the mouths of the old
Roman kings, consuls, and generals, such orations as
would be delivered by an accomplished advocate of the
Livian era, and which strikingly contrast with the genuine traditions of Roman antiquity (*e.g.* the fable of
Menenius Agrippa).   In the same way he gives us
descriptions of battles, as if he had been an actual
spectator; but whose features would serve well enough
for battles in any period, and whose distinctness contrasts on the other hand with the want of connexion and
the inconsistency that prevail elsewhere, even in his
treatment of chief points of interest.   The difference
between such a compiler and an original historian may be
best seen by comparing Polybius himself with the style
in which Livy uses, expands, and abridges his annals in
those periods of which Polybius's account has been pre-

served. Johannes von Müller has given a stiff, formal, pedantic aspect of his history, in the endeavour to remain faithful in his portraiture to the times he describes. We much prefer the narratives we find in old Tschudy. All is more naïve and natural than it appears in the garb of a fictitious and affected archaism.

A history which aspires to traverse long periods of time, or to be universal, must indeed forego the attempt to give individual representations of the past as it actually existed. It must foreshorten its pictures by abstractions; and this includes not merely the omission of events and deeds, but whatever is involved in the fact that Thought is, after all, the most trenchant epitomist. A battle, a great victory, a siege, no longer maintains its original proportions, but is put off with a bare mention. When Livy *e.g.* tells us of the wars with the Volsci, we sometimes have the brief announcement: "This year war was carried on with the Volsci."

2. A second species of Reflective History is what we may call the *Pragmatical*. When we have to deal with the Past, and occupy ourselves with a remote world, a Present rises into being for the mind—produced by its own activity, as the reward of its labour. The occurrences are, indeed, various; but the idea which pervades them—their deeper import and connexion—is *one*. This takes the occurrence out of the category of the Past and makes it virtually Present. Pragmatical (didactic) reflections, though in their nature decidedly abstract, are truly and indefeasibly of the Present, and quicken the annals of the dead Past with the life of to-day. Whether, indeed, such reflections are truly interesting and enlivening, depends on the writer's own spirit. Moral reflections must here be specially noticed,—the moral teaching expected from history; which latter has not unfrequently been treated with a direct view to the former.

It may be allowed that examples of virtue elevate the soul, and are applicable in the moral instructions of children for impressing excellence upon their minds. But the destinies of peoples and states, their interests, relations, and the complicated tissue of their affairs, present quite another field. Rulers, Statesmen, Nations, are wont to be emphatically commended to the teaching which experience offers in history. But what experience and history teach is this,—that peoples and governments never have learned anything from history, or acted on principles deduced from it. Each period is involved in such peculiar circumstances, exhibits a condition of things so strictly idiosyncratic, that its conduct must be regulated by considerations connected with itself, and itself alone. Amid the pressure of great events, a general principle gives no help. It is useless to revert to similar circumstances in the Past. The pallid shades of memory struggle in vain with the life and freedom of the Present. Looked at in this light, nothing can be shallower than the oft-repeated appeal to Greek and Roman examples during the French Revolution. Nothing is more diverse than the genius of those nations and that of our times. Johannes v. Müller, in his Universal History as also in his History of Switzerland, had such moral aims in view. He designed to prepare a body of political doctrines for the instruction of princes, governments and peoples (he formed a special collection of doctrines and reflections,—frequently giving us in his correspondence the exact number of apophthegms which he had compiled in a week); but he cannot reckon this part of his labour as among the best that he accomplished. It is only a thorough, liberal, comprehensive view of historical relations (such *e.g.* as we find in Montesquieu's "Esprit des Loix"), that can give truth and interest to reflections of this order. One Reflective

History therefore, supersedes another. The materials are patent to every writer: each is likely enough to believe himself capable of arranging and manipulating them; and we may expect that each will insist upon his own spirit as that of the age in question. Disgusted by such reflective histories, readers have often returned with pleasure to a narrative adopting no particular point of view. These certainly have their value; but for the most part they offer only material for history. We Germans are not content with such. The French, on the other hand, display great genius in reanimating bygone times, and in bringing the past to bear upon the present conditions of things.

3. The third form of Reflective History is the *Critical*. This deserves mention as preëminently the mode of treating history, now current in Germany. It is not history itself that is here presented. We might more properly designate it as a History of History; a criticism of historical narratives and an investigation of their truth and credibility. Its peculiarity in point of fact and of intention, consists in the acuteness with which the writer extorts something from the records which was not in the matters recorded. The French have given as much that is profound and judicious in this class of composition. But they have not endeavoured to pass a merely critical procedure for substantial history. They have duly presented their judgments in the form of critical treatises. Among us, the so-called "higher criticism," which reigns supreme in the domain of philology, has also taken possession of our historical literature. This "higher criticism" has been the pretext for introducing all the anti-historical monstrosities that a vain imagination could suggest. Here we have the other method of making the past a living reality; putting subjective fancies in the place of historical data; fancies

whose merit is measured by their boldness, that is, the scantiness of the particulars on which they are based, and the peremptoriness with which they contravene the best established facts of history.

4. The last species of Reflective History announces its fragmentary character on the very face of it. It adopts an abstract position; yet, since it takes general points of view (*e.g.* as the History of Art, of Law, of Religion), it forms a transition to the Philosophical History of the World. In our time this form of the history of ideas has been more developed and brought into notice. Such branches of national life stand in close relation to the entire complex of a people's annals; and the question of chief importance in relation to our subject is, whether the connexion of the whole is exhibited in its truth and reality, or referred to merely external relations. In the latter case, these important phenomena (Art, Law, Religion, &c.) appear as purely accidental national peculiarities. It must be remarked that, when Reflective History has advanced to the adoption of general points of view, if the position taken is a true one, these are found to constitute—not merely external thread, a superficial series—but are the inward guiding soul of the occurrences and actions that occupy a nation's annals. For, like the soul-conductor Mercury, the Idea is in truth, the leader of peoples and of the World; and Spirit, the rational and necessitated will of that conductor, is and has been the director of the events of the World's History. To become acquainted with Spirit in this its office of guidance, is the object of our present undertaking. This brings us to

III. The third kind of history,—the *Philosophical.* No explanation was needed of the two previous classes; their nature was self-evident. It is otherwise with this last, which certainly seems to require an exposition or justification. The most general definition that can be given, is, that the Philosophy of History means nothing but the *thoughtful consideration of it.* Thought is, indeed, essential to humanity. It is this that distinguishes us from the brutes. In sensation, cognition and intellection; in our instincts and volitions, as far as they are truly human, Thought is an invariable element. To insist upon Thought in this connexion with history, may, however, appear unsatisfactory. In this science it would seem as if Thought must be subordinate to what is given, to the realities of fact; that this is its basis and guide: while Philosophy dwells in the region of self-produced ideas, without reference to actuality. Approaching history thus prepossessed, Speculation might be expected to treat it as a mere passive material; and, so far from leaving it in its native truth, to force it into conformity with a tyrannous idea, and to construe it, as the phrase is, *"à priori."* But as it is the business of history simply to adopt into its records what is and has been, actual occurrences and transactions; and since it remains true to its character in proportion as it strictly adheres to its data, we seem to have in Philosophy, a process diametrically opposed to that of the historiographer. This contradiction, and the charge consequent brought against speculation, shall be explained and confuted. We do not, however, propose to correct the innumerable special misrepresentations, trite or novel, that are current respecting the aims, the interests, and the modes of treating history, and its relation to Philosophy.

The only Thought which Philosophy brings with it to the contemplation of History, is the simple conception of *Reason;* that Reason is the Sovereign of the World; that the history of the world, therefore, presents us with a rational process. This conviction and intuition is a hypothesis in the domain of history as such. In that of Philosophy it is no hypothesis. It is there proved by speculative cognition, that Reason—and this term may here suffice us, without investigating the relation sustained by the Universe to the Divine Being,—is *Substance,* as well as *Infinite Power;* its own *Infinite Material* underlying all the natural and spiritual life which it originates, as also the *Infinite Form,*—that which sets this Material in motion. On the one hand, Reason is the *substance* of the Universe; viz. that by which and in which all reality has its being and subsistence. On the other hand, it is the *Infinite Energy* of the Universe; since Reason is not so powerless as to be incapable of producing anything but a mere ideal, a mere intention—having its place outside reality, nobody knows where; something separate and abstract, in the heads of certain human beings. It is *the infinite complex of things,* their entire Essence and Truth. It is its own material which it commits to its own Active Energy to work up; not needing, as finite action does, the conditions of an external material of given means from which it may obtain its support, and the objects of its activity. It supplies its own nourishment, and is the object of its own operations. While it is exclusively its own basis of existence, and absolute final aim, it is also the energising power realising this aim; developing it not only in the phenomena of the Natural, but also of the Spiritual Universe—the History of the World. That this "Idea" or "Reason" is the *True,* the *Eternal,* the absolutely *powerful* essence; that it reveals itself in the World, and that in that World nothing else is revealed but this and its honour and glory—is the thesis which, as we have said, has been proved in Philosophy, and is here regarded as demonstrated.

In those of my hearers who are not acquainted with

Philosophy, I may fairly presume, at least, the existence of a *belief* in Reason, a desire, a thirst for acquaintance with it, in entering upon this course of Lectures. It is, in fact, the wish for rational insight, not the ambition to amass a mere heap of acquirements, that should be presupposed in every case as possessing the mind of the learner in the study of science. If the clear idea of Reason is not already developed in our minds, in beginning the study of Universal History, we should at least have the firm, unconquerable faith that Reason *does* exist there; and that the World of intelligence and conscious volition is not abandoned to chance, but must shew itself in the light of the self-cognizant Idea. Yet I am not obliged to make any such preliminary demand upon your faith. What I have said thus provisionally, and what I shall have further to say, is, even in reference to *our* branch of science, not to be regarded as hypothetical, but as a summary view of the whole; the *result of the investigation* we are about to pursue; a result which happens to be known to *me*, because I have traversed the entire field. It is only an inference from the history of the World, that its development has been a rational process; that the history in question has constituted the rational necessary course of the World-Spirit—that Spirit whose nature is always one and the same, but which unfolds this its one nature in the phenomena of the World's existence. This must, as before stated, present itself as the ultimate *result* of History. But we have to take the latter as it is. We must proceed historically—empirically. Among other precautions we must take care not to be misled by professed historians who (especially among the Germans, and enjoying a considerable authority), are chargeable with the very procedure of which they accuse the Philosopher —introducing *à priori* inventions of their own into the

records of the Past. It is, for example, a widely current
fiction, that there was an original primaeval people,
taught immediately by God, endowed with perfect insight and wisdom, possessing a thorough knowledge of
all natural laws and spiritual truth; that there have been
such or such sacerdotal peoples; or, to mention a more
specific averment, that there was a Roman Epos, from
which the Roman historians derived the early annals of
their city, &c. Authorities of this kind we leave to those
talented historians by profession, among whom (in Germany at least) their use is not uncommon.—We might
then announce it as the first condition to be observed,
that we should faithfully adopt all that is historical.
But in such general expressions themselves, as "faithfully" and "adopt," lies the ambiguity. Even the ordinary, the "impartial" historiographer, who believes
and professes that he maintains a simply receptive attitude; surrendering himself only to the data supplied
him—is by no means passive as regards the exercise of
his thinking powers. He brings his categories with
him, and sees the phenomena presented to his mental
vision, exclusively through these media. And, especially
in all that pretends to the name of science, it is indispensable that Reason should not sleep—that reflection
should be in full play. To him who looks upon the
world rationally, the world in its turn, presents a rational aspect. The relation is mutual. But the various
exercises of reflection—the different points of view—
the modes of deciding the simple question of the relative
importance of events (the first category that occupies
the attention of the historian), do not belong to this
place.

I will only mention two phases and points of view
that concern the generally diffused conviction that Reason has ruled, and is still ruling in the world, and

consequently in the world's history; because they give us, at the same time, an opportunity for more closely investigating the question that presents the greatest difficulty, and for indicating a branch of the subject, which will have to be enlarged on in the sequel.

I.—One of these points is, that passage in history, which informs us that the Greek Anaxagoras was the first to enunciate the doctrine that νοῦς, Understanding generally, or Reason, governs the world. It is not intelligence as self-conscious Reason,—not a Spirit as such that is meant; and we must clearly distinguish these from each other. The movement of the solar system takes place according to unchangeable laws. These laws are Reason, implicit in the phenomena in question. But neither the sun nor the planets, which revolve around it according to these laws, can be said to have any consciousness of them.

A thought of this kind,—that Nature is an embodiment of Reason; that it is unchangeably subordinate to universal laws, appears nowise striking or strange to us. We are accustomed to such conceptions, and find nothing extraordinary in them. And I have mentioned this extraordinary occurrence, partly to shew how history teaches, that ideas of this kind, which may seem trivial to us, have not always been in the world; that on the contrary, such a thought makes an epoch in the annals of human intelligence. Aristotle says of Anaxagoras, as the originator of the thought in question, that he appeared as a sober man among the drunken. Socrates adopted the doctrine from Anaxagoras, and it forthwith became the ruling idea in Philosophy,—except in the school of Epicurus, who ascribed all events to chance. "I was delighted with the sentiment,"—Plato makes Socrates say,—"and hoped I had found a teacher who would shew me Nature in harmony with Reason, who would demonstrate in each particular phenomenon its specific aim, and in the whole, the grand object of the Universe. I would not have surrendered this hope for a great deal. But how very much was I disappointed, when, having zealously applied myself to the writings of Anaxagoras, I found that he adduces only external causes, such as Atmosphere, Ether, Water, and the like." It is evident that the defect which Socrates complains of respecting Anaxagoras's doctrine, does not concern the principle itself, but the shortcoming of the propounder in applying it to Nature in the concrete. Nature is not deduced from that principle: the latter remains in fact a mere abstraction, inasmuch as the former is not comprehended and exhibited as a development of it,—an organisation produced by and from Reason. I wish, at the very outset, to call your attention to the important difference between a conception, a principle, a truth limited to an *abstract* form and its determinate application, and concrete development. This distinction affects the whole fabric of philosophy; and among other bearings of it there is one to which we shall have to revert at the close of our view of Universal History, in investigating the aspect of political affairs in the most recent period.

We have next to notice the rise of this idea—that Reason directs the orld—in connexion with a further application of it, well known to us,—in the form, viz. of the *religious truth,* that the world is not abandoned to chance and external contingent causes, but that a *Providence* controls it. I stated above, that I would not make a demand on your faith, in regard to the principle announced. Yet I might appeal to your belief in it, *in this religious aspect,* if, as a general rule, the nature of philosophical science allowed it to attach authority to presuppositions. To put it in another shape,—this appeal is forbidden, because the science of which we have to treat, proposes itself to furnish the proof (not indeed of the abstract *Truth* of the doctrine, but) of its correctness as compared with facts. The truth, then, that a Providence (that of God) presides over the events of the World—consorts with the proposition in question; for *Divine* Providence is Wisdom, endowed with an infinite Power, which realises its aim, viz. the absolute rational design of the World. Reason is Thought conditioning itself with perfect freedom. But a difference—rather a contradiction—will manifest itself, between this belief and our principle, just as was the case in reference to the demand made by Socrates in the case of Anaxagoras's dictum. For that belief is similarly indefinite; it is what is called a belief in a general Providence, and is not followed out into definite application, or displayed in its bearing on the grand total—the entire course of human history. But to *explain* History is to depict the passions of mankind, the genius, the active powers, that play their part on the great stage; and the providentially determined process which these exhibit, constitutes what is generally called the "plan" of Providence. Yet it is this very plan which is supposed to be concealed from our view: which it is deemed presumption, even to wish to recognise. The ignorance of Anaxagoras, as to how intelligence reveals itself in actual existence, was ingenuous. Neither in his consciousness, nor in that of Greece at large, had that thought been further expanded. He had not attained the power to apply his general principle to the concrete, so as to deduce the latter from the former. It was Socrates who took the first step in comprehending the union of the Concrete with the Universal. Anaxagoras, then, did not take up a *hostile* position towards such an application. The common belief in Providence *does;* at least it opposes the use of the principle on the large scale, and denies the possibility of discerning the plan of Providence. In isolated cases this plan is supposed to be manifest. Pious persons are encouraged to recognise in particular circumstances, something more than mere chance; to acknowledge the guiding hand of God; *e.g.* when help has unexpectedly come to an individual in great perplexity and need. But these instances of providential design are of a limited kind, and concern the accomplishment of nothing more than the desires of the individual in question. But in the history of the World, the *Individuals* we have to do with are *Peoples;* Totalities that are States. We cannot, therefore, be satisfied with what we may call this "peddling" view of Providence, to which the belief alluded to limits itself. Equally unsatisfactory is the merely abstract, undefined belief in a Providence, when that belief is not brought to bear upon the details of the process which it conducts. On the contrary our earnest endeavour must be directed to the recognition of the ways of Providence, the means it uses, and the historical phenomena in which it manifests itself; and we must shew their connexion with the general principle above mentioned. But in noticing the recognition of the plan of Divine Providence generally, I have implicitly touched upon a prominent question of the day; viz. that of the possibility of knowing God: or rather—since public opinion has ceased to allow it to be a matter of *question*—the *doctrine* that it is impossible to know God. In direct contravention of what is commanded in holy Scripture as the highest duty,—that we should not merely love, but *know* God,—the prevalent dogma involves the denial of what is there said; viz. that it is the Spirit (der Geist) that leads into Truth, knows all things, penetrates even into the deep things of the Godhead. While the Divine

Being is thus placed beyond our knowledge, and outside the limit of all human things, we have the convenient licence of wandering as far as we list, in the direction of our own fancies. We are freed from the obligation to refer our knowledge to the Divine and True. On the other hand, the vanity and egotism which characterise it, find, in this false position, ample justification; and the pious modesty which puts far from it the knowledge of God, can well estimate how much furtherance thereby accrues to its own wayward and vain strivings. I have been unwilling to leave out of sight the connexion between our thesis—that Reason governs and has governed the World—and the question of the possibility of a knowledge of God, chiefly that I might not lose the opportunity of mentioning the imputation against Philosophy of being shy of noticing religious truths, or of having occasion to be so; in which is insinuated the suspicion that it has anything but a clear conscience in the presence of these truths. So far from this being the case, the fact is, that in recent times Philosophy has been obliged to defend the domain of religion against the attacks of several theological systems. In the Christian religion God has revealed Himself,—that is, he has given us to understand what He is; so that He is no longer a concealed or secret existence. And this possibility of knowing Him, thus afforded us, renders such knowledge a duty. God wishes no narrow-hearted souls or empty heads for his children; but those whose spirit is of itself indeed, poor, but rich in the knowledge of Him; and who regard this knowledge of God as the only valuable possession. That development of the thinking spirit, which has resulted from the revelation of the Divine Being as its original basis, must ultimately advance to the *intellectual* comprehension of what was presented in the first instance, to *feeling* and *imagina-*

tion. The time must eventually come for understanding that rich product of active Reason, which the History of the World offers to us. It was for a while the fashion to profess admiration for the wisdom of God, as displayed in animals, plants, and isolated occurrences. But, if it be allowed that Providence manifests itself in such objects and forms of existence, why not also in Universal History? This is deemed too great a matter to be thus regarded. But Divine Wisdom, *i.e.* Reason, is one and the same in the great as in the little; and we must not imagine God to be too weak to exercise his wisdom on the grand scale. Our intellectual striving aims at realising the conviction that what was *intended* by eternal wisdom, is actually *accomplished* in the domain of existent, active Spirit, as well as in that of mere Nature. Our mode of treating the subject is, in this aspect, a Theodicaea,—a justification of the ways of God,—which Leibnitz attempted metaphysically, in his method, *i.e.* in indefinite abstract categories,—so that the ill that is found in the World may be comprehended, and the thinking Spirit reconciled with the fact of the existence of evil. Indeed, nowhere is such a harmonising view more pressingly demanded than in Universal History; and it can be attained only by recognising the *positive* existence, in which that negative element is a subordinate, and vanquished nullity. On the one hand, the ultimate design of the World must be perceived; and, on the other hand, the fact that this design has been actually realised in it, and that evil has not been able permanently to assert a competing position. But this conviction involves much more than the mere belief in a superintending νοῦς or in "Providence." "Reason," whose sovereignty over the World has been maintained, is as indefinite a term as "Providence," supposing the term to be used by those who are unable to characterise it distinctly,—to shew wherein it consists, so as to enable us to decide whether a thing is rational or irrational.   An adequate definition of Reason is the first desideratum; and whatever boast may be made of strict adherence to it in explaining phenomena,—without such a definition we get no farther than mere words.   With these observations we may proceed to the second point of view that has to be considered in this Introduction.

II.—The enquiry into the *essential destiny* of Reason —as far as it is considered in reference to the World— is identical with the question, *what is the ultimate design of the World?*   And the expression implies that that design is destined to be realised.   Two points of consideration suggest themselves: first, the *import* of this design—its abstract definition; and secondly, its *realisation.*

It must be observed at the outset, that the phenomenon we investigate—Universal History—belongs to the realm of *Spirit*.   The term "World," includes both physical and psychical Nature.   Physical Nature also plays its part in the World's History, and attention will have to be paid to the fundamental natural relations thus involved.   But Spirit, and the course of its development, is our substantial object.   Our task does not require us to contemplate Nature as a Rational System in itself— though in its own proper domain it proves itself such— but simply in its relation to *Spirit*.   On the stage on which we are observing it,—Universal History—Spirit displays itself in its most concrete reality.   Notwithstanding this (or rather for the very purpose of comprehending the *general* principles which this, its form of *concrete reality,* embodies) we must premise some abstract characteristics of the *nature of spirit*.   Such an explanation, however, cannot be given here under any other form than that of bare assertion.   The present is

not the occasion for unfolding the idea of Spirit specu-
latively; for whatever has a place in an Introduction,
must, as already observed, be taken as simply historical;
something assumed as having been explained and proved
elsewhere; or whose demonstration awaits the sequel
of the Science of History itself.

We have therefore to mention here:

(1.) The abstract characteristics of the nature of
Spirit.

(2). What means Spirit uses in order to realise its
Idea.

(3.) Lastly, we must consider the shape which the
perfect embodiment of Spirit assumes—the
State.

(1.) The nature of Spirit may be understood by a
glance at its direct opposite—*Matter.* As the essence
of Matter is Gravity, so, on the other hand, we may
affirm that the substance, the essence of Spirit is Freedom. All will readily assent to the doctrine that Spirit,
among other properties, is also endowed with Freedom;
but philosophy teaches that all the qualities of Spirit
exist only through Freedom; that all are but means for
attaining Freedom; that all seek and produce this and
this alone. It is a result of speculative Philosophy, that
Freedom is the sole truth of Spirit. Matter possesses
gravity in virtue of its tendency towards a central point.
It is essentially composite; consisting of parts that *exclude* each other. It seeks its Unity; and therefore
exhibits itself as self-destructive, as verging towards its
opposite [an indivisible point]. If it could attain this,
it would be Matter no longer, it would have perished.
It strives after the realisation of its Idea; for in Unity
it exists *ideally.* Spirit, on the contrary, may be defined
as that which has its centre in itself. It has not a unity

outside itself, but has already found it; it exists *in* and *with itself*. Matter has its essence out of itself; Spirit is *self-contained existence* (Bei-sich-selbst-seyn). Now this is Freedom, exactly. For if I am dependent, my being is referred to something else which I am not; I cannot exist independently of something external. I am free, on the contrary, when my existence depends upon myself. This self-contained existence of Spirit is none other than self-consciousness—consciousness of one's own being. Two things must be distinguished in consciousness; first, the fact *that I know;* secondly, *what I know*. In *self* consciousness these are merged in one; for Spirit *knows itself*. It involves an appreciation of its own nature, as also an energy enabling it to realise itself; to make itself *actually* that which it is *potentially*. According to this abstract definition it may be said of Universal History, that it is the exhibition of Spirit in the process of working out the knowledge of that which it is potentially. And as the germ bears in itself the whole nature of the tree, and the taste and form of its fruits, so do the first traces of Spirit virtually contain the whole of that History. The Orientals have not attained the knowledge that Spirit—Man *as such*— is free; and because they do not know this they are not free. They only know that *one is free*. But on this very account, the freedom of that one is only caprice; ferocity—brutal recklessness or passion, or a mildness and tameness of the desires, which is itself only an accident of Nature—mere caprice like the former.—That *one* is therefore only a Despot; not a *free man*. The consciousness of Freedom first arose among the Greeks, and therefore they were free; but they, and the Romans likewise, knew only that *some* are free,—not man as such. Even Plato and Aristotle did not know this. The Greeks, therefore, had slaves; and their whole life and the maintenance of their splendid liberty, was implicated with the institution of slavery: a fact moreover, which made that liberty on the one hand only an accidental, transient and limited growth; on the other hand, constituted it a rigorous thraldom of our common nature—of the Human.   The German nations, under the influence of Christianity, were the first to attain the consciousness, that man, as man, is free: that it is the *freedom* of Spirit which constitutes its essence. This consciousness arose first in religion, the inmost region of Spirit; but to introduce the principle into the various relations of the actual world, involves a more extensive problem than its simple implantation; a problem whose solution and application require a severe and lengthened process of culture.   In proof of this, we may note that slavery did not cease immediately on the reception of Christianity.   Still less did liberty predominate in States; or Governments and Constitutions adopt a rational organization, or recognise freedom as their basis. That application of the principle to political relations; the thorough moulding and interpenetration of the constitution of society by it, is a process identical with history itself.   I have already directed attention to the distinction here involved, between a principle as such, and its *application; i.e.* its introduction and carrying out in the actual phenomena of Spirit and Life.   This is a point of fundamental importance in our science, and one which must be constantly respected as essential. And in the same way as this distinction has attracted attention in view of the *Christian* principle of self-consciousness—Freedom; it also shews itself as an essential one, in view of the principle of Freedom *generally*. The History of the world is none other than the progress of the consciousness of Freedom; a progress whose development according to the necessity of its nature, it is our business to investigate.

The general statement given above, of the various grades in the consciousness of Freedom—and which we applied in the first instance to the fact that the Eastern nations knew only that *one* is free; the Greek and Roman world only that *some* are free; whilst *we* know that all men absolutely (man *as man*) are free,—supplies us with the natural division of Universal History, and suggests the mode of its discussion. This is remarked, however, only incidentally and anticipatively; some other ideas must be first explained.

The destiny of the spiritual World, and,—since this is the *substantial World,* while the physical remains subordinate to it, or, in the language of speculation, has no truth *as against* the spiritual,—the *final cause of the World at large,* we allege to be the *consciousness* of its own freedom on the part of Spirit, and *ipso facto,* the *reality* of that freedom. But that this term "Freedom," without further qualification, is an indefinite, and incalculable ambiguous term; and that while that which it represents is the *ne plus ultra* of attainment, it is liable to an infinity of misunderstandings, confusions and errors, and to become the occasion for all imaginable excesses,—has never been more clearly known and felt than in modern times. Yet, for the present, we must content ourselves with the term itself without farther definition. Attention was also directed to the importance of the infinite difference between a principle in the abstract, and its realisation in the concrete. In the process before us, the essential nature of freedom— which involves in it absolute necessity,—is to be displayed as coming to a consciousness of itself (for it is in its very nature, self-consciousness) and thereby realising its existence. Itself is its own object of attainment, and the sole aim of Spirit. This result it is, at which the process of the World's History has been continually aiming; and to which the sacrifices that have ever and anon been laid on the vast altar of the earth, through the long lapse of ages, have been offered. This is the only aim that sees itself realised and fulfilled; the only pole of repose amid the ceaseless change of events and conditions, and the sole efficient principle that pervades them. This final aim is God's purpose with the world; but God is the absolutely perfect Being, and can, therefore, will nothing other than himself—his own Will. The Nature of His Will—that is, His Nature itself—is what we here call the Idea of Freedom; translating the language of Religion into that of Thought. The question, then, which we may next put, is: What means does this principle of Freedom use for its realisation? This is the second point we have to consider.

(2.) The question of the *means* by which Freedom develops itself to a World, conducts us to the phenomenon of History itself. Although Freedom is, primarily, an undeveloped idea, the means it uses are external and phenomenal; presenting themselves in History to our sensuous vision. The first glance at History convinces us that the actions of men proceed from their needs, their passions, their characters and talents; and impresses us with the belief that such needs, passions and interests are the sole springs of action—the efficient agents in this scene of activity. Among these may, perhaps, be found aims of a liberal or universal kind—benevolence it may be, or noble patriotism; but such virtues and general views are but insignificant as compared with the World and its doings. We may perhaps see the Ideal of Reason actualized in those who adopt such aims, and within the sphere of their influence; but they bear only a trifling proportion to the mass of the human race; and the extent of that influence is limited accordingly. Passions, private aims, and the satisfaction of selfish desires, are on the other hand, most effective springs of action. Their power lies in the fact that they respect none of the limitations which justice and morality would impose on them; and that these natural impulses have a more direct influence over man than the artificial and tedious discipline that tends to order and self-restraint, law and morality. When we look at this display of passions, and the consequences of their violence; the Unreason which is associated not only with them, but even (rather we might say *especially*) with *good* designs and righteous aims; when we see the evil, the vice, the ruin that has befallen the most flourishing kingdoms which the mind of man ever created, we can scarce avoid being filled with sorrow at this universal taint of corruption: and, since this decay is not the work of mere Nature, but of the Human Will —a moral embitterment—a revolt of the Good Spirit (if it have a place within us) may well be the result of our reflections. Without rhetorical exaggeration, a simply truthful combination of the miseries that have overwhelmed the noblest of nations and polities, and the finest exemplars of private virtue,—forms a picture of most fearful aspect, and excites emotions of the profoundest and most hopeless sadness, counter-balanced by no consolatory result. We endure in beholding it a mental torture, allowing no defence or escape but the consideration that what has happened could not be otherwise; that it is a fatality which no intervention could alter. And at last we draw back from the intolerable disgust with which these sorrowful reflections threaten us, into the more agreeable environment of our individual life—the Present formed by our private aims and interests. In short we retreat into the selfishness that stands on the quiet shore, and thence enjoy in safety the distant spectacle of "wrecks confusedly hurled." But even regarding History as the slaughter-bench at which the happiness of peoples, the wisdom of States, and the virtue of individuals have been victimised —the question involuntarily arises—to what principle, to what final aim these enormous sacrifices have been offered. From this point the investigation usually proceeds to that which we have made the general commencement of our enquiry. Starting from this we pointed out those phenomena which made up a picture so suggestive of gloomy emotions and thoughtful reflections—as *the very field* which we, for our part, regard as exhibiting only the means for realising what we assert to be the essential destiny—the absolute aim, or —which comes to the same thing—the true *result* of the World's History. We have all along purposely eschewed "moral reflections" as a method of rising from the scene of historical specialties to the general principles which they embody. Besides, it is not the interest of such sentimentalities, really to rise above those depressing emotions; and to solve the enigmas of Providence which the considerations that occasioned them, present. It is essential to their character to find a gloomy satisfaction in the empty and fruitless sublimities of that negative result. We return then to the point of view which we have adopted; observing that the successive steps (Momente) of the analysis to which it will lead us, will also evolve the conditions requisite for answering the enquiries suggested by the panorama of sin and suffering that history unfolds.

The *first* remark we have to make, and which—though already presented more than once—cannot be too often repeated when the occasion seems to call for it,—is that what we call *principle, aim, destiny,* or the nature and

idea of Spirit, is something merely general and abstract.
Principle—Plan of Existence—Law—is a hidden, undeveloped essence, which *as such*—however true in itself—is not completely real. Aims, principles, &c.,
have a place in our thoughts, in our subjective design
only; but not yet in the sphere of reality. That which
exists for itself only, is a possibility, a potentiality; but
has not yet emerged into Existence. A *second* element
must be introduced in order to produce actuality—viz.
actuation, realization; and whose motive power is the
Will—the activity of man in the widest sense. It is
only by this activity that that Idea as well as abstract
characteristics generally, are realised, actualised; for of
themselves they are powerless. The motive power that
puts them in operation, and gives them determinate existence, is the need, instinct, inclination, and passion of
man. That some conception of mine should be developed into act and existence, is my earnest desire: I
wish to assert my personality in connection with it: I
wish to be satisfied by its execution. If I am to exert
myself for any object, it must in some way or other be
my object. In the accomplishment of such or such
designs I must at the same time find *my* satisfaction;
although the purpose for which I exert myself includes
a complication of results, many of which have no interest for me. This is the absolute right of personal existence—to find *itself* satisfied in its activity and labour.
If men are to interest themselves for anything, they
must (so to speak) have part of their existence involved in it; find their individuality gratified by its
attainment. Here a mistake must be avoided. We intend blame, and justly impute it as a fault, when we say
of an individual, that he is "interested" (in taking part
in such or such transactions) that is, seeks only his
private advantage. In reprehending this we find fault

with him for furthering his personal aims without any regard to a more comprehensive design; of which he takes advantage to promote his own interest, or which he even sacrifices with this view. But he who is active in *promoting an object,* is not simply "interested," but interested in that object itself. Language faithfully expresses this distinction.—Nothing therefore happens, nothing is accomplished, unless the individuals concerned, seek their own satisfaction in the issue. They are particular units of society; *i.e.* they have special needs, instincts, and interests generally, peculiar to themselves. Among these needs are not only such as we usually call necessities—the stimuli of individual desire and volition—but also those connected with individual views and convictions; or—to use a term expressing less decision— leanings of opinion; supposing the impulses of reflection, understanding, and reason, to have been awakened. In these cases people demand, if they are to exert themselves in any direction, that the object should commend itself to them; that in point of opinion,—whether as to its goodness, justice, advantage, profit,—they should be able to "enter into it" (dabei seyn). This is a consideration of especial importance in our age, when people are less than formerly influenced by reliance on others, and by authority; when, on the contrary, they devote their activities to a cause on the ground of their own understanding, their independent conviction and opinion.

We assert then that nothing has been accomplished without interest on the part of the actors; and—if interest be called passion, inasmuch as the whole individuality, to the neglect of all other actual or possible interests and claims, is devoted to an object with every fibre of volition, concentrating all its desires and powers upon it—we may affirm absolutely that *nothing great* in *the World* has been accomplished without *passion*. Two elements, therefore, enter into the object of our investigation; the first the Idea, the second the complex of human passions; the one the warp, the other the woof of the vast arras-web of Universal History. The concrete mean and union of the two is Liberty, under the conditions of morality in a State. We have spoken of the Idea of Freedom as the nature of Spirit, and the absolute goal of History. Passion is regarded as a thing of sinister aspect, as more or less immoral. Man is required to have no passions. Passion, it is true, is not quite the suitable word for what I wish to express. I mean here nothing more than human activity as resulting from private interests—special, or if you will, self-seeking designs—with this qualification, that the whole energy of will and character is devoted to their attainment; that other interests (which would in themselves constitute attractive aims), or rather all things else, are sacrificed to them. The object in question is so bound up with the man's will, that it entirely and alone determines the "hue of resolution," and is inseparable from it. It has become the very essence of his volition. For a person is a specific existence; not man in general (a term to which no real existence corresponds), but a particular human being. The term "character" likewise expresses this idiosyncrasy of Will and Intelligence. But *Character* comprehends all peculiarities whatever; the way in which a person conducts himself in private relations, &c., and is not limited to his idiosyncrasy in its practical and active phase. I shall, therefore, use the term "passion;" understanding thereby the particular bent of character, as far as the peculiarities of volition are not limited to private interest, but supply the impelling and actuating force for accomplishing deeds shared in by the community at large.

Passion is in the first instance the *subjective,* and therefore the *formal* side of energy, will, and activity—leaving the object or aim still undetermined. And there is a similar relation of formality to reality in merely individual conviction, individual views, individual conscience. It is always a question, of essential importance, what is the purport of my conviction, what the object of my passion, in deciding whether the one or the other is of a true and substantial nature. Conversely, if it is so, it will inevitably attain actual existence—be realised.

From this comment on the second essential element in the historical embodiment of an aim, we infer—glancing at the institution of the State in passing—that a State is then well constituted and internally powerful, when the private interest of its citizens is one with the common interest of the State; when the one finds its gratification and realization in the other,—a proposition in itself very important. But in a State many institutions must be adopted, much political machinery invented, accompanied by appropriate political arrangements,—necessitating long struggles of the understanding before what is really appropriate can be discovered,—involving, moreover, contentions with private interest and passions, and a tedious discipline of these latter, in order to bring about the desired harmony. The epoch when a State attains this harmonious condition, marks the period of its bloom, its virtue, its vigour, and its prosperity. But the history of mankind does not begin with a *conscious* aim of any kind, as it is the case with the particular circles into which men form themselves of set purpose. The mere social instinct implies a conscious purpose of security for life and property; and when society has been constituted, this purpose becomes more comprehensive. The History of the World begins with its general aim—the realization of the Idea of Spirit—only in an *implicit* form (*an sich*) that is, as Nature; a hidden, most profoundly hidden, unconscious instinct; and the whole process of History (as already observed), is directed to rendering this unconscious impulse a conscious one. Thus appearing in the form of merely natural existence, natural will—that which has been called the subjective side,—physical craving, instinct, passion, private interest, as also opinion and subjective conception,—spontaneously present themselves at the very commencement. This vast congeries of volitions, interests and activities, constitute the instruments and means of the World-Spirit for attaining its object; bringing it to consciousness, and realising it. And this aim is none other than finding itself—coming to itself— and contemplating itself in concrete actuality. But that those manifestations of vitality on the part of individuals and peoples, in which they seek and satisfy their own purposes, are, at the same time, the means and instruments of a higher and broader purpose of which they know nothing,—which they realise unconsciously,— might be made a matter of question; rather has been questioned, and in every variety of form negatived, decried and contemned as mere dreaming and "Philosophy." But on this point I announced my view at the very outset, and asserted our hypothesis,—which, however, will appear in the sequel, in the form of a legitimate inference,—and our belief, that Reason governs the world, and has consequently governed its history. In relation to this independently universal and substantial existence—all else is subordinate, subservient to it, and the means for its development.—The Union of Universal Abstract Existence generally with the Individual,—the Subjective—that this alone is Truth, belongs to the department of speculation, and is treated in

this general form in Logic.—But in the process of the
World's History itself,—as still incomplete,—the abstract final aim of history is not yet made the distinct
object of desire and interest.   While these limited sentiments are still unconscious of the purpose they are fulfilling, the universal principle is implicit in them, and is
realizing itself through them.   The question also assumes
the form of the union of *Freedom* and *Necessity;* the
latent abstract process of Spirit being regarded as *Necessity,* while that which exhibits itself in the conscious
will of men, as their interest, belongs to the domain of
Freedom.   As the metaphysical connection (*i.e.* the connection in the Idea) of these forms of thought, belongs
to Logic, it would be out of place to analyse it here.
The chief and cardinal points only shall be mentioned.

Philosophy shews that the Idea advances to an infinite
antithesis; that, viz. between the Idea in its free, universal form—in which it exists for itself—and the contrasted form of abstract introversion, reflection on itself,
which is formal existence-for-self, personality, formal
freedom, such as belongs to Spirit only.   The universal
Idea exists thus as the substantial totality of things on
the one side, and as the abstract essence of free volition
on the other side.   This reflection of the mind on itself is
individual self-consciousness—the polar opposite of the
Idea in its general form, and therefore existing in absolute Limitation.   This polar opposite is consequently
limitation, particularization, for the universal absolute
being; it is the side of its *definite existence;* the sphere
of its formal reality, the sphere of the reverence paid to
God.—To comprehend the absolute connection of this
antithesis, is the profound task of metaphysics.   This
Limitation originates all forms of particularity of whatever kind.   The formal volition [of which we have
spoken] wills itself; desires to make its own personality

valid in all that it purposes and does: even the pious individual wishes to be saved and happy. This pole of the antithesis, existing for itself, is—in contrast with the Absolute Universal Being—a special separate existence, taking cognizance of speciality only, and willing that alone. In short it plays its part in the region of mere phenomena. This is the sphere of particular purposes, in effecting which individuals exert themselves on behalf of their individuality—give it full play and objective realization. This is also the sphere of happiness and its opposite. He is happy who finds his condition suited to his special character, will, and fancy, and so enjoys himself in that condition. The History of the World is not the theatre of happiness. Periods of happiness are blank pages in it, for they are periods of harmony,—periods when the antithesis is in abeyance. Reflection on self,—the Freedom above described—is abstractly defined as the formal element of the activity of the absolute Idea. The realizing *activity* of which we have spoken is the middle term of the Syllogism, one of whose extremes is the Universal essence, the *Idea,* which reposes in the penetralia of Spirit; and the other, the complex of external things, objective matter. That activity is the medium by which the universal latent principle is translated into the domain of objectivity.

I will endeavour to make what has been said more vivid and clear by examples.

The building of a house is, in the first instance, a subjective aim and design. On the other hand we have, as means, the several substances required for the work,— Iron, Wood, Stones. The elements are made use of in working up this material: fire to melt the iron, wind to blow the fire, water to set wheels in motion, in order to cut the wood, &c. The result is, that the wind, which has helped to build the house, is shut out by the house;

so also are the violence of rains and floods, and the destructive powers of fire, so far as the house is made
fire-proof.   The stones and beams obey the law of
gravity,—press downwards,—and so high walls are carried up.   Thus the elements are made use of in accordance with their nature, and yet to co-operate for a product, by which their operation is limited.   Thus the
passions of men are gratified; they develop themselves
and their aims in accordance with their natural tendencies, and build up the edifice of human society; thus
fortifying a position for Right and Order *against themselves*.

The connection of events above indicated, involves
also the fact, that in history an additional result is
commonly produced by human actions beyond that which
they aim at and obtain—that which they immediately
recognise and desire.   They gratify their own interest;
but something farther is thereby accomplished, latent
in the actions in question, though not present to their
consciousness, and not included in their design.   An
analogous example is offered in the case of a man who,
from a feeling of revenge,—perhaps not an unjust one,
but produced by injury on the other's part,—burns that
other man's house.   A connection is immediately established between the deed itself and a train of circumstances not directly included in it, taken abstractedly.
In itself it consisted in merely presenting a small flame
to a small portion of a beam.   Events not involved in
that simple act follow of themselves.   The part of the
beam which was set fire to is connected with its remote
portions; the beam itself is united with the woodwork
of the house generally, and this with other houses; so
that a wide conflagration ensues, which destroys the
goods and chattels of many other persons besides his
against whom the act of revenge was first directed; per-

haps even costs not a few men their lives. This lay
neither in the deed abstractedly, nor in the design of the
man who committed it. But the action has a further
general bearing. In the design of the doer it was only
revenge executed against an individual in the destruction
of his property, but it is moreover a crime, and that involves punishment also. This may not have been present
to the mind of the perpetrator, still less in his intention; but his deed itself, the general principles it calls
into play, its substantial content entails it. By this
example I wish only to impress on you the consideration, that in a simple act, something farther may be implicated than lies in the intention and consciousness of
the agent. The example before us involves, however,
this additional consideration, that the substance of the
act, consequently we may say the act itself, recoils upon
the perpetrator,—reacts upon him with destructive tendency. This union of the two extremes—the embodiment of a general idea in the form of direct reality, and
the elevation of a speciality into connection with universal truth—is brought to pass, at first sight, under the
conditions of an utter diversity of nature between the
two, and an indifference of the one extreme towards the
other. The aims which the agent set before them are
limited and special; but it must be remarked that the
agents themselves are intelligent thinking beings. The
purport of their desires is interwoven with *general, essential* considerations of justice, good, duty, &c; for
mere desire—volition in its rough and savage forms—
falls not within the scene and sphere of Universal History. Those general considerations, which form at the
same time a norm for directing aims and actions, have
a determinate purport; for such an abstraction as "good
for its own sake," has no place in living reality. If
men are to act, they must not only intend the Good, but

must have decided for themselves whether this or that particular thing is a Good. What special course of action, however, is good or not, is determined, as regards the ordinary contingencies of private life, by the laws and customs of a State; and here no great difficulty is presented. Each individual has his position; he knows on the whole what a just, honourable course of conduct is. As to ordinary, private relations, the assertion that it is difficult to choose the right and good,—the regarding it as the mark of an exalted morality to find difficulties and raise scruples on that score,—may be set down to an evil or perverse will, which seeks to evade duties not in themselves of a perplexing nature; or, at any rate, to an idly reflective habit of mind—where a feeble will affords no sufficient exercise to the faculties,—leaving them therefore to find occupation within themselves, and to expend themselves on moral self-adulation.

It is quite otherwise with the comprehensive relations that History has to do with. In this sphere are presented those momentous collisions between existing, acknowledged duties, laws, and rights, and those contingencies which are adverse to this fixed system; which assail and even destroy its foundations and existence; whose tenor may nevertheless seem good,—on the large scale advantageous,—yes, even indispensable and necessary. These contingencies realise themselves in History: they involve a general principle of a different order from that on which depends the *permanence* of a people or a State. This principle is an essential phase in the development of the *creating* Idea, of Truth striving and urging towards [consciousness of] itself. Historical men—*World-Historical Individuals*—are those in whose aims such a general principle lies.

Caesar, in danger of losing a position, not perhaps at that time of superiority, yet at least of equality with

the others who were at the head of the State, and of
succumbing to those who were just on the point of becoming his enemies,—belongs essentially to this category.
These enemies—who were at the same time pursuing
their personal aims—had the form of the constitution,
and the power conferred by an appearance of justice,
on their side.   Caesar was contending for the maintenance of his position, honour, and safety; and, since the
power of his opponents included the sovereignty over the
provinces of the Roman Empire, his victory secured for
him the conquest of that entire Empire; and he thus
became—though leaving the form of the constitution—
the Autocrat of the State.   That which secured for him
the execution of a design, which in the first instance was
of negative import—the Autocracy of Rome,—was, however, at the same time an independently necessary feature in the history of Rome and of the world.   It was
not, then, his private gain merely, but an unconscious
impulse that occasioned the accomplishment of that for
which the time was ripe.   Such are all great historical
men,—whose own particular aims involve those large
issues which are the will of the World-Spirit.   They may
be called Heroes, inasmuch as they have derived their
purposes and their vocation, not from the calm, regular
course of things, sanctioned by the existing order; but
from a concealed fount—one which has not attained to
phenomenal, present existence,—from that inner Spirit,
still hidden beneath the surface, which, impinging on the
outer world as on a shell, bursts it in pieces, because
it is another kernel than that which belonged to the
shell in question.   They are men, therefore, who appear
to draw the impulse of their life from themselves; and
whose deeds have produced a condition of things and
a complex of historical relations which appear to be
only *their* interest, and *their* work.

Such individuals had no consciousness of the general
Idea they were unfolding, while prosecuting those aims
of theirs; on the contrary, they were practical, political
men.   But at the same time they were thinking men, who
had an insight into the requirements of the time—*what
was ripe for development.*   This was the very Truth
for their age, for their world; the species next in order,
so to speak, and which was already formed in the womb
of time.   It was theirs to know this nascent principle;
the necessary, directly sequent step in progress, which
their world was to take; to make this their aim, and to
expend their energy in promoting it.   World-historical
men—the Heroes of an epoch—must, therefore, be recognised as its clear-sighted ones; *their* deeds, *their* words
are the best of that time.   Great men have formed purposes to satisfy themselves, not others.   Whatever pru-
dent designs and counsels they might have learned from
others, would be the more limited and inconsistent features in their career; for it was they who best understood affairs; from whom *others* learned, and approved,
or at least acquiesced in—their policy.   For that Spirit
which had taken this fresh step in history is the inmost
soul of all individuals; but in a state of unconsciousness
which the great men in question aroused.   Their fel-
lows, therefore, follow these soul-leaders; for they feel
the irresistible power of their own inner Spirit thus embodied.   If we go on to cast a look at the fate of these
World-Historical persons, whose vocation it was to be
the agents of the World-Spirit,—we shall find it to have
been no happy one.   They attained no calm enjoyment;
their whole life was labour and trouble; their whole nature was nought else but their master-passion.   When
their object is attained they fall off like empty hulls
from the kernel.   They die early, like Alexander; they
are murdered, like Caesar; transported to St. Helena,

like Napoleon. This fearful consolation—that historical men have not enjoyed what is called happiness, and of which only private life (and this may be passed under very various external circumstances) is capable,—this consolation those may draw from history, who stand in need of it; and it is craved by Envy—vexed at what is great and transcendant,—striving, therefore, to depreciate it, and to find some flaw in it. Thus in modern times it has been demonstrated *ad nauseam* that princes are generally unhappy on their thrones; in consideration of which the possession of a throne is tolerated, and men acquiesce in the fact that not themselves but the personages in question are its occupants. The Free Man, we may observe, is not envious, but gladly recognises what is great and exalted, and rejoices that it exists.

It is in the light of those common elements which constitute the interest and therefore the passions of individuals, that these historical men are to be regarded. They are *great* men, because they willed and accomplished something great; not a mere fancy, a mere intention, but that which met the case and fell in with the needs of the age. This mode of considering them also excludes the so-called "psychological" view, which—serving the purpose of envy most effectually—contrives so to refer all actions to the heart,—to bring them under such a subjective aspect—as that their authors appear to have done everything under the impulse of some passion, mean or grand,—some *morbid craving,*—and on account of these passions and cravings to have been not moral men. Alexander of Macedon partly subdued Greece, and then Asia; therefore he was possessed by a *morbid craving* for conquest. He is alleged to have acted from a craving for fame, for conquest; and the proof that these were the impelling motives is that he did that which resulted in fame. What pedagogue has not

demonstrated of Alexander the Great—of Julius Caesar
—that they were instigated by such passions, and were
consequently immoral men?—whence the conclusion immediately follows that he, the pedagogue, is a better
man than they, because he has not such passions; a proof
of which lies in the fact that he does not conquer Asia,—
vanquish Darius and Porus,—but while he enjoys life
himself lets others enjoy it too.   These psychologists
are particularly fond of contemplating those peculiarities
of great historical figures which appertain to them as
private persons.   Man must eat and drink; he sustains
relations to friends and acquaintances; he has passing
impulses and ebullitions of temper.   "No man is a hero
to his valet-de-chambre," is a well-known proverb; I
have added—and Goethe repeated it ten years later—
"but not because the former is no hero, but because
the latter is a valet."   He takes off the hero's boots,
assists him to bed, knows that he prefers champagne,
&c.   Historical personages waited upon in historical
literature by such psychological valets, come poorly
off; they are brought down by these their attendants
to a level with—or rather a few degrees below the
level of—the morality of such exquisite discerners of
spirits.   The Thersites of Homer who abuses the kings
is a standing figure for all times.   Blows—that is beating with a solid cudgel—he does not get in every age,
as in the Homeric one; but his envy, his egotism, is the
thorn which he has to carry in his flesh; and the undying
worm that gnaws him is the tormenting consideration
that his excellent views and vituperations remain absolutely without result in the world.   But our satisfaction
at the fate of Thersitism also, may have its sinister side.

A World-historical individual is not so unwise as to
indulge a variety of wishes to divide his regards.   He
is devoted to the One Aim, regardless of all else.   It

is even possible that such men may treat other great,
even sacred interests, inconsiderately; conduct which
is indeed obnoxious to moral reprehension. But so
mighty a form must trample down many an innocent
flower—crush to pieces many an object in its path.

The special interest of passion is thus inseparable
from the active development of a general principle:
for it is from the special and determinate and from its
negation, that the Universal results. Particularity con-
tends with its like, and some loss is involved in the
issue. *It* is not the general idea that is implicated in
opposition and combat, and that is exposed to danger.
It remains in the background, untouched and uninjured.
This may be called the *cunning of reason,*—that it
sets the passions to work for itself, while that which
develops its existence through such impulsion pays the
penalty, and suffers loss. For it is *phenomenal* being
that is so treated, and of this, part is of no value, part
is positive and real. The particular is for the most part
of too trifling value as compared with the general: individuals are sacrificed and abandoned. The Idea pays
the penalty of determinate existence and of corrupti-
bility, not from itself, but from the passions of individuals.

But though we might tolerate the idea that individuals, their desires and the gratification of them, are thus
sacrificed, and their happiness given up to the empire
of chance, to which it belongs; and that as a general
rule, individuals come under the category of means
to an ulterior end,—there is one aspect of human individuality which we should hesitate to regard in that
subordinate light, even in relation to the highest; since
it is absolutely no subordinate element, but exists in
those individuals as inherently eternal and divine. I
mean *morality, ethics, religion.* Even when speaking of

the realization of the great ideal aim by means of individuals, the *subjective* element in them—their interest and that of their cravings and impulses, their views
and judgments, though exhibited as the merely formal
side of their existence,—was spoken of as having an
infinite right to be consulted. The first idea that
presents itself in speaking of *means* is that of something external to the object, and having no share in
the object itself. But merely natural things—even the
commonest lifeless objects—used as means, must be of
such a kind as adapts them to their purpose; they must
possess something in common with it. Human beings
least of all, sustain the bare external relation of mere
means to the great ideal aim. Not only do they in the
very act of realising it, make it the occasion of satisfying personal desires, whose purport is diverse from that
aim—but they share in that ideal aim itself; and are
for that very reason objects of their own existence;
not *formally* merely, as the world of living beings generally is—whose individual life is essentially subordinate to that of man, and is properly used *up* as an
instrument. Men, on the contrary, are objects of existence to themselves, as regards the intrinsic import
of the aim in question. To this order belongs that in
them which we would exclude from the category of
mere means,—Morality, Ethics, Religion. That is to
say, man is an object of existence in himself only in
virtue of the Divine that is in him,—that which was
designated at the outset as *Reason;* which, in view of its
activity and power of self-determination, was called
Freedom. And we affirm—without entering at present
on the proof of the assertion—that Religion, Morality,
&c. have their foundation and source in that principle,
and so are essentially elevated above all alien necessity
and chance. And here we must remark that individuals,

to the extent of their freedom, are responsible for the depravation and enfeeblement of morals and religion. This is the seal of the absolute and sublime destiny of man—that he knows what is good and what is evil; that his destiny *is* his very ability to will either good or evil,—in one word, that he is the subject of moral imputation, imputation not only of evil, but of good; and not only concerning this or that particular matter, and all that happens *ab extrâ,* but *also* the good and evil attaching to his individual freedom. The brute alone is simply innocent. It would, however, demand an extensive explanation—as extensive as the analysis of moral freedom itself—to preclude or obviate all the misunderstandings which the statement that what is called innocent imports the entire unconsciousness of evil—is wont to occasion.

In contemplating the fate which virtue, morality, even piety experience in history, we must not fall into the Litany of Lamentations, that the good and pious often —or for the most part—fare ill in the world, while the evil-disposed and wicked prosper. The term *prosperity* is used in a variety of meanings—riches, outward honour, and the like. But in speaking of something which in and for itself constitutes an aim of existence, that so-called well or ill-faring of these or those iso-lated individuals cannot be regarded as an essential element in the rational order of the universe. With more justice than happiness,—or a fortunate environment for individuals,—it is demanded of the grand aim of the world's existence, that it should foster, nay involve the execution and ratification of good, moral, righteous pur-poses. What makes men morally discontented (a dis-content, by the bye, on which they somewhat pride themselves), is that they do not find the present adapted to the realization of aims which they hold to be right and just (more especially in modern times, ideals of political constitutions); they contrast unfavourably things as they *are*, with their idea of things as they *ought* to be.   In this case it is not private interest nor passion that desires gratification, but Reason, Justice, Liberty; and equipped with this title, the demand in question assumes a lofty bearing, and readily adopts a position not merely of discontent, but of open revolt against the actual condition of the world.   To estimate such a feeling and such views aright, the demands insisted upon, and the very dogmatic opinions asserted, must be examined.   At no time so much as in our own, have such general principles and notions been advanced, or with greater assurance.   If in days gone by, history seems to present itself as a struggle of passions; in our time   though displays of passion are not wanting—it exhibits partly a predominance of the struggle of notions assuming the authority of principles; partly that of passions and interests essentially subjective, but under the mask of such higher sanctions.   The pretensions thus contended for as legitimate in the name of that which has been stated as the ultimate aim of Reason, pass accordingly, for absolute aims,—to the same extent as Religion, Morals, Ethics.   Nothing, as before remarked, is now more common than the complaint that the *ideals* which imagination sets up are not realised— that these glorious dreams are destroyed by cold actuality.   These Ideals—which in the voyage of life founder on the rocks of hard reality—may be in the first instance only subjective, and belong to the idiosyncrasy of the individual, imagining himself the highest and wisest.   Such do not properly belong to this category.   For the fancies which the individual in his isolation indulges, cannot be the model for universal reality; just as *universal* law is not designed for the units of the mass. These as such may, in fact, find their interests decidedly thrust into the background. But by the term "Ideal," we also understand the ideal of Reason, of the Good, of the True. Poets, as *e.g.* Schiller, have painted such ideals touchingly and with strong emotion, and with the deeply melancholy conviction that they could not be realised. In affirming, on the contrary that the Universal Reason *does* realise itself, we have indeed nothing to do with the individual empirically regarded. That admits of degrees of better and worse, since here chance and speciality have received authority from the Idea to exercise their monstrous power. Much, therefore, in particular aspects of the grand phenomenon might be found fault with. This subjective fault-finding,—which, however, only keeps in view the individual and its deficiency, without taking notice of Reason pervading the whole,—is easy; and inasmuch as it asserts an excellent intention with regard to the good of the whole, and seems to result from a kindly heart, it feels authorized to give itself airs and assume great consequence. It is easier to discover a deficiency in individuals, in states, and in Providence, than to see their real import and value. For in this merely negative fault-finding a proud position is taken,—one which overlooks the object, without having entered into it,— without having comprehended its positive aspect. Age generally makes men more tolerant; youth is always discontented. The tolerance of age is the result of the ripeness of a judgment which, not merely as the result of indifference, is satisfied even with what is inferior; but, more deeply taught by the grave experience of life, has been led to perceive the substantial, solid worth of the object in question. The insight then to which—

in contradistinction from those ideals—philosophy is to
lead us, is, that the real world is as it ought to be—that
the truly good—the universal divine reason—is not a
mere abstraction, but a vital principle capable of realising itself. This *Good,* this *Reason,* in its most concrete
form, is God. God governs the world; the actual working of his government—the carrying out of his plan—
is the History of the World. This plan philosophy
strives to comprehend; for only that which has been
developed as the result of it, possesses *bonâ fide* reality.
That which does not accord with it, is negative, worth-
less existence. Before the pure light of this divine
Idea—which is no mere Ideal—the phantom of a world
whose events are an incoherent concourse of fortuitous
circumstances, utterly vanishes. Philosophy wishes to
discover the substantial purport, the real side of the
divine Idea, and to justify the so much despised Reality of things; for Reason is the comprehension of the
Divine work. But as to what concerns the perversion,
corruption, and ruin of religious, ethical and moral
purposes, and states of society generally, it must be affirmed, that in their *essence* these are infinite and eternal; but that the forms they assume may be of a limited
order, and consequently belong to the domain of mere
nature, and be subject to the sway of chance. They
are therefore perishable, and exposed to decay and corruption. Religion and morality—in the same way as
inherently universal essences—have the peculiarity of
being present in the individual soul, in the full extent
of their Idea, and therefore truly and really; although
they may not manifest themselves in it *in extenso,* and
are not applied to fully developed relations. The religion, the morality of a limited sphere of life—that of a
shepherd or a peasant, *e.g.*—in its intensive concentration and limitation to a few perfectly simple relations

of life,—has infinite worth; the same worth as the religion and morality of extensive knowledge, and of an
existence rich in the compass of its relations and actions.
This inner focus—this simple region of the claims of
subjective freedom,—the home of volition, resolution,
and action,—the abstract sphere of conscience,—that
which comprises the responsibility and moral value of
the individual, remains untouched; and is quite shut out
from the noisy din of the World's History—including
not merely external and temporal changes, but also
those entailed by the absolute necessity inseparable
from the realization of the Idea of Freedom itself.
But as a general truth this must be regarded as settled,
that whatever in the world possesses claims as noble
and glorious, has nevertheless a higher existence above
it. The claim of the World-Spirit rises above all special
claims.

These observations may suffice in reference to the
means which the World-Spirit uses for realising its
Idea. Stated simply and abstractly, this mediation involves the activity of personal existences in whom
Reason is present as their absolute, substantial being;
but a basis, in the first instance, still obscure and unknown to them. But the subject becomes more complicated and difficult when we regard individuals not
merely in their aspect of activity, but more concretely,
in conjunction with a particular manifestation of that
activity in their religion and morality,—forms of existence which are intimately connected with Reason, and
share in its absolute claims. Here the relation of mere
means of an end disappears, and the chief bearings
of this seeming difficulty in reference to the absolute
aim of Spirit, have been briefly considered.

(3.) The third point to be analysed is, therefore—
what is the object to be realised by these means; i.e.

what is the form it assumes in the realm of reality.
We have spoken of *means;* but in the carrying out of
a subjective, limited aim, we have also to take into
consideration the element of a *material,* either already
present or which has to be procured.   Thus the question would arise: What is the material in which the
Ideal of Reason is wrought out?   The primary answer
would be,—Personality itself—human desires—Subjectivity generally.   In human knowledge and volition, as
its material element, Reason attains positive existence.
We have considered subjective volition where it has an
object which is the truth and essence of a reality, viz.
where it constitutes a great world-historical passion.
As a subjective will, occupied with limited passions, it
is dependent, and can gratify its desires only within
the limits of this dependence.   But the subjective will
has also a substantial life— a reality,—in which it moves
in the region of *essential* being and has the essential
itself as the object of its existence.   This essential being
is the union of the *subjective* with the *rational* Will: it
is the moral Whole, the State, which is that form of
reality in which the individual has and enjoys his freedom; but on the condition of his recognition, believing
in and willing that which is common to the Whole.   And
this must not be understood as if the subjective will
of the social unit attained its gratification and enjoyment through that common Will; as if this were a means
provided for its benefit; as if the individual, in his relations to other individuals, thus limited his freedom,
in order that this universal limitation—the mutual constraint of all—might secure a small space of liberty
for each.   Rather, we affirm, are Law, Morality, Government, and they alone, the positive reality and completion of Freedom.   Freedom of a low and limited

order, is mere caprice; which finds its exercise in the sphere of particular and limited desires.

Subjective volition—Passion—is that which sets men in activity, that which effects "practical" realization. The Idea is the inner spring of action; the State is the actually existing, realised moral life. For it is the Unity of the universal, essential Will, with that of the individual; and this is "Morality." The Individual living in this unity has a moral life; possesses a value that consists in this substantiality alone. Sophocles in his Antigone, says, "The divine commands are not of yesterday, nor of today; no, they have an infinite existence, and no one could say whence they came." The laws of morality are not accidental, but are the essentially Rational. It is the very object of the State that what is essential in the practical activity of men, and in their dispositions, should be duly recognised; that it should have a manifest existence, and maintain its position. It is the absolute interest of Reason that this moral Whole should exist; and herein lies the justification and merit of heroes who have founded states,— however rude these may have been. In the history of the World, only those peoples can come under our notice which form a state. For it must be understood that this latter is the realization of Freedom, i.e. of the absolute final aim, and that it exists for its own sake. It must further be understood that all the worth which the human being possesses—all spiritual reality, he possesses only through the State. For his spiritual reality consists in this, that his own essence—Reason—is objectively present to him, that it possesses objective immediate existence for him. Thus only is he fully conscious; thus only is he a partaker of morality—of a just and moral social and political life. For Truth is the Unity of the universal and subjective Will; and the

Universal is to be found in the State, in its laws, its universal and rational arrangements. The State is the Divine Idea as it exists on Earth. We have in it, therefore, the object of History in a more definite shape than before; that in which Freedom obtains objectivity, and lives in the enjoyment of this objectivity. For Law is the objectivity of Spirit; volition in its true form. Only that will which obeys law, is free; for it obeys itself—it is independent and so free. When the State or our country constitutes a community of existence; when the subjective will of man submits to laws,— the contradiction between Liberty and Necessity vanishes. The Rational has necessary existence, as being the reality and substance of things, and we are free in recognising it as law, and following it as the substance of our own being. The objective and the subjective will are then reconciled, and present one identical homogeneous whole. For the morality (Sittlichkeit) of the State is not of that ethical (moralische) reflective kind, in which one's own conviction bears sway; this latter is rather the peculiarity of the modern time, while the true antique morality is based on the principle of abiding by one's duty [to the state at large]. An Athenian citizen did what was required of him, as it were from instinct; but if I reflect on the object of my activity, I must have the consciousness that my will has been called into exercise. But morality is Duty—substantial Right—a *"second* nature" as it has been justly called; for the *first* nature of man is his primary merely animal existence.

The development *in extenso* of the Idea of the State belongs to the Philosophy of Jurisprudence; but it must be observed that in the theories of our time various errors are current respecting it, which pass for established truths, and have become fixed prejudices.

We will mention only a few of them, giving prominence
to such as have a reference to the object of our history.

The error which first meets us is the direct contradictory of our principle that the state presents the realization of Freedom; the opinion, viz., that man is free
by *nature,* but that in *society,* in the State—to which
nevertheless he is irresistibly impelled—he must limit
this natural freedom. That man is free by Nature is
quite correct in one sense; viz., that he is so according
to the Idea of Humanity; but we imply thereby that
he is such only in virtue of his destiny—that he has an
undeveloped power to become such; for the "Nature"
of an object is exactly synonymous with its "Idea."
But the view in question imports more than this. When
man is spoken of as "free by Nature," the mode of his
existence as well as his destiny is implied. His merely
natural and primary condition is intended. In this
sense a "state of Nature" is assumed in which mankind at large are in the possession of their natural rights
with the unconstrained exercise and enjoyment of their
freedom. This assumption is not indeed raised to the
dignity of the historical fact; it would indeed be difficult, were the attempt seriously made, to point out any
such condition as actually existing, or as having ever
occurred. Examples of a savage state of life can be
pointed out, but they are marked by brutal passions and
deeds of violence; while, however rude and simple their
conditions, they involve social arrangements which (to
use the common phrase) *restrain* freedom. That assumption is one of those nebulous images which theory
produces; an idea which it cannot avoid originating,
but which it fathers upon real existence, without sufficient historical justification.

What we find such a state of Nature to be in actual
experience, answers exactly to the Idea of a *merely*

THE PHILOSOPHY OF HISTORY 391

natural condition. Freedom as the *ideal* of that which is original and natural, does not exist *as original and natural*. Rather must it be first sought out and won; and that by an incalculable medial discipline of the intellectual and moral powers. The state of Nature is, therefore, predominantly that of injustice and violence, of untamed natural impulses, of inhuman deeds and feelings. Limitation is certainty produced by Society and the State, but it is a limitation of the mere brute emotions and rude instincts; as also, in a more advanced stage of culture, of the premeditated self-will of caprice and passion. This kind of constraint is part of the instrumentality by which only, the consciousness of Freedom and the desire for its attainment, in its true—that is Rational and Ideal form—can be obtained. To the Ideal of Freedom, Law and Morality are indispensably requisite; and they are in and for themselves, universal existences, objects and aims; which are discovered only by the activity of thought, separating itself from the merely sensuous, and developing itself, in opposition thereto; and which must on the other hand, be introduced into and incorporated with the originally sensuous will, and that contrarily to its natural inclination. The perpetually recurring misapprehension of Freedom consists in regarding that term only in its *formal*, subjective sense, abstracted from its essential objects and aims; thus a constraint put upon impulse, desire, passion—pertaining to the particular individual as such—a limitation of caprice and self-will is regarded as a fettering of Freedom. We should on the contrary look upon such limitation as the indispensable proviso of emancipation. Society and the State are the very conditions in which Freedom is realised.

We must notice a second view, contravening the prin-

ciple of the development of moral relations into a legal
form. The *patriarchal* condition is regarded—either in
reference to the entire race of man, or to some branches
of it—as exclusively that condition of things, in which
the legal element is combined with a due recognition
of the moral and emotional parts of our nature; and in
which justice as united with these, truly and really influences the intercourse of the social units. The basis
of the patriarchal condition is the family relation; which
develops the *primary* form of conscious morality, succeeded by that of the State as its *second* phase. The
patriarchal condition is one of transition, in which the
family has already advanced to the position of a race or
people; where the union, therefore, has already ceased
to be simply a bond of love and confidence, and has become one of plighted service. We must first examine
the ethical principle of the Family. The Family may
be reckoned as virtually a single person; since its members have either mutually surrendered their individual
personality, (and consequently their legal position towards each other, with the rest of their particular interests and desires) as in the case of the Parents; or
have not yet attained such an independent personality,
—(the Children,—who are primarily in that merely
natural condition already mentioned.) They live, therefore, in a unity of feeling, love, confidence, and faith
in each other. And in a relation of mutual love, the
one individual has the consciousness of himself in the
consciousness of the other; he lives out of self; and
in this mutual self-renunciation each regains the life
that had been virtually transferred to the other; gains,
in fact, that other's existence and his own, as involved
with that other. The farther interests connected with
the necessities and external concerns of life, as well
as the development that has to take place within their

circle, *i.e.* of the children, constitute a common object
for the members of the Family.   The Spirit of the
Family—the Penates—form one substantial being, as
much as the Spirit of a People in the State; and morality
in both cases consists in a feeling, a consciousness, and a
will, not limited to individual personality and interest,
but embracing the common interests of the members generally.   But this unity is in the case of the Family
essentially one of *feeling;* not advancing beyond the
limits of the merely *natural.*   The piety of the Family
relation should be respected in the highest degree by
the State; by its means the State obtains as its members individuals who are already moral (for as mere
persons they are not) and who in uniting to form a
state bring with them that sound basis of a political
edifice—the capacity of feeling one with a Whole.   But
the expansion of the Family to a patriarchal unity carries us beyond the ties of blood-relationship—the simply
natural elements of that basis; and outside of these
limits the members of the community must enter upon
the position of independent personality.   A review of
the patriarchal condition, *in extenso,* would lead us to
give special attention to the Theocratical Constitution.
The head of the patriarchal clan is also its priest.   If
the Family in its general relations, is not yet separated
from civic society and the state, the separation of religion from it has also not yet taken place; and so
much the less since the piety of the hearth is itself a
profoundly subjective state of feeling.

We have considered two aspects of Freedom,—the
objective and the subjective; if, therefore, Freedom is
asserted to consist in the individuals of a State all agree-
ing in its arrangements, it is evident that only the subjective aspect is regarded.   The natural inference from
this principle is, that no law can be valid without the

approval of all. This difficulty is attempted to be obviated by the decision that the minority must yield to the majority; the majority therefore bear the sway. But long ago J. J. Rousseau remarked, that in that case there would be no longer freedom, for the will of the *minority* would cease to be respected. At the Polish Diet each single member had to give his consent before any political step could be taken; and this kind of freedom it was that ruined the State. Besides, it is a dangerous and false prejudice, that the People *alone* have reason and insight, and know what justice is; for each popular faction may represent itself as the People, and the question as to what constitutes the State is one of advanced science, and not of popular decision.

If the principle of regard for the individual will is recognised as the only basis of political liberty, viz., that nothing should be done by or for the State to which all the members of the body politic have not given their sanction, we have, properly speaking, no *Constitution*. The only arrangement that would be necessary, would be, first, a centre having no *will* of its own, but which should take into consideration what appeared to be the necessities of the State; and, secondly, a contrivance for calling the members of the State together, for taking the votes, and for performing the arithmetical operations of reckoning and comparing the number of votes for the different propositions, and thereby deciding upon them. The State is an *abstraction*, having even its generic existence in its citizens; but it is an actuality, and its simply generic existence must embody itself in individual will and activity. The want of government and political administration in general is felt; this necessitates the selection and separation from the rest of those who have to take the helm in political affairs, to decide concerning them, and to give orders to other citizens, with a view to the execution of their plans. If, *e. g.*, even the people in a Democracy resolve on a war, a general must head the army. It is only by a Constitution that the *abstraction*—the State—attains life and reality; but this involves the distinction between those who command and those who obey.—Yet obedience seems inconsistent with liberty, and those who command appear to do the very opposite of that which the fundamental idea of the State, viz., that of Freedom, requires. It is, however, urged that,—though the distinction between commanding and obeying is absolutely necessary, because affairs could not go on without it—and indeed this seems only a compulsory limitation, external to and even contravening freedom in the abstract—the constitution should be at least so framed, that the citizens may obey as little as possible, and the smallest modicum of free volition be left to the commands of the superiors;—that the substance of that for which subordination is necessary, even in its most important bearings, should be decided and resolved on by the People—by the will of many or of all the citizens; though it is supposed to be thereby provided that the State should be possessed of vigour and strength as a reality—an individual unity.— The primary consideration is, then, the distinction between the governing and the governed, and political constitutions in the abstract have been rightly divided into Monarchy, Aristocracy, and Democracy; which gives occasion, however, to the remark that Monarchy itself must be further divided into Despotism and Monarchy proper; that in all the divisions to which the leading Idea gives rise, only the generic character is to be made prominent,—it being not intended thereby that the particular category under review should be exhausted as a Form, Order, or Kind in its *concrete* de-

velopment. But especially it must be observed, that
the above-mentioned divisions admit of a multitude of
particular modifications,—not only such as lie within
the limits of those classes themselves,—but also such
as are mixtures of several of these essentially distinct
classes, and which are consequently misshapen, unstable,
and inconsistent forms. In such a collision, the concerning question is, what is the *best constitution;* that
is, by what arrangement, organization, or mechanism
of the power of the State its object can be most surely
attained. This object may indeed be variously understood; for instance, as the calm enjoyment of life on
the part of the citizens, or as Universal Happiness.
Such aims have suggested the so-called Ideals of Constitution, and,—as a particular branch of the subject,
—Ideals of the Education of Princes (Fenelon), or of
the governing body—the aristocracy at large (Plato);
for the chief point they treat of is the condition of those
subjects who stand at the head of affairs; and in these
Ideals the concrete details of political organization are
not at all considered. The inquiry into the best constitution is frequently treated as if not only the theory
were an affair of subjective independent conviction,
but as if the introduction of a constitution recognised
as the best,—or as superior to others,—could be the
result of a resolve adopted in this theoretical manner;
as if the form of a constitution were a matter of free
choice, determined by nothing else but reflection. Of
this artless fashion was that deliberation,—not indeed
of the Persian *people,* but of the Persian *grandees,* who
had conspired to overthrow the pseudo-Smerdis and the
Magi, after their undertaking had succeeded, and when
there was no scion of the royal family living,—as to
what constitution they should introduce into Persia;

and Herodotus gives an equally naïve account of this deliberation.

In the present day, the Constitution of a country and people is not represented as so entirely dependent on free and deliberate choice. The fundamental but abstractly (and therefore imperfectly) entertained conception of Freedom, has resulted in the Republic being very generally regarded—in *theory*—as the only just and true political constitution. Many even, who occupy elevated official positions under monarchical constitutions—so far from being opposed to this idea—are actually its supporters; only they see that such a constitution, though the best, cannot be realised under all circumstances; and that—while men are what they are —we must be satisfied with less freedom; the monarchical constitution—under the given circumstances, and the present moral condition of the people—being even regarded as the most advantageous. In this view also, the necessity of a particular constitution is made to depend on the condition of the people in such a way as if the latter were non-essential and accidental. This representation is founded on the distinction which the reflective understanding makes between an idea and the corresponding reality; holding to an abstract and consequently untrue idea; not grasping it in its complete ness, or—which is virtually, though not in point of form, the same—not taking a concrete view of a people and a state. We shall have to shew further on, that the constitution adopted by a people makes one substance—one spirit—with its religion, its art and philosophy, or, at least, with its conceptions and thoughts —its culture generally; not to expatiate upon the additional influences, *ab extrâ,* of climate, of neighbours, of its place in the world. A State is an individual totality, of which you cannot select any particular side, although a supremely important one, such as its political constitution; and deliberate and decide respecting it in that isolated form. Not only is that constitution most intimately connected with and dependent on those other spiritual forces; but the form of the entire moral and intellectual individuality—comprising all the forces it embodies—is only a step in the development of the grand Whole,—with its place preappointed in the process; a fact which gives the highest sanction to the constitution in question, and establishes its absolute necessity.—The origin of a State involves imperious lordship on the one hand, instinctive submission on the other. But even obedience—lordly power, and the fear inspired by a ruler—in itself implies some degree of voluntary connection. Even in barbarous states this is the case; it is not the isolated will of individuals that prevails; individual pretensions are relinquished, and the general will is the essential bond of political union. This unity of the general and the particular is the Idea itself, manifesting itself as a *State,* and which subsequently undergoes further development within itself. The abstract yet necessitated process in the development of truly independent states is as follows:—They begin with regal power, whether of patriarchal or military origin. In the next phase, particularity and individuality assert themselves in the form of Aristocracy and Democracy. Lastly, we have the subjection of these separate interests to a single power; but which can be absolutely none other than one outside of which those spheres have an independent position, viz., the Monarchical. Two phases of royalty, therefore, must be distinguished,—a primary and a secondary one. This process is necessitated, so that the form of government assigned to a particular stage of development *must* present itself: it is therefore no matter of choice, but is that form which is adapted to the spirit of the people.

In a Constitution the main feature of interest is the self-development of the *rational*, that is, the *political* condition of a people; the setting free of the successive elements of the Idea: so that the several powers in the State manifest themselves as separate,—attain their appropriate and special perfection,—and yet in this independent condition, work together for one object, and are held together by it—*i. e.*, form an organic whole. The State is thus the embodiment of rational freedom, realizing and recognizing itself in an objective form. For its objectivity consists in this,—that its successive stages are not merely ideal, but are present in an appropriate reality; and that in their separate and several working, they are absolutely merged in that agency by which the totality—the soul—the individual unity—is produced, and of which it is the result.

The State is the Idea of Spirit in the external manifestation of human Will and its Freedom. It is to the State, therefore, that change in the aspect of History indissolubly attaches itself; and the successive phases of the Idea manifest themselves in it as distinct political *principles*. The Constitutions under which World-Historical peoples have reached their culmination, are peculiar to them; and therefore do not present a generally applicable political basis. Were it otherwise, the differences of similar constitutions would consist only in a peculiar method of expanding and developing that generic basis; whereas they really originate in diversity of principle. From the comparison therefore of the political institutions of the ancient World-Historical peoples, it so happens, that for the most recent principle of a Constitution—for the principle of our own times—nothing (so to speak) can be learned. In science and art it is quite otherwise; e. g., the ancient philosophy is so decidedly the basis of the modern, that it is inevitably contained in the latter, and constitutes its basis. In this case the relation is that of a continuous development of the same structure, whose foundation-stone, walls, and roof have remained what they were. In Art, the Greek itself, in its original form, furnishes us the best models. But in regard to political constitution, it is quite otherwise: here the Ancient and the Modern have not their essential principle in common. Abstract definitions and dogmas respecting just government,—importing that intelligence and virtue ought to bear sway—are, indeed, common to both. But nothing is so absurd as to look to Greeks, Romans, or Orientals, for models for the political arrangements of our time. From the East may be derived beautiful pictures of a patriarchal condition, of paternal government, and of devotion to it on the part of peoples; from Greeks and Romans, descriptions of popular liberty. Among the latter we find the idea of a Free Constitution admitting all the citizens to a share in deliberations and resolves respecting the affairs and laws of the Commonwealth. In our times, too, this is its general acceptation; only with this modification, that—since our States are so large, and there are so many of "the Many," the latter,—direct action being impossible,—should by the indirect method of elective substitution express their concurrence with resolves affecting the common weal; that is, that for legislative purposes generally, the people should be represented by deputies. The so-called Representative Constitution is that form of government with which we connect the idea of a free constitution, and this notion has become a rooted prejudice. On this theory People and Government are separated. But there is a perversity in this antithesis; an ill-intentioned *ruse* designed to insinuate that the People are the totality of the State. Besides, the basis of this view is the principle of isolated individuality—the absolute validity of the subjective will—a dogma which we have already investigated. The great point is, that Freedom in its Ideal conception has not subjective will and caprice for its principle, but the recognition of the universal will; and that the process by which Freedom is realised is the free development of its successive stages. The subjective will is a merely formal determination—a *carte blanche*—not including what it is that is willed. Only the *rational* will is that universal principle which independently determines and unfolds its own being, and develops its successive elemental phases as organic members. Of this Gothic-cathedral architecture the ancients knew nothing.

At an earlier stage of the discussion, we established the two elemental considerations: first, the *idea* of freedom as the absolute and final aim; secondly, the *means* for realising it, *i. e.* the subjective side of knowledge and will, with its life, movement, and activity. We then recognised the State as the moral Whole and the Reality of Freedom, and consequently as the objective unity of these two elements. For although we make this distinction into two aspects for our consideration, it must be remarked that they are intimately connected; and that their connection is involved in the idea of each when examined separately. We have, on the one hand, recognised the Idea in the definite form of Freedom conscious of and willing itself,—having itself alone as its object: involving at the same time, the pure and simple Idea of Reason, and likewise, that which we have called subject—self-consciousness—Spirit actually existing in the World. If, on the other hand, we consider Subjectivity, we find that subjective knowledge and will is Thought. But by the very act of thoughtful cognition and volition, I will the universal object —the substance of absolute Reason. We observe, therefore, an essential union between the objective side— the Idea,—and the subjective side—the personality that conceives and wills it.—The *objective* existence of this union is the State, which is therefore the basis and centre of the other concrete elements of the life of a people,—of Art, of Law, of Morals, of Religion, of Science. All the activity of Spirit has only this object—the becoming conscious of this union, *i.e.,* of its own Freedom. Among the forms of this conscious union *Religion* occupies the highest position. In it, Spirit —rising above the limitations of temporal and secular existence—becomes conscious of the Absolute Spirit, and in this consciousness of the self-existent Being, renounces its individual interest; it lays this aside in Devotion—a state of mind in which it refuses to occupy itself any longer with the limited and particular. By Sacrifice man expresses his renunciation of his property, his will, his individual feelings. The religious concentration of the soul appears in the form of feeling; it nevertheless passes also into reflection; a form of worship (*cultus*) is a result of reflection. The second form of the union of the objective and subjective in the human spirit is *Art*. This advances farther into the realm of the actual and sensuous than Religion. In its noblest walk it is occupied with representing, not indeed, the Spirit of God, but certainly the Form of God; and in its secondary aims, that which is divine and spiritual generally. Its office is to render visible the Divine; presenting it to the imaginative and intuitive faculty. But the True is the object not only of conception and feeling, as in Religion,—and of intuition, as in Art,—but also of the thinking faculty; and this gives us the third form of the union in question—*Philosophy*. This is consequently the highest, freest, and wisest phase. Of course we are not intending to investigate these three phases here; they have only suggested themselves in virtue of their occupying the same general ground as the object here considered—the *State*.

The general principle which manifests itself and becomes an object of consciousness in the State,—the form under which all that the State includes is brought,— is the whole of that cycle of phenomena which constitutes the *culture* of a nation. But the definite *substance* that receives the form of universality, and exists in that concrete reality which is the State,—is the Spirit of the People itself. The actual State is animated by this spirit, in all its particular affairs—its Wars, Institutions, &c. But man must also attain a conscious realization of this his Spirit and essential nature, and of his original identity with it. For we said that morality is the identity of the *subjective* or *personal* with the *universal* will. Now the mind must give itself an express consciousness of this; and the focus of this knowledge is *Religion*. Art and Science are only various aspects and forms of the same substantial being. In considering Religion, the chief point of enquiry is, whether it recognises the True—the Idea—only in its separate, abstract form, or in its true unity; in *separation*—God being represented in an abstract form as the Highest Being, Lord of Heaven and Earth, living in a remote region far from human actualities,—or in its *unity*,—God, as Unity of the Universal and Individual; the Individual itself assuming the aspect of positive and real existence in the idea of the Incarnation. Religion is the sphere in which a nation gives itself the definition of that which it regards as the True. A definition contains everything that belongs to the essence of an object; reducing its nature to its simple characteristic predicate, as a mirror for every predicate,—the generic soul pervading all its details. The conception of God, therefore, constitutes the general basis of a people's character.

In this aspect, religion stands in the closest connection with the political principle. Freedom can exist only where Individuality is recognised as having its positive and real existence in the Divine Being. The connection may be further explained thus:—Secular existence, as merely temporal—occupied with particular interests—is consequently only relative and unauthorized; and receives its validity only in as far as the universal soul that pervades it—its principle—receives absolute validity; which it cannot have unless it is recognised as the definite manifestation, the phenomenal existence of the Divine Essence. On this account it is that the State rests on Religion. We hear this often repeated in our times, though for the most part nothing further is meant than that individual subjects as God-fearing men would be more disposed and ready to perform their duty; since obedience to King and Law so naturally follows in the train of reverence for God. This reverence, indeed, since it exalts the general over the special, may even turn upon the latter,—become fanatical,—and work with incendiary and destructive violence against the State, its institutions, and arrangements. Religious feeling, therefore, it is thought, should be sober—kept in a certain degree of coolness,—that it may not storm against and bear down that which should be defended and preserved by it. The possibility of such a catastrophe is at least latent in it.

While, however, the correct sentiment is adopted,

that the State is based on Religion, the position thus
assigned to Religion supposes the State already to exist;
and that subsequently, in order to maintain it, Religion
must be brought into it—buckets and bushels as it were
—and impressed upon people's hearts. It is quite true
that men must be trained to religion, but not as to something whose existence has yet to begin. For in affirming that the State is based on Religion—that it has its
roots in it—we virtually assert that the former has proceeded from the latter; and that this derivation is going
on now and will always continue; *i. e.*, the principles
of the State must be regarded as valid in and for themselves, which can only be in so far as they are recognised as determinate manifestations of the Divine Nature. The form of Religion, therefore, decides that of
the State and its constitution. The latter actually originated in the particular religion adopted by the nation;
so that, in fact, the Athenian or the Roman State was
possible only in connection with the specific form of
Heathenism existing among the respective peoples; just
as a Catholic State has a spirit and constitution different from that of a Protestant one.

If that outcry—that urging and striving for the implantation of Religion in the community—were an utterance of anguish and a call for help, as it often seems
to be, expressing the danger of religion having vanished, or being about to vanish entirely from the State,
—that would be fearful indeed,—worse, in fact, than
this outcry supposes; for it implies the belief in a re-
source against the evil, viz., the implantation and in-
culcation of religion; whereas religion is by no means
a thing to be so produced; its *self-production* (and there
can be no other) lies much deeper.

Another and opposite folly which we meet with in
our time, is that of pretending to invent and carry out

political constitutions independently of religion. The Catholic confession, although sharing the Christian name with the Protestant, does not concede to the State an inherent Justice and Morality,—a concession which in the Protestant principle is fundamental. This tearing away of the political morality of the Constitution from its natural connection, is necessary to the genius of that religion, inasmuch as it does not recognise Justice and Morality as independent and substantial. But thus excluded from intrinsic worth,—torn away from their last refuge—the sanctuary of conscience—the calm retreat where religion has its abode,—the principles and institutions of political legislation are destitute of a real centre, to the same degree as they are compelled to remain abstract and indefinite.

Summing up what has been said of the State, we find that we have been led to call its vital principle, as actuating the individuals who compose it,—Morality. The State, its laws, its arrangements, constitute the rights of its members; its natural features, its mountains, air, and waters, are *their* country, their fatherland, their outward material property; the history of this State, *their* deeds; what their ancestors have produced, belongs to them and lives in their memory. All is their possession, just as they are possessed by it; for it constitutes their existence, their being.

Their imagination is occupied with the ideas thus presented, while the adoption of these laws, and of a fatherland so conditioned is the expression of their will. It is this matured totality which thus constitutes *one* Being, the spirit of *one* People. To it the individual members belong; each unit is the Son of his Nation, and at the same time—in as far as the State to which he belongs is undergoing development—the Son of his Age. None remains behind it, still less advances be-

yond it. This spiritual Being (the Spirit of his Time)
is his; he is a representative of it; it is that in which he
originated, and in which he lives. Among the Athenians the word Athens had a double import; suggesting
primarily, a complex of political institutions, but no
less, in the second place, that Goddess who represented
the Spirit of the People and its unity.

This Spirit of a People is a *determinate* and particular Spirit, and is, as just stated, further modified by
the degree of its historical development. This Spirit,
then, constitutes the basis and substance of those other
forms of a nation's consciousness, which have been noticed. For Spirit in its self-consciousness must become
an object of contemplation to itself, and objectivity involves, in the first instance, the rise of differences which
make up a total of distinct spheres of objective spirit;
in the same way as the Soul exists only as the complex
of its faculties, which in their form of concentration in
a simple unity produce that Soul. It is thus *One Individuality* which, presented in its essence as God, is
honoured and enjoyed in *Religion;* which is exhibited
as an object of sensuous contemplation in *Art*; and is
apprehended as an intellectual conception, in *Philosophy*. In virtue of the original identity of their essence,
purport, and object, these various forms are insepara-
bly united with the Spirit of the State. Only in connection with this particular religion, can this particular
political constitution exist; just as in such or such a
State, such or such a Philosophy or order of Art.

The remark next in order is, that each particular National genius is to be treated as only One Individual in
the process of Universal History. For that history is
the exhibition of the divine, absolute development of
Spirit in its highest forms,—that gradation by which
it attains its truth and consciousness of itself. The forms

which these grades of progress assume are the characteristic "National Spirits" of History; the peculiar tenor of their moral life, of their Government, their Art, Religion, and Science. To realise these grades is the boundless impulse of the World-Spirit—the goal of its irresistible urging; for this division into organic members, and the full development of each, is its Idea. —Universal History is exclusively occupied with shewing how Spirit comes to a recognition and adoption of the Truth: the dawn of knowledge appears; it begins to discover salient principles, and at last it arrives at full consciousness.

Having, therefore, learned the abstract characteristics of the nature of Spirit, the means which it uses to realise its Idea, and the shape assumed by it in its complete realisation in phenomenal existence—namely, the State—nothing further remains for this introductory section to contemplate but

III. *The course of the World's History.* The mutations which history presents have been long characterised in the general, as an advance to something better, more perfect. The changes that take place in Nature —how infinitely manifold soever they may be—exhibit only a perpetually self-repeating cycle; in Nature there happens "nothing new under the sun," and the multiform play of its phenomena so far induces a feeling of *ennui;* only in those changes which take place in the region of Spirit does anything new arise. This peculiarity in the world of mind has indicated in the case of man an altogether different destiny from that of merely natural objects—in which we find always one and the same stable character, to which all change reverts;— namely, a *real* capacity for change, and that for the better,—an impulse of *perfectibility.* This principle, which reduces change itself under a law, has met with an unfavourable reception from religions—such as the Catholic—and from States claiming as their just right a stereotyped, or at least a stable position. If the mutability of worldly things in general—political constitutions, for instance—is conceded, either Religion (as the Religion of *Truth*) is absolutely excepted, or the difficulty escaped by ascribing changes, revolutions, and abrogations of immaculate theories and institutions, to accidents or imprudence,—but principally to the levity and evil passions of man. The principle of Perfectibility indeed is almost as indefinite a term as mutability in general; it is without scope or goal, and has no standard by which to estimate the changes in question: the improved, more perfect, state of things towards which it professedly tends is altogether undetermined.

The principle of *Development* involves also the existence of a latent germ of being—a capacity or potentiality striving to realise itself. This formal conception finds actual existence in Spirit; which has the History of the World for its theatre, its possession, and the sphere of its realisation. It is not of such a nature as to be tossed to and fro amid the superficial play of accidents, but is rather the absolute arbiter of things; entirely unmoved by contingencies, which, indeed, it applies and manages for its own purposes. Development, however, is also a property of organized natural objects. Their existence presents itself, not as an exclusively dependent one, subjected to external changes, but as one which expands itself in virtue of an external unchangeable principle; a simple essence,—whose existence, i. e., as a germ, is primarily simple,—but which subsequently develops a variety of parts, that become involved with other objects, and consequently live through a continuous process of changes;—a process nevertheless, that results in the very contrary of change, and is even transformed into a *vis conservatrix* of the organic principle, and the form embodying it. Thus the organized *individuum* produces itself; it expands itself *actually* to what it was always *potentially*: So Spirit is only that which it attains by its own efforts; it makes itself *actually* what it always was *potentially*.—That development (of *natural organisms*) takes place in a direct, unopposed, unhindered manner. Between the Idea and its realisation—the essential constitution of the original germ and the conformity to it of the existence derived from it—no disturbing influence can intrude. But in relation to Spirit it is quite otherwise. The realisation of *its* Idea is mediated by consciousness and will; these very faculties are, in the first instance, sunk in their primary *merely* natural life; the first object and goal of their striving is the realisation of their merely natural destiny,—but which, since it is Spirit that animates it, is possessed of vast attractions and displays great power and [moral] richness. Thus Spirit is at war with itself; it has to overcome itself as its most formidable obstacle. That development which in the sphere of Nature is a peaceful growth, is in that of Spirit, a severe, a mighty conflict with itself. What Spirit really strives for is the realisation of its Ideal being; but in doing so, it hides that goal from its own vision, and is proud and well satisfied in this alienation from it.

Its expansion, therefore, does not present the harmless tranquillity of mere growth, as does that of organic life, but a stern reluctant working against itself. It exhibits, moreover, not the mere formal conception of development, but the attainment of a definite result. The goal of attainment we determined at the outset: it is Spirit in its *completeness,* in its essential nature, *i. e.,* Freedom. This is the fundamental object, and there-

fore also the leading principle of the development,—
that whereby it receives meaning and importance (as
in the Roman history, Rome is the object—consequently
that which directs our consideration of the facts related); as, conversely, the phenomena of the process
have resulted from this principle alone, and only as
referred to it, possess a sense and value.   There are
many considerable periods in History in which this
development seems to have been intermitted; in which,
we might rather say, the whole enormous gain of previous culture appears to have been entirely lost; after
which, unhappily, a new commencement has been necessary, made in the hope of recovering—by the assistance
of some remains saved from the wreck of a former civil-
lization, and by dint of a renewed incalculable expenditure of strength and time,—one of the regions which
had been an ancient possession of that civilization.   We
behold also *continued* processes of growth; structures
and systems of culture in particular spheres, rich in
kind, and well developed in every direction.   The merely
formal and indeterminate view of development in general can neither assign to one form of expansion superiority over the other, nor render comprehensible the object of that decay of older periods of growth; but must
regard such occurrences,—or, to speak more particularly, the retrocessions they exhibit,—as external contingencies; and can only judge of particular modes of
development from indeterminate points of view; which
—since the development as such, is all in all—are relative and not absolute goals of attainment.
Universal History exhibits the *gradation* in the development of that principle whose substantial *purport*
is the consciousness of Freedom.   The analysis of the
successive grades, in their abstract form, belongs to
Logic; in their concrete aspect to the Philosophy of

Spirit. Here it is sufficient to state that the first step in the process presents that immersion of Spirit in Nature which has been already referred to; the second shows it as advancing to the consciousness of its freedom. But this initial separation from Nature is imperfect and partial, since it is derived immediately from the merely natural state, is consequently related to it, and is still encumbered with it as an essentially connected element. The third step is the elevation of the soul from this still limited and special form of freedom to its pure universal form; that state in which the spiritual essence attains the consciousness and feeling of itself. These grades are the ground-principles of the general process; but how each of them on the other hand involves within *itself* a process of formation,— constituting the links in a dialectic of transition,—to particularise this may be reserved for the sequel.

Here we have only to indicate that Spirit begins with a germ of infinite possibility, but *only* possibility,—containing its substantial existence in an undeveloped form, as the object and goal which it reaches only in its resultant—full reality. In actual existence Progress appears as an advancing from the imperfect to the more perfect; but the former must not be understood abstractly as *only* the imperfect, but as something which involves the very opposite of itself—the so-called perfect—as a *germ* or impulse. So—reflectively, at least —*possibility* points to something destined to become actual; the Aristotelian δύναμις is also *potentia,* power and might. Thus the Imperfect, as involving its opposite, is a contradiction, which certainly exists, but which is continually annulled and solved; the instinctive movement—the inherent impulse in the life of the soul—to break through the rind of mere nature, sensuousness,

and that which is alien to it, and to attain to the light
of consciousness, *i. e.* to itself.

We have already made the remark how the commencement of the history of Spirit must be conceived so as
to be in harmony with its Idea—in its bearing on the
representations that have been made of a primitive
"*natural* condition," in which freedom and justice are
supposed to exist, or to have existed.   This was, however, nothing more than an assumption of historical
existence, conceived in the twilight of theorising reflection.   A pretension of quite another order,—not a mere
inference of reasoning, but making the claim of historical fact, and that supernaturally confirmed,—is put
forth in connection with a different view that is now
widely promulgated by a certain class of speculatists.
This view takes up the idea of the primitive paradisai-
cal condition of man, which had been previously expanded by the Theologians, after their fashion,—involving, *e.g.*, the supposition that God spoke with Adam
in Hebrew,—but re-modelled to suit other requirements.
The high authority appealed to in the first instance is
the biblical narrative.   But this depicts the primitive
condition, partly only in the few well-known traits, but
partly either as in man generically,—human nature at
large,—or, so far as Adam is to be taken as an individual, and consequently one person,—as existing and
completed in *this one,* or *only in one* human pair.   The
biblical account by no means justifies us in imagining
a *people,* and an historical condition of such people, existing in that primitive form; still less does it warrant
us in attributing to them the possession of a perfectly
developed knowledge of God and Nature.   "Nature," so
the fiction runs, "like a clear mirror of God's creation,
had originally lain revealed and transparent to the un-

clouded eye of man." * Divine Truth is imagined to have
been equally manifest. It is even hinted, though left
in some degree of obscurity, that in this primary condition men were in possession of an indefinitely extended
and already expanded body of religious truths immediately revealed by God. This theory affirms that all
religions had their historical commencement in this
primitive knowledge, and that they polluted and obscured the original Truth by the monstrous creations
of error and depravity; though in all the mythologies
invented by Error, traces of that origin and of those
primitive true dogmas are supposed to be present and
cognizable. An important interest, therefore, accrues
to the investigation of the history of ancient peoples,
that, viz., of the endeavour to trace their annals up
to the point where such fragments of the primary revelation are to be met with in greater purity than lower
down.*

* Fr. von Schlegel, "Philosophy of History," p. 91, Bohn's
Standard Library.

* We have to thank this interest for many valuable dis-
coveries in Oriental literature, and for a renewed study of
treasures previously known, in the department of ancient
Asiatic Culture, Mythology, Religions, and History. In Catholic countries, where a refined literary taste prevails, Governments have yielded to the requirements of speculative inquiry,
and have felt the necessity of allying themselves with learning
and philosophy. Eloquently and impressively has the Abbé
Lamennais reckoned it among the criteria of the true religion,
that it must be the universal—that is, catholic—and the oldest
in date; and the Congregation has laboured zealously and
diligently in France towards rendering such assertions no
longer mere pulpit tirades and authoritative dicta, such as
were deemed sufficient formerly. The religion of Buddha—
a god man—which has prevailed to such an enormous extent,
has especially attracted attention. The Indian Timûrtis, as

We owe to the interest which has occasioned these investigations, very much that is valuable; but this investigation bears direct testimony against itself, for it would seem to be awaiting the issue of an historical demonstration of that which is presupposed by it as historically established. That advanced condition of the knowledge of God, and of other scientific, *e.g.,* astronomical knowledge (such as has been falsely attributed to the Hindoos); and the assertion that such a condition occurred at the very beginning of History, —or that the religions of various nations were traditionally derived from it, and have developed themselves in degeneracy and depravation (as is represented in the rudely-conceived so-called "Emanation System,"); —all these are suppositions which neither have, nor,— if we may contrast with their arbitrary subjective origin,

---

also the Chinese abstraction of the Trinity, has furnished clearer evidence in point of subject matter. The savants, M. Abel Remusat and M. Saint Martin, on the one hand, have undertaken the most meritorious investigations in the Chinese literature, with a view to make this also a base of operations for researches in the Mongolian and, if such were possible, in the Thibetian; on the other hand, Baron von Eckstein, in his way (*i.e.,* adopting from Germany superficial physical conceptions and mannerisms, in the style of Fr. v. Schlegel, though with more geniality than the latter) in his periodical, "Le Catholique,"—has furthered the cause of that primitive Catholicism generally, and in particular has gained for the savants of the Congregation the support of the Government; so that it has even set on foot expeditions to the East, in order to discover there treasures still concealed; (from which further disclosures have been anticipated, respecting profound theological questions, particularly on the higher antiquity and sources of Buddhism), and with a view to promote the interest of Catholicism by this circuitous but scientifically interesting method.

the true conception of History,—can attain historical confirmation.

The only consistent and worthy method which philosophical investigation can adopt, is to take up History where Rationality begins to manifest itself in the actual conduct of the World's affairs (not where it is merely an undeveloped potentiality),—where a condition of things is present in which it realises itself in consciousness, will and action. The inorganic existence of Spirit —that of abstract Freedom—unconscious *torpidity* in respect to good and evil (and consequently to laws), or, if we please to term it so, "blessed ignorance,"— is itself not a subject of History. *Natural,* and at the same time *religious* morality, is the piety of the *family.* In this social relation, morality consists in the members behaving towards each other *not as individuals*—possessing an independent will; not as persons. The Family therefore, is excluded from that process of development in which History takes its rise. But when this self-involved spiritual Unity steps beyond this circle of feeling and natural love, and first attains the consciousness of personality, we have that dark, dull centre of indifference, in which neither Nature nor Spirit is open and transparent; and for which Nature and Spirit can become open and transparent only by means of a further process,—a very lengthened culture of that Will at length become self-conscious. Consciousness alone is clearness; and is that alone for which God (or any other existence) can be revealed. In its true form,— in absolute universality—nothing can be manifested except to consciousness made percipient of it. Freedom is nothing but the recognition and adoption of such universal substantial objects as Right and Law, and the production of a reality that is accordant with them— the State. Nations may have passed a long life before arriving at this their destination, and during this period, they may have attained considerable culture in some directions.   This ante-historical period—consistently with what has been said—lies out of our plan; whether a real history followed it, or the peoples in question never attained a political constitution.—It is a great discovery in history—as of a new world—which has been made within rather more than the last twenty years, respecting the Sanscrit and the connection of the European languages with it.   In particular, the connection of the German and Indian peoples has been demonstrated, with as much certainty as such subjects allow of.   Even at the present time we know of peoples which scarcely form a society, much less a State, but that have been long known as existing; while with regard to others, which in their advanced condition excite our especial interest, tradition reaches beyond the record of the founding of the State, and they experienced many changes prior to that epoch.   In the connection just referred to, between the languages of nations so widely separated, we have a result before us, which proves the diffusion of those nations from Asia as a centre, and the so dissimilar development of what had been originally related, as an incontestable fact; not *as* an inference deduced by that favourite method of combining, and reasoning from, circumstances grave and trivial, which has already enriched and will continue to enrich history with so many fictions given out as facts.   But that apparently so extensive range of events lies beyond the pale of history; in fact preceded it.

In our language the term *History* * unites the objective with the subjective side, and denotes quite as much the *historia rerum gestarum,* as the *res gestae* themselves; on the other hand it comprehends not less what

* German, "Geschichte," from "Geschehen," to happen. Tr.

has *happened,* than the *narration* of what has happened. This union of the two meanings we must regard as of a higher order than mere outward accident; we must suppose historical narrations to have appeared contemporaneously with historical deeds and events. It is an internal vital principle common to both that produces them synchronously. Family memorials, patriarchal traditions, have an interest confined to the family and the clan. The uniform course of events which such a condition implies, is no subject of serious remembrance; though distinct transactions or turns of fortune, may rouse Mnemosyne to form conceptions of them,— in the same way as love and the religious emotions provoke imagination to give shape to a previously formless impulse. But it is the State which first presents subject-matter that is not only *adapted* to the prose of History, but involves the production of such history in the very progress of its own being. Instead of merely subjective mandates on the part of government,—sufficing for the needs of the moment,—a community that is acquiring a stable existence, and exalting itself into a State, requires formal commands and laws—comprehensive and universally binding prescriptions; and thus produces a record as well as an interest concerned with intelligent, definite—and, in their results—lasting transactions and occurrences; on which Mnemosyne, for the behoof of the perennial object of the formation and constitution of the State, is impelled to confer perpetuity. Profound sentiments generally, such as that of love, as also religious intuition and its conceptions, are in themselves complete—constantly present and satisfying; but that outward existence of a political constitution which is enshrined in its rational laws and customs, is an *imperfect* Present; and cannot be thoroughly understood without a knowledge of the past.

The periods—whether we suppose them to be centuries or millennia—that were passed by nations before history was written among them,—and which may have been filled with revolutions, nomadic wanderings, and the strangest mutations,—are on that very account destitute of *objective* history, because they present no *subjective* history, no annals. We need not suppose that the records of such periods have accidentally perished; rather, because they were not possible, do we find them wanting. Only in a State cognizant of Laws, can distinct transactions take place, accompanied by such a clear consciousness of them as supplies the ability and suggests the necessity of an enduring record. It strikes every one, in beginning to form an acquaintance with the treasures of Indian literature, that a land so rich in intellectual products, and those of the profoundest order of thought, has no History; and in this respect contrasts most strongly with China—an empire possessing one so remarkable, one going back to the most ancient times. India has not only ancient books relating to religion, and splendid poetical productions, but also ancient codes; the existence of which latter kind of literature has been mentioned as a condition necessary to the origination of History—and yet History itself is not found. But in that country the impulse of organization, in beginning to develop social distinctions, was immediately petrified in the merely natural classification according to *castes;* so that although the laws concern themselves with civil rights, they make even these dependent on natural distinctions; and are especially occupied with determining the relations (Wrongs rather than Rights) of those classes towards each other, *i.e.,* the privileges of the higher over the lower. Consequently, the element of morality is banished from the pomp of Indian life and from its political institutions. Where that iron bondage of distinctions derived from nature prevails, the connection of society is nothing but wild arbitrariness,—transient activity, —or rather the play of violent emotion without any goal of advancement or development. Therefore no intelligent reminiscence, no object for Mnemosyne presents itself; and imagination—confused though profound —expatiates in a region, which, to be capable of History, must have had an aim within the domain of Reality, and, at the same time, of substantial Freedom.

Since such are the conditions indispensable to a history, it has happened that the growth of Families to Clans, of Clans to Peoples, and their local diffusion consequent upon this numerical increase,—a series of facts which itself suggests so many instances of social complication, war, revolution, and ruin,—a process which is so rich in interest, and so comprehensive in extent,—has occurred without giving rise to History: moreover, that the extension and organic growth of the empire of articulate sounds has itself remained voiceless and dumb,—a stealthy, unnoticed advance. It is a fact revealed by philological monuments, that languages, during a rude condition of the nations that have spoken them, have been very highly developed; that the human understanding occupied this theoretical region with great ingenuity and completeness. For Grammar, in its extended and consistent form, is the work of thought, which makes its categories distinctly visible therein. It is, moreover, a fact, that with advancing social and political civilization, this systematic completeness of intelligence suffers attrition, and language thereupon becomes poorer and ruder: a singular phenomenon—that the progress towards a more highly intellectual condition, while expanding and cultivating rationality, should disregard that intelligent amplitude and expressiveness—should find it an obstruction and contrive to do without it.   Speech is the act of theoretic intelligence in a special sense; it is its *external* manifestation.   Exercises of memory and imagination, without language, are direct, [non-speculative] manifestations.   But this act of theoretic intelligence itself, as also its subsequent development, and the more concrete class of facts connected with it,—viz. the spreading of peoples over the earth, their separation from each other, their comminglings and wanderings—remain involved in the obscurity of a voiceless past.   They are not acts of Will becoming self-conscious—of Freedom, mirroring itself in a phenomenal form, and creating for itself a proper reality.   Not partaking of this element of substantial, veritable existence, those nations—notwithstanding the development of language among them —never advanced to the possession of a *history*.   The rapid growth of language, and the progress and dispersion of Nations, assume importance and interest for concrete Reason, only when they have come in contact with States, or begin to form political constitutions themselves.

After these remarks, relating to the form of the *commencement* of the World's History, and to that antehistorical period which must be excluded from it, we have to state the direction of its course: though here only formally.   The further definition of the subject in the concrete, comes under the head of arrangement.

Universal history—as already demonstrated—shews the development of the consciousness of Freedom on the part of Spirit, and of the consequent realization of that Freedom.   This development implies a gradation— a series of increasingly adequate expressions or manifestations of Freedom, which result from its Idea.   The logical, and—as still more prominent—the *dialectical*

nature of the Idea in general, viz. that it is self-determined—that it assumes successive forms which it successively transcends; and by this very process of transcending its earlier stages, gains an affirmative, and, in
fact, a richer and more concrete shape;—this necessity
of its nature, and the necessary series of pure abstract
forms which the Idea successively assumes—is exhibited
in the department of *Logic*. Here we need adopt only
one of its results, viz. that every step in the process,
as differing from any other, has its determinate peculiar
principle. In history this principle is idiosyncrasy of
Spirit—peculiar National Genius. It is within the limitations of this idiosyncrasy that the spirit of the nation,
concretely manifested, expresses every aspect of its
consciousness and will—the whole cycle of its realization. Its religion, its polity, its ethics, its legislation,
and even its science, art, and mechanical skill, all bear
its stamp. These special peculiarities find their key
in that common peculiarity,—the particular principle
that characterises a people; as, on the other hand, in the
facts which History presents in detail, that common
characteristic principle may be detected. That such or
such a specific quality constitutes the peculiar genius
of a people, is the element of our inquiry which must
be derived from experience, and historically proved. To
accomplish this, pre-supposes not only a disciplined
faculty of abstraction, but an intimate acquaintance with
the Idea. The investigator must be familiar *à priori*
(if we like to call it so), with the whole circle of conceptions to which the principles in question belong—
just as Keppler (to name the most illustrious example
in this mode of philosophizing) must have been familiar
à priori with ellipses, with cubes and squares, and with
ideas of their relations, before he could discover, from
the empirical data, those immortal "Laws" of his, which

are none other than forms of thought pertaining to those
classes of conceptions. He who is unfamiliar with the
science that embraces these abstract elementary conceptions, is as little capable—though he may have gazed
on the firmament and the motions of the celestial bodies
for a life-time—of *understanding* those Laws, as of
discovering them. From this want of acquaintance with
the ideas that relate to the development of Freedom,
proceed a part of those objections which are brought
against the philosophical consideration of a science
usually regarded as one of mere experience; the so-
called *à priori* method, and the attempt to insinuate
ideas into the empirical data of history, being the chief
points in the indictment. Where this deficiency exists,
such conceptions appear alien—not lying within the
object of investigation. To minds whose training has
been narrow and merely subjective,—which have not
an acquaintance and familiarity with ideas,—they are
something strange—not embraced in the notion and conception of the subject which their limited intellect
forms. Hence the statement that Philosophy does not
understand such sciences. It must, indeed, allow that
it has not that kind of Understanding which is the prevailing one in the domain of those sciences that it does
not proceed according to the categories of such Understanding, but according to the categories of *Reason*
—though at the same time recognising that Understanding, and its true value and position. It must
be observed that in this very process of scientific *Understanding,* it is of importance that the essential should
be distinguished and brought into relief in contrast with
the so-called non-essential. But in order to render this
possible, we must know what *is essential;* and that is—
in view of the History of the World in general—the
Consciousness of Freedom, and the phases which this

consciousness assumes in developing itself. The bearing of historical facts on this category, is their bearing on the truly Essential. Of the difficulties stated, and the opposition exhibited to comprehensive conceptions in science, part must be referred to the inability to grasp and understand Ideas. If in Natural History some monstrous hybrid growth is alleged as an objection to the recognition of clear and indubitable classes or species, a sufficient reply is furnished by a sentiment often vaguely urged,—that "the exception confirms the rule;" *i.e.,* that is the part of a well-defined rule, to shew the conditions in which it applies, or the deficiency or hybridism of cases that are abnormal. Mere Nature is too weak to keep its genera and species pure, when conflicting with alien elementary influences. If, *e.g.,* on considering the human organization in its concrete aspect, we assert that brain, heart, and so forth are essential to its organic life, some miserable abortion may be adduced, which has on the whole the human form, or parts of it,—which has been conceived in a human body and has breathed after birth therefrom,—in which nevertheless no brain and no heart is found. If such an instance is quoted against the general conception of a human being—the objector persisting in using the name, coupled with a superficial idea respecting it— it can be proved that a real, concrete human being, is a truly different object; that such a being must have a brain in its head, and a heart in its breast.

A similar process of reasoning is adopted, in reference to the correct assertion that genius, talent, moral virtues, and sentiments, and piety, may be found in every zone, under all political constitutions and conditions; in confirmation of which examples are forthcoming in abundance. If in this assertion, the accompanying distinctions are intended to be repudiated

as unimportant or non-essential, reflection evidently
limits itself to abstract categories; and ignores the
specialities of the object in question, which certainly
fall under no principle recognised by such categories.
That intellectual position which adopts such merely
formal points of view, presents a vast field for ingenious questions, erudite views, and striking compari-
sons; for profound seeming reflections and declamations,
which may be rendered so much the more brilliant in
proportion as the subject they refer to is indefinite,
and are susceptible of new and varied forms in inverse
proportion to the importance of the results that can be
gained from them, and the certainty and rationality of
their issues.   Under such an aspect the well known
Indian Epopees may be compared with the Homeric;
perhaps—since it is the vastness of the imagination by
which poetical genius proves itself—preferred to them;
as, on account of the similarity of single strokes of
imagination in the attributes of the divinities, it has
been contended that Greek mythological forms may be
recognised in those of India.   Similarly the Chinese
philosophy, as adopting the One [τὸ ἕν] as its basis,
has been alleged to be the same as at a later period
appeared as Eleatic philosophy and as the Spinozistic
System; while in virtue of its expressing itself also in
abstract numbers and lines, Pythagorean and Christian principles have been supposed to be detected in
it.   Instances of bravery and indomintable courage,—
traits of magnanimity, of self-denial, and self-sacrifice,
which are found among the most savage and the most
pusillanimous nations,—are regarded as sufficient to
support the view that in these nations as much of social
virtue and morality may be found as in the most civilized
Christian states, or even more.   And on this ground a
doubt has been suggested whether in the progress of

history and of general culture mankind have become better; whether their morality has been increased,—morality being regarded in a subjective aspect and view, as founded on what the agent holds to be right and wrong, good and evil; not on a principle which is considered to be in and for itself right and good, or a crime and evil, or on a particular religion believed to be the true one.

We may fairly decline on this occasion the task of tracing the formalism and error of such a view, and establishing the true principles of morality, or rather of social virtue in opposition to false morality. For the History of the World occupies a higher ground than that on which morality has properly its position, which is personal character,—the conscience of individuals,— their particular will and mode of action; *these* have a value, imputation, reward or punishment proper to themselves. What the absolute aim of Spirit requires and accomplishes,—what Providence does,—transcends the obligations, and the liability to imputation and the ascription of good or bad motives, which attach to individuality in virtue of its social relations. They who on moral grounds, and consequently with noble intention, have resisted that which the advance of the Spiritual Idea makes necessary, stand higher in moral worth than those whose crimes have been turned into the means —under the direction of a superior principle—of realising the purposes of that principle. But in such revolutions both parties generally stand within the limits of the same circle of transient and corruptible existence. Consequently it is only a formal rectitude—deserted by the living Spirit and by God—which those who stand upon ancient right and order maintain. The deeds of great men, who are the Individuals of the World's History, thus appear not only justified in view of that in-

trinsic result of which they were not conscious, but also
from the point of view occupied by the secular moralist.
But looked at from this point, moral claims that are irrelevant, must not be brought into collision with world-
historical deeds and their accomplishment. The Litany
of private virtues—modesty, humility, philanthropy and
forbearance—must not be raised against them. The
History of the World might, on principle, entirely ignore the circle within which morality and the so much
talked of distinction between the moral and the politic
lies—not only in abstaining from judgments, for the
principles involved, and the necessary reference of the
deeds in question to those principles, are a sufficient
judgment of them—but in leaving Individuals quite
out of view and unmentioned. What it has to record is
the activity of the Spirit of Peoples, so that the individual forms which that spirit has assumed in the sphere
of outward reality, might be left to the delineation of
special histories.

The same kind of formalism avails itself in its peculiar manner of the indefiniteness attaching to genius,
poetry, and even philosophy; thinks equally that it finds
these everywhere. We have here products of reflective
thought; and it is familiarity with those general conceptions which single out and name real distinctions
without fathoming the true depth of the matter,—that
we call Culture. It is something merely formal, inasmuch as it aims at nothing more than the analysis of
the subject, whatever it be, into its constituent parts,
and the comprehension of these in their logical definitions and forms. It is not the free universality of conception necessary for making an abstract principle the
object of consciousness. Such a consciousness of
Thought itself, and of its forms isolated from a particular object, is Philosophy. This has, indeed, the condi-

tion of its existence in culture; that condition being the taking up of the object of thought, and at the same time clothing it with the form of universality, in such a way that the material content and the form given by the intellect are held in an inseparable state;—inseparable to such a degree that the object in question—which, by the analysis of one conception into a multitude of conceptions, is enlarged to an incalculable treasure of thought —is regarded as a merely empirical datum in whose formation thought has had no share.

But it is quite as much an act of Thought—of the Understanding in particular—to embrace in one simple conception object which of itself comprehends a concrete and large significance (as Earth, Man,—Alexander or Caesar) and to designate it by one word,—as to *resolve* such a conception—duly to isolate in idea the conceptions which it contains, and to give them particular names. And in reference to the view which gave occasion to what has just been said, thus much will be clear,—that as reflection produces what we include under the general terms Genius, Talent, Art, Science,— formal culture on every grade of intellectual development, not only can, but must grow, and attain a mature bloom, while the grade in question is developing itself to a State, and on this basis of civilization is advancing to intelligent reflection and to general forms of thought, —as in laws, so in regard to all else. In the very association of men in a state, lies the necessity of formal culture—consequently of the rise of the sciences and of a cultivated poetry and art generally. The arts designated "plastic," require besides, even in their technical aspect, the civilized association of men. The poetic art—which has less need of external requirements and means, and which has the element of immediate existence, the voice, as its material—steps forth with great boldness and with matured expression, even under the conditions presented by a people not yet united in a political combination; since, as remarked above, language attains on its own particular ground a high intellectual development, prior to the commencement of civilization.

Philosophy also must make its appearance where political life exists; since that in virtue of which any series of phenomena is reduced within the sphere of culture, as above stated, is the Form strictly proper to Thought; and thus for philosophy, which is nothing other than the consciousness of this form itself—the Thinking of Thinking,—the material of which its edifice is to be constructed, is already prepared by *general* culture. If in the development of the State itself, periods are necessitated which impel the soul of nobler natures to seek refuge from the Present in ideal regions, —in order to find in them that harmony with itself which it can no longer enjoy in the discordant real world, where the reflective intelligence attacks all that is holy and deep, which had been spontaneously inwrought into the religion, laws and manners of nations, and brings them down and attenuates them to abstract godless generalities,—Thought will be compelled to become Thinking Reason, with the view of effecting in its own element, the restoration of its principles from the ruin to which they had been brought.

We find then, it is true, among all world-historical peoples, poetry, plastic art, science, even philosophy; but not only is there a diversity in style and bearing generally, but still more remarkably in subject-matter; and this is a diversity of the most important kind, affecting the rationality of that subject-matter. It is useless for a pretentious aesthetic criticism to demand that our good pleasure should not be made the rule for the matter—the substantial part of their contents—and to maintain that it is the beautiful form as such, the grandeur of the fancy, and so forth, which fine art aims at, and which must be considered and enjoyed by a liberal taste and cultivated mind. A healthy intellect does not tolerate such abstractions, and cannot assimilate productions of the kind above referred to. Granted that the Indian Epopees might be placed on a level with the Homeric, on account of a number of those qualities of form—grandeur of invention and imaginative power, liveliness of images and emotions, and beauty of diction; yet the infinite difference of matter remains; consequently one of substantial importance and involving the interest of Reason, which is immediately concerned with the consciousness of the Idea of Freedom, and its expression in individuals. There is not only a classical *form,* but a classical order of *subject-matter;* and in a work of art form and subject-matter are so closely united that the former can only be classical to the extent to which the latter is so. With a fantastical, indeterminate material—the *Rule* is the essence of *Reason*—the form becomes measureless and formless, or mean and contracted. In the same way, in that comparison of the various systems of philosophy of which we have already spoken, the only point of importance is overlooked, namely, the character of that Unity which is found alike in the Chinese, the Eleatic, and the Spinozistic philosophy—the distinction between the recognition of that Unity as abstract and as concrete—concrete to the extent of being a unity in and by itself—a unity synonymous with Spirit. But that co-ordination proves that it recognises only such an abstract unity; so that while it gives judgment respecting philosophy, it is ignorant of that very point which constitutes the interest of philosophy.

But there are also spheres which, amid all the variety

that is presented in the substantial content of a particular form of culture, remain the same. The difference above mentioned in art, science, philosophy, concerns the thinking Reason and Freedom, which is the self-consciousness of the former, and which has the same one root with Thought. As it is not the brute, but only the man that thinks, he only—and only because he is a thinking being—has Freedom. *His* consciousness imports this, that the individual comprehends itself as a *person,* that is, recognises itself in its single existence as possessing universality,—as capable of abstraction from, and of surrendering all speciality; and, therefore, as inherently infinite. Consequently those spheres of intelligence which lie beyond the limits of this consciousness are a common ground among those substantial distinctions. Even morality, which is so intimately connected with the consciousness of freedom, can be very pure while that consciousness is still wanting; as far, that is to say, as it expresses duties and rights only as *objective* commands; or even as far as it remains satisfied with the merely formal elevation of the soul—the surrender of the sensual, and of all sensual motives—in a purely negative, self-denying fashion. The *Chinese* morality—since Europeans have become acquainted with it and with the writings of Confucius—has obtained the greatest praise and proportionate attention from those who are familiar with the Christian morality. There is a similar acknowledgement of the sublimity with which the *Indian* religion and poetry, (a statement that must, however, be limited to the higher kind), but especially the Indian philosophy, expatiate upon and demand the removal and sacrifice of sensuality. Yet both these nations are, it must be confessed, *entirely* wanting in the essential consciousness of the Idea of Freedom. To the Chinese their moral laws are just like natural laws,—external, positive commands,—claims established by force,—compulsory duties or rules of courtesy towards each other. Freedom, through which alone the essential determinations of Reason become moral sentiments, is wanting. Morality is a political affair, and its laws are administered by officers of government and legal tribunals. Their treatises upon it (which are not law books, but are certainly addressed to the subjective will and individual disposition) read,—as do the moral writings of the Stoics,—like a string of commands stated as necessary for realising the goal of happiness; so that it seems to be left free to men, on their part, to adopt such commands,—to observe them or not; while the conception of an abstract subject, "a wise man" [Sapiens] forms the culminating point among the Chinese, as also among the Stoic moralists. Also in the Indian doctrine of the renunciation of the sensuality of desires and earthly interests, positive moral freedom is not the object and end, but the annihilation of consciousness—spiritual and even physical privation of life.

It is the concrete spirit of a people which we have distinctly to recognise, and since it is Spirit it can only be comprehended spiritually, that is, by thought. It is this alone which takes the lead in all the deeds and tendencies of that people, and which is occupied in realising itself,—in satisfying its ideal and becoming self-conscious,—for its great business is self-production. But for spirit, the highest attainment is self-knowledge; an advance not only to the *intuition,* but to the *thought*—the clear conception of itself. This it must and is also destined to accomplish; but the accomplishment is at the same time its dissolution, and the rise of another spirit, another world-historical people, another epoch of Universal History. This transition and connection leads us to the connection of the whole—the idea of the World's History as such —which we have now to consider more closely, and of which we have to give a representation.

History in general is therefore the development of Spirit in *Time,* as Nature is the development of the Idea in *Space*.

If then we cast a glance over the World's History generally, we see a vast picture of changes and transactions; of infinitely manifold forms of peoples, states, individuals, in unresting succession. Everything that can enter into and interest the soul of man—all our sensibility to *goodness, beauty, and greatness*—is called into play. On every hand aims are adopted and pursued, which we recognise, whose accomplishment we desire—we hope and fear for them. In all these occurrences and changes we behold human action and suffering predominant; everywhere something akin to ourselves, and therefore everywhere something that excites our interest for or against. Sometimes it attracts us by beauty, freedom, and rich variety, sometimes by energy such as enables even vice to make itself interesting. Sometimes we see the more comprehensive mass of some general interest advancing with comparative slowness, and subsequently sacrificed to an infinite complication of trifling circumstances, and so dissipated into atoms. Then, again, with a vast expenditure of power a trivial result is produced; while from what appears unimportant a tremendous issue proceeds. On every hand there is the motliest throng of events drawing us within the circle of its interest, and when one combination vanishes another immediately appears in its place.

The general thought—the category which first presents itself in this restless mutation of individuals and peoples, existing for a time and then vanishing—is that of *change* at large. The sight of the ruins of some ancient sovereignty directly leads us to contemplate this thought of change in its negative aspect. What traveller among the ruins of Carthage, of Palmyra, Persepolis, or Rome, has not been stimulated by reflections on the transiency of kingdoms and men, and to sadness at the thought of a vigorous and rich life now departed—a sadness which does not expend itself on personal losses and the uncertainty of one's own undertakings, but is a disinterested sorrow at the decay of a splendid and highly cultured national life! But the next consideration which allies itself with that of change, is, that change while it imports dissolution, involves at the same time the rise of *a new life*—that while death is the issue of life, life is also the issue of death. This is a grand conception; one which the Oriental thinkers attained, and which is perhaps the highest in their metaphysics. In the Idea of *Metempsychosis* we find it evolved in its relation to individual existence; but a myth more generally known, is that of the *Phoenix* as a type of the Life of *Nature;* eternally preparing for itself its funeral pile, and consuming itself upon it; but so that from its ashes is produced the new, renovated, fresh life. But this image is only Asiatic; oriental not occidental. Spirit—consuming the envelope of its existence—does not merely pass into another envelope, nor rise rejuvenescent from the ashes of its previous form; it comes forth exalted, glorified, a purer spirit. It certainly makes war upon itself—consumes its own existence; but in this very destruction it works up with existence into a new form, and each successive phase becomes in its turn a material, working on which it exalts itself to a new grade.

If we consider Spirit in this aspect—regarding its changes not merely as rejuvenescent transitions, *i.e.,* returns to the same form, but rather as manipulations of

itself, by which it multiplies the material for future
endeavours—we see it exerting itself in a variety of
modes and directions; developing its powers and grati-
fying its desires in a variety which is inexhaustible; because every one of its creations, in which it has already
found gratification, meets it anew as material, and is
a new stimulus to plastic activity. The abstract conception of mere change gives place to the thought of
Spirit manifesting, developing, and perfecting its powers in every direction which its manifold nature can
follow. What powers it inherently possesses we learn
from the variety of products and formations which it
originates. In this pleasurable activity, it has to do
only with itself. As involved with the conditions of
mere nature—internal and external—it will indeed meet
in these not only opposition and hindrance, but will
often see its endeavours thereby fail; often sink under
the complications in which it is entangled either by
Nature or by itself. But in such case it perishes in fulfilling its own destiny and proper function, and even
thus exhibits the spectacle of self-demonstration as
spiritual activity.

The very essence of Spirit is activity; it realises its
potentiality—makes itself its own deed, its own work—
and thus it becomes an object to itself; contemplates itself as an objective existence. Thus is it with the Spirit
of a people: it is a Spirit having strictly defined characteristics, which erects itself into an objective world,
that exists and persists in a particular religious form of
worship, customs, constitution and political laws,—in
the whole complex of its institutions,—in the events and
transactions that make up its history. That is its work
—that is what this particular Nation *is*. Nations are
what their deeds are. Every Englishman will say: We
are the men who navigate the ocean, and have the com-

merce of the world; to whom the East Indies belong
and their riches; who have a parliament, juries, &c.—
The relation of the individual to that Spirit is that he
appropriates to himself this substantial existence; that
it becomes his character and capability, enabling him
to have a definite place in the world—to be *something*.
For he finds the being of the people to which he belongs
an already established, firm world—objectively present
to him—with which he has to incorporate himself. In
this its work, therefore—its world—the Spirit of the
people enjoys its existence and finds its satisfaction.
—A Nation is moral—virtuous—vigorous—while it is
engaged in realising its grand objects, and defends its
work against external violence during the process of
giving to its purposes an objective existence. The contradiction between its potential, subjective being—its
inner aim and life—and its *actual* being is removed; it
has attained full reality, has itself objectively present
to it. But this having been attained, the activity displayed by the Spirit of the people in question is no
longer needed; it has its desire. The Nation can still
accomplish much in war and peace at home and abroad;
but the living substantial soul itself may be said to
have ceased its activity. The essential, supreme interest
has consequently vanished from its life, for interest is
present only where there is opposition. The nation lives
the same kind of life as the individual when passing
from maturity to old age,—in the enjoyment of itself,—
in the satisfaction of being exactly what it desired and
was able to attain. Although its imagination might have
transcended that limit, it nevertheless abandoned any
such aspirations as objects of *actual endeavour,* if the
real world was less than favourable to their attainment—
and restricted its aim by the conditions thus imposed.
This mere *customary life* (the watch wound up and

going on of itself) is that which brings on natural death.
Custom is activity without opposition, for which there
remains only a formal duration; in which the fulness and
zest that originally characterised the aim of life is out
of the question,—a merely external sensuous existence
which has ceased to throw itself enthusiastically into
its object. Thus perish individuals, thus perish peoples
by a natural death; and though the latter may continue
in being, it is an existence without intellect or vitality;
having no need of its institutions, because the need for
them is satisfied,—a political nullity and tedium.   In
order that a truly universal interest may arise, the Spirit
of a People must advance to the adoption of some new
purpose: but whence can this new purpose originate?
It would be a higher, more comprehensive conception
of itself—a transcending of its principle—but this very
act would involve a principle of a new order, a new
National Spirit.

Such a new principle does in fact enter into the Spirit
of a people that has arrived at full development and
self-realisation; it dies not a simply natural death,—
for it is not a mere single individual, but a spiritual,
generic life; in its case natural death appears to imply
destruction through its own agency. The reason of
this difference from the single natural individual, is
that the Spirit of a people exists as a *genus,* and consequently carries within it its own negation, in the very
generality which characterises it.   A people can only
die a violent death when it has become naturally dead
in itself, as *e.g.,* the German Imperial Cities, the German Imperial Constitution.

It is not of the nature of the all-pervading Spirit to
die this merely natural death; it does not simply sink
into the senile life of mere custom, but—as being a
National Spirit belonging to Universal History—attains

to the consciousness of what its work is; it attains to a conception of itself. In fact it is world-historical only in so far as a *universal principle* has lain in its fundamental element,—in its grand aim: only so far is the work which such a spirit produces, a moral, political organization. If it be mere desires that impel nations to activity, such deeds pass over without leaving a trace; or their traces are only ruin and destruction. Thus, it was first Chronos—Time—that ruled; the Golden Age, without moral products; and what was produced—the offspring of that Chronos—was devoured by it. It was Jupiter—from whose head Minerva sprang, and to whose circle of divinities belong Apollo and the Muses—that first put a constraint upon Time, and set a bound to its principle of decadence. He is the Political god, who produced a moral work—the State.

In the very element of an achievement the quality of generality, of thought, is contained; without thought it has no objectivity; that is its basis. The highest point in the development of a people is this,—to have gained a conception of its life and condition,—to have reduced its laws, its ideas of justice and morality to a science; for in this unity [of the objective and subjective] lies the most intimate unity that Spirit can attain to in and with itself. In its work it is employed in rendering itself an object of its own contemplation; but it cannot develop itself objectively in its essential nature, except in *thinking* itself.

At this point, then, Spirit is acquainted with its principles—the general character of its acts. But at the same time, in virtue of its very generality, this work of thought is different in point of form from the actual achievements of the national genius, and from the vital agency by which those achievements have been performed. We have then before us a *real* and an *ideal* existence of the Spirit of the Nation. If we wish to gain the general idea and conception of what the Greeks were, we find it in Sophocles and Aristophanes, in Thucydides and Plato. In these individuals the Greek spirit conceived and thought itself. This is the profounder kind of satisfaction which the Spirit of a people attains; but it is "ideal," and distinct from its "real" activity.

At such a time, therefore, we are sure to see a people finding satisfaction in the *idea* of virtue; putting *talk* about virtue partly side by side with actual virtue, but partly in the place of it. On the other hand pure, universal thought, since its nature is universality, is apt to bring the Special and Spontaneous—Belief, Trust, Customary Morality—to reflect upon itself, and its primitive simplicity; to shew up the limitation with which it is fettered,—partly suggesting reasons for renouncing duties, partly itself *demanding reasons,* and the connection of such requirements with Universal Thought; and not finding that connection, seeking to impeach the authority of duty generally, as destitute of a sound foundation.

At the same time the isolation of individuals from each other and from the Whole makes its appearance; their aggressive selfishness and vanity; their seeking personal advantage and consulting this at the expense of the State at large. That inward principle in transcending its outward manifestations is subjective also in *form*—viz., selfishness and corruption in the unbound passions and egotistic interests of men.

Zeus, therefore, who is represented as having put a limit to the devouring agency of Time, and staid this transiency by having established something inherently and independently durable—Zeus and his race are themselves swallowed up, and that by the very power that produced them—the principle of thought, perception, reasoning, insight derived from rational grounds, and the requirement of such grounds.

Time is the negative element in the sensuous world. Thought is the same negativity, but it is the deepest, the infinite form of it, in which therefore all existence generally is dissolved; first *finite* existence,—*determinate,* limited form: but existence *generally,* in its objective character, is limited; it appears therefore as a mere datum—something immediate—authority;—and is either intrinsically finite and limited, or presents itself as a limit for the thinking subject, and its infinite reflection on itself [unlimited abstraction].

But first we must observe how the life which proceeds from death, is itself, on the other hand, only individual life; so that, regarding the species as the real and substantial in this vicissitude, the perishing of the individual is a regress of the species into individuality. The perpetuation of the race is, therefore, none other than the monotonous repetition of the same kind of existence. Further, we must remark how perception, —the comprehension of being by thought,—is the source and birthplace of a new, and in fact higher form, in a principle which while it preserves, dignifies its material. For Thought is that *Universal*—that *Species* which is immortal, which preserves identity with itself. The particular form of Spirit not merely passes away in the world by natural causes in Time, but is annulled in the automatic self-mirroring activity of consciousness. Because this annulling is an activity of Thought, it is at the same time conservative and elevating in its operation. While then, on the one side, Spirit annuls the reality, the permanence of that which it *is,* it gains on the other side, the essence, the Thought, the Universal element of that which *it only was* [its transient conditions]. Its principle is no longer that immediate import and aim which it was previously, but the *essence* of that import and aim.

The result of this process is then that Spirit, in rendering itself objective and making this its being an object of thought, on the one hand destroys the determinate form of its being, on the other hand gains a comprehension of the universal element which it involves, and thereby gives a new form to its inherent principle. In virtue of this, the substantial character of the National Spirit has been altered,—that is, its principle has risen into another, and in fact a higher principle.

It is of the highest importance in apprehending and comprehending History to have and to understand the thought involved in this transition. The individual traverses as a unity various grades of development, and remains the same individual; in like manner also does a people, till the Spirit which it embodies reaches the grade of universality. In this point lies the fundamental, the Ideal necessity of transition. This is the soul —the essential consideration—of the philosophical comprehension of History.

Spirit is essentially the result of its own activity; its activity is the transcending of immediate, simple, unreflected existence,—the negation of that existence, and the returning into itself. We may compare it with the seed; for with this the plant begins, yet it is also the result of the plant's entire life. But the weak side of life is exhibited in the fact that the commencement and the result are disjoined from each other. Thus also is it in the life of individuals and peoples. The life of a people ripens a certain fruit; its activity aims at the complete manifestation of the principle which it embodies. But this fruit does not fall back into the bosom of the people that produced and matured it; on the contrary, it becomes a poison-draught to it. That poison-draught it cannot let alone, for it has an insatiable thirst for it: the taste of the draught is its annihilation, though at the same time the rise of a new principle.

We have already discussed the final aim of progression. The principles of the successive phases of Spirit that animate the Nations in a necessitated gradation, are themselves only steps in the development of the one universal Spirit, which through them elevates and completes itself to a self-comprehending *totality*.

While we are thus concerned exclusively with the Idea of Spirit, and in the History of the World regard everything as only its manifestation, we have, in traversing the past,—however extensive its periods,—only to do with what is *present;* for philosophy, as occupying itself with the True, has to do with the *eternally present*. Nothing in the past is lost for it, for the Idea is ever present; Spirit is immortal; with it there is no past, no future, but an essential *now*. This necessarily implies that the present form of Spirit comprehends within it all earlier steps. These have indeed unfolded themselves in succession independently; but what Spirit is it has always been essentially; distinctions are only the development of this essential nature. The life of the ever present Spirit is a circle of progressive embodiments, which looked at in one respect still exist beside each other, and only as looked at from another point of view appear as past. The grades which Spirit seems to have left behind it, it still possesses in the depths of its present.

X

THE PHILOSOPHY OF LAW *

Selected and translated by J. Loewenberg

THE STATE

IDEA AND AIM OF THE STATE

THE State is the realization of the ethical Idea. It is the ethical spirit as revealed, self-conscious, substantial will. It is the will which thinks and knows itself, and carries out what it knows, and in so far as it knows. The unreflected existence of the State rests on custom, and its reflected existence on the self-consciousness of the individual, on his knowledge and activity. The individual, in return, has his substantial freedom in the State, as the essence, purpose, and product of his activity.

The true State is the ethical whole and the realization of freedom. It is the absolute purpose of reason that freedom should be realized. The State is the spirit, which lives in the world and there realizes itself consciously; while in nature it is actual only as its own other or as dormant spirit. Only as present in consciousness, knowing itself as an existing object, is it the State. The State is the march of God through the world, its ground is the power of reason realizing

* From Hegel's *Die Philosophie des Rechts.*

itself as will. The idea of the State should not denote
any particular State, or particular institution; one must
rather consider the Idea only, this actual God, by itself.
Because it is more easy to find defects than to grasp
the positive meaning, one readily falls into the mistake
of emphasizing so much the particular nature of the
State as to overlook its inner organic essence. The
State is no work of art. It exists in the world, and
thus in the realm of caprice, accident, and error. Evil
behavior toward it may disfigure it on many sides. But
the ugliest man, the criminal, the invalid, and the crip-
ple, are still living human beings. The affirmative, life,
persists in spite of defects, and it is this affirmative
which alone is here in question.

In the State, everything depends upon the unity of
the universal and the particular. In the ancient States
the subjective purpose was absolutely one with the
will of the State. In modern times, on the contrary, we
demand an individual opinion, an individual will and
conscience. The ancients had none of these in the modern sense; the final thing for them was the will of the
State. While in Asiatic despotisms the individual had
no inner self and no self-justification, in the modern
world man demands to be honored for the sake of his
subjective individuality.

The union of duty and right has the twofold aspect
that what the State demands as duty should directly
be the right of the individual, since the State is nothing
but the organization of the concept of freedom. The
determinations of the individual will are given by the
State objectivity, and it is through the State alone that
they attain truth and realization. The State is the sole
condition of the attainment of the particular end and
good.

Political disposition, called patriotism—the assurance

resting in truth and the will which has become a custom
—is simply the result of the institutions subsisting in
the State, institutions in which reason is actually
present.

Under patriotism one frequently understands a mere
willingness to perform extraordinary acts and sacrifices. But patriotism is essentially the sentiment of regarding, in the ordinary circumstances and ways of life,
the weal of the community as the substantial basis and
the final end. It is upon this consciousness, present
in the ordinary course of life and under all circumstances, that the disposition to heroic effort is founded.
But as people are often rather magnanimous than just,
they easily persuade themselves that they possess the
heroic kind of patriotism, in order to save themselves
the trouble of having the truly patriotic sentiment, or
to excuse the lack of it.

Political sentiment, as appearance, must be distinguished from what people truly will. What they at
bottom will is the real cause, but they cling to particular interests and delight in the vain contemplation of
improvements. The conviction of the necessary stability of the State in which alone the particular interests can be realized, people indeed possess, but custom
makes invisible that upon which our whole existence
rests; it does not occur to any one, when he safely
passes through the streets at night, that it could be
otherwise. The habit of safety has become a second
nature, and we do not reflect that it is the result of
the activity of special institutions. It is through force
—this is frequently the superficial opinion—that the
State coheres, but what alone holds it together is the
fundamental sense of order, which is possessed by all.

The State is an organism or the development of the
idea into its differences. These different sides are the

different powers of the State with their functions and
activities, by means of which the universal is constantly
and necessarily producing itself, and, being presupposed in its own productive function, it is thus always
actively present. This organism is the political constitution. It eternally springs from the State, just as the
State in turn maintains itself through the constitution.
If these two things fall asunder, if both different sides
become independent of each other, then the unity which
the constitution produces is no longer operative; the
fable of the stomach and the other organs may be applied to it. It is the nature of an organism that all its
parts must constitute a certain unity; if one part asserts its independence the other parts must go to destruction. No predicates, principles, and the like suffice
to express the nature of the State; it must be comprehended as an organism.

The State is real, and its reality consists in the interest of the whole being realized in particular ends. Actuality is always the unity of universality and particularity, and the differentiation of the universal into
particular ends. These particular ends seem independent, though they are borne and sustained by the whole
only. In so far as this unity is absent, no thing is real,
though it may exist. A bad State is one which merely
exists. A sick body also exists, but it has no true
reality. A hand, which is cut off, still looks like a
hand and exists, but it has no reality. True reality is
necessity. What is real is eternally necessary.

To the complete State belongs, essentially, consciousness and thought. The State knows thus what it wills,
and it knows it under the form of thought.

The essential difference between the State and religion consists in that the commands of the State have
the form of legal duty, irrespective of the feelings ac-

companying their performance; the sphere of religion, on the other hand, is in the inner life.   Just as the State, were it to frame its commands as religion does, would endanger the right of the inner life, so the church, if it acts as a State and imposes punishment, degenerates into a tyrannical religion.

In the State one must want nothing which is not an expression of rationality.   The State is the world which the spirit has made for itself; it has therefore a determinate and self-conscious course.   One often speaks of the wisdom of God in nature, but one must not believe that the physical world of nature is higher than the world of spirit.   Just as spirit is superior to nature, so is the State superior to the physical life.   We must therefore worship the State as the manifestation of the divine on earth, and consider that, if it is difficult to comprehend nature, it is infinitely harder to grasp the essence of the State.   It is an important fact that we, in modern times, have attained definite insight into the State in general and are much engaged in discussing and making constitutions; but that does not advance the problem much.   It is necessary to treat a rational matter in the light of reason, in order to learn its essential nature and to know that the obvious does not always constitute the essential.

When we speak of the different functions of the powers of the State, we must not fall into the enormous error of supposing each power to have an abstract, independent existence, since the powers are rather to be differentiated as elements in the conception of the State. Were the powers to be in abstract independence, however, it is clear that two independent things could never constitute a unity, but must produce war, and the result would be destruction of the whole or restoration of unity by force.   Thus, in the French Revolution, at one time the legislative power had swallowed up the executive, at another time the executive had usurped the legislative power.

THE CONSTITUTION

The constitution is rational, in so far as the State defines and differentiates its functions according to the nature of its concept.

Who shall make the constitution? This question seems intelligible, yet on closer examination reveals itself as meaningless, for it presupposes the existence of no constitution, but only a mere mass of atomic individuals. How a mass of individuals is to come by a constitution, whether by its own efforts or by those of others, whether by goodness, thought, or force, it must decide for itself, for with a disorganized mob the concept of the State has nothing to do. But if the question does presuppose an already existing constitution, then to make a constitution means only to change it. The presupposition of a constitution implies, however, at once, that any modification in it must take place constitutionally. It is absolutely essential that the constitution, though having a temporal origin, should not be regarded as made. It (the principle of constitution) is rather to be conceived as absolutely perpetual and rational, and therefore as divine, substantial, and above and beyond the sphere of what is made.

Subjective freedom is the principle of the whole modern world—the principle that all essential aspects of the spiritual totality should develop and attain their right. From this point of view one can hardly raise the idle question as to which form is the better, monarchy or democracy. One can but say that the forms of all constitutions are one-sided that are not able to tolerate the principle of free subjectivity and that do not know how to conform to the fully developed reason.

Since spirit is real only in what it knows itself to be, and since the State, as the nation's spirit, is the law permeating all its affairs, its ethical code, and the consciousness of its individuals, the constitution of a people chiefly depends upon the kind and the character of its self-consciousness. In it lies both its subjective freedom and the reality of the constitution.

To think of giving people a constitution *a priori,* though according to its content a more or less rational one—such a whim would precisely overlook that element which renders a constitution more than a mere abstract object. Every nation, therefore, has the constitution which is appropriate to it and belongs to it.

The State must, in its constitution, permeate all situations. A constitution is not a thing just made; it is the work of centuries, the idea and the consciousness of what is rational, in so far as it is developed in a people. No constitution, therefore, is merely created by the subjects of the State. The nation must feel that its constitution embodies its right and its status, otherwise the constitution may exist externally, but has no meaning or value. The need and the longing for a better constitution may often indeed be present in individuals, but that is quite different from the whole multitude being permeated with such an idea—that comes much later. The principle of morality, the inwardness of Socrates originated necessarily in his day, but it took time before it could pass into general self-consciousness.

THE POWER OF THE PRINCE

Because sovereignty contains in ideal all special privileges, the common misconception is quite natural, which

takes it to be mere force, empty caprice, and synonymous with despotism. But despotism means a state of
lawlessness, in which the particular will as such,
whether that of monarch or people *(ochlocracy)*, is the
law, or rather instead of the law. Sovereignty, on the
contrary, constitutes the element of ideality of particular spheres and functions under lawful and constitutional conditions.

The sovereignty of the people, conceived in opposition to the sovereignty residing in the monarch, stands
for the common view of democracy, which has come
to prevail in modern times. The idea of the sovereignty
of the people, taken in this opposition, belongs to a confused idea of what is commonly and crudely understood
by "the people." The people without its monarch and
without that whole organization necessarily and directly
connected with him is a formless mass, which is no
longer a State. In a people, not conceived in a lawless
and unorganized condition, but as a self-developed and
truly organic totality—in such a people sovereignty is
the personality of the whole, and this is represented in
reality by the person of the monarch.

The State must be regarded as a great architectonic
edifice, a hieroglyph of reason, manifesting itself in
reality. Everything referring merely to utility, externality, and the like, must be excluded from its philosophic treatment. That the State is the self-determining and the completely sovereign will, the final decision being necessarily referred to it—that is easy to
comprehend. The difficulty lies in grasping this "I
will" as a person. By this it is not meant that the
monarch can act arbitrarily. He is bound, in truth, by
the concrete content of the deliberations of his council,
and, when the constitution is stable, he has often nothing more to do than sign his name—but this name is

important; it is the point than which there is nothing higher.

It may be said that an organic State has already existed in the beautiful democracy of Athens. The Greeks, however, derived the final decision from entirely external phenomena, from oracles, entrails of sacrificed animals, and from the flight of birds. Nature they considered as a power which in this wise made known and gave expression to what was good for the people. Self-consciousness had at that time not yet attained to the abstraction of subjectivity; it had not yet come to the realization that an "I will" must be pronounced by man himself concerning the decisions of the State. This "I will" constitutes the great difference between the ancient and the modern world, and must therefore have its peculiar place in the great edifice of the State. Unfortunately this modern characteristic is regarded as merely external and arbitrary.

It is often maintained against the monarch that since he may be ill-educated or unworthy to stand at the helm chance. It is therefore absurd to assume the rationality of the institution of the monarch. The presupposition, however, that the fortunes of the State depend upon the particular character of the monarch is false. In the perfect organization of the State the important thing is only the finality of formal decision and the stability against passion. One must not therefore demand objective qualification of the monarch; he has but to say "yes" and to put the dot upon the "i." The crown shall be of such a nature that the particular character of its bearer is of no significance. Beyond his function of administering the final decision, the monarch is a particular being who is of no concern. Situations may indeed arise in which his particularity alone asserts itself, but in that case the State is not yet fully developed, or else is ill constructed. In a well-ordered monarchy the law alone has objective power to which the monarch has but to affix the subjective "I will."

Monarchs do not excel in bodily strength or intellect, and yet millions permit themselves to be ruled by them. To say that the people permit themselves to be governed contrary to their interests, aims, and intentions is preposterous, for people are not so stupid. It is their need, it is the inner power of the idea, which, in opposition to their apparent consciousness, urges them to this situation and retains them therein.

Out of the sovereignty of the monarch flows the prerogative of pardoning criminals. Only to the sovereignty belongs the spiritual power to undo what has been done and to cancel the crime by forgiving and forgetting.

Pardon is the remission of punishment, but does not abolish right. Right remains, and the pardoned is a criminal as he was before the pardon. The act of mercy does not mean that no crime has been committed. This remission of punishment may be effected in religion, for by and in spirit what has been done can be made undone. But in so far as remission occurs in the world, it has its place only in majesty and is due only to its arbitrary decision.

THE EXECUTIVE

The main point upon which the function of the government depends is the division of labor. This division is concerned with the transition from the universal to the particular and the individual; and the business is to be divided according to the different branches. The difficulty lies in harmonizing the superior and the in-

ferior functions. For some time past the main effort
has been spent in organizing from above, the lower and
bulky part of the whole being left more or less unorganized; yet it is highly important that it should become organic, for only thus is it a power and a force;
otherwise it is but a heap or mass of scattered atoms.
Authoritative power resides only in the organic state
of the particular spheres.

The State cannot count on service which is capricious
and voluntary (the administration of justice by knights-
errant, for instance), precisely because it *is* capricious
and voluntary. Such service presupposes acting according to subjective opinion, and also the possibility of
neglect and of the realization of private ends. The
opposite extreme to the knight-errant in reference to
public service would be the State-servant who was attached to his task solely by want, without genuine duty
and right.

The efficiency of the State depends upon individuals,
who, however, are not entitled to carry on the business
of the State through natural [or untutored] fitness, but
according to their objective qualifications. Ability, skill,
character, belong to the particular nature of the individual; for a particular office, however, he must be specially educated and trained. An office in the State can,
therefore, be neither sold nor bequeathed.

Public service demands the sacrifice of independent
self-satisfaction, and the giving up of the pursuit of
private ends, but grants the right of finding these in
dutiful service, and in it only. Herein lies the unity
of the universal and the particular interests which
constitutes the concept and the inner stability of the
State.

The members of the executive and the officials of the
State form the main part of the middle class which rep-

resents the educated intelligence and the consciousness of right of the mass of a people. This middle class is prevented by the institutions of sovereignty from above and the rights of corporation from below, from assuming the exclusive position of an aristocracy and making education and intelligence the means for caprice and despotism. Thus the administration of justice, whose object is the proper interest of all individuals, had at one time been perverted into an instrument of gain and despotism, owing to the fact that the knowledge of the law was hidden under a learned and foreign language, and the knowledge of legal procedure under an involved formalism.

In the middle class, to which the State officials belong, resides the consciousness of the State and the most conspicuous cultivation; the middle class constitutes therefore the ground pillar of the State in regard to uprightness and intelligence. The State in which there is no middle class stands as yet on no high level.

THE LEGISLATURE

The legislature is concerned with the interpretation of the laws and with the internal affairs of the State, in so far as they have a universal content. This function is itself a part of the constitution and thus presupposes it. Being presupposed, the constitution lies, to that degree, outside the direct province of the legislature, but in the forward development of the laws and the progressive character of the universal affairs of government, the constitution receives its development also.

The constitution must alone be the firm ground on which the legislature stands; hence it must not be created for purposes of legislation. But the constitution not only *is,* its essence is also to *become*—that is, it progresses with the advance of civilization. This progress is an alteration which is imperceptible, but has not the form of an alteration. Thus, for example, the emperor was formerly judge, and went about the empire administering justice. Through the merely apparent advance of civilization it has become practically necessary that the emperor should gradually yield his judicial function to others, and thus came about the transition of the judicial function from the person of the prince to a body of judges; thus the progress of any condition is an apparently calm and imperceptible one. In this way and after a lapse of time a constitution attains a character quite different from what it had before.

In the legislative power as a whole are operative both the monarchical element and the executive. To the former belongs the final decision; the latter as advisory element possesses concrete knowledge, perspective over the whole in all its ramifications, and acquaintance with the objective principles and wants of the power of the State. Finally, in the legislature the different classes or estates are also active. These classes or estates represent in the legislature the element of subjective formal freedom, the public consciousness, the empirical totality of the views and thought of the many.

The expression "The Many" (οἱ πολλοί) characterizes the empirical totality more correctly than the customary word "All." Though one may reply that, from this "all," children, women, etc., are obviously meant to be excluded, yet it is more obvious that the definite expression "all" should not be used when something quite indefinite is in question.

There are, in general, current among the public so unspeakably many distorted and false notions and phrases about the people, the constitution, and the classes, that it would be a vain task to mention, explain, and correct them. The prevalent idea concerning the necessity and utility of an assembly of estates amounts to the assumption that the people's deputies, nay, the people itself, best understand what would promote the common weal, and that they have indubitably the good will to promote it. As for the first point, the case is just the reverse. The people, in so far as this term signifies a special part of the citizens, stands precisely for the part that does not know what it wills. To know what one wills, and, what is more difficult, to know what the absolute will, viz., reason, wills, is the fruit of deep knowledge and insight; and that is obviously not a possession of the people. As for the especially good will, which the classes are supposed to have for the common good, the usual point of view of the masses is the negative one of suspecting the government of a will which is evil or of little good.

The attitude of the government toward the classes must not be essentially a hostile one. Belief in the necessity of this hostile relation is a sad mistake. The government is not one part in opposition to another, so that both are engaged in wrestling something from each other. When the State is in such a situation it is a misfortune and not a mark of health. Furthermore, the taxes, for which the classes vote, are not to be looked upon as gifts, but are consented to for the best interests of those consenting. What constitutes the true meaning of the classes is this—that through them the State enters into the subjective consciousness of the people and thus the people begin to share in the State.

In despotic countries, where there are only princes and people, the people assert themselves, whenever they act, as a destructive force directed against the organization, but the masses, when they become organically related to the State, obtain their interests in a lawful and orderly way. When this organic relation is lacking, the self-expression of the masses is always violent; in despotic States the despot shows, therefore, indulgence for his people, and his rage is always felt by those surrounding him. Moreover, the people of a despotic State pay light taxes, which in a constitutional State are increased through the very consciousness of the people. In no other country are taxes so heavy as they are in England.

There exists a current notion to the effect that, since the private class is raised in the legislature to a participation in the universal cause, it must appear in the form of individuals—either that representatives are chosen for the function, or that every individual exercises a vote. This abstract atomic view prevails neither in the family nor in civic society, in both of which the individual appears only as a member of a universal. The State, however, is in essence an organization of members, and these members are themselves spheres; in it no element shall show itself as an unorganized mass. The many, as individuals, whom one chooses to call the people, are indeed a collection, but only as a multitude, a formless mass, whose movement and action would be elemental, irrational, savage, and terrible.

The concrete State is the whole, organized into its particular spheres, and the member of the State is a member of such a particular class. Only in this objective determination can the individual find recognition in the State. Only in his coöperative capacity, as member of the community and the like, can the individual first find a real and vital place in the universal. It remains, of course, open to him to rise through his skill to any class for which he can qualify himself, including even the universal class.

It is a matter of great advantage to have among the delegates representatives of every special branch of society, such as trade, manufacture, etc.—individuals thoroughly familiar with their branch and belonging to it. In the notion of a loose and indefinite election this important matter is left to accident; every branch, however, has the same right to be represented as every other. To view the delegates as representatives has, then, an organic and rational meaning only if they are not representatives of mere individuals, of the mere multitude, but of one of the essential spheres of society and of its large interests. Representation thus no longer means substitution of one person by another, but it means, rather, that the interest itself is actually present in the representative.

Of the elections by many separate individuals it may be observed that there is necessarily an indifference, especially in large States, about using one's vote, since one vote is of such slight importance; and those who have the right to vote will not do so, no matter how much one may extol the privilege of voting. Hence this institution turns into the opposite of what it stands for. The election becomes the business of a few, of a single party, of a special interest, which should, in fact, be neutralized.

Through the publicity of the assembly of classes public opinion first acquires true thoughts and an insight into the condition and the notion of the State and its affairs, and thus develops the capacity of judging more rationally concerning them; it learns, furthermore, to know and respect the routine, talents, virtues, and skill of the authorities and officers of the State. While publicity stimulates these talents in their further development and incites their honorable display, it is also an antidote for the pride of individuals and of the multi-

tude, and is one of the greatest opportunities for their
education.

It is a widespread popular notion that everybody
already knows what is good for the State, and that it
is this common knowledge which finds expression in the
assembly. Here, in the assembly, are developed virtues,
talents, skill, which have to serve as examples. To be
sure, the ministers may find these assemblies onerous,
for ministers must possess large resources of wit and
eloquence to resist the attacks which are hurled against
them. Nevertheless, publicity is one of the best means
of instruction in the interests of the State generally,
for where publicity is found the people manifest an
entirely different regard for the State than in those
places where there are no assemblies or where they are
not public. Only through the publication of every one
of their proceedings are the chambers related to the
larger public opinion; and it is shown that what one
imagines at home with his wife and friends is one thing,
and what happens in a great assembly, where one feat
of eloquence wrecks another, is quite a different thing.

PUBLIC OPINION

Public opinion is the unorganized way in which what
a people wants and thinks is promulgated. That which
is actually effective in the State must be so in an organic fashion. In the constitution this is the case.
But at all times public opinion has been a great power,
and it is particularly so in our time, when the principle
of subjective freedom has such importance and significance. What shall now prevail, prevails no longer
through force, little through use and custom, but rather
through insight and reasons.

Public opinion contains, therefore, the eternal sub-

stantial principles of justice, the true content, and the
result of the whole constitution, legislation, and the
universal condition in general. The form underlying
public opinion is sound common sense, which is a fundamental ethical principle winding its way through everything, in spite of prepossessions. But when this inner
character is formulated in the shape of general propositions, partly for their own sake, partly for the purpose of actual reasoning about events, institutions, relations, and the recognized wants of the State, there
appears also the whole character of accidental opinion,
with its ignorance and perversity, its false knowledge
and incorrect judgment.

It is therefore not to be regarded as merely a difference in subjective opinion when it is asserted on the
one hand ——

"Vox populi, vox dei";
and on the other (in Ariosto, for instance) ——*
"Che'l Volgare ignorante ogn' un riprenda
E parli più di quel che meno intenda."

Both sides co-exist in public opinion. Since truth and
endless error are so directly united in it, neither one nor
the other side is truly in earnest. Which one is in
earnest, is difficult to decide—difficult, indeed, if one con-
fines oneself to the direct expression of public opinion.
But as the substantial principle is the inner character of
public opinion, this alone is its truly earnest aspect;
yet this insight cannot be obtained from public opinion
itself, for a substantial principle can only be apprehended apart from public opinion and by a considera-

* Or in Goethe:
"Zuschlagen kann die Masse,
Da ist sie respektabel;
Urteilen gelingt ihr miserabel."

tion of its own nature. No matter with what passion
an opinion is invested, no matter with what earnestness
a view is asserted, attacked, and defended, this is no
criterion of its real essence. And least of all could
public opinion be made to see that its seriousness is
nothing serious at all.

A great mind has publicly raised the question whether
it is permissible to deceive a people. The answer is
that a people will not permit itself to be deceived concerning its substantial basis, the essence, and the definite character of its spirit, but it deceives *itself* about
the way in which it knows this, and according to which
it judges of its acts, events, etc.

Public opinion deserves, therefore, to be esteemed as
much as to be despised; to be despised for its concrete
consciousness and expression, to be esteemed for its essential fundamental principle, which only shines, more
or less dimly, through its concrete expression. Since
public opinion possesses within itself no standard of
discrimination, no capacity to rise to a recognition of
the substantial, independence of it is the first formal
condition of any great and rational enterprise (in actuality as well as in science). Anything great and rational is eventually sure to please public opinion, to be
espoused by it, and to be made one of its prepossessions.

In public opinion all is false and true, but to discover
the truth in it is the business of the great man. The
great man of his time is he who expresses the will and
the meaning of that time, and then brings it to completion; he acts according to the inner spirit and essence of his time, which he realizes. And he who does
not understand how to despise public opinion, as it
makes itself heard here and there, will never accomplish
anything great.

FREEDOM OF THE PRESS

The freedom of public utterance (of which the press is one means, having advantage over speech in its more extended reach, though inferior to it in vivacity), the gratification of that prickling impulse to express and to have expressed one's opinion, is directly controlled by the police and State laws and regulations, which partly hinder and partly punish its excesses. The indirect guarantee lies in its innocuousness, and this again is mainly based on the rationality of the constitution, the stability of the government, and also on the publicity given to the assemblies of the classes. Another security is offered by the indifference and contempt with which insipid and malicious words are, as a rule, quickly met.

The definition of the freedom of the press as freedom to say and write what one pleases, is parallel to the one of freedom in general, viz., as freedom to do what one pleases. Such view belongs to the uneducated crudity and superficiality of naïve thinking. The press, with its infinite variety of content and expression, represents what is most transient, particular, and accidental in human opinion. Beyond the direct incitation to theft, murder, revolt, etc., lies the art of cultivating the expression which in itself seems general and indefinite enough, but which, in a measure, conceals a perfectly definite meaning. Such expressions are partly responsible for consequences of which, since they are not actually expressed, one is never sure how far they are contained in the utterances and really follow from them. It is this indefiniteness of the content and form of the press which prevents the laws governing it from assuming that precision which one demands of laws. Thus the extreme subjectivity of the wrong, injury, and crime committed by the press, causes the decision and sentence to be equally subjective. The laws are not only indefinite, but the press can, by the skill and subtlety of its expressions, evade them, or criticise the judgment of the court as wholly arbitrary. Furthermore, if the utterance of the press is treated as an offensive deed, one may retort that it is not a deed at all, but only an opinion, a thought, a mere saying. Consequently, impunity is expected for opinions and words, because they are merely subjective, trivial, and insignificant, and, in the same breath, great respect and esteem is demanded for these opinions and words—for the opinions, because they are mine and my mental property, and for the words, because they are the free expression and use of that property. And yet the basic principle remains that injury to the honor of individuals generally, abuse, libel, contemptuous caricaturing of the government, its officers and officials, especially the person of the prince, defiance of the laws, incitement to revolt, etc., are all offenses and crimes of different grades.

However, the peculiar and dangerous effect of these acts for the individuals, the community, and the State depends upon the nature of the soil on which they are committed, just as a spark, if thrown upon a heap of gunpowder, has a much more dangerous result than if thrown on the mere ground, where it vanishes and leaves no trace. But, on the whole, a good many such acts, though punishable by law, may come under a certain kind of Nemesis which internal impotence is forced to bring about. In entering upon opposition to the superior talents and virtues, by which impotence feels oppressed, it comes to a realization of its inferiority and to a consciousness of its own nothingness, and the Nemesis, even when bad and odious, is, by treating it with contempt, rendered ineffectual. Like the public, which forms a circle for such activity, it is confined to a harmless malicious joy, and to a condemnation which reflects upon itself.

MEANING OF WAR

There is an ethical element in war. It must not be regarded as an absolute ill, or as merely an external calamity which is accidentally based upon the passions of despotic individuals or nations, upon acts of injustice, and, in general, upon what ought not to be. The recognition of the finite, such as property and life, as accidental, is necessary. This necessity is at first wont to appear under the form of a force of nature, for all things finite are mortal and transient. In the ethical order, in the State, however, nature is robbed of its force, and the necessity is exalted to a work of freedom, to an ethical law. The transient and negative nature of all things is transformed in the State into an expression of the ethical will. War, often painted by edifying speech as a state in which the vanity of temporal things is demonstrated, now becomes an element whereby the ideal character of the particular receives its right and reality. War has the deep meaning that by it the ethical health of the nations is preserved and their finite aims uprooted. And as the winds which sweep over the ocean prevent the decay that would result from its perpetual calm, so war protects the people from the corruption which an everlasting peace would bring upon it. History shows phases which illustrate how successful wars have checked internal unrest and have strengthened the entire stability of the State.

In peace, civic life becomes more extended, every sphere is hedged in and grows immobile, and at last all men stagnate, their particular nature becoming more and more hardened and ossified. Only in the unity of a body is health, and, where the organs become still, there is death. Eternal peace is often demanded as an ideal toward which mankind should move. Thus Kant proposed an alliance of princes, which should settle the controversies of States, and the Holy Alliance probably aspired to be an institution of this kind. The State, however, is individual, and in individuality negation is essentially contained. A number of States may constitute themselves into a family, but this confederation, as an individuality, must create an opposition and so beget an enemy. Not only do nations issue forth invigorated from their wars, but those nations torn by internal strife win peace at home as a result of war abroad. War indeed causes insecurity in property, but this real insecurity is only a necessary commotion. From the pulpits much is preached concerning the insecurity, vanity, and instability of temporal things, and yet every one, though he may be touched by his own words, thinks that he, at least, will manage to hold on to his possessions. Let the insecurity finally come, in the form of Hussars with glistening sabres, and show its earnest activity, and that touching edification which foresaw all this now turns upon the enemy with curses. In spite of this, wars will break out whenever necessity demands them; but the seeds spring up anew, and speech is silenced before the grave repetitions of history.

The military class is the class of universality. The defense of the State is its privilege, and its duty is to realize the ideality contained in it, which consists in self-sacrifice. There are different kinds of bravery. The courage of the animal, or the robber, the bravery which arises from a sense of honor, the chivalrous bravery, are not yet the true forms of bravery. In civilized

nations true bravery consists in the readiness to give oneself wholly to the service of the State, so that the individual counts but as one among many. Not personal
valor alone is significant; the important aspect of it
lies in self-subordination to the universal cause.

To risk one's life is indeed something more than mere
fear of death, but this is only negative; only a positive
character—an aim and content—gives meaning to bravery. Robbers and murderers in the pursuit of crime,
adventurers in the search of their fanciful objects, etc.,
also possess courage, and do not fear death. The principle of the modern world—the power of thought and
of the universal—has given to bravery a higher form;
the higher form causes the expression of bravery to
appear more mechanical. The brave deeds are not the
deeds of any particular person, but those of the members of a whole. And, again, since hostility is directed,
not against separate individuals, but against a hostile
whole, personal valor appears as impersonal. This principle it is which has caused the invention of the gun; it
is not a chance invention that has brought about the
change of the mere personal form of bravery into the
more abstract.

INTERNATIONAL RELATIONS

Just as the individual is not a real person unless
related to other persons, so the State is no real individuality unless related to other States. The legitimate power of a State, and more especially its princely
power, is, from the point of view of its foreign relations, a wholly internal affair. A State shall, therefore, not interfere with the internal affairs of another
State. On the other hand, for a complete State, it is
essential that it be recognized by others; but this recog-

nition demands as a guarantee that it shall recognize those States which recognize it, and shall respect their independence. Hence its internal affairs cannot be a matter of indifference to them.

When Napoleon, before the peace of Campoformio, said, "The French Republic requires recognition as little as the sun needs to be recognized," his words suggest nothing but the strength of existence, which already carries with it the guarantee of recognition, without needing to be expressed.

When the particular wills of the State can come to no agreement their controversy can be decided only by war. What offense shall be regarded as a breach of treaty, or as a violation of respect and honor, must remain indefinite, since many and various injuries can easily accrue from the wide range of the interests of the States and from the complex relations of their citizens. The State may identify its infinitude and honor with every one of its single aspects. And if a State, as a strong individuality, has experienced an unduly protracted internal rest, it will naturally be more inclined to irritability, in order to find an occasion and field for intense activity.

The nations of Europe form a family according to the universal principle of their legislation, their ethical code, and their civilization. But the relation among States fluctuates, and no judge exists to adjust their differences. The higher judge is the universal and absolute Spirit alone—the World-Spirit.

The relation of one particular State to another presents, on the largest possible scale, the most shifting play of individual passions, interests, aims, talents, virtues, power, injustice, vice, and mere external chance. It is a play in which even the ethical whole, the independence of the State, is exposed to accident. The principles which control the many national spirits are limited. Each nation as an existing individuality is guided by its particular principles, and only as a particular individuality can each national spirit win objectivity and self-consciousness; but the fortunes and deeds of States in their relation to one another reveal the dialectic of the finite nature of these spirits. Out of this dialectic rises the universal Spirit, the unlimited World-Spirit, pronouncing its judgment—and its judgment is the highest—upon the finite nations of the world's history; for the history of the world is the world's court of justice.